THE POLITICS OF COLLECTING

EUNSONG KIM

# The Politics of Collecting

## Race and the Aestheticization of Property

DUKE UNIVERSITY PRESS
DURHAM AND LONDON
2024

Project Editor: Livia Tenzer
Designed by Matthew Tauch
Typeset in Garamond Premier Pro by Westchester Publishing Services

Library of Congress Cataloging-in-Publication Data
Names: Kim, Eunsong, author.
Title: The politics of collecting : race and the aestheticization of property / Eunsong Kim.
Description: Durham : Duke University Press, 2024. | Includes bibliographical references and index.
Identifiers: LCCN 2023045082 (print)
LCCN 2023045083 (ebook)
ISBN 9781478030485 (paperback)
ISBN 9781478026242 (hardcover)
ISBN 9781478059479 (ebook)
Subjects: LCSH: Museums—Collection management—United States. | Cultural property—Political aspects. | Cultural property—Moral and ethical aspects. | Art—History. | Art—Political aspects. | Art and race. | Art and society. | BISAC: ART / History / General | ART / Museum Studies
Classification: LCC AM133 .K56 2024 (print) | LCC AM133 (ebook) | DDC 069/.40973—dc23/eng/20240225
LC record available at https://lccn.loc.gov/2023045082
LC ebook record available at https://lccn.loc.gov/2023045083

Cover art: Juwon Jun, *Handwork*. Courtesy of the artist.

*For my brother,*
*Sung Gi Kim*

# CONTENTS

# PRELUDE

## *On Motivations*

In 2011, the Getty Museum hired James Cuno from the Art Institute of Chicago (AIC). As preordained by neoliberalism, his primary contribution at the AIC had been dismantling the education department and replacing the staff with volunteers. During his tenure at the AIC he wrote a number of books against repatriation and in favor of the elevation of the encyclopedic museum—a rhyme scheme, if you will. When he was hired as the CEO of the Getty Museum—an institution previously embroiled in its own criminal negligence of provenance—the Getty prepared a press release stating that, while it had been noted that Cuno's personal views on repatriation are "liberal," he would abide by the museum's official policy, which we could surmise was less "liberal" (or more ethical?) than his own.

Much as one would expect, on joining the Getty, Cuno took apart the education department, replacing educators with volunteers (who, in turn, needed to be trained and replaced often, which turned out not to be as cost effective as Cuno had initially laid out). This was done to relieve the endowment deficit, as the endowment had dipped from $5 billion to $4 billion. It is not clear how much this "dippage" had to do with the operations budget, but nevertheless, the budget for the departments of education, building, foods, and services were cut to ease anxiety.

The utilization of unpaid, *free* educational volunteers in lieu of wage laborers and public accountability with regard to education under the guise of community service—a liberal good misappropriated to serve the interests of a private institution—is part and parcel of the maintenance of neoliberal institutions. Here, the rhetoric of inclusion and expansion comes at the cost of labor expropriation and property entrenchment, together with the disavowal of colonial history and a hostility toward reparations. That the Getty continues to maintain its operations through both its refusal to pay workers and its refusal to repatriate objects is unexceptional to the general practice of the neoliberal schema.[1]

I was officially at the Getty to acculturate myself to the world of museums and gain professional experience, coaxing myself into the violent flexibilities demanded by the neoliberal academic "market." I was personally there to learn more about the politics of provenance research and institutional provenance claims. As an eager student of Marxist feminism, but also as an ethnographer of sorts, I attended all the town hall meetings and budget proposals. I took copious notes. When Cuno declared in the same meeting both that the Getty is the "richest museum in the world" and that volunteers make up fifty-four full-time positions, I wondered if there would be a secondary meeting afterward for its IWW-aspiring members. When scientists were brought in to discuss the optimal temperature for artworks to live in (i.e., the best refrigerators in the world), I understood that all of this was the backdrop for how colonial theft becomes normalized, and how repatriation and redistribution is narrated as cannot be.

Thus I, of course, attended all the acquisitions meetings where newly purchased items were shown and told. I was particularly surprised by the acquisition of the Knoedler Gallery archives, not because the Getty had bothered to purchase them, but because of what the presenting curator deemed to be their importance. It was discussed how, in the sales books, we could see that Henry Clay Frick was buying and returning paintings as if he was shopping at a department store. Cue laughter. It is indeed funny and peculiar to trace through acquisition records the figures of union busters, robber barons. In this book, I work to display these figures' desires and efforts to extract, to destroy, to segregate, along with the desire and effort to memorialize themselves through collections.

But my desire to research capitalism, colonialism, philanthropy, patronage, and expression has roots deeper than graduate school. I was raised by parents who grew up in a Korea full of white missionaries, and who then wanted to become missionaries. Having this goal, our family was dependent on the charity of wealthy Christians, the desires of churchgoers and their pastors. This is to say, we grew up very poor, and they remain very poor. My personal understanding of poverty was the act of waiting for the rich to decide whether we were a cause worthy of support.

Since my parents never owned a home and most likely will never own very much, all my memories of growing up in Korea, and then at times in the United States, revolve around staying in the homes of wealthy Christians as they vacationed elsewhere. To say we moved a lot would be an understatement; we moved endlessly. In Canada, the apartment we lived in was owned by a Christian organization and was supposedly free. This meant poorly kept, rodent-infested, and uncared for. Free has a cost: free means you don't complain. Free means enforced gratitude.

My brother and I would routinely ask my parents to select a different kind of job. We didn't articulate it as such, but we hated this life of waiting to be moved by the rich and of accepting the untenably "free." As I began to gnaw at the research of this book, at the theoretical questions that were, in fact, deeply personal, I began to see how the material dynamics of wealth, desire, and legacy play out visibly yet are mystified in arts and poetry spaces. Prominent museums, archives, and poetry spaces become so via colonial accumulation. That is, they require the transfer of the commons, Black and Indigenous dispossession, and labor expropriation to a concentrated figure of wealth, and then to his desired aesthetic pursuit. I am interested in what is lost in this transfer because I imagine there is much. I remain interested in the desires of those fighting, waiting.

My positionality serves as both the possibility and limitation of grappling with the various stakes of property, US settler colonialism, chattel slavery, aesthetics, poetics, labor, and representation. The experiences of my life before and at the Getty prompted me to trace a transfer that I believe extrapolates labor and aesthetic congruences, and, as I stated at the beginning, my interest in tackling this history is about the present. As another dawn of robber barons is upon us, as individual wings of museums and aestheticized techno-utopian schemes are presented to the public with applause, I work to denaturalize their historical and political continuums.[2] If we are to abolish them, it is imperative to understand the politics carried forth as sacred aesthetic expression, and to repatriate these havens in their entirety.

# ACKNOWLEDGMENTS

This book encompasses over a decade of love, friendship, struggle, antagonism, and more. Graduate school was an incredibly vibrant time in my life, and this work began there under the guidance of Fatima El-Tayeb and Page duBois. From the beginning, Fatima provided the closest reading of each argument and displayed how critique works as care. Page mused on every question with me and asked me to push beyond the contemporary and into the continuums in which the present becomes forged. This book exists because of their mentorship and beauty. There's not a day that goes by where Grace Kyungwon Hong's incisive ideas do not float in and out of all that I read and consider, and I sit up straighter each time I remember (and I remember often) Luis Martín-Cabrera telling me *you don't change money, money changes you.* Camille Forbes's associative and investigative reading practices and Grant Kester's candid method of inquiry grounded the first iteration of this research. I could not have asked for better guidance.

Like so many others, I wanted to pursue scholarship after reading Lisa Lowe's *Immigrant Acts*; the book illuminated how much I wanted to study processes of unlearning and learning, thinking and the unthought. Lisa read an early draft of this manuscript and her feedback challenged and shaped this project into its current form. This monograph exists because of and through her critical support.

Much of my research was supported by a postdoctoral Ford Fellowship and by Northeastern University. Dean Uta Poiger provided a research leave to draft this book and has been an advocate for research in the humanities. I've been fortunate to be part of a department and college where I can build my work with my colleagues: K. J. Rawson, Lori Lefkovitz, Marina Leslie, Elizabeth Britt, Sari Altschuler, Patrick Mullen, Ellen Cushman, Carla Kaplan, Hillary Chute, Chris Gallagher, Julia Flanders, Qianqian Zhang-Wu, Nicole Guidotti-Hernández, Mya Poe, Lillian-Yvonne Bertram, Sebastian Stockman, Erika Boeckeler, Melissa Berry-Woods, Somy Kim, Elizabeth Maddock Dillion, Sasha Sabherwal,

Denise Khor, Philip Thai. The intellectual vibrancy of Carmel Salhi, Ilham Khuri-Makdisi, Kris Manjapra, Régine Michelle Jean-Charles, Rachel Rosenbloom, Naomi Boase, Tiffany Joseph, and Caitlin Thornbrugh has allowed for spaces of contestation and creation to be formed in Boston. The fact that I can exchange drafts with Theo Davis has been a tremendous gift. Neal Learner's championing of my career and cycling passion has shaped my days for the better. Doreen Lee's intellectual range and foresight is unparalleled; I'm so grateful that I get to call her, Nick Harkness, and Lewis my confidants. Nicole Aljoe's wisdom has instructed each step of my trajectory through teaching, research, and beyond—I cannot thank her enough. Patricia Williams has gifted me with her counsel and strength; I cannot believe I get to call my favorite writer a friend.

I am so very thankful for the communities that welcomed me throughout this project. Kimberly Juanita Brown spoke with me on the phone for hours before ever having met me, and her intellectual rigor and generosity has become my life's aspiration. Shawn Wong and Chandan Reddy mentored me through so many life stages: they are always on my mind. Dorothy Wang encouraged this research before it was even a project; her scholarship paved the way for racial critiques in poetry studies. Bhanu Kapil urged me to continue writing and dreaming; her commitment to transformation remains a blueprint. There are people who stun you and transform your life and work for the better: Shalanda Baker, J. Kehaulani Kauanui, Karen Leong, Myla Vicenti Carpio, H. L. T. Quan, Crystal Griffin, Anita Huizar-Hernandez, Alexandria Agloro, Matt Hooley, John Keene, Casey Boyle, Liz Losh, David Marriott, Karl Klare, Brian Reed, Andrew Feld, Krista Ratcliffe, Lila Sharif, Seung B. Kye, Ash Kini, Janet Kim, Kiik Araki-Kawaguchi, Ellen Wu, Mari Matsuda, Tamara Lanier, Pedro Vélez, Aisha Sabatini Sloan, Tisa Bryant, Joseph Rezek, and Josen Diaz have all left deep marks on this work.

Divya Mehra graciously shared her practice with me, and Sasha Huber has been speaking to me about her practice since 2013, when I first began research for chapter 5. For chapter 4, Harryette Mullen and Ryan Wong generously shared their ideas and histories with me. Page duBois contextualized the history of the Archive for New Poetry, which made the chapter possible; Ricky Punzalan and Michelle Caswell offered crucial insights into appraisal literature. Stephanie A. Jones offered initial critiques of chapter 6 that altered it for the better. Carrie Nakamura and Wayne Modest invited me to present on the monograph at the Research Center for Material Culture; support from the Art Writers Grant and Pradeep

Dalal jump-started my inquiries; and Margot Norton, Jamillah James, Karsten Lund, Leo Genji Amino, and Kim Nguyen opened their respective art spaces for my research, which challenged and expanded how I approached questions of aesthetics.

Archivists at the Frick Art Reference Library, Ryan Henderson and Ron Baraff at Rivers of Steel, Zachary Brodt at the University of Pittsburgh, Heather Smedberg and Colleen Garcia at University of California San Diego, Christine Oka at Northeastern, and many others have been indispensable to this research. Max Haiven, Hrag Vartanian, and Elizabeth Dillion formatively read drafts of the book in 2017, and I have returned to their notes throughout the years. Erik Baker, Justin Hogg, and Manu Karuka read drafts at the final stages of editing, and anonymous readers provided critical insights that lead to its rewriting.

I have been fortunate to work with brilliant students over the course of this making: the projects and writings of Jesica Bak, Hana Shapiro, Cari Munoz, Moni Garcia, Aida Campos, Margaret Schultz, Matthew Flores, Sasha Wodtke, Diya Navlakha, Patricio Pino, Patrick Svensson, Ash Liu, Ivy, Michael Davis, Whinter Collins, Raiya Suliman, Rhya Brooke, Aerial Starks, and Alanna Prince have impacted my research. There are artists and writers whose work reverberated throughout the writing and editing of this monograph: Carmen Gimenz Smith, Solmaz Sharif, Santee Frazier, Sarah Viren, Willyce Kim, Mona Kareem, Juwon Jun, Joan Kane, Felicia Zamora, Amanda Wallace, Michelle Dizon, Jessica Lynne, S*an H. Smith, Cassandra Gillig, Nikki Wallschlaeger, Kameelah Janan Rasheed, Lisa Vinebaum, Robyn Schiff, Nick Twemlow, Enzo Camacho, Ami Lien, Sarah Jackson, Ricardo Alberto Maldonado, Mary Sutton, Judith Goldman, Farid Matuk, Susan Briante, Jacob Wren, Hae Yeon Choo, Hong-An Troung, Dwayne Dixon, Avery Meinen, Thea Quiray Tagle, Reuben Roqueñi, Olive Demar, Tito Garza Lopez, Michael Dowdy, Safiya Sinclair, Junie Alrich, micha cardenas, Dionne Brand, and Christina Sharpe. I look and look again to their work and presence.

The friendship of Kareli Lizarraga, Naomi Tom, Jarrett M. Drake, Allia Griffin, Kylie King, Criss Moon, Lewis Cheung, Sam Yim, Maya Mackrandilal, Jennie Freeburg, Georges, Cassie, Jean-Baptiste, and Ella Toulouse sustained me at all stages of this process, and writing retreats with my pom partners extraordinaire Moya Bailey and Grace Sanders Johnson were where this book was completed. Yelena Bailey helped me move not once but twice in a year, and has offered indispensable interpretation throughout the years. I looked and look to activists who research the international arms trade in Korea, particularly the possibilities presented by Jungmin Choi and Minyeong Kim Han, for their constant reminders as to the stakes of critique, use, and action.

So much labor went to all iterations of this book: I am grateful to Isla Ng and Jesica Bak for their research assistance; to Juwon Jun, who worked again and again on all the details, large and small; to Ellis Kim for the bibliography; and to Tom Aldrich, who helped shape the chapters into what it looks like now—having a composer suggest cuts has been a dream. Carrie Nakamura read the earliest to the last draft and lovingly pushed me toward precision and clarity.

Livia Tenzer, Ann Boisvert, and Benjamin Kossak provided support during the final stages of this work and Elizabeth Ault believed in this work from the very beginning; this project would not have an existence without her guidance.

William C. Anderson has been a foundation for this research: I learn about all of life's vital components because of our friendship.

There isn't a day I don't think about Nam Hwa Ja, who lived the life she wanted, no matter the dictums.

Lastly, because he is always first, this book is dedicated to my brother, Sung Gi Kim, who is my ideal reader and my chosen family.

This book is indebted to the above and to all those *I do not yet know how to name*. All insights have been borrowed and cited to the best of my abilities. Only the errors are mine.

# Introduction

here we lie in folds, collected stones
in the museum of spectacles,
our limbs displayed, fract and soluble
were this a painting, it would combust canvases,
this lunate pebble, this splintered phalanx,
I can hardly hold their sincere explosions

**Dionne Brand, *Ossuaries***

The inspection of finance within museums and institutions has become an object of study, whether by buyers and dealers evaluating the art market or by researchers who study the privatization of culture.[1] A peculiar debate concerning the terrain of aesthetics and finance occurred when the news network CBS aired a thirteen-minute segment on *60 Minutes* titled "Even in Tough Times, Contemporary Art Sells."[2] The 2012 coverage was immediately met with controversy, disdain, and discourse across news outlets. In the segment, journalist Morley Safer visits Miami's Art Basel art fair to speak with dealers and buyers about the market. [3] The piece is full of quotes from infamous dealers such as Timothy Blum and Larry Gagosian. Gagosian remarks about the fair to the onetime American International Group owner turned venture capitalist Eli Broad, "It's a place to sell art, it's a place to make money." In response, Broad declares with a large smile, "We just bought this," in front of a piece by Kara Walker. Safer narrates the segment with mundane or controversial statements, such as "Contemporary art has become a global commodity, just like oil or soybeans or pork belly and there seems to be no shortage of people wanting to speculate in it, and no shortage of billions willing to invest in it. As a haven for their cash, love of art, or status symbol . . . to feed those beasts, there are virtually art fairs every weekend around the globe. . . . The collectors are bubble proof—it's only their mad money they're spending anyway."[4]

Within twenty-four hours of the segment airing, two noted US art critics, Jerry Saltz and Roberta Smith, wrote nearly identical responses to the report.[5] Both rebuttals emphasized the importance of "looking at the art" and argued against Safer's concentration on inevitable issues such as money and access, which they argued prevented him from looking closely. Neither critic attempted to address or question the function of finance in the art world; instead, they dismissed its inspection as something that takes away from art appreciation. Emphasizing Safer's lack of positive affect, Smith's response in the *New York Times* included framings such as "Mr. Safer clearly has no time for love, and no one bothers to explain that even speculators and the superrich don't stay interested too long unless they have some knowledge of and attraction to art."[6] In a subtle defense of the *superrich*, Smith subsumes the connection between aesthetics and finance and postulates that Safer's reductive understanding of art and focus on its market have to do with how he is affectively disconnected from aesthetics.

It is noteworthy that, while Safer candidly critiques high art's clear partnership with finance, his ideological position is revealed in other comments, such as "There's very little sense of an aesthetic experience here."[7] Safer claims that today's art fairs do not present an "aesthetic experience" but rather are a "cacophony of cash," and does not consider how the two could be related or even erotically entwined. To Safer, the corrosion of art is caused not by the influx of finance or money, but by the way that money and finance have shifted the definition of aesthetic value to include conceptual art, multimedia art, and other such forms and mediums purposefully untouched by the artist's hand. One potential subtext of Safer's antics in Miami is a nostalgia for an Enlightenment-driven understanding of aesthetics, where the artist provides the experience for contemplation, and his creation of beauty is believed to be the entrance into the sublime.

Notably, both the critics and the journalist reenact a false dichotomy where one can either (1) inspect the mode of circulation or (2) look for meaning, when in fact it is the cohesion of the two that opens up a set of pivotal questions and challenging provocations. This book seeks to pursue these tenets together and demonstrate how they are, in fact, integrally enmeshed and interdependent. I seek to materialize the relationship between finance and aesthetics or, as I frame it throughout the book, between property, race, and aesthetics. Racial capitalism mediated all aspects of the twentieth century, including the development of US museums and aesthetic forms, and I document the expansion of conceptualized forms together with racial capitalism to show how immaterialism—which underwrites most "innovation" in avant-garde forms and spans collecting imperatives from found art to digital artifacts such as NFTs (nonfungible tokens)—does not move away from possessive materialism but further cements it through the aestheticization of property. Holding this particular context in focus throughout the book, I explore how objects and collections become valued, and how the ideas linked to the objects are essential for understanding how meaning is managed, distributed, and archived.

Debates concerning materiality/immateriality have been waged across Western epistemes with little agreement and consensus. Sometimes situated as the Cartesian binary, other times aligned with the sublime and transcendence, Lacanian critiques of the real, or contemporary notions of the virtual and digital, *materiality* and *immateriality* have resisted settled definitions.[8] What seems consistent in the debates is how the fragility affixed to the immaterial remains at the helm of aestheticized property and art capital. Marxist analysis instructs how it is through mediation that the material realizes value, and further, it is through a cerebrality removed from the body that material becomes property. Cedric Robinson situates the epistemological foundation of materialism/immaterialism as a religious venture beginning with Plato and Aristotle and traceable throughout the formation of European Christianity. He argues that fixations of the material (earth, body) and the ideal/immaterial (not of the earth, not of the body) spring out of religious critiques, whether in favor of radicalizing the church or protecting its authority. As the church synonymized itself with power, those vested in its protection worked to define divinity through concepts of the ideal/immaterial, situated dialectically and above what was material and earthly. Rejection of the material became conflated with submission to the divine.[9] Taking from Robinson, I argue that the capitalist dichotomy of mind- and handwork mirrors the lines drawn from immateriality to materiality, conceptual to racialized, and artist/manager to worker. In this light, I examine theories concerning deskilling and immateriality, and notions of separating concept from craft, idea from body.

Museums and archives are spaces that have been delegated as environments where aesthetics can be propertized. The conversation between Safer and Smith concerning aesthetics and finance situates the political and historical backdrop of this book, as it demonstrates how issues of financial value become bracketed off from debates over aesthetic value and experience. But in my experience as an arts and culture writer, I have found that directly talking about money, labor, and our relationships with(in) institutions is the only way to clarify the mystification process predicated upon culture. The conferral of aesthetic value does not happen prior to but rather through financialized and racialized processes of indoctrination. Clarifying the stakes—such as how an artist enters the permanent collection of a prominent museum, how poets enter the archives of an institution, how a personal collection becomes a museum—will allow me to set up arguments about how we might like to proceed in this realm, be it inside of it, and perhaps reimagine rupturing such formations.

This book follows paths opened up by transnational activists to trace the colonial and material history of immaterialism, which requires an examination of both the rise of immaterial and conceptual aesthetic forms and the creation of personal and private collections of objects that become normalized as the site of the museum.[10] In describing the structure of this book, I return to the *60 Minutes* segment in which Safer inspects the evidence that leads him to conclude that Art Basel—one of the biggest art fairs in the world—is devoid of an "aesthetic experience." In the clip, Safer mocks installation art, video art, and what appear to be found- and appropriated-art sculptures. He finds a large installation of a hat and stands under it, rolling his eyes. The clip seeks to demonstrate that, while the works examined are stupid and probably "not-art," they are expensive and collected and, therefore, validated as art.

It is true that aesthetics require indoctrination. But rather than scrutinize and delve into the relationship between finance and aesthetics, the public discourse between Safer and his critics reveals that there are people who have accepted the expansion of art as aesthetic experience, and there are people who continue to believe art should induce an aesthetic experience. To be of the latter category speaks to one's class position.[11] For those of the former, money, while an annoying reality of the art world, deserves no place in any aesthetic or affective discussion of it. Hence, those in the former cannot conceive of why money is even being discussed.

The fusion of finance, aesthetics, and politics abounds across mediums and institutions.[12] In 2010, two years prior to Safer's report, the Poetry Foundation would be transformed from being a platform for a little magazine (*Poetry*) into one of the most powerful poetry organizations in the United States, thanks to a $100 million donation of Lilly pharmaceutical stock from Ruth Lilly.[13] The foundation would receive part of Lilly's inheritance of the giant pharmaceutical corporation that produced antidepressants such as Prozac and Zyprexa and other drugs.[14] The corporation's development process included nonconsensual testing on incarcerated persons, who developed issues ranging from diabetes to long-term disabilities.[15]

Akin to the discourse generated by Safer's report, writing on the donation vacillated between praise for increased arts funding and moralization of finance in the field of poetry.[16] Neither produced tools for examining how certain kinds of poetry become synonymized with immateriality and function as the form of mediation. This becomes most apparent in scholarship about new and experimental poetry, discussed in chapter 4.

The most common response to conceptual, avant-garde art and experimental poetry is often flat rejection. Safer's belittlement of found object art, while clearly in awe of its financial value, is one of the ideological frameworks I explore throughout this book. I address how found art—art that works against familiar forms of "aesthetic experience" and expectation—becomes theorized, valued, and then permanently collected in museum spaces and archives. I ask: How does a urinal become sculpture; appropriation, an innovative new form; exploitation, a performance; management, an aesthetic impulse? What are the historic and socioeconomic forces that situate the variegated developments of aesthetic forms and their institutions? In addressing these questions, I demonstrate how the context of racial capitalism and settler colonialism is vital to understanding how the category of art becomes expanded and vital to materializing the building of institutions that house their collections. I do so in order to investigate the political framework that protects the categorical expansion of art, while simultaneously restricting the subject position of those who occupy the subject of the artist.

Many of us—particularly in critical ethnic studies and American studies—are familiar with how race is made real through laws, social structures, and forms of power. In this book, I demonstrate how the usage of the terms *experimental*, *innovative*, *conceptual*, and *immaterial* in the arts and their collecting institutions works in tandem with the ongoing process of making race real. Collected objects are situated as the highest order of aesthetic importance and formal invention have been understood as some of art's greatest achievements. This book situates historical and contemporary articulations of formalist experimentation and innovation in the arts and argues that the primary signifier of innovation has been and remains the propertization of race, and of anti-Blackness in particular.[17]

I argue that what demarcates the expansive possibilities of modern and postmodern art is the racialized and gendered labor that is imperative to the notion of aesthetic freedom. In pursuing this inquiry, I explore the relationship between whiteness and freedom, and argue, as Cheryl Harris has so pivotally laid out, that whiteness as property has tethered whiteness to freedom in all aspects of aesthetic cultures, materializing how racialized property becomes interpolated as innovation. In order to examine the relationship between whiteness and expansion in the arts, I treat art collections as property, and then pursue the political implications of their aesthetics in order to analyze the socioeconomic ideological freedoms said to be found in their work.[18] Examining the political implications of property and artistic freedom allows me to engage with artists such as Noah Purifoy and Sasha Huber, whose practices intervene into the provenance of property claims.

My reading of property is fundamentally grounded in Harris's scholarship. Harris shows that the construction of property was the legal definition of whiteness, and thus, all discussions regarding property are racialized formations. She demonstrates that, in the US context, the origins of property are "rooted in racial domination," and extends how this US-specific understanding comes from a longer tradition of European thought that analyzed property as a metaphysical right to exclude.[19] In this book, I am connecting the right to exclude and racial domination to what Harryette Mullen has described as *aesthetic apartheid*: the ways in which aesthetic and literary institutions work to segregate genres, forms, and objects.[20] Through this, I would add the ways in which they limit and define the scope of art's expansion. I use Harris to inspect property claims theorized as formal innovation, such as the found object, as well as the forging of the personal collection, to reveal how racialized concepts of "new" and "experimental" are at the core of the expansion of the arts. It is through this legal framework that I examine the "neutralizing" space of the museum and the archive, and arguments that put forth how aesthetic spaces afford deracialized and depoliticized abstraction. Debates that polarize one against the other, such as Safer and Smith's about Art Basel, or that underdescribe the impact of propertization, such as that around Ruth Lilly's donation to the Poetry Foundation, subsume finance as either a minor detail or misunderstanding, rather than as the opportunity to inspect the role of racial capitalism and settler colonialism as cultural production.[21]

## On the Making of US Museums

Aesthetic debates concerning form, such as those around found object, appropriation, and conceptual art, as well as new and experimental poetry, are property concerns, as I will discuss in chapters 3 and 4. However, the current discourse about form—as unattached to material, economic, and historical contexts—has yet to broach this framework. Legal understandings of property must be taken into consideration when we discuss aesthetic forms that reify the collecting and archiving of its object, as the term *property* clarifies the stakes of the debate. Property remains, per Harris's analysis, a form historically rooted in exclusion and not in physical objecthood, or even in an individual sense of ownership.

It is through property relations that I inspect the politics that have expanded the category of aesthetics. In taking seriously the accepted modernist argument that Marcel Duchamp opens up the possibility of art—as in, he triumphantly delinks labor from concept and thereby offers and elevates the immateriality of the concept—I posit that the gesture did not open up the possibilities of the subject called the artist. Rather, it opened up possibilities only for a particular chosen subset. The elevated artist remains to this day primarily white and male. Susan Cahan has demonstrated that for Black and nonwhite artists, even placement in permanent collections at premiere institutions has not resulted in "lifelong membership"—a curious duality.[22] It is not much better in poetry. One can witness these debates whenever an anthology is published. When Pulitzer Prize–winning former poet laureate Rita Dove edited an anthology of US poetry in 2011 that included more Black poets than previous anthologies, the anti-Black backlash became so intense that headlines reviewing the debate unironically announced that there was a "Bloodletting over an Anthology."[23] How is it that what "counts" as art expands, while who counts as artist remains? I situate this conundrum as one of property relations.

Moreover, the exclusion of nonwhite artists and poets from historically white institutions is more than a question of representation; it is about the materiality required to maintain what Hortense Spillers calls "their new world."[24] Rather than a progressive narrative of *new* world culture, it is the wealth dispossessed in the *new* colonial world that upholds the traditions and artifacts of the *old* world order; the United States is entrusted with the role of global leader because of its commitment to the continuum of colonial rule. It is by design that this continuum is duly extended through the composition of contemporary museum boards and prize committees.[25] What has received much less attention is how formative this new world culture was and is to the material development of art institutions and aesthetic practice.

The developmental narrative of museums posits that encyclopedic museums began as "cabinets of curiosities" that European colonialists would bring back in order to display "curiosities" in their homes, and that this colonial structure grew until it became a home unto itself. This origin is reflected in the collecting practices and policies of museums, as in the Louvre's collection of Indigenous remains and the British Museum's refusal to repatriate objects, as well as in the narration of US museums. European art dealers such as Joseph Duveen and US art galleries such as Knoedler worked exclusively between twentieth-century robber barons—Andrew Carnegie, Andrew Mellon, Henry Clay Frick, John D. Rockefeller, John Pierpont Morgan—and European aristocrats, in the sale and transfer of objects.[26] In identifying the artifact possibilities of US *new* money with European *old*-world dynasty, Duveen and other functionary bureaucrats mediated the wealth and objects of the US through the creation of the personal collection museum. In particular, Duveen worked with Andrew Mellon to establish the objects that would come to constitute the National Gallery in Washington, DC, and was pivotal to the Frick Collection, in New York, procuring and offloading European artifacts to the United States on behalf of European aristocrats and US billionaires.[27] His assistance in establishing single-minded US museums was one of explicit effort. The structural legacies shared by Europe and the United States are explained through this competitive and colonial partnership, and colonial notions of linear time are essential to how this dynasty becomes justified.

The direct connection between museums and industry is also largely subsumed under specific aesthetic periods, even as it is continuous. Though the extraction of coke, coal, and steel by robber barons Carnegie, Frick, Rockefeller, and, later, John D. Rockefeller Jr., is widely known, it is less advertised that the family of Duchamp's primary patron, Walter Arensberg, operated a steel company along the same Allegheny River where Carnegie and Frick based their operations, and that this industry generated a dynastic wealth that exempted the Arensbergs (particularly Walter and his wife, Louise) from the lifelong exploitation of wage labor, that is, work. The coal extracted and generated into steel from this region would become the building blocks of what we now understand as the modern world: the sky-high buildings, architectural gems, the Brooklyn Bridge, navy ships—the very marrow of US empire.

In situating my argument, I look to the historical parameters that transfigure property into art and examine sites that have been disconnected or misconnected in this process. Toward this end, my first chapter politicizes the provenance of the Frick Collection, today a museum housed in Frick's New York City mansion. I read the development of the Frick

Collection through the disavowal of union culture and the segregation primary to labor dispossession in the late nineteenth and early twentieth centuries. In examining the violence that grounds the materialization of the personal collection museum space, I provoke connections between this history and the rise of twentieth-century scientific management. The dispossession pivotal to situating the exceptional collecting space parallels the dispossession primary to the rise of institutions of collecting and forms such as the found object and conceptual practices.

In making my argument, I present a macro-examination of the museum and the archive, as well as a micro-inspection of elevated aesthetic objects. I consider art museums and aesthetic archives to be symbols, property, and symbolic property. For this reason, I do not discuss the variegated nuances between the encyclopedic and the specialized collection, their purported democratic ideals for artistic citizenship, or exceptional examples of stellar management or ethical collecting practices. I avoid these discussions because I am interested in demystifying symbolic property and examining the connections among aesthetics, property, and labor writ large. In addition, while I find examples of deviance to be necessary to the imagination, I am arguing that museum and archives are already constructed sites of exception, and therefore, I have devoted my energy to de-exceptionalizing this state.

Michel Foucault described museums as "heterotopias," spaces "beyond" time and space.[28] He wrote that the site of the archive "is the first law of what can be said, the system that governs the appearance of statements as unique events."[29] Considering that the museum space originated through the expansion of the colonial cabinet of curiosities, my argument is one that traces how colonialism continues to structure our relations, aesthetics, and otherwise through the space of the archive and the museum.

Heterotopic idealizations of museums as dead and consigned to the past bypass the genealogical imperative that roots how museums were founded as the *first law*: property. As property, they exist through the valence of power afforded by law. If reparations, redress, and disappearance are movements of the dead that the dying make, and the calls that some make on their behalf, I argue that a better framing of museums is their undying. They are constant reminders of how colonialism is maintained: the objects of the museums cannot be repatriated, redressed, or burned down; to do so would be an affront to our foundational relationship to the preservation of colonial aesthetics and, by extension, freedom. The recent return of a small number of objects bears no existential threat to any such institution.

This maintenance of property is afforded through the dynamics of colonial time. As Indigenous critical theorists such as Mishuana Goeman and Jodi Byrd have demonstrated, discussions of settler colonial structures solely through time-based frameworks are limited by the discourse of progressive history and its articulations of past, present, and future.[30] The undercurrents of time-based framings make inevitable the continuous presence of the colonial order. As in, if there is no way to go back to how things were, rather than grappling with what J. Kēhaulani Kauanui situates as "enduring indigeneity"—both in that "indigeneity itself is enduring" and in that "settler colonialism is a structure that endures indigeneity, as it holds out against it"—the present colonial order is indemnified as the *natural* order of things.[31] In this hierarchy, property and dispossession are naturalized foundations for the liberal world.

In *Ossuaries*, poet Dionne Brand evokes the underground to unmask this developmental European fantasy. The fifteen-part epic poem centers on Yasmine, the object/subject imprisoned by the colonial museumification of life. Though the target of violence, Yasmine is refused an innocence, an "outside" elevation to her predicament.[32] Brand labors against aesthetics as a cure ("a mild narcotic") for the malady of colonial existence.[33] Opening with the testament that even her body and her dreams are incarcerated, the epic traces imprisonment as the museum form.[34] This voice is living yet denied life; Brand's epic encircles the tempo and conditions of objecthood. Thus, if Kauanui's enduring indigeneity is foregrounded with Brand's archaeological politicization of the museum form, rather than centralizing colonial time and positing a developmental narrative of movement—from European cabinets of curiosities to encyclopedic museums in Europe and the United States, from European dynasty to US settler-colonial extractive wealth, and from modernist to postmodernist forms—the museum apologia would have no standing. When orienting with Kauanui and Brand, colonial notions of the past are not treated as holding the evidence of colonization; the very metric of "the past" *is* evidence of settler colonialism. Reform would be inconceivable if the progressive lineage from artifacts procured to uphold chattel slavery to objects of aesthetic merit is pressed upon *who endures* and who cannot rather than the elapsed time in which such collections were developed. This consideration materializes the way in which US and European museums are not collections that hold the proof of their crimes, but rather that their continued spatial existence constitutes the crime. They do not hold the proof, they *are* the proof.[35]

A critical intervention into time is necessary, as the function of colonial time has also worked to uphold the archive's explicit entitlement to ownership and dispossession: colonial time legitimates property.[36] When museum CEOs defend their illegitimate records and their lack of provenance against repatriation, it is often through the metaphor of time as guardianship. It is rationalized that the colonial institution protected the artifact from destruction. The decades or centuries of preservation serve as evidence of institutional care, and the longer the institution has confined the object, the deeper its entitlement. I look to historical materialist thinkers to undo this collapse. In *Slaves and Other Objects*, Page duBois discusses how the field of classics, while fundamentally dependent on objects from antiquity, often fails to contextualize the materiality of the object. She posits that the fields of classics and cultural studies—in their efforts to analyze the object—pry themselves away from the context or the *dirt* of the object; in this case, how each and every object the field of classics studies was made available through enslaved persons and derived through chattel slavery. Following duBois's call for "embeddedness," I likewise insist that objects cannot be separated from their material conditions and their culture.[37]

Walter Benjamin has famously articulated that "there is no document of civilization which is not at the same time a document of barbarism."[38] My case study of the Homestead Strike of 1892 and the Frick Collection in chapter 1 takes seriously duBois's and Benjamin's theorizations, and I aim to link most explicitly the documents of civilization to barbarism *and* the aesthetic theories that have worked to mystify these connections. In resuscitating the Homestead Strike, the Frick Collection, the Carnegie libraries, and the rise of Taylorism to consider alongside notions of artistic rupture and "enduring indigeneity," I work to challenge our theories concerning the museum space, innovation, and appropriation—the kinds of expression often deemed progressive by modern and contemporary theories. I contend that such forms are not only consistent with how property is understood but are also the documents of civilization.

There are liberal notions of the art object and the museum space, and both liberal and illiberal notions of striking; the fact that neither leads to abolition (of property or otherwise) has been undertheorized. It has become normalized to look to the museum space and the private collection for evidence of art and aesthetics.[39] How might we reformulate our understanding of expression (and aesthetics) given a history where collections have been forged through disavowal? I am asking: What has been unthought through our acceptance of the painting, of the object as that which must be preserved, saved, publicized? The scope of this project is to explore *expression*: the museum collection and the poetry archive have become registered sources of aesthetic expression; strikes and protests have become legitimate and illegitimate forms of recognized political expression; and then there are unaccounted forms of unregistered impressions. I interrogate the first two forms, to make space for the third, the fourth, and more.[40]

As the frameworks conjoined in this book historically have been considered disparate, their amalgamation demands much from its interlocutors. The configuration presented—from institutions to forms, conceptual art to labor theory, immaterialism to settler colonialism, and collecting practices to racial capitalism—strains disciplinary confines and thus will ask those engaged with the text to grapple with the difficulties and pleasures of its coalescence. In writing the book, I grappled with the complex ways in which the frameworks have been made structurally separate and tended to both the maintenance of ideological continuums and the permutations that have occurred from disciplinary maintenance. I aim for this book to open up critical insights into how colonialism and discourses on race and gender (via property) have informed and continue to inform aesthetic emergence in order to aid the ongoing efforts to center emergent and anticolonial epistemologies across institutions. This project seeks to bridge the perceived political and aesthetic gaps between what has been categorized as material- and concept-driven aesthetics and what is classified as immaterial, through understanding both as praxes of property. In the remainder of this introduction, I delineate debates concerning property, materiality, immateriality, and the avant-garde that will be vital to the theoretical stakes of this project.

## Aesthetic Shields

Cheryl Harris's insight that property is the right to exclude and thus should be characterized as metaphysical and not physical situates how the interrelationship between the physical and metaphysical exists beyond the mythology of Western civilization and thrives to this day.[41] During antiquity, this dichotomy was understood as realism and idealism. From there, the binary has been discussed as the mind/body division of the Enlightenment; scientific management's brainwork/handwork, later transmuted into skilled/unskilled work; and the concept/object division in the tradition of avant-garde and conceptual art. This last category, however, does not name its negation; it does not name the function and labor it has abandoned to the other.

We can trace whiteness as property and the right to exclude to fundamental operations concerning forms writ large, as well as to contemporary aesthetics and their institutions. Some artists assume the freedom to expand the category of art—for example, urinals as fountains—and these objects and ideas have historically been considered their property. It is in and through whiteness that property claims can be registered, and objects and ideas become witnessed as the owners' property through the discourse of exclusion (as in, not all urinals are fountains or art, just those found by Duchamp). That the symbols of segregation (urinals/fountains) become mistranslated as symbols of aesthetic liberation—for those already considered legally free—exposes the relationship between racial capitalism, settler colonialism, and modernism and the characteristics that formalize the aestheticization of property.

The tradition of racialized appropriation continues today, from Richard Prince's endless theft of works by Black photographers, to Joe Scanlan's "Donnelle Woodford" blackface project, to Santiago Sierra's entire oeuvre, which is examined in this book. Exemplifying this practice, in 2015, MoMA's first poet laureate, Kenneth Goldsmith, attempted to present the autopsy report of Michael Brown, the young Black man shot by police in Ferguson, Missouri, in 2014, as his poem in a reading at Brown University. Immediately afterward, he releasing a statement that read, "Appropriation and plagiarism are here to stay."[42] In the effort to defend Goldsmith's anti-Black "found object" poetry from criticism, a 2015 *New Yorker* piece proclaimed that "conceptual art and conceptual poetry embody ideas, and both descend from Duchamp."[43] The invocation of Duchamp was to serve as the closing argument. If racialized and gendered formations provide the expansive and conceptual possibilities of modern and postmodern art imperative to the concept of artistic freedom, then we should ask: For whom is decontextualized appropriation—transformations of the urinal—the site of aesthetic liberation? As situated by my research—from Duchamp's *Fountain* to the digitization of daguerreotypes and the Archive for New Poetry—the usage, control, and modification of an imagined Blackness (one that can and should *aesthetically* be removed from its embodiments) becomes the primary mode of innovative art, aesthetic rupture, and originality.

While my research begins in the late nineteenth and early twentieth century, I am interested in laying out the colonial history of immaterial/conceptual art in order to clarify the racial dynamics of the present. For these reasons, I fixate on the praxis of property and traverse forms and movements usually considered politically and aesthetically differentiated. I read concept- and idea-oriented aesthetic projects, be they defined as postmodern, modern, avant-garde, conceptual, or otherwise within the vital scope of art historical periodization, as also needing to be understood within economic and legal processes. Throughout the book, I track the ways in which the building of artistic institutions and institutionalized aesthetic forms is in close conversation with contested and naturalized labor divisions. For example, in one case, I ask: How do the distinctions and parallels between the labor *experiments* forced onto steel workers in the early twentieth century by Fredrick Taylor and the burgeoning categorizations of experimental aesthetic forms provide insight into the antagonistic and cooperative relationship between art and capital?

In this study, I am distinguishing property from commodity, as property claims remain with their supposed owners.[44] While we are allowed and encouraged to purchase and consume commodities, and even to commodify (e.g., purchasing a coffee mug of a painting at the museum gift shop), the ability to profit from, indeed own, the object of profit, and exclude by controlling access to said object (e.g., the painting upstairs represented on the coffee mug) is altogether and purposefully denied. This book pushes for a petty materialist approach to interrogating the ownership of "liberatory" art objects for the purposes of clarifying the racial and gender dispossessions embedded in the discourse of property, and one day, of dismantling property altogether.

For those outside of the incestuous cloisters of contemporary art and poetry, the avant-garde may be a topic of disinterest. In this book, I demonstrate how theories invented for modernism and the avant-garde are foundational shielding arguments for the mediation of settler colonialism and the anti-Blackness of cultural forms into the present.[45] Recent protests of art institutions, while vibrant, have approached singular board members and actors, rather than the institutions' history and the construction of the boards more broadly. Thus, I hope to aid in what can become an ongoing investigation into institutional finance, history, land, and more. I seek to examine the racialized contours that marked immaterialism in the avant-garde as innovative and trace the theories that naturalized narratives of experimentation via colonization, in order to denaturalize them.

Throughout the book I take up what I call *shields*: people, objects, and forms that have been so thoroughly defended that their names themselves come to serve as a shelter from critique—the shield of glory that is the museum form, the shield of Duchamp that invokes the avant-garde and the authority of the artist-manager, the shield that terminology such as *new* and *experimental* provides against material analysis, the shield of archival preservation, the shield of an immaterial removed of material. As Duchampian ideological promulgations have only been extended, rather than limited, by art historians and literary scholars, an unfamiliarity with the terrains of his name and its function also serves to shame and discipline young new artists and field outsiders. In other instances, figures like Santiago Sierra have used Marxism as a shield to re-create and aestheticize exploitation, wherein Marxism engenders neat class critiques that accommodate rather than destroy the economy of the gallery space. I take apart these shields to create a window through which we may speak to each other about violence, imagination, dreams, and more.

Across the chapters, I grapple with the relationship between finance and aesthetics and the routes they traverse to create corresponding systems of colonial logic. Each chapter deals with the mutations between racial capitalism and modern aesthetic institutions. When reading an earlier draft of this manuscript, theorist Max Haiven graciously pointed to the ways in which the rise of certain financial products corresponds to financial periods; as in, the financialization of life and death begins in the late 1970s, as does the rise of terms such as "intangible economy"—much later than the rise of immaterial art that I track here. However, while the precision of vocabulary is important, so too is understanding its contradictions and developments. The wealth legacies of Frick, Carnegie, and the Arensbergs share a primary extractive source: the coke, coal, and steel industries mentioned above. This continuity is an instructive depiction of late nineteenth-century colonial accumulation.[46] Further, the Carnegie Steel Company became the first billion-dollar company in the world through its partnership with J. P. Morgan, who worked to financialize extractive industries. So while financial capitalism and conceptual/immaterial art as we currently understand them may not have existed at this time, their forms were in the making. If immaterial labor has been commodified under capitalism (as Antonio Negri and Michael Hardt have recently argued), in this book, I argue that immaterial labor and art were invented in late capitalism to distinguish *forms* of labor.[47]

This book's focus on New York institutions is not merely a detail, but is the book's very grounding. In grappling with the *longue durée* of public silence, Joanne Barker writes of how Manna-hata means "island of the many hills" in Lenape and became "Manhattan" through mistranslation by "an Englishman working for the Dutch West India Company."[48] While the traditional homeland of the Lenape people (Manna-hata) has become synonymous with financial capitalism, museums, entertainment, and culture (Manhattan), Barker's scholarship establishes how the city with all its famous scenery remains a site of dispossession, a settler city founded as a barrier fort built to restrict the movement of the Lenape people in the effort to remove them from their homelands.[49] The presence of the Lenape people is made explicit through the name, and it is through this clarity that their presence lives and remains disavowed. This book shows how aesthetic traditions have not merely participated in this violence, but have actively formalized it into what are considered immaterial and transcendent aesthetics.

Each chapter of this book thus opens by discussing the land on which the subject's histories and ideas take shape. Manhattan, the Allegheny River in Pittsburgh, Philadelphia, the Kumeyaay land known as La Jolla in California, and Massachusetts are all variations of colonial mistranslated or borrowed Indigenous words and names. This methodology aims to consider English in light of Kauanui's "enduring indigeneity." Though US empire actively works against Indigenous presence, its language is full of Indigenous words and names. And so, perhaps another failing of modernist structuralism, and even postmodernist poststructuralism, is how the relationship between the stable signifier and the unstable signified does not open into an engagement with Native presence or reparation; and thus, I return to the root.

There are arguments that have been made privately to me, and sometimes not so privately, that some nonwhite artists consider themselves to be conceptual, or have been branded conceptual posthumously, or have been theorized as avant-garde in the present. That select nonwhite artists have been granted the title of *experimental*, or may have taken up the term voluntarily, does not invalidate the arguments I make regarding the found form, aesthetics, racial capitalism, or collecting imperatives. I do not see the presence of exceptions as evidence against the structure; nor do I believe in the utilization of nonwhite peoples to nullify the overwhelming facts of white supremacy. One could make the argument that certain nonwhite artists and poets truly believe their lineage is sincerely linked to the white avant-garde; I would respond that the sincerity of their feelings is not a shield for the history and violence of institutionalized aesthetics. Others might make the case that my arguments collapse certain nonwhite artists further into the white canon; I would ask for the field to reexamine nonwhite artists and writers who may be vulnerable to such forms of erasure. Furthermore, while whiteness continues to be protected legally, the perpetuation of anti-Blackness does not require legalized whiteness. It may be that in this contemporary moment, non-Black artists of color take up what has been normalized by white avant-garde and white institutional practices to perpetuate anti-Blackness in their aesthetics, sincerely, as their own expression.

The focus of this project is not the visual marker of whiteness or white persons, but the formations of property. Throughout my analysis, I press into how certain objects, materials, and people are assumed to be vacant, empty vessels and how notions of *found*, *readymade*, *collected* depend on notions of previous indeterminacy, transient vacancy, and the legal division between the object and property. The rest of this introduction tracks the frameworks that support this analysis—and against which it sometimes strains. The various case studies in this book—the Frick Collection, scientific management, Duchamp's *Fountain*, the Archive for New Poetry, Harvard's claim to the daguerreotypes of enslaved persons, and the uncritical criticism concerning Santiago Sierra—have been selected for their formal and material logics. I am interested in the invention of the forms of *collecting* and *propertizing*, from the dispossession that is the museum space to the discourse of *found* and *readymade*, and how these forms were and remain the aesthetic mediations of racial capitalism. By exploring these cases, I argue that the discourse of formal aesthetic innovation is rooted in materialized notions of possession and dispossession; it occurs through an affirmation of the racialization of property. In arguing this, I seek to connect the language of form with the politics of property in order to amplify the stakes of this *excess* realm.[50] I have selected these particular case studies as they are exemplary of a dominant mode of art and literature that has normalized itself as abstract, immaterial, and avant-garde. In this normalization, I track the origin tale of vacancy and property so that their abrogation may one day be plotted.

## On Form and Property

Throughout this book I ask: How and why are certain spaces imagined as vacant, as available for discovery?[51] And in return: How does abstraction construct emptiness? Further, though constructed through an emptiness that cannot be, how do forms of exclusion appear so consistently without contradiction? It was and is a particularity that the aestheticization of property is witnessed as innovative and new. It was and is a particular positionality that carries out the aestheticization of property as one's own unique expression—art, anti-art, or otherwise.

Cheryl Harris's foundational "Whiteness as Property" opens with an excerpt of Harris's unpublished poem and an extract from the petition in *Plessy v. Ferguson*. I read this gesture as the text's porous ambition to interact with all contours of language, from legal to aesthetic and otherwise. Harris harrows into how the legitimation of settler colonialism and racial capitalism takes root in European philosophy. She situates how whiteness in the US was invented to uphold the legal distinction between enslaved persons and free persons (white), and in this, whiteness becomes the vehicle for legal notions of freedom. Thus, to own property (including one's body and labor) was the material manifestation of freedom. In this legal formulation, property is not the demonstration of *having* things, but of "the right to exclude" others from the categorical imperative of freedom. Exclusion demarcates property. Further, Harris demonstrates that through this definition of property, US settlers insisted that the land they "discovered" was *vacant*, and this conversion from vacancy into occupation was crystalized through the discourse of property that defined the legalization of chattel slavery.[52] The legalization of settler colonialism and chattel slavery worked in tandem to construct *whiteness as property*. Whiteness was and remains the positionality to insist on something (or someone) as vacant when they are full and alive.[53]

Anticapitalist traditions often trace previous European philosophies in order to press the discourse of revolution and decolonization. Harris's methodology of tracking European philosophy in order to critique the foundation of violence is a shared procedure among Marxist, feminist, and postcolonial scholars. However, Harris's critique of property may not necessarily be Marxist; as Harris renders race a priori to understanding historical and contemporary forms of property, affecting how its abolition would be theorized and imagined. Marx's critique of the property form varied throughout his life, from the discourse on the protection of the private property of workers, to his formidable critique of the commons, to his ambivalence or affirmation toward socialist forms of colonization.[54] Though Marx's groundbreaking intervention was to reframe Hegel's understanding of progressive history from the dialectic between master and slave to one between the bourgeoisie and the proletariat, Marx's ideal proletariat was European and, as examined in my final chapter, uninvolved in aesthetics.[55]

Most masterfully, Cedric Robinson's oeuvre demonstrates a critique of Marx and Marxism by situating how it is not the transformation of the proletariat and bourgeoisie that is a priori to revolution; rather it is the lumpenproletariat, the enslaved, the colonized, the Indigenous, and the older tradition of peasant revolts that ground ontological transformation. In *Black Marxism*, Robinson situates three key components of his critique: (1) the historical context of German nationalism and its importance to understanding the rise of communism; (2) the erasure of slave revolts and marronage from the historization of capitalism and colonization and the subsequent misgivings of frameworks such as primitive accumulation and labor; and (3) how the history and presence of Black Radical Tradition pushes Marxism further than what it could ever imagine.[56] In *Anthropology of Marxism*, Robinson extends his critique into Western civilization to trace how the genealogy of Western socialism comes not out of Marx or capitalism, but from heretics, peasants, and their revolts against the church and state. By situating how a critique of property and capital preexist capitalism and modern colonization, Robinson forges a primary critique of Marx, whose developmental understanding of liberation and socialism situates capitalism as prefiguring socialism, erroneously marking capitalism as a central stage of global liberation.

Similar to Kauanui's critique of colonial time, Robinson's epistemological critique is vital to denying the developmental narrative of progress predicated upon exploitation and to denying *any* necessity of capitalism and colonization, and it serves as a model for rejecting narratives of property and its forms writ large. The toils of labor and exploitation do not prefigure the liberated subject; Robinson demonstrates that capitalism does not exist to liberate, nor can it eventually be fashioned into liberation. Capitalism is not the grounds upon which liberation can be built; the foundation for the fight lies elsewhere.

Furthermore, Robinson argues that an orthodox Marxist understanding of property and history does not and cannot account for chattel slavery but rather fails to understand the relationship between colonialism and what becomes considered primitive accumulation. Thus, Robinson situates capitalism as always racial capitalism.[57] Previously, W. E. B. Du Bois delineated the ongoing conflicts between the terms *Black* and *worker*.[58] Under racial capitalism, the categories of *Black* and *worker* are witnessed as terms of separation and contradiction.[59] Affixed to chattel slavery, Black labor is not recognized as a site of wage labor or private property. In the term *worker*, whiteness is presumed, and thus Black labor remains a site of dispossession. In this trajectory, Black, Indigenous, immigrant, and undocumented persons are often left out of the discourse of the working class because US rhetoric tends to situate the working class as a static position belonging specifically to white persons, rather than, as Harry Braverman notes, "an ongoing social process."[60] Such distinctions remain palpable in ongoing tensions between white Marxist theorists on the one hand, and postcolonial and anticolonial Black Marxists and Black studies and Indigenous critical theory scholars on the other. Some of these tensions will be explored in my first chapter, on the Homestead Strike and the anti-Black discourse of "scab" labor.

I depart from previous Marxist scholarship, such as Adorno's and Horkheimer's work on the culture industry and more recent examinations of arts funding, in key ways. While I am sympathetic to Adorno's political project of reading culture as symptomatic of capitalism (which prescribes the "art of resistance" as immutable surface refractions at best, co-optation at worst) such a reading practices what Lewis Gordon theorized as "epistemic closure"[61] and refuses what Gayatri Spivak has described as "intimate sabotage."[62] Museums, archives, and cultural production do not exist outside of racial capitalism, *and* the critiques made in this book do not serve to foreclose what cannot be seen by the politicized critic, be it ruptures, weapons, silences, absences, continuums, more.[63]

Furthermore, my approach to historical materialism is without moral indictments, without some faulty prescription for artists, writers, persons, without an illusive guidance for better funding, path, or space. Unlike contemporary scholarship that traces the financial documents of an institution in order to ultimately level an individualistic critique of (too often) nonwhite artists and writers who have interacted with said institutions, the aims of my critiques are structurally more ambitious and uncurative. The embeddedness of specific individual artists and writers of color within institutions speaks to the larger structures of colonialism and capitalism. The concentration on how they operate—as if they could operate outside of colonialism while we remain inside of it—speaks to the misguided popularity of morally condemning particular individuals rather than the gatekeepers, colonial agents and their ancestors, and the ways in which the property form becomes naturalized through this dynamic.

The neoliberal mutations that continue to occur between criticism, the institution, the artist, and the critic almost demand constant apprehension toward the instrumentalization of critical theory and its selected artist, such as the scholarship surrounding Santiago Sierra (discussed in chapter 6) and the usage of Marxism as a shield to recreate and aestheticize exploitation. Critics interested in work and labor have often approached this issue as cased in the pursuit of individual artists, and, in a positivistic sense, they approach artists interested in legible protest, artists interested in wage negotiation, through a deracialized framework, as case studies of artists with "better politics."[64] In their scholarship, Marxism becomes reframed as a class critique suited for the confines of a gallery space, while the abolition of private property, field examinations of labor practices, or the mild pursuit of a socialist future entirely fall off the map. Thus, the framework Harris provides allows for history to be materially reexamined, and I use her framework to interrogate modernism and the avant-garde in necessary ways. "Whiteness as property" offers the framework and vocabulary by which avant-garde origin stories might be fundamentally perforated.

## On the Racial Politics of the Avant-Garde

The desire to leave behind older traditions in the pursuit of newer ones should be understood as part of the theoretical justification of colonization. Fatima El-Tayeb has powerfully demonstrated how, contrary to the assertion of "race" as a US concern, race was constructed in Europe for the purposes of colonization, and European racial hierarchy was exported around the globe to uphold colonialism.[65] Thus, theorizations that obscure the racial politics of the avant-garde can only do so through a conflation of liberalism with racialization, and, as Lisa Lowe has so exquisitely laid out, by mistaking "liberalism as the primary ideology of—and not the source of critique for—colonized civilization."[66] In aesthetic inquiry, there has been little distinction between these political formations. Lowe posits, "The genealogy of modern liberalism is thus also a genealogy of modern race; racial differences and distinctions designate the boundaries of the human and endure as remainders attesting to the violence of liberal universality."[67] Modern understandings of the world were racialized perspectives—they were colonial formations that informed the definitions of universality and freedom.

To hone in on a defining moment for modernist freedom, in 1917 in New York City, at the height of modernist momentum, the Society of Independent Artists held a show that promised to accept all submitted works of art. The call is a revolutionary claim against the forces of institutional gatekeeping, against the spaces of authority that had worked for centuries to keep art exclusive.[68] By refusing to evaluate expression through the discourse of selection, the society promised an art show that would prioritize personal expression above all else. Duchamp tests the boundaries of this progressive gesture by submitting an object that he terms a "ready-made." He claims to have found the object and declares it his work of art. This gesture forces the Society of Independent Artists to reveal the limits of their initial call: all legible artworks will be accepted, but this call is not an opening for illegible or emergent aesthetic forms. For the society, art is made or designed by the author. Their rejection of Duchamp's object marks a compression within modernist understandings of art, which were without ambition to rupture the links between the artist, expression, and craft. The modernists reveal the limitation of their understanding of aesthetics, thus anointing themselves, in the view of the forthcoming avant-gardists, as the outdated, aging former vanguard—and the discovery of this limitation propels the avant-gardist project of expansion forward.

Neither the expansion of the category of artist nor that of art expanded the category of the human—I do not state this as a recuperative gesture of longing, but as fact.[69] The endless expansion of artist and art exists within the realm of settler colonialism, neocolonialism, and racial capitalism. That the committee members of the society consisted of white men (Duchamp was also part of the committee) and one white woman rarely factors into the narrative of avant-garde invention and liberation. That the show—irrespective of Duchamp's rejection or inclusion—would have been a segregated show, in a settler nation-state, has not been part of the discourse of artistic freedom and experimentalism. I further explore how aesthetic movements become divided into racialized timelines in the fourth chapter of this book, to elucidate the naturalization of what Mullen describes as *aesthetic apartheid*.[70]

Scholars interested in thinking across colonialism, slavery, and aesthetics have often been looped into a cycle of disenfranchisement, amnesia, dehistoricization, deconxtexualization, and misreadings. I believe the tool that continues this cycle to be the negation of property. I politicize the neutrality pivotal to the discourse of forms and aesthetic spaces by centering property claims, be it the innovation of a form, their objects, or collections. While primary to their constructions, theorization, and circulation, the politics of property remain wholly absent in discussions concerning museums, modern art, and poetry.

Property is an important differentiator to the said freedoms of conceptual art, as conceptual art is fundamentally exclusive. While it is true that figures such as Duchamp worked to expand the category of what was considered art, they did so through the confines of the legible subject, expanding only what was already and only available to them. *Whiteness as property* was vital to the narration of innovation and freedom of conceptual art, as it is only through the vehicle of property that the category of art is expanded. This is the ontological problem of immaterialism: its author is required to be a property-eligible subject.

In liberal New York City, whiteness as property and colorblind rhetoric became woven into the liberalism of the avant-garde. My reading of aesthetics with racial capitalism is symptomatic, as canonical modern artworks such as *Fountain* emerged in the presence of Jim Crow law and culture.[71] Given this history, it is no accident that the most important works of modern art, avant-garde forms, and museums have all been rendered universal and therefore outside the purview of racial analysis. It is precisely this narrative of universal aesthetic liberation that racializes and contextualizes *Fountain*. As Lowe has demonstrated, liberal freedom is predicated upon racial and gender dispossession, and thus it is through the expansion of artistic freedom that its racial signification becomes pronounced.[72]

My decision to fold art and poetry together stems from my desire to examine the dynamics between racial capitalism and modernism. In a critique of Language poetry, David Marriott argues that finance is not about value or representation, but instead about forms of communication.[73] While advocates of modernist abstraction and modernist-driven conceptualist practices focus on theories of production, Marriott materializes how finance is "fundamentally dependent on communication."[74] The communiqué narrated from one seller in finding another purchaser operates through abstracted form. A materialist reading of the genre differences between poetry and visual art is immensely helpful in understanding why and how particular notions of property, form, and innovation arise and are adopted across genres. Their similarities as well as their differences lead to new analyses about the underlying politics of the modernist tradition.

Though cross-media aesthetic movements have mostly waned, contemporary artists and writers continue to look to each other as part of generative practice and to establish the necessity of their formal pursuits. Genre-shielding can be witnessed back and forth throughout the twentieth and twenty-first centuries. In 1959, Brion Gysin declared that "writing is fifty years behind painting," and this phrase has been endlessly cited by conceptualist writers to justify their racially appropriative practices.[75] Furthermore, the difference in material stakes between media amplifies the politics in place. While artists exhibiting in museums and producing objects may have clear financial incentives to produce objects for sale, the financial goals of the poetry market have not always been so transparent.[76] Though poetry is without an immediate object value—which constitutes its claim to moral superiority—and currently there is no "poetry blue chip market," the normalization of modernist found-art occurred in tandem with found poetic practices.[77] If abstract modernist forms in visual art are displays of white property claims, abstract modernist forms in poetry situate the language space in which such objects can reside.[78]

## On Work/Labor

The affective appeal of avant-garde forms is in their suppression of the category of labor. Modernist expression remained linked to artistic craft, which implicitly carries with it questions of access *and* work: the artist paints their new vision; the poet expresses feelings by writing new lines. Taking from Duchamp's reification of ideas, conceptual art insists that art can move away from the object altogether through a denigration of non-art forms and objects, all of which will be decided by the recognized artist. The work of thinking, conceptualizing, and art-doing becomes bracketed from the labor of making, using, and being, and as such, a hierarchical elevation from one to the other is created. More than anything else, found and conceptual art reify the processes of dispossession and division of labor. In avant-garde found practices, who enacts what kinds of labor and where, how much (or if) they are paid, what is made invisible and why, and how non-art work differs from art work are questions that become fundamentally passé, or affectively uninteresting, and their pursuit is only taken up by conservative modernists or ill-informed killjoys.[79] Situated as one of the most important works of modern art—the origin point of its mythology—*Fountain* is the gesture that allowed some to move beyond questions of materiality, context, work, and place, and as such, it continues to deflect such questions in the present.

When presenting my research at conferences, I often hear the rebuttal that artists have always outsourced their labor in the form of painting schools and factories. I would agree that large-scale canonical art productions have paralleled the various economic structures of the societies in which they take place. The fact that Rembrandt and the "old European masters" employed uncredited persons to paint and make is an important dimension of the political economy of art, but not the emphasis of this book. My contention here is not that avant-garde and contemporary artists and poets are *unlike* the European tradition from which they descend, but rather that their narratives concerning art *too* parallel the societal and economic shifts of their present and should be examined in that light. Their emphasis on dividing *idea* (art) from *object* (material, labor, person) is a way to understand the aestheticized meditations of racial capitalism and settler colonialism. Therefore, how the rise of racial and economic systems becomes animated through forms pronounced as immaterial remains my focus.

The implications of the question of mental work—a vestige of the Cartesian binary—impact academia as much as the discourse of aesthetics. To ask what the labor and role of thinking might be, particularly amid the neoliberalization of academia and the normalization of white supremacy, may feel either excessive or self-laudatory. In the former vein, I have seen radical academics, artists, and writers (professionalized thinkers) apologize for their profession. It does not seem *enough* to write and think. *Real work* seems like more. A critical examination of labor divisions created during the early twentieth century in deunionized steel mills, and then aestheticized through the avant-garde, is required to track how the fields of writing and art perpetuate ideas of mind work as removed from hand work in both their critique and solidarity. In accepting this division, the artist/writer/academic identifies as the guilty mind-worker/manager, perhaps romanticizing the hand work they are not paid to perform and laboring to articulate projects that elevate the hand-worker above the mind-worker. The elevation from one to the other is supposed to become their gesture of worker solidarity. But what to make of this? Surely we do not accept the implication that some people live without their minds and others live without their bodies. Rejecting this division does not erase the serious exploitation that many face in their daily lives while others do not.

Conceptual art has often been akin to management, and bureaucracy has been narrated as pivotal to modern and contemporary art forms.[80] The elevation of conceptual forms is neither exceptional to nor innovative of the logic of racial capitalism and colonialism but rather is the *aestheticization of its politics.*[81] The emancipation of some is produced through the work of others. As immaterial fantasies are continually expounded, labor becomes the darkest matter.[82] What do the material foundations of immaterial aesthetics reveal about the foundational violence of aesthetics and freedom? In the second and third chapters, I take up how the categorical expansion of art for white artists adheres to the new labor divisions created in the twentieth and twenty-first centuries. Frederick Winslow

Taylor created the categories of "mind work" and "hand work" by observing newly deunionized steel mills, describing them in texts such as *Shop Management* and *The Principles of Scientific Management*. His work remains foundational in business schools, managerial studies, and, I argue, aesthetic movements.[83] The goal of scientific management was to displace the knowledge of production into units of managerial control, so much so that workers would be unable to point to their exact contribution. It was also a tactic to deny claims of creativity and ownership from those considered low-wage workers. Such labor divisions have been normalized and remain in place, and labor scholars continue to study the structural dispossession created by Taylorism.

The freedoms offered through conceptual divides are the same freedoms offered by segregation. The gesture of aesthetic appropriation replicates the dispossession that labor divisions exact in the form of private property. Tracking the divisions drawn between elevated mind workers and unionized hand workers, deunionized hand workers, and segregated and immigrant "scabs" is vital to understanding the inventions of avant-garde forms and notions of the artist today. In this project, I analyze the transformation of each category in conjunction with the movements taking place in aesthetics. How is the labor of artists and intellectuals understood and defined? How do we define ourselves in a moment in which mental activity is taken away and then "given back" to workers (as a mechanism of further disempowerment)?

## Structure of the Book

Divided into six chapters, this book inspects the various historical parameters that transfigure the aestheticization of property. Throughout, I connect histories and sites that have been disconnected, such as labor studies and art history, or misconnected, such as property and form. To this end, my opening chapter politicizes the provenance of the Frick Collection in New York City. In order to read the development of the Frick Collection through the disavowal of union culture and the segregation primary to labor dispossession in the late nineteenth and early twentieth centuries, I first turned to Frick's acquisition records of art objects from the Knoedler Gallery alongside his role in the Homestead Strike of 1892. The strike at the Homestead Steel Works outside Pittsburgh, Pennsylvania, took place during union renegotiations with Frick and Carnegie and is still known as one of the largest union strikes, as well as one of the most violent union clashes with private security forces in US history. Labor historians have theorized that the violence workers faced at Homestead degraded US union culture. Though it is the breaking of steel unions that led to the rapacious wealth that Carnegie and Frick remain known for, I complicate even this class-conscious narrative through an examination of racial segregation within late nineteenth-century unions and the anti-Black riots executed by the Homestead union members during the strike. In racializing every aspect of this labor and art history, I situate how the distance between illegible person, dignified laborer, and aesthetic expression continues to be maintained.

I begin with the Frick because I seek to highlight the political linkages between patrons of European masters, patrons of the avant-garde, and patrons of experimental poetics in the growth of neoliberal aesthetics. The differences in their objects serve to illuminate the consistency with which they fortified their collections and legacies. In addition, I am staking that collectors of the old European masters and the avant-garde overlap in key ways when accounting for their racialized collecting efforts: from the impetus to leave behind their aesthetic vision to the narrative of aesthetic preservation as a benevolent gesture of public good. Why leave behind an art collection for a future public when one's relationship to the present public has been one of scorn, degradation, violence, and murder? What do we make of this ongoing, contradictory repetition?

In making connections between the personal-art-collection-as-museum and the procedure of donating one's art collection to an established museum, my second chapter looks at the parallel histories of scientific management and conceptual art. It is through scientific management that the materialist histories of the Frick Collection and the Arensberg collection of works by Duchamp—though seemingly disparate in aesthetic styles—are crystallized. I track how the rise of Fredrick Winslow Taylor's scientific management was made possible by deunionization, and I analyze the colonial history of scientific management itself—particularly how Taylor's conception was modeled after his deep admiration of the slave plantation as the most efficient site of management. I explore the parallel rise of scientific management and conceptual art because I want us to consider: How does exploitation become metastasized as innovation in economic and aesthetic spheres? How does it become naturalized that some people work without their minds and others are celebrated for an idea removed from the body? How did questions concerning the expropriation of labor and material become removed from considerations of what becomes defined as innovative?

The traditions of found art as understood by Duchamp, his patrons, and the art establishment are rooted in racialized understandings of property fundamentally unavailable to nonwhite persons, legally and as institutional practice. Thus, in the third chapter, I examine how financial patronage operated and remains vital to how the modernist canon is understood. I question ahistorical, apolitical, and meritocratic readings of found art, and instead read the politics of found object art as developed by Duchamp and his patrons. The correspondence between Duchamp and the Arensbergs firmly demonstrates the processes of museum donor acquisition—a phenomena that is both known and understudied. I contextualize this argument through an examination of Noah Purifoy's work and outdoor museum.

Further, I argue in chapter 3 that historicizing *Fountain* allows us to witness how pivotal colonialism and segregation have been to previous understandings of modernists' innovation and their collections. In conjunction, while appropriation becomes celebrated and normalized for avant-garde writers and artists, the violence of enforced assimilation becomes a key theme for many Black, Asian American, and postcolonial cultural producers. The tensions that foreground the celebration of the found object practice are the same processes that attempt to normalize assimilation. By examining the operations of property and property management in the arts, I propose that alongside the literature and art that expose the freedom of appropriation there exists a haunted and haunting archive of cultural texts that lay out dreams for liberation.

I set up all that I do with art, museums, labor, finance, and property in order to tend to the development of poetry archives, which has important convergences and divergences with the former. In chapter 4, I trace how *experimental* and *conceptual* remain racialized terms in poetic discourse and their archival formations. In this pursuit I examine the collecting priorities of the University of California San Diego's Archive for New Poetry (ANP). I begin by delineating how race becomes pivotal to the collection development priorities of the ANP, and how this prioritization is institutionally processed by literary scholarship that links innovation to whiteness. Under the banner of "new," the ANP created a segregated repository—its current collecting priorities are 100 percent white—with a historical dedication to Language poetry. The indexing of whiteness as the sole and proprietary manifestation of experimentation can be witnessed in the ANP's collection, appraisal, and acquisition processes. I argue that there is little institutional possibility for collecting imperatives to become desegregated if whiteness continues to be indexed to "new" forms—be it in poetry, art, or otherwise. As long as race remains at the margins of literary scholarship and archival praxis, segregated and segregating collections will remain the institutional norm.[84]

The ANP resides on Indigenous land—Kumeyaay, Cupeño, Luiseño, and Cahuilla land—and as such, the collection remains a settlement. And though containing poetry rather than art objects, the operations of exclusionary property function similarly to the Frick Collection. Thus, while not dismissing their differences, chapter 4 notes the similarities between these institutions as rooted in settler colonialism and racial capitalism: from their inception to their collection and organization, property remains their foregrounding logic.

Following my examination of race and experimental literary archives, I look at the racial politics of the ostensibly revolutionary form of digitization. As Kalindi Vora and Neda Atanasoski have demonstrated, digital technologies have fundamentally depended on preexisting racialized labor formations, and celebratory pronouncements of how new technologies will displace the human worker are simply advertisements to evade discussing the continuums of neocolonialism.[85] In my fifth chapter, I examine the institutional provenance of daguerreotypes of enslaved persons held by the Getty Museum and Harvard University—particularly how digital images continue the regimes of racialized property—and consider the ways contemporary Black artists have intervened in narratives of institutional ownership. By examining the critical framework offered by Carrie Mae Weems's artwork, the anticolonial extensions of Divya Mehra's practice, and Sasha Huber's performances, chapter 5 explores how US ideals of property and art become compounded by the digital present.

My critiques of property and the terms of immateriality will be instructive for analyzing the future operations of digital forms, as many reactions to digital property forms conjure outlandish statements from those who insist that it was different before. David Joselit provides the most recent summation of the transcendent mythology of the readymade form. In order to critique nonfungible tokens (NFTs), Joselit sets the tokens up against Duchamp's readymade, and argues that the digital financial tool is a "reverse of Duchamp's gesture."[86] He distinguishes property from free information, desublimation from deskilling, and abandonment from what could be assumed as dispossession, and then claims that generous readings of art have the potential to destabilize and reject the property form. In this reading, non-NFT readymade art is outside the bounds of property, and it is outside of property where we might somehow become destabilized. Joselit's definition, which situates "the legacy of slavery (the human becoming property)," reveals the liberal position from which the readymade remains mythologized away from material history: through an insistence on *becoming*.[87] In this liberal iteration, the human is naturalized before the enslaved, evading how the category of the human was invented during the Enlightenment to enslave and colonize.[88] The human does not become property and is not a container for transient or mobile relationships; rather, the *human* is the category afforded to those who possessed property. What Joselit instructively misses is how Duchamp's readymades have always been property through the colonial construction of the human, and, in this, could be considered prescient NFTs.

My last chapter outlines the continuation of *whiteness as property* and scientific management in contemporary art by discussing Santiago Sierra's body of work, particularly *250 cm Line Tattoo on 6 Paid People*, in which Sierra paid six day laborers thirty dollars each to have a line tattooed across their backs in front of an art gallery audience in Cuba. Taking up the labor and material conditions as well as the financial and rhetorical forces surrounding the series, I interrogate the Taylorist, managerial logics pivotal to the current milieu of contemporary gallery art. Though fundamentally dependent on humiliating vulnerable communities (homeless Black and brown women, unemployed men, undocumented persons, poor children), Sierra's performances have been described as "better politics" and as anticapitalist art by art historians, museum catalogs, and his gallery's PR statements.[89] I examine the theorems offered by Sierra, his gallery representations, and the arguments promulgated by prominent art critics to situate an evolving definition of neoliberal aesthetics. I locate neoliberal aesthetics as the aestheticized practice of Taylorism, dependent on the ongoing dispossession of race, gender, and labor discussed in chapters 1 and 2. Furthermore, in rejecting the replication of exploitation, which stems from the fetishization of production as the apex of criticality and innovation—my working definition of neoliberal aesthetics—I offer a loose antagonistic framework against this tradition.

There are no images from Sierra's catalog in this book because I take up what Kimberly Juanita Brown has theorized as the "repeating body" as a call for praxis.[90] While Brown speaks specifically about the images and representations of enslaved persons, I find her ethical puncturing key to discussing contemporary images of Black persons and useful for problematizing the discourse of aesthetic representation. Some readers may be interested to look up referenced images, to do their own investigation of my reading, and to fault my citation of Sierra as perpetuating violence. I would respond that I believe we can discuss Sierra's catalog and the practice of neoliberal aesthetics without the image, as the image has been made purposefully uninteresting and without importance. I am interested in examining the prevailing narratives and undoing the powers of its circulation rather than compounding them.

Examining the political implications of artistic freedom essential to the Duchampian tradition has allowed me to describe how artists and poets such as Noah Purifoy, Sasha Huber, Divya Mehra, Wafaa Bilal, and Wanda Coleman intervene into the provenance of property claims. These artists engage with practices of reparations and work against colonial aesthetics. Specifically, they reject the abstraction that serves the imagination of colonialism and racial capitalism and confer a precise engagement with time, space, and materiality. As Gayatri Chakravorty Spivak deftly demonstrates how access to self-representation is the threshold for subalternity, these artists and writers are not subaltern.[91] They also do not perform the false alterity demanded by liberal inclusionary measures; rather they implicate their threshold positionality in their practice. Their positions as racialized, gendered subjects pressure rudimentary understandings of politicized and aesthetic action, and in each of their oeuvres we can witness a sustained and variegated engagement with the liminalities of liberation. While they differ from each other in complex and critical ways, I argue that when read together, artists and poets who materialize what continues to be dematerialized demand a commitment to the dissolution of normalized colonial forms, practices, and foundations, and allow us to approach the pleasures/pain of other things to come.

Rather than pretending to resolve the contradictions opened by aesthetics (be they formal, political, or otherwise) the work imagined by these artists and poets compounds their mediums' irresolution. Art and poetry do not work as an alibi, nor as the passive observer (perpetrator) that aestheticizes the structures and frameworks of historical violence to offer false solutions where none can exist; instead, they pressurize even the best representational answers as in need of more inquiry and dissolution. In offering unresolvable questions as part of their practice and in their work, they complicate the relationship between immaterial and material, and deny the transcendent ideology of aesthetics. Aesthetics without glory, without salvation, without cure. Here aesthetics works through reparations for those the world has denied and toward the world in which we can and must live.

The ambition of this book is to aid in the deracination of the present world order by examining the colonial roots of art, poetry, museums, and archives. As stated by many before me, the liberation of aesthetics will require the liberation of all its dependent and constitutive spaces. In line with the long and ongoing call to abolish the police and prisons, recent arguments have been put forth by activists that, just as the police do not keep people safe, museums do not keep culture safe and therefore must be abolished. I agree and would extend the reach for abolition into the conceptualization and formation of property. I am not alone in rejecting a siloed exceptionalist freedom, a siloed transcendence, a freedom predicated upon the oppression of others. I begin in art because, though it advertises itself as a beautiful, wonderful space removed from the *messiness* of the world, it is in fact a space where this messiness becomes metastasized.[92] I begin in aesthetics to take up the world. I begin in art and poetry because all of the roots must be pulled out—especially and particularly colonial aesthetics.[93]

I am starting small with hopes that other case studies will arise, connecting or countering my arguments, which would, in effect, help it grow. I welcome contestations and criticism of this thesis as a method of growth. I also welcome partnerships and parallel projects from all spectrums, so that we might together grow toward the end.

ONE

# Personal Collection and the Museum Form

## *Racial Capitalism, Settler Colonialism, and the Legacies of the Homestead Strike of 1892*

if it doesn't cost me my life, it doesn't cost anything at all. **S*an D. Henry-Smith, *Wild Peach***

Akin to how modern-day computing and contemporary machinery industries are environmentally extractive and require water, steel plants were built near rivers.[1] Andrew Carnegie and Henry Clay Frick's steel plants, and the franchises that would become U.S. Steel, were located next to the Monongahela and Allegheny Rivers. In the introduction to this book, we discussed, via Joanne Barker's scholarship, that Manhattan is a mistranslation of the Lenape Manna-hata, and the names Monongahela and Allegheny also derive from Lenape.[2] Allegheny is from Alikehane, which translates as "River where the footprints can be seen," and its etymology points to the Allegewi tribe who were known to live along this river.[3] This area remains the unceded regions in which the Seneca tribe and the Iroquois and Lenape peoples, among others, lived and live, and where now, twenty miles from the river, the Allegheny Indian Reservation is located. The presence of Indigeneity is both rooted and obscured through the name.

The Allegheny River flows from Pennsylvania to New York for about 50 miles, then 250 miles back into Pennsylvania, where it joins the Monongahela River—the name of which is thought to derive from the Lenape Mënaonkihëla, "Where banks cave in or erode"—into what is called the Ohio River.[4] It is on the Allegheny and Monongahela Rivers where Carnegie's steel plants operated, where he became the richest man in the world, and where Frick became the globe's largest railway stockholder. It is on these rivers that the steel plants were forcibly deunionized, including during the Homestead Strike of 1892, as examined in this chapter.

This chapter situates the interconnections between museums and racial capitalism, philanthropy, and settler colonialism. While contemporary public memory of the Homestead Strike and the Gilded Age remains faint, the memory of the period's owners and managers permeates contemporary discourse.[5] The Homestead Steel Works was owned in a partnership between Andrew Carnegie and Henry Clay Frick, whom many of us might know as wealthy philanthropists, arts benefactors, robber barons, or disaster capitalists and settlers. Throughout the 1870s and 1880s Frick became a millionaire by acquiring plants that produced coke, a refined form of coal that is indispensable in the production of iron and steel.[6] By the 1880s he ran a monopoly in Pennsylvania, becoming known as "the Coke King."[7] After the death of Carnegie's partner in 1888, Frick joined the Carnegie Steel Company. The wealth of Carnegie and Frick, which grounded the philanthropic art projects they are best known for today, can be traced to steel and more directly to the 1892 strike, suggesting an intimate relationship between labor, property, and the politics of aesthetics.

How did we arrive at a present with flailing labor protections laws—politically attached to the figure of the white working class yet hostile toward unions—and full of museums (there are currently more museums than Starbucks and McDonalds locations combined)[8] that purport to be political havens? In answering this question, I work to examine mimetically disparate and recurring histories: (1) the dispossession of labor as the presence of wealth, (2) the rise and politics of personal collection museums, and (3) the aestheticization of property. The Frick Collection in New York City and the Homestead Strike of 1892 will be my case studies in examining the connections between labor dispossession and the rise of the personal collection museum. I look to Homestead because labor historians across the political spectrum have examined this strike as the tipping point for how and when US labor became delegitimized, forcefully reorganized, and managed.[9] I look at the acquisition records of the Frick's founding collection because the museum is the direct product of Henry Clay Frick, a central figure whom the strikers fought against. By studying the Homestead Strike with the Frick Collection, I argue that in the developmental history of personal art collections, there is a tandem history of worker, racial, and land dispossession. I seek to materialize the wealth accumulated through the admonishment of collective bargaining and the dismantling of labor, which was transferred to the site of the neutral and yet expressive art collection.

Scholars of modernism and the avant-garde have long argued that collecting—what Jeremy Braddock describes as the "collecting aesthetic"—was in itself the "paradigmatic form of modernist art."[10] Such readings invite us to account for the materiality and the material history of collecting imperatives and to view collecting as an individual expression of desire and idiosyncrasy. Through this understanding one can push to question *how* the collector amassed wealth in order to collect, what the colonial context was that made such an amassing possible, and what the dynamics of racial property and the archive are. Modern art too often becomes grounded in and defined through a dehistoricized, decontextualized notion of collecting. I seek to reframe property relations in art and position how *whiteness as property* functions in granting ownership in modern, postmodern, and museum art. In denaturalizing the museum's histories of wealth extraction, I display how the eradication of striking and labor rights and the segregation of labor have been and remain pivotal to the museum's foundation.

## The Homestead Strike of 1892

For scholars of labor and capitalism, the Homestead Strike of 1892 has become central to understanding anti-unionization in the United States. The strikers' ultimate defeat led to the dismantling of steel unions and union culture for more than forty years, until the Wagner Act of 1935. The strategies used by Frick and the Carnegie Steel Company, including hiring a former union employee to conduct counterinsurgency, bringing in private militia, receiving support from the National Guard to forcefully break the strike, and employing corporate spies to prevent future strikes altogether, have been vastly duplicated to this day. Lastly, the conclusion of the 1892 strike becomes a way to examine the nascence of corporate entitlements, and a portent of wealth transfers and labor dispossessions to come.[11]

Unlike Carnegie, Frick was not known in his lifetime or thereafter as a philanthropist or populist; in fact, he had been and remained openly anti-union.[12] Conversely, Carnegie, a Scottish immigrant whose wealth was accumulated through a series of insider trading tips,[13] took his preliminary millions by consolidating independently operated steel mills and was known to be a "progressive" businessman who often spoke publicly in favor of unions and wrote widely on the profitability of good labor relations.[14] He was publicized as a fair and honest businessman during his lifetime—a reputation to which he attached great importance.[15] His rhetorical strategy of remaining pro-union publicly, yet collaborating with Frick, who was known to behave otherwise, is not a contradiction, but a way to understand the foundation of philanthropy. I will explore this point further in the chapter.

In practice, Carnegie was not and had never been pro-union. By the late 1880s, unions in his factories had been systematically denied, and by the 1900s, not a single mill under his ownership recognized union membership. The primary arguments made for their dissolution had been that a global drop in steel prices made the agreed-upon wage minimum uneconomic for the company, that technological improvements needed to be factored into the plant's operations budget, and that these improvements would alleviate the need for "skilled" laborers enforced by union contracts.[16] This rhetoric is refuted by the astronomical increase of Carnegie's and Frick's overall net wealth during their lifetime and beyond, and by the actuality that technological improvements did not abolish the need for "skilled" workers but instead variegated and altered the kinds of skills required.[17] It is vital to sequester the subtext of Carnegie and Frick's economic rationale, which is better read as capitalism and entitlement, since labor injustice is rarely the result of economic "necessity" or "difficulty."[18]

The previous union agreement set forth a minimum ($25 dollars per produced ton, which is about $690 today), to ensure a safety net for the workers if the market price dropped too far. The agreement also settled on eight-hour workdays, which previously had extended twelve to eighteen hours. Carnegie and Frick worked to break the conditions of the minimum threshold, the eight-hour workday, and the powers of collective bargaining.[19] By late June, the workers had attempted to accept all of Frick's demands except, crucially, the dissolution of their union.[20]

The Homestead Strike began on June 30, 1892. In an effort to block the strikers in advance, Frick had built a fort around the mill and hired three hundred Pinkerton men.[21] The Pinkertons are a private police force that had been deployed by Frick and Carnegie in previous labor disputes and who were known to infiltrate union organizations as spies in order to sabotage negotiations and the striking process.[22] The Pinkertons found difficulty docking their ships and, upon landing, became engaged in an armed conflict—known as the "Battle of Homestead"—with the strikers. During this battle, the Pinkertons were armed, violent, and outnumbered. They killed seven strikers and injured countless others before surrendering. On July 12, the National Guard sent in 8,500 troops to arrest the strikers and open the mill. Within twenty minutes of their arrival, the plant was reopened. The National Guard then occupied Homestead until October 13 and worked for Frick as he reopened the mill with non-union workers.[23]

Workers who had participated in the strike were barred from gaining employment at the mill, and became blacklisted at all other mills locally and sometimes nationally.[24] By July 18, a number of strikers were charged with conspiracy and treason and were then involved in a congressional hearing that lasted for over two years.[25] In contrast, the injuries, murders, and blacklisting of strikers have yet to be redressed by the state as a grievance, or—why not?—treason.

## Whiteness as Property

On July 6, 1892, seven days after the workers had been locked out of Homestead, the Carnegie Steel Company released a statement asserting, "We contend that we have a legal right to the *enjoyment* of our property, and to operate it and control it as we please. . . . But for years our works have been managed . . . by men who do not own a dollar in them. This will stop right here. The Carnegie Steel Company will hereafter control their works in the employment of labor."[26] Frick and Carnegie insist that they are victims of wrongdoing straining to regain control. Traversing terms for property and appropriating the discourse of work, they claim they are being managed by workers "who do not own a dollar." They remind their imagined audience that their entitlements are legally bound, a claim the workers cannot make. They write as if theirs too is a public plea. They imply that any perceived injury the workers face is an a priori condition of the labor system; it is the injury workers are to consume as adjudicated by the governance of property. The fact that this routine is questioned and unearthed is the injustice that *will stop right here*.

I want to spend a moment focusing on the term *enjoyment* as the resolution to the breaking of the strike, and in defining the contours of property. The affective turn toward enjoyment can be understood through liberal sociologist Thorstein Veblen's breakdown of class and labor divisions.[27] Veblen argues that in the late nineteenth and early twentieth centuries, the elite class engaged in forms of leisure and the working class was captured in forms of exploit. The terms are exactly as they sound and form a dialectical relationship: *leisure* is forms of activity without function; *exploit* is forms of labor that correlate to function. *Leisure* denotes a sense of individual presence and agency concerning the nonfunctional form of activity; *exploit* denotes a loss, a commodification of one's labor. Rather than implying idleness, Veblen articulated how forms of leisure required copious amounts of time. The learning of ancient languages and refined manners and the collecting of rare artifacts carried a notion of rarefied expertise and, arguably, an understanding of merit and dedication. What is assumed in this quasi-Marxist analysis is that the upper classes exploit to sustain their leisure. Thus, it can be resummarized that it is not so much that the upper class is the leisure class, but rather that they are the exploiting class. Leisure is predicated upon exploitation.[28]

To press, how does one enjoy property? This tension is clarified in the press release as the noun (*property*) is followed up with "to operate it and control it as we please." One might deduce that the operation and control of property is not defined by leisure, but enjoyment. Conversely, Rebecca Harding Davis's *Life in the Iron Mills*, a novella published in 1861, navigates the lived experience of exploitation, elucidating the mutations of "structures of feeling," as theorized by Raymond Williams.[29] Davis presses into the lives of those exploited in the mills: "What do you make of a case like that, amateur psychologist? You call it an altogether serious thing to be alive: to these men it is a drunken jest, a joke,—horrible to angels perhaps, to them commonplace enough."[30] Rejecting the notions of reader identification and analysis, Davis challenges the clarity with which the elite classes assess *and* dismiss abject poverty and exploitation. Situated in a moment in which public education and literacy would have been signals of the "leisure class," Davis provokes the difference between what a reader of this class might consider "being alive" and the lived experience of the workers in the mill. "You call it an altogether serious thing to be alive" foreshadows and uncloaks the moral clarity with which proclamations such as "to operate it and control it as we please" come to be made.

This is the context in which *enjoyment* might be read and reread. If the antithesis of leisure is exploitation, then the antithesis of enjoyment is dispossession. In this legalized affective hierarchy, the expropriation of labor is normalized, and the obedience of the worker is its congruence. The rupturing of this dynamic is not violence but a moment in which we may antagonize why the violence of private property remains intact while the socialization of property fails to suture.

To further this point, on July 4, a few days after the strike began and before the press release, Frick informed Carnegie about the use of private militia, the position of the press, and the legality of their position. I quote the letter in detail to illustrate the exactitude of their claims and the clarity with which they fight:

> The workmen seem to be well organized, and have things, so far, very much their own way, that is to say, are guarding every avenue to the works; stopping all who may, or try, to get in the works. This is rather in our favor in view of our arrangements. *We have a thorough understanding with the sheriff.*
>
> 300 Watchmen obtained from Pinkerton will leave . . . and take passage on two barrages. . . . One of the Deputy Sheriffs will . . . accompany the guards or watchmen in our property at Homestead without much trouble, and this once accomplished we are, we think, in good position.
>
> The newspapers, as usual, are inclined towards the enemy, and doubtless will raise a great howl when they discover that we have the audacity to attempt to guard and protect our property.
>
> I had the article, written by Mr. Weeks from data furnished by us to him, reproduced in all of the morning and evening papers of this City, so that I think our position is well defined. *We shall, of course, keep within the law*, and do nothing that is not entirely legal.[31]

As in the press release, Frick emphasizes the legality of their situation. While it is repeatedly acknowledged that the law is on their side, the undercurrents acknowledge how violence (the law) will be necessary to overturn a social norm. Walter Benjamin cites the law described here as "mythic violence."[32] The violence of the law, the violence of the police, and the violence authorized to the Pinkertons situate the mythology of Western democracy and the United States. It is formalized and accepted as the practice of the law. Frick and Carnegie do not need to operate outside of the bounds of the law—history rarely paints them as violent, illegal felons. They navigate the terrain of public perception, the law, and the *feelings* of their position as they plot to dismantle the structures of collective bargaining. While labor unions for white workers were a norm in the mid-to-late nineteenth century, the enjoyment of private property ownership had yet to be actualized. With the police and private militia on their side, Frick and Carnegie finalize the realization of ownership. The violence that transfigures socialized property into private property is the violence agreed upon by the law. If enjoyment constitutes the affective possibilities of private ownership, then violence is the legal condition of objecthood.

It is important to point out that these actions—the hiring of private militia and the dissemination of propaganda in city newspapers—were only in response to the strike. The workers had agreed to Frick and Carnegie's lowered minimum threshold but would not accept the dissolution of the union. This is to ask, What is the imagined threat they are reacting to? Benjamin clarifies how work and general strikes fall outside the bounds of law and into the language of violence. What the police and law do is authority; what strikers do (in refusing to work) is "a danger undermining the legal system."[33] Benjamin articulates, "The right to strike conceded to labor is certainly not a right to exercise violence but, rather, to escape from a violence indirectly exercised by the employer."[34] An indirect form of employer violence can be seen in the leadup to the strike in the form of workplace injury and death. On September 19, 1891, the *National Labor Tribune* reported three deaths at Homestead due to machine injuries, and the April 9 issue of 1892 reported additional fatalities.[35] Examination of the *National Labor Tribune* archives from 1890 to 1896 reveals that workplace injuries and deaths far outstrip reportage of strikes. Rather than identifying violence as isolated actions or events taken up by individuals—such as a strike—it is far more useful to examine the ongoing violence of the state and those afforded state protection.

An attempted escape from indirect violence is illuminated by a central character in Davis's novella, Hugh Wolfe. A worker in the mill, Hugh is charged with theft and receives a nineteen-year sentence of hard labor in a penitentiary.[36] The novel displays the reaction of Doctor May and his wife, the only characters from the leisure class presented in the novella: "His wife said something about the ingratitude of that kind of people, and then they began to talk of something else."[37] During the trial, the narrator states of Hugh that "when the sentence was read, he just looked up, and said the money was his by rights, and that all the world had gone wrong."[38] I offer this scene next to Frick's letter to examine the antagonism of the leisure class toward the exploited class. While he first described them as *workmen*, Frick then proceeds to clarify the strikers as *the enemy*. Both Frick and Doctor May are matter of fact about their distance from "that kind of people"—the enemy—and as if to illustrate, they turn to the next topic. The management of "that kind of people" is but one topic among the rest. Enjoyment lies in distance, not presence. It is structurally flippant, dismissive, and abstracting. I am exacting here that what is being worked out—not clarified but massaged—is mythic violence. The exploitation of "that kind of people" and the planning of violence against "the enemy" becomes a conversational feat.

Paul Krause postulates that the nucleus of the Homestead Strike was property to which all parties felt equally entitled.[39] As Hugh comments, "The money was his by rights," and, by extension, the escape from the abjection of poverty was also his right. Unlike Frick and Carnegie, the unionized and non-unionized workers lived in Homestead, and a large number of them rented company housing or had purchased homes near the mill.[40] Though the strikers do not make this ideological claim, the strike of 1892 makes a case for socialized collective property: the strikers fought to protect forms of their property—their homes, their labor power, and the protection that they would remain needed and valuable.

In a conflict between forms of property, Frick's assertion of private property becomes formalized by the law. Krause describes how Frick requested the intervention of the local sheriff "to protect our property from violence, damage and destruction, and to protect us in its free use and enjoyment."[41] Enjoyment again. The sheriff complied with this request, as did the National Guard. As demonstrated by the swift deployment of armed private and public militia against the workers, the law exemplifies that owners are entitled to property enjoyment. Their explicit property claims demonstrate a *structure of feeling*: the affective desire for systems of inescapable mythic violence.

## Underdescribed Components: The Assassination Attempt on Frick and Anti-Black Riots

With this serious conflict laid out, I want to introduce two key components that complicate the narrative and its outcome: first, the attempted assassination of Frick; second, and most important, the deployment of Black workers by the National Guard. Both are integral to understanding the conflicting property/affective claims made by Frick and Carnegie and the striking workers. However, both components have often been relegated to the footnotes in formative retellings of Homestead, or they have been chronologically distanced.[42] Linking these events to the larger narrative of the strike will intimately provoke populist narratives concerning unions while challenging the political horizons of socialized property.

The Homestead Strike began with national support. The working conditions in the mills were unimaginably difficult and, with some understanding of the challenges the working class faced, there was public support for unions. Newspaper reportage was initially sympathetic with the strikers. This sentiment is theorized to have universally turned with the assassination attempt on Frick, made on July 23 by Russian anarchist Andrew Berkman, the former lover of Emma Goldman. Berkman was not one of the strikers but a committed supporter of strikes against capitalist industries; as Berkman was not a trained assassin, Frick survived with minimal injuries. Labor historians have been careful in their analysis of the attempted assassination, remarking unanimously that the strikers were opposed to Frick's assassination, and that Berkman's action was taken without the strikers' consent, knowledge, or approval.

The assassination attempt became a crisis for the strikers.[43] Optically, the workers did not want to be associated with the radical violence of assassination.[44] In light of Berkman's actions, the strikers became concerned that their cause would appear less ethical, or without moral superiority. Beverly Gage and Philip Taft have posited that while union strikes in the United States have been distinctly violent—most often in the form of violence against workers, or workers resisting the violence of state and private militia—unions have refused association and participation with radical violence.[45] Such tendencies have led historians to argue that US unions have disengaged from ideological conflicts.[46] Gage contextualizes this argument through the Homestead strikers, as assassination was outside the purview of the strikers' aims.[47] Even after the arrival of the National Guard and the reopening of the mills on July 12—two events that were profound losses for the strikers—it is Berkman's assassination attempt on July 23 that led to discussions of surrender. The union worked to protect and reform the rights they had won for their selected members, but it was not necessarily attached to clarifying the dynamics of wealth through anticapitalist, anticolonialist, and revolutionary actions.

Most importantly, race has been pronouncedly and conveniently obscured in the celebrated version of the Homestead narrative for a specific reason. A key and lauded point of Homestead's remembrance is how the town and workers systematically organized against non-union, out-of-town "scab" workers. Unlike in other instances of fractured alliance during strikes, the workers of the mill and the town stood in "solidarity."[48] The town refused services to "scab" laborers, maintaining a united front against their presence and employment. When the strike is recounted, it is often told dramatically through the gaze of a bold and victimized white working class. Other events are often misleadingly omitted or disconnected—namely, that unions in this moment were de facto segregated, and that the strikers rioted against Black workers.

To provide more historical context, the largest US labor union in the late nineteenth century, the Knights of Labor, began accepting Black workers in 1878 but maintained racially segregated assemblies and at times practiced outright exclusion of nonwhite members.[49] As a method and policy of segregation, Black workers were either completely barred from joining unions or denied membership for being unskilled, enclosing them in a suffocating circle. This occurrence was so routine that the term *scab* began to signal Black workers. From the 1890s well into the 1920s, Black workers were viewed as the "enemy of unionized workers."[50] The majority of mills had most likely utilized enslaved persons and later employed Black workers as operators of blast furnaces in steel mills and iron plantations, which was considered to be the worst and most dangerous job.[51] Davis's novella alludes to the gendered and racial composite of workers. In *Life in the Iron Mills,* she depicts how both women and men—some identified as "mulatto"—congregated around the mill.[52] Nonwhite persons and women are interwoven into the structure of the iron and steel enterprise. Black operators were included in the mills to work the blast furnaces but excluded as workers from the unions.

The strikers rioted against Black workers, destroyed their living quarters, and spoke of lynching.[53] Contextually, then, the town's refusal of services to the "scab" workers would not have been just in solidarity with the white laborers local to Homestead but also in line with national practices of segregation and the tenets of racial violence central to property claims.[54] Imagined to be outside the framework of both private and socialized property, as well as that of collective bargaining, Black workers remained the target of the violence of the law and its authority. Their presence redirected the strikers' anger away from the corporation that had so intricately worked to exploit them—previously and presently—and which would go on to bar them entirely from employment in the near future.

In contrast, when the National Guard arrived, the town greeted them with song.[55] The strikers, having engaged in their own campaign for state protection—as they had been wrongfully injured and killed—believed the militia could be converted to their cause, and hoped that the new police presence was a protection for the strike to continue. However, when it became clear that this was not the case, there was no rioting against the National Guard.[56] There was no rioting or support for the attempted assassination of Frick. Instead, violence would be directed toward Black workers.[57]

Here, I want to recall Frick's assertion of the "enemy." For Frick, the enemy represented the striking workmen; the inverse was not true for the unionized strikers. This dynamic has been theorized by W. E. B. Du Bois and Cedric Robinson.[58] As Du Bois lays out in *Black Reconstruction in America*, the presence of Black workers destroys the political narrative of fair wage employment, dismantling the fantasy of the capitalist worker's hard-earned rise. Black workers were without legible claims—to the strikers, management, or the state. "Scabs"—Black workers—disavowed the triumphant narrative of liberal wage work.[59] "Scabs" demarcate *correct* and *incorrect* participation in the labor market, highlighting the fallacy of any justice within capitalism and of the possibility of a just system of labor. The presence of "scabs" became a signal of refused work, denied work, notwork. It was the work that could not be taken up, but would be—work without the narrative of subjectivity or pride.[60]

Although the notion of Black *and* worker functioned as a misnomer for the European, white-identified proletariat, references to slavery, and in particular fears of white slavery, were routinely invoked by unions.[61] William H. Sylvis, leader of the Knights of Labor, declared in a speech in 1869, "We are all one family of slaves together. The labor movement is a second Emancipation Proclamation."[62] Unions utilized slavery as a political metaphor to fight capitalism. The righteousness of unions and labor movements held slavery as the border that could not be crossed. The rhetoric of slavery can also be found leading up to the Homestead Strike of 1892. Krause writes that the Amalgamated Association of Iron and Steel Workers and the *National Labor Tribune* found the working conditions not only unacceptable, but *like* slavery. On July 9, 1881, the *Tribune* reported: "Slavery at Homestead. . . . Talk about foreign despotism! We venture the assertion that no such rules . . . can be found anywhere in Europe, and in a free country like this it is a lasting shame and disgrace that free men tolerate it. Until the men there free themselves from it, they will be looked upon as absolute slaves."[63]

This invocation of slavery by labor unions serves to stress the severity, the absolute limit and desperation, of their situation. Christina Sharpe diagnoses this phenomenon in discussing the relationship between freedom and slavery: "We must think about Black flesh, Black optics, and ways of producing enfleshed work . . . the hold remains in the form of the semiotics of the slave ship hold, the prison, the womb, and elsewhere in and as the tension between being and instrumentality that is Black being in the wake."[64] Sharpe's articulation of the tension between being and instrumentality describes the violence of abstraction, particularly the violence of slavery as metaphor. The working conditions are undignified for white workers, and slavery is instrumentalized by the writers of the *National Labor Tribune* to articulate their grievance. That Black workers remain segregated from the possibility of work cannot enter the invocation so long as Black workers, Black persons, remain instrumentality rather than being.

I want to pair Sylvis and reports from the *National Labor Tribune* with a passage from Du Bois's *Black Reconstruction in America*, in which he elucidates the failures of post–Civil War reconstruction. "The emancipation of man," he writes, "is the emancipation of labor and the emancipation of labor is the freeing of that basic majority of workers who are yellow, brown and black."[65] Unlike the *Tribune*, Du Bois links the exploitation of white workers to the exploitation of Black laborers as both unfold capitalism. While the editorial from the *Tribune* creates a hierarchy between *men* and *slaves*, implicitly acknowledging how, in both the absence and the presence of abolition, workers must be differentiated from slaves, Du Bois presses forth how the emancipation of Black laborers—those previously enslaved, and those indentured—is necessary to the emancipation of all labor. Though slavery has never been work, nor labor, nor metaphor, it is invoked by the *Tribune* to support the futurity of labor claims: the life and property of the white laborer. Du Bois preemptively situates this move as "the real modern problem." The language of slavery did not transfigure into the identification with and integration of Black workers. Rather, the language of slavery became weaponized to further abstract then perpetuate anti-Black violence, as labor tensions mutated into race riots throughout the mid-nineteenth century in Cincinnati, Philadelphia, and elsewhere.[66]

Banned from joining a larger labor movement, Black workers were refused the category of worker; it is this very refusal that makes their "employment" by private enterprises through state intervention possible. The 1892 strike is the composite of segregated labor; it is a circumstance made possible through segregation. The presence of Black laborers did not break the strike—this was the doing of the National Guard. The National Guard enters the event to force segregated "employment" into further dispossession, and the "opportunity" for such employment exists because it has been systematically relegated to outside the realm of collective bargaining.

Speaking on the legal and cultural formations of whiteness as property, Cheryl Harris writes that "possession—the act necessary to lay the basis for rights in property—was defined to include only the cultural practices of whites. This definition laid the foundation for the idea that whiteness—that which whites alone possess—is valuable and is property."[67] While not white owners, or even white police officers, these white workers considered the possession of property exclusively theirs. And because property and whiteness functioned as a symbiosis, Harris writes, "white workers perceived that they had more in common with the bourgeoisie than with fellow workers who were Black."[68] This can be witnessed in the numerous articles appearing in the *National Labor Tribune* in Pittsburgh. While fully supporting essential labor reforms such as the eight-hour workday and collective bargaining, the *Tribune* published explicitly anti-Black and anti-immigrant editorials. On April 30, 1892, just two months before the strike, several articles concerning "John Chinaman" and supporting the Chinese Exclusion Act appeared. On September 17, 1892, a series of articles concerning the "Southern Negro" as strike breaker were featured. In December 1892, several months after the strike, the paper declared how "moral courage" is necessary to reject immigrant families, to send them *back*, as their presence interferes with the pursuit of US labor goals.[69] The differing notions of property claims (as forged by Krause) between the workers and the "owners" (as theorized by Harris) are pivotal to understanding the crux of property. Harris writes, "Property is thus said to be a right, not a thing, characterized as metaphysical, not physical."[70] The stakes are the immaterial gains rooted in material life. Frick and Carnegie describe property in terms of affect—*enjoyment*—and Krause describes the workers' claims, which echo Marx's right to the socialization of property; in both instances, Black workers are excluded.

If the successful horizon of the Homestead Strike could lead to the socialization of private property or the protection of workers' existing property claims, a successful strike would also have continued to uphold the segregation pivotal to their claims. However, to repeat Du Bois, the emancipation of labor could not be achieved through a negation of Black labor. In the context of Homestead, striking and worker "rights" remain loyal to a vision of a segregated workforce. What becomes assumed is Blackness as the baseline of dispossession.

The rioting against Black workers was not movement toward divine violence but the keeping of law-protecting violence that Benjamin critiques, expected of capitalist maintenance. Through Gage, we can see how the union riots against Black workers were ideological property claims and more specifically anti-Black continuations of property claims.[71] Property relations as desired by Frick and as analyzed by Harris and Marx would continue to exist irrespective of "scab" workers, as the strikers were not engaged in ideological conflicts. Furthermore, violence against "scab" workers is not radical violence against the forces of the Carnegie Steel Company, the Pinkertons, or the National Guard. Rather than affirming radical violence, the strikers affirmed the operations of state violence. The defeat's prehistory and future uphold the labor dispossession pivotal to segregation, in the form of the Black-worker separation critiqued in Robinson's scholarship. The stakes for unions of the Gilded Age were high—I do not dismiss their adversities and the abjection of poverty. Rather than a dismissal, this is to take most seriously the political aims of the strikers, and to ask how and why the aggression and violence became so singularly directed toward segregated Black workers—a tendency that remains to this day.

The legacy of Homestead is the breakdown of union culture *and* the way in which segregated labor remains unprotected and depoliticized. The presence of Black workers in this conflict offered the possibility of transforming the horizon from the socialization of property to an imagination of its abolishment. The possibility.

## Extractive Capitalism and Wealth Transfer: The Library System, Philanthropy, and the Frick Collection

After the strike, new workers were forced to sign individual contracts, and the working day increased to twelve hours. Five hundred jobs were eliminated, wages were reduced and became inconsistent, and, most importantly, segregated labor deployment and the breakdown of unions occurred throughout the United States.[72] Additionally, deunionization gave way to forms of dispossession called scientific management, which aimed to remove the "mental activity" from work once more. I will discuss the structural impact of these losses in chapter 2.

And of the gains? Krause writes, "It was common knowledge that the monumental profits earned by Carnegie Steel in the 1890s grew directly from the defeat of unionism at Homestead."[73] This point has been agreed upon across political spectrums, field emphases, and historical periods.[74] But it must be stressed repeatedly that Carnegie Steel had been wildly profitable even before the strike. Carnegie himself was then and remained the richest man in the world, with the Carnegie Steel Company netting an average profit of $4 million ($110 million today) each year leading up to the strike, although post-strike, its excesses were rapacious—history-altering. By 1901, with J. P. Morgan's backing, the Carnegie Steel Company became the U.S. Steel Corporation, the first global billion-dollar company (approximately $51.3 billion today).[75] The term *robber baron* illuminates the genesis of the company's value.[76]

Before tracing the wealth derived from the Homestead Strike of 1892 to the Frick Collection, I want to situate the legacies of the steel and coke industries. In 2014, the Food and Agriculture Organization of the United Nations announced that if soil degradation continues at its current rate, "all of the world's top soil could be gone in 60 years," which would conclude the possibility of current farming practices.[77] The agency noted how "generating three centimeters of top soil takes 1,000 years," and how due to chemical-heavy farming, deforestation, and industries that intensify global warming, soil regeneration has become difficult, if not completely impossible in most parts of the world.[78] It is now known that coal mining, which began as an early settler-colonial enterprise and gave way to the infrastructure of the Industrial Revolution—steel and iron, the *bones* of railroads, bridges, and buildings—depletes the earth, destroying the topsoil so that it cannot be used in the future for farming.[79] Additionally, coal has been the largest contributor to the human-made increase of $CO_2$. The Carbon Majors Report released in 2017 tracked the one hundred companies most responsible for the world's greenhouse gas emissions since 1988, and while the companies included oil and other gas projects, China Coal, Coal India, and other international coal companies dominated the top twenty.[80]

Carnegie and Frick accumulated wealth by selling steel, a human-made material catalyzed by coke, a type of fuel derived from heating coal. The rise of steel industries in Pittsburgh coincides with coal mining that began during the mid-eighteenth century in the Allegheny county across the Monongahela River. The steel manufactured at the Carnegie Steel Company and U.S. Steel Corporation would continue to be used in railroads across the United States, in the Brooklyn Bridge, and, later, for US Navy ships during World War I, setting the tenor for corporate-military alliances remaining to this day.[81]

Predicated on settler colonialism, which insists on the vacancy of land, and chattel slavery, which insists on the vacancy of people, extractive industries work toward a depletion of materiality and possibility. Du Bois prompts, "That dark and vast sea of human labor in China and India, the South Seas and all Africa; in the West Indies and Central America and in the United States—that great majority of mankind, on whose bent and broken backs rest today the founding stones of modern industry—shares a common destiny . . . spawning the world's raw material and luxury—cotton, wool, coffee, tea, cocoa, palm oil, fibers, spices, rubber, silks, lumber, copper, gold, diamonds, leather—how shall we end the list and where?"[82] This remains our pressing question, as extracting natural resources from the earth is the process of world-altering capitalism and quarantines dispossession *into the future*. The legacies of the robber barons, their philanthropic projects, their leisure, and their ideas live with us today. "The richest man in the world" in the 1890s is linked directly to our present moment: from library systems, philanthropy, and museums, to capitalism *and* the number of harvests we may have left.

While by 1900 the partnership between Carnegie and Frick had ended in conflict, this did not signal the end to their profits. Frick brought a legal suit against Carnegie for a percentage of the company's shares, won, and then spent the rest of his life as one of the directors of U.S. Steel; effectively, he remained at the helm of the steel empire. There, Frick became the "largest individual railway stockholder in the world" and acquired art for what would become the Frick Collection.[83] Carnegie would spend the remainder of his days engaged in the philanthropic projects he is known for today.

Liberalism is the ideology that formed the modern capitalist world. In constructing the liberal subject, we see the development of education, libraries, museums, and philanthropy—the tools for advancement and betterment, or so we are told. Carnegie was then and is now known for his gifts: the gifted library, the gifted concert hall, the gifted learning spaces. He is often noted as the father of modern philanthropy—to repeat: this version of philanthropy was developed in tandem with the dismantling of unions during the Gilded Age.[84] Carnegie's philanthropic work sought to naturalize exploitative systems through the forging of liberal subjecthood. As Lisa Lowe demonstrates, liberalism is the ideology that amalgamated slavery, colonialism, and freedom.[85] In liberalism, slavery and colonialism became the parameters in which freedom was constructed and defined. Within liberalist ideology, philanthropy is the promulgation of the "positive" outcome of capitalism. It rationalizes—to this day—that the violence of capitalism, expropriation, and segregation will be the grounds on which a new and better subject can be forged. With regard to Carnegie and Frick, Krause writes, "it is a matter not of 'Yes, a robber baron, but a benefactor' but rather of 'Yes, a robber baron and a benefactor.'"[86] In replacing the conjunction "but" with "and," I am interested in scrutinizing the narrative once more to press: What is a benefactor?

Three years before the Homestead Strike, Carnegie foreshadowed himself in a speech at Braddock, Pennsylvania. David P. Demarest Jr. writes: "The union had been broken in Braddock in 1888, and when Carnegie gave his workers there a library in 1889, he looked forward to Homestead in his dedicatory remarks: 'I should like to see a Library [in Homestead] . . . [but] our men there are not partners. They are not interested with us. On the contrary, an Amalgamated Association has for years compelled us to pay one-third more in the principal department of our work [there].' Homestead got its library in 1898."[87] Carnegie declares that his libraries come only through a "partnership"—here *partnership* is a euphemism for the condition of segregating and segregated, of a dispossessed labor force. Philanthropy in this sense becomes the narrative that legitimizes capitalism. The town is without a union, and because of this, the philanthropist explains, the capitalist is able to be more generous in other ways. Is involuntary dispossession also a kind of partnership, if we consider how it comes with the perk of a cultural hub?

And Carnegie wasn't just providing any library. Carnegie describes the kind of library "his workers" would have. At the 1889 opening of the Carnegie Library in Braddock, he urged the now deunionized workmen to be careful while reading trade journals and newspapers as they "report even rumors." After disparaging an education that teaches Greek and Latin, as these are "no more practical use to them Choctaw," he describes how those who read about Ulysses and Agamemnon or take in Shakespeare "have been 'educated' as if they were destined for life upon some other planet than this. . . . What they have obtained has served to imbue them with false ideas and to give them a distaste for practical life."[88] He then muses on the knowledge the workers should have: "If you want to make labour what it should be, educate yourself in useful knowledge. This is the moral I would emphasize."[89] The library was to proliferate Carnegie's understanding of morality; education as the exodus from moral deprivation is standard liberalist ideology. Importantly, Carnegie distinguished the morality the workers would need to learn from his own. Krause describes how Carnegie attempted to write literature, befriending the likes of Mark Twain and Herbert Spencer, while operating with a very specific notion of education for his "partners" at the mill.[90] Concretely, Carnegie's libraries would house "useful knowledge." Krause writes, "'Useful knowledge' did not embrace classical learning, what we today call the liberal arts. Rather, the 'new idea of education' was to concentrate, as the new library most assuredly would, on the study of business and science alone."[91]

I was surprised to learn that Carnegie made this distinction during the Gilded Age, as it is both familiar and contemporary. It reminded me of the countless op-eds and university debates concerning the practicality of the "liberal arts." The collapse of public arts education and the defunding of humanities programs in higher education have been consistently rationalized in terms of economics and practicality. The rationale for these programs' disappearance is their lack of use value. Both aesthetic inquiry and the humanities—categories that do not appear to be outright business-driven—and legible sciences that purport to support capitalism directly by creating a profit-driven product are simply not useful *for them*.[92] The disparity is revealed as artificial when it is observed that the very directors and managers of this "new" system have had much contact with *not useful knowledge* and continue to have an abundance of access to its forms. This rationale reifies Veblen's distinction between leisure (activity without function) and exploit (functional labor). The disparity between knowledge systems—imaginaries—is reserved for the abstracted worker-to-be.[93] Historical and contemporary debates regarding "useful knowledge" rarely push: What *use* are the arts for the wealthy? It is simply agreed that for them it is a space of leisure and non-use, a reservation for a life where *use* is not the primary goal. Considering the consistency of this rhetoric, a historical and linguistic timeline of the attacks on the liberal arts and the humanities would be most *useful*.

Carnegie identified his wealth as providing him with the powers to adjudicate use and access. Extrapolating on Carnegie's thoughts on libraries and philanthropy by pulling from Carnegie's own writing, Krause writes, "The successful businessman was a '*trustee for the poor*' and for the entire community; the charge of the trustee is to administer the wealth of the community '*far better than it could or would have done for itself.*' To Carnegie the most appealing expression of this public trusteeship was the establishment of free public libraries, because the library offered to 'the industrious and the ambitious' the surest means of self-advancement."[94] Wealth is articulated as a vessel allotted to some and not others for the purposes of *correct* distribution—not redistribution. Carnegie's wealth mimics the responsibilities of the father; the children—the poor—are by structural and narrative placement without the facilities for correct comprehension, imagination, or desire. The distribution of Carnegie's wealth is the charity of objects he believes would instruct the proper trustees' replication. In this light, the library must only contain knowledge that Carnegie believes is sympathetic to the system that created the structures that placed him, the trustee of wealth and power, at the top.

The towns with which Carnegie "partnered" often refused his "gift" or disparaged the gesture. Carnegie's formula of breaking unions and then offering the town a library was transparent to the workers. Krause cites one Homestead worker as stating, "Carnegie builds libraries for the working men, but what good are libraries to me, working practically eighteen hours a day?"[95] The library, filled with curated, supposedly replicant literature, intended to "improve the minds"[96] of the poor and constructed only after the town's union was destroyed, was the ultimate gesture of liberalism. Philanthropy was the conclusion to the moralizing narrative of wealth. From the violence of capitalism, it heralded a narrative afterlife for the benefactor: Carnegie would go on to build 2,811 libraries, multiple concert halls, peace centers, and a university.[97]

## Wealth Transfer and the Frick Collection

Art collecting falls into the pursuits of the leisure class and speaks to the narrative ambitions of the ruling class to dictate the terms of aesthetic importance. In grappling with this phenomenon, previous Marxist critiques of the museum have tended to its imparting narratives, its monetary relationship to individual artists, and its architecture.[98] While it is imperative to discuss the physical and metaphysical symbols of the museum space, I want to dive further into the conditions of its making. I have yet to precisely distinguish between the encyclopedic or personal collection and the specializing arts museum. This is because I am less invested in quantifying their differences, or taxonomizing and individualizing their particularities, than in thinking about their political convergences.

There is a profound explicitness with which national museums understand themselves to be loot havens. After the Louvre became a public space in 1792, the French minister of the interior Jean-Marie Rolard declared that it would display the "nation's great riches."[99] This was clarified six years later to mean national loot. A banner of a 1798 sculpture exhibition stated, "Monuments of Ancient Sculpture. Greece gave them up. Rome lost them. Their fate has changed twice. It will not change again."[100] Of the British parallel, Lord Gowrie, the minister of arts under Margaret Thatcher, rejected the Greek government's repatriation of the Elgin Marbles stating, "I know it's loot, but it's our loot."[101] Far from an epithet, "loot" in the context of museums rarely comes with the association of restitution, repatriation, or reparation. As will be discussed in chapter 5, loot simply becomes the fact that cannot be denied and the space in which everything continues to be built. By comparison, wealth extraction is a kinder euphemism than national loot.

Both Carnegie and Frick built universities, museums, and parks. The University of Pittsburgh was founded on a land grant provided by Frick, and the central parks in Pittsburgh are the site of Frick's and Carnegie's former residences. While Carnegie distinguished the kinds of knowledge the workers might possess from his own, and Frick did not bother, we should be underwhelmed to discover that both actively collected from the "not useful" category, and in particular, paintings.[102]

Before I began my research into the acquisition records, my hypothesis was that Frick was motivated to deny the strikers their wages and the union because he was occupied with the activity of art acquisition. It is a hypothesis that directly conflated the timeline of Frick's antagonisms with his desires. However, after inspecting the Knoedler Gallery's sales records from 1881 to 1919, along with Frick's papers at the Frick Collection, I realized that, though Frick had made one purchase in 1883, he made no other purchases until 1894, two full years after the strike.

The Knoedler sales books display how the Frick Collection was built after the Homestead Strike of 1892. In forging this collection, Frick primarily purchased paintings through them, and then through his dealer—infamous dealer to the robber barons—Joseph Duveen. In the 1900s, the Knoedler Gallery in New York was a central hub for art sales. Museums like the Metropolitan Museum of Art and the Museum of Modern Art and individuals like John D. Rockefeller acquired art through the Knoedler Gallery. Frick accumulated art through their sales department from 1883 to the time of his death in 1919, becoming one of the gallery's most important and central patrons.

In my examination of the politics of wealth extraction, I analyzed acquisition records. My objects of analysis became the Knoedler Gallery's sales books from 1881 to 1919, the Knoedler's inventory cards from 1859 to 1971, Frick's will and personal papers from the Frick Collection, and the Frick Collection's acquisition records. The Knoedler's sale books provide information regarding the date of sale, price, delivery location, name of the artist, and title of the object. They also provide the number of purchases a patron made in a set number of years, and the monthly net of gallery sales. The inventory cards also provide some of this information and note when and if the object in question was resold and to whom. As both documents are at times fragmented and mismatched, without a chronological or discernible order and difficult to decipher, I cross-referenced between them for maximum accuracy.[103]

Throughout the last part of his life, Frick amassed an enormous art collection, and in his will, he established a corporation—valued at $50 million ($984 million today)—and left $15 million (approximately $218.5 million today) for the collection's endowment.[104] Additionally, his Fifth Avenue mansion on New York's Upper East Side was to house what he designated as the "Frick Collection." In the United States, the Frick is known as the premiere collection of paintings by the "Old European Masters." This is no hyperbole, as with his new wealth—so vast he couldn't spend it all or take it with him when he died[105]—Henry Clay Frick fastidiously collected from 1894 to the end of his life.

To map the outlines of Frick's patronage, according to Knoedler's sales books, he purchased a single painting in 1883, by Otis T. Weber, titled *Homeward Bound*, for $125 (about $3,000 today).[106] From here, there is no mention of Frick in the sales or inventory records for ten years.[107] After the strike of 1892, from 1894 to 1900, Frick appears forty-eight times in the sales books.[108] Each appearance denotes a sale, many of which comprised multiple paintings. To illustrate the financial crescendo of his acquisition: in 1894 he purchased one painting for $1,350 ($39,500 today), and in 1895 he acquired artworks totaling $115,600 (approximately $3.47 million today).[109]

At this point, Frick's business often accounted for more than half of the gallery's sales, making his account one of the gallery's most important. For example, during August of 1896 the gallery made $63,778, while Frick paid $38,260 ($1.5 million today) for six paintings.[110] Beginning in 1898, he acquired paintings almost every month. On August 9, 1898, Frick acquired two paintings for $49,000 ($1.5 million today).[111] The gallery's net profit for the month was $58,792.22 ($1.7 million today), indicating that Frick's two paintings made up more than 83 percent of the gallery's total sales.

The year 1899 saw some of Frick's biggest purchases yet, which totaled $176,125 ($5.4 million today)[112] and portended the numbers that would continue from here on. In August 1899, Frick acquired seven paintings for $100,350 ($3.05 million today) and then exchanged them in October for other paintings. By 1900 he was no longer the chairman at the Carnegie Steel Company; at this point, he had won his suit against Carnegie and was at U.S. Steel. In September of 1901, he purchased Vermeer's *The Music Lesson* and Wouwerman's *The Cavalry Camp* for $87,000 ($2.58 million

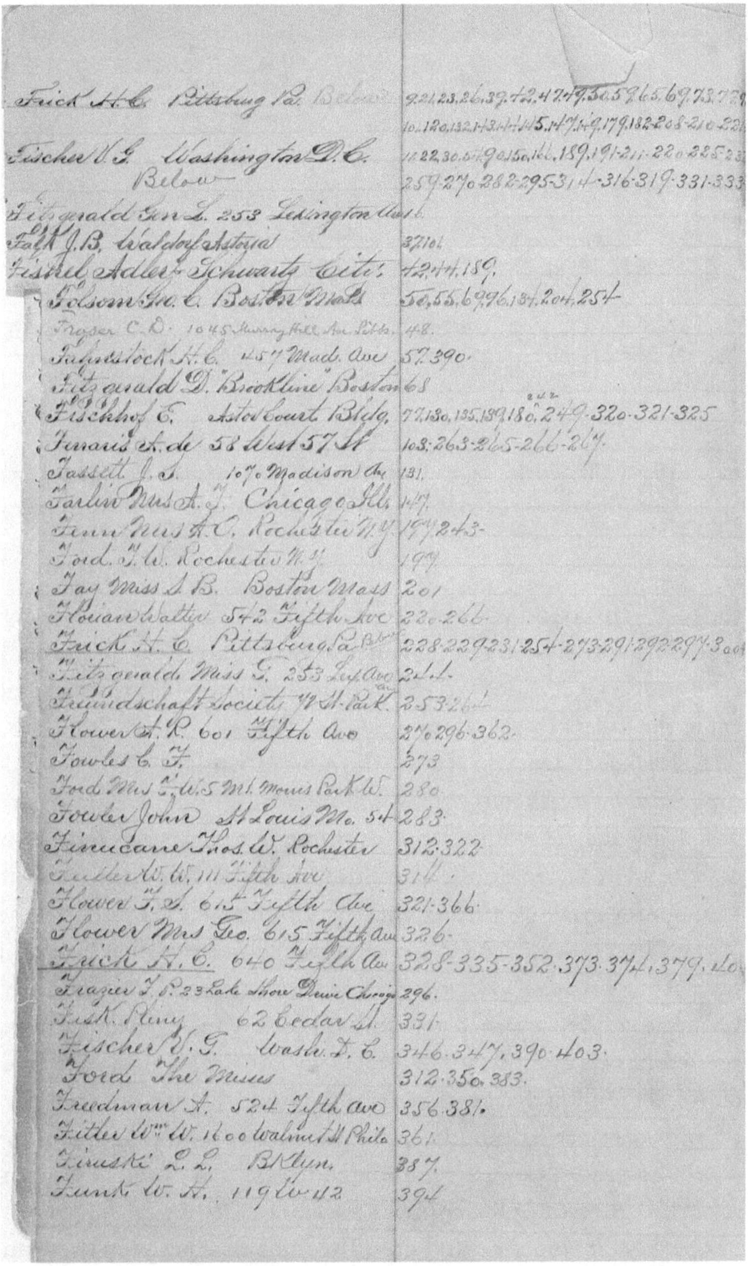

1.1 Knoedler Gallery, Sales book 8, November 1900–April 1907. Henry Clay Frick appears three times on this page and more often than any other buyer in the sales book. He appears on pages 9, 21, 23, 26, 39, 42, 47, 49, 50, 59, 65, 69, 73, 77, 91, 96, 101, 120, 132, 143, 144, 145, 147, 149, 179, 182, 208, 210, 222, 228, 229, 231, 254, 273, 291, 292, 297, 300, 311, 328, 335, 352, 373, 374, 379, and 405. Knoedler Gallery Archive, Getty Research Center, Los Angeles.

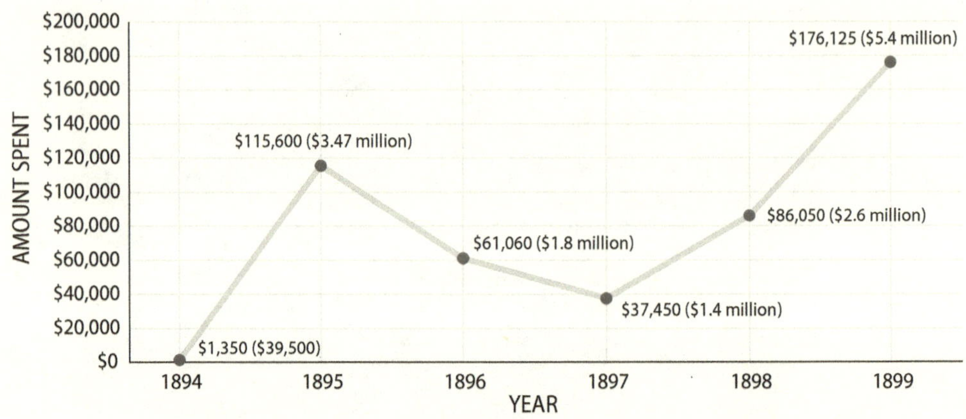


**1.2** Henry Clay Frick's expenditures on artworks after the Homestead Strike of 1892. Amounts in parentheses show values in today's dollars. Graph by Isla Ng.

today).[113] This trend toward bigger sales continued into 1907—when he retired from U.S. Steel but remained a shareholder—and beyond.[114] From 1900 to 1907, he made forty-six unique purchases. He was the biggest client at the gallery by at least tenfold.[115]

Frick's tendency to acquire the most expensive paintings would continue until his death in 1919.[116] While his acquisitions become less frequent with Knoedler, he acquired four paintings in his last years for the approximate total of $1,010,000 ($28 million today).[117] Acquisitions continued throughout 1912–16, with twenty-six unique sales[118] totaling $2,323,582, ($53 million today).[119] As to the wealth accumulation that made this possible, Krause writes, "two years before the strike on November 20th, 1890, Carnegie and Frick gained a $4 million contract with the navy to produce 5,909 tons of battleship armor."[120] Given that the company netted a profit of over $4 million that year ($110 million today), this would not have been the only contract. The union's proposed minimum was $25 per ton, which would be $147,725 of a $4 million contract; this would've amounted to about 27.5 percent of the contract for labor costs. At Frick's suggestion of $23 per ton, it would be $135,907. The difference between these numbers would not amount to *one* of Frick's painting purchases during 1912–16.[121] From 1916 until his death in December 1919, Frick continued to acquire paintings by the European masters.[122] His final transaction with Knoedler occurred in March, seven months before his death. It was a painting by Gilbert Stuart, *Portrait of George Washington*, purchased for $65,000

($947,000 today).[123] This is the historical materialist process in which a personal collection becomes a museum.

I want to be blunt and careful in my analysis of these findings. My interest in financial and material excavations is not that we might replace systems of colonialist, racist, and exploitative funding sources with good and better capitalist funding. My engagement with the Homestead Strike, with the Frick Collection, and with Carnegie's philanthropy is not to create a division between improper and proper funding. If this is what a reader extracts from this text, I have failed in the project entirely. My aim in materializing one timeline of wealth by situating its foundational labor dispossession and segregation is to contribute a small and slivered offering to the abolition of property. Insofar as our current art and cultural institutions operate through philanthropy and wealth transfer, and are legally, ideologically, and aesthetically grounded in property claims, all those who work in this realm are involved.

Additionally, and most importantly: there are no good or better capitalist means of accumulation. Absolutely none. The idea of the good funding source is akin to the mythology of the neutral museum, neutral artist, neutral form: it exists as a political, narrative construction for the benefit of those who desire the mirage of depoliticization.

It is important to clarify that the politicization of Frick's wealth is not a depoliticization of the artworks he would come to collect.[124] Too often, the argument against financial provenance is framed as a moral question or a developmental narrative. The current genre of financial accountability has formulated a depoliticization (shame) of the artist in order to politicize the funding source. Such is the narrative that frames that if X artist boycotts or refuses Y money or institution, then something else could be achieved. While such an analytical move is routine and expected of current financial analysis, I object to and reject the politics of this approach. This is a quotidian, moralizing tactic whose mission is to discipline the potential artist, while preserving the sanctity and expression of robber barons 1.0 and robber barons 2.0. Searching for positions of innocence purported to be exempted from shame and violence is a tactic I find to be deeply at odds with historical materialist and feminist theory. It is a method that assumes an innocence or a moral rectitude of the critic unlike those of the artist.

My trepidation and rejection of a simplified moral narrative stems from Gayatri Chakravorty Spivak's critique of materialist discourse in the United States. By highlighting the word processing machine from which the writer from the Global North makes legible their critique, Spivak reveals how an enclosed nationalist understanding of labor and exploitation is maintained through the privileging of the critic's US nationalist orientation. As the expropriation of women in the third world becomes effaced in academic debates concerning the labor theory of value, Spivak posits how "the question of Value in its 'materialist' articulation must be asked as the cappuccino-drinking worker and the word-processing critic actively forget the actual price-in-exploitation of the machine producing coffee and words."[125] From the word processor and coffee utilized by critics in the United States to the personal collection museum and the philanthropic library, such materializations are but single instances in long and complicated timelines that involve global and colonial routes. Thus, a nonreductive and nonenclosed materialization of the means of production is required for the critique to be applicable beyond its (anti)nationalist borders and in its invitation to international partners and Indigenous connections.

A more apt approach to funding, and more specifically to wealth extraction, would be to question, how has it come to be that public support for labor movements wanes as private collections sprout? How does the presence of unceded Indigenous land connect with calls to repatriate objects? What is the relationship between land, environment, and that which becomes legible as art? What are the labor politics within institutions? What is the institutionalization of labor politics, and how does it align with the theoretical framework that institutions celebrate? Rather than depoliticizing specific artists, writers, and curators in order to politicize funding sources, I am suggesting an examination into the public wealth transfer that has occurred and is occurring and to interrogate its constructed obfuscations.

In tandem, poet Diane di Prima's line "not all the works of Mozart worth one human life" needs to be taken up with the sentiment above.[126] The financial and ideological tyranny materialized in Carnegie's formula of breaking unions for 2,811 "useful" libraries that cannot be used by workers and in Frick's pursuit of the Frick Collection reveals that lives and bodies and methods and expressions have been exchanged *for*. Is it didactic and dire to know that one painting would have met the bargaining demands at Homestead for a year? What is it to know that it is the Frick Collection that the Pinkertons and the National Guard came to protect? If the imperative for museum making is the fortressing of ceremonial monuments and the imperative to remember, yet the site of the museum is a concentration of plunder, might we query: What and who is being remembered?

### Conclusion: Museum Boards and Financializing Immorality

Frick's collection displays the condensation of wealth transfer, but it also speaks to a certain notion of beauty, achievement, and transcendence. Without depoliticizing artists like Turner and Whistler, what is a collection of only them? The paintings collected by Frick post-strike were not a random assortment of his tastes, his evaluation of art history. Rather, they crystallize the economies of distribution. With the assistance and guidance of Joseph Duveen, Frick arranged a collection of objects with strenuous specificity to European art; his management here is as politicized as his management of the workers. In his will, Frick formed a committee—a board—for his collection, made up to protect his legacy; this is a historical and financial formation that has remained underanalyzed.

The composition of the board reflected Frick's social and corporate circles, rather than expertise with art, public education, or culture. In the *New York Times* on November 19, 1927, an article titled "Frick Gallery Gets Two Art Treasures: Paintings by Duccio and Berna Purchased for the Public for about $500,000" detailed the trustees of Frick's estate: Mrs. H. C. Frick, Miss. Helen Frick, Childs Frick, Walker D. Hines, John D. Rockefeller Jr., George F. Baker Jr., Lewis Cass Ledyard, J. Horace Harding, and Horace Havemeyer.[127] By 1930, Secretary of the Treasury Andrew Mellon had also joined the board. The selected board members were not educators or artists but well-known wealthy persons and, like Frick, orchestrators of national union and labor disputes, such as the 1914 Ludlow Massacre executed by Rockefeller.

The archive at the Frick displays how each member of the board of trustees painstakingly discussed every potential painting purchase.[128] For instance, on March 10, 1930, Mellon wrote to Helen Frick, the board's chair—on his "The Secretary of the Treasury, Washington" letterhead—regarding the acquisition of Veneziano's *Coronation of the Virgin*: "I am sorry that I have been delayed in writing you further about the painting of 'The Coronation of the Virgin' by Paola [*sic*] Veneziano. It arrived here and I inspected it carefully. . . . The price asked, $190,000, seems to me quite reasonable considering present day values but I did not consider that I had to do with any negotiation for it. I feel justified in recommending it and feel sure that you will make no mistake in acquiring it at the price mentioned."[129] The price, $190,000, is $2.9 million today. In each letter to the chair, the writer apologizes for the slightest delay. It becomes clear through the letters that the painting object in question was either sent to each individual board member or was displayed in a convenient viewing location. The price, while consistently gaudy (compared to what the workers demanded), is almost always accepted without negotiation.[130]

To attest to this tenor, one day after Mellon's letter to Helen Frick, John D. Rockefeller wrote to the chair about the painting. He begins the letter by apologizing for not viewing the work in a more timely manner. I will quote the letter at length:

> The picture seems to me beautiful and well painted. It gave me much pleasure. There was just one feature that I found a little disturbing, but that may be something purely personal to me and not in any way affecting the merit or worthwhileness of the picture. It was the fresh, crude and rather hard and obtruding character of the architecture of the bench upon which the two figures are seated, particularly of the upper part of the back where the two circles appear near the heads of the figures. While otherwise *I found the picture very charming and should enjoy having it myself,* I am not quite sure whether this one feature would give me pause, *so far as my personal ownership or enjoyment of the picture is concerned.*
>
> Having made this comment, which is merely the expression of an *untutored individual* who is frankly always appealed to in a work of art by its beauty and charm, I am quite willing to cast my vote for the purchase of the painting, if the judgement of the other trustees approves its purchase. *This I say without knowing anything about the price which is asked or the value of the painting.*[131]

Rockefeller, Mellon, and the other board members each provided their individual accounts of the painting. At times, they express their personal desire for ownership ("should enjoy having it myself"), and we are to assume that their ownership is the barometer of institutional ownership. While professing to be "untutored" on the subject at hand, Mellon declares individualized desire, as well as an eagerness to be agreeable to the board.

The growth of Frick's obsequious endowment was taken most seriously by the board. Each painting proposition was vetted, every decision debated and democratized. It needs not be said, but to avoid confusion, I will state that the care afforded to the acquisition of the objects in the Frick Collection is a care that the workers at Carnegie Steel Company and U.S. Steel—white union workers, segregated Black workers, as well as the land and its rivers—were, and have remained, without. Is this because workers and the land were sites of abstraction for the board, while the pursuits of the museum, not? Robinson implores: "Expropriation, impoverishment, alienation, and the formations of class consciousness and expression will be treated not as abstraction or the residual effects of a system of production but as living categories. We are concerned with how real men and women (and children) experienced dislocation, poverty, and the exploitation of their labor and reacted to them; how they employed the intellectual and emotional inventories available to them to come to terms with their experience."[132] Often when philanthropy is discussed, it is done through the discourse of "their money," "their desires," and "their ideas." It is rationalized that capitalism *affords* them the right to spend their earnings—*winnings*—as they see fit. Demonstrated in this chapter is how it is not possible to accumulate wealth: it is possible to sequester the future. What is built is not a museum but the abstraction of poverty and of the land and its people. A consequential configuration of wealth that incorporates not only the desires and rights of capitalists, but also the impacts of their ventures, is an unaccepted math. The computation concerning racial capitalism, colonialism, and the environment remains one in which ample evidence continues to be supplied, and it gestures toward an environmental analysis of the Carnegie Steel Company and coal mining during the Gilded Age as an invitation for deeper debates into the *legacies* of capitalism and philanthropy.

In the following chapter, I situate how the abstraction enforced by the robber barons to create the property understood as the collection and museum became transmuted across economic sectors and aesthetic forms as new divisions of labor. The breakdown of unions and the deployment of segregated labor is of particular interest as it leads to the rise of "scientific management," which advocated "removing the mental activity" from "hand work." In thinking about the parallels between labor history and the museum space and in building from this research, I argue that Taylorism is a crucial frame through which to grapple with the politics of artistic forms such as the readymade, found object art, immaterial art, experimentalism, and conceptualism. I examine how the aestheticization of property continues into the twentieth century, popularized and celebrated in standardized divisions of labor and emergent forms of art.

TWO

# Scientific Management and Conceptual Art

## *The Invention of the Artist Manager*

As in the steel industry, the core of these new labor systems was the creation of artificial job hierarchies and the transfer of skills away from workers to the managers. **Katherine Stone, "Origins of Job Structures in the Steel Industry"**

Objects are thus reduced to "ideas," and as a result we get "Conceptual Art." Compared to isolated objects, isolated ideas in the metaphysical context of a gallery offer the random art audience an aesthetic bargain. **Robert Smithson, "Production for Production's Sake"**

The efforts of Andrew Carnegie, Henry Clay Frick, and the industrial robber barons to dismantle unions had wide-reaching consequences. As discussed in the previous chapter, the 1892 Homestead Strike located a pivotal nineteenth-century "battle between capital and labor," and labor historians have thus interrogated the legacy of Homestead as a focal point for subsequent deunionization efforts.[1] I would add that it was also a focal point for labor segregation and the evasion of land dispossession.[2] In pursuing what emerged from the deunionization of steel, the location of this chapter remains Pennsylvania's steel industries and their contrapuntal relationship with Manhattan's high art spaces. However, rather than tracing the material history of a personal collection with the history of a strike, in this chapter, I examine the ideological impact of deunionization.

I look at the late nineteenth- and early twentieth-century development of "scientific management" by Fredrick Winslow Taylor and the deunionized Midvale Steel mill in Nicetown, Philadelphia, as a way of understanding the racial and colonial ideology of contemporaneous avant-garde art forms such as "found," "readymade," and the post-studio aesthetic practices afforded under their banner. Avant-garde manifestos paired with Taylor's ideas demonstrate the metastasizing of divisions of labor in what became known as conceptual art, as well as in "New" and experimental poetry. Moreover, as chapter 3 will demonstrate, the relationship between scientific management and modernism can be situated through their patrons. In the creation of "mind work," scientific management and the managerial function attempted to standardize the vocabulary and rationale of exploitation; it is a system that serves factory owners, the bourgeoisie, and those who seek to expropriate. Modernism and museum art in the United States—though at times advertised with leftist politics—exists through the patronage of the ruling class. With the advent of forms such as the readymade and the normalization of post-studio practices, collected art becomes both leisure and exploit, then merit and exploit. Irrespective of intention and narrative pursuits, art remains at the threshold of the dominant class as a signifier of leisure and wealth. The rich of today—in continuum with the robber barons of the previous generation—continue to collect art and build museums around their personal collections and to reify forms that uphold the divisions of labor that place them at the top.

Simultaneously, as the artist separates himself from the artisan (the hand worker), the function of art becomes a cerebral activity reserved for the echelons of abstract thought and play. To be a conceptual artist, and to collect conceptual art, signifies one as an esteemed abstract thinker, ahead of and beyond the dirt of one's time and place. These narratives come with objects, which remain collected by the very rich who promulgate the mythology that conceptualism and the avant-garde are about the fantastical separation from past forms of work; they attempt to nullify the narrative of excess through theory. Through all and because of this, exploitation (the displacement of work and its dispossession) does not disappear.

The parallel popularity of scientific management and found object art in the twentieth century prompts consideration of how certain forms of labor become deskilled in both managerial studies and modern art. In extending my examination of the aestheticization of property, I investigate in this chapter how "mind work" becomes a distinctive and elevated labor position. Wanting to understand the ideological imperative of the idea, I address a continuum between those identified with *the idea* in corporate and aesthetic spheres. In making this connection I ask: Why and how do occupations associated with thinking become valued over those disassociated from it? Taking up labor process theory and deskilling, I ask: How do divisions of labor become aestheticized in modern and contemporary art? Were modern and contemporary artists deskilled, or is the labor position of the artist akin to technocrats who supervise and profit from the mechanisms of deskilling? Is modern art the aestheticization of deskilling, in which the artist too becomes the manager of dispossession? In exploring these questions, the aim of this chapter is twofold: first, I seek to track the continuum of racial capitalism in US labor formations, with particular emphasis on how, in its conception of "mental" and "hand" work, scientific management naturalized racial capitalism; and second, in doing so, I examine how divisions of labor become aestheticized and taken up as new forms of art.

In the early twentieth century, the efforts at Midvale Steel to standardize labor dispossession in steel mills across the region took place on Indigenous land: racial capitalism and settler colonialism operate in this conjunction. Much like how the names of the Allegheny and Monongahela Rivers are derived from Lenape words, what is understood as present-day Pennsylvania was settled by the colonialists through the "Walking Purchase," which the Delaware Nation have continued to contest.[3] I situate their ongoing Indigenous presence here to harken to what J. Kēhaulani Kauanui describes as "enduring Indigeneity" and to refute the progressive liberal notion of history and time.

My methodology for this chapter weaves together conversations from labor studies, Marxist theory, critical race studies, Black studies, and visual critical studies. I examine the rise and function of scientific management and the powerful critiques made of it throughout the century. Through my examination of scientific management, I analyze how white artists such as Marcel Duchamp and his critical champions have promulgated the scientific management approach to divisions of labor through the readymade, which they too situated as a new and innovative form. For this reason, I pay particular attention to art historians often cited as providing theoretical interventions into understandings of labor and aesthetics; I utilize labor theory to argue that their analyses work to abstract power and history in order to exceptionalize subjectivity, disregarding class and racial oppositions writ large. In this reading, I urge visual and literary studies to consider racial and class antagonism *as* the site of the museum and the artist subject, as these configurations will need to be addressed to challenge the subsumption of aestheticized management/exploitation.

My attention to the labor process in this chapter is antagonistic to contemporary fetishisms of process, as found in conceptual art that fixates on an abstracted notion of process, or rhetorical gestures that applaud nonhierarchical approaches or romanticize decentralization with no regard for the materialization of power. This chapter instead seeks to critically expose hierarchies that are formed through divisions of labor in order to materialize the exploitation made abstract in capitalist and aesthetic forms.

## The Rise of Scientific Management

In the early twentieth century, Fredrick Winslow Taylor published a series of essays and books on "scientific management," a method of management that differentiated between "mental" and "hand" workers. Also known as Taylorism and then Fordism, scientific management attributes corporate and organizational success to the result of managers (those best suited for "mind work," or the knowledge of production) efficiently instructing the shop's "hand workers" (those deemed suited to manual and physical labor) toward more profitable output. While observing and managing workers in the deunionized Midvale mill and pursuing the standardization of work, Taylor timed workers (in what he called "time-motion studies"), created abstract output goals based on his desires, and sought to dispossess the worker of production knowledge, shifting this knowledge exclusively to management. This reinscription of labor justified exploitation as "scientific" efficiency. And as capitalists and socialists alike wanted to make work more technocratic and standardized, Taylorist notions were circulated globally.[4]

Workers' unions and Marxists objected to scientific management as an accelerated form of dehumanization. One key critic, Harry Braverman, synthesized scientific management's actual contribution as the rigorous and enthusiastic deskilling of workers.[5] This rigor is in service of dispossession as, "in a society based on the purchase and sale of labor power, dividing the craft *cheapens* its individual parts."[6] The creation of the term "hand work" leads to the articulation of "unskilled workers." Critiques of scientific management have situated how workers categorized as unskilled are not unskilled; they have been deskilled. The process of deskilling forcefully extracted the knowledge of production to management, naturalizing the notion that some people think and other people do not think. Without romanticizing past forms of work, Braverman contends that, before scientific management's artificial labor divisions, workers participated in some processes of work, meaning that they had knowledge and control of how their work was coordinated, organized, and performed. Under scientific management, workers were systematically removed from the labor process, which was transported to the realm of management. Scientific management was the wholesale attempt at the standardization of worker dispossession.

Arguing that Marx's crucial contribution to the analysis of capitalism was his analysis of the labor process, in which capital is extracted from one class to another, Braverman contended that Marxist scholarship over the twentieth century pivoted toward theorizing revolutions (potential or otherwise), transforming socialist states, and documenting the conditions of exploitation throughout the world. Although all important tracks, Braverman notes that without attending to the process in which labor unfolds, the form of capitalism remains global and pivotal to *even* socialist states.[7] When the process of labor remains unaccounted for, capitalist and colonially derived labor processes become situated as "natural," "inevitable," and "eternal," when they are, in fact, constructed and artificial.[8]

In materializing the composite that becomes social inevitability, scientific management is tethered to what Daniel Markovits describes as the transition from aristocracy to meritocracy. Returning to Thorstein Veblen's *The Theory of the Leisure Class*, Markovits posits a transfiguration of the bourgeoisie in the late twentieth and early twenty-first centuries. At the height of the Industrial Revolution, Veblen theorized class disparities through the discourse of "leisure" and "exploit." Situating the philanthropic and artistic pursuits of the robber baron class, he argued that the aristocracy was understood as such because it engaged in forms of leisure: art, conspicuous consumption, and other forms of what was understood as "non-work." Markovits updates Veblen's thesis regarding the aristocracy through the discourse of merit, arguing that the tenets of aristocracy have been replaced by the system of meritocracy, whereby the rich remain dominant through the artificial restructuring of educational and work processes that create the discourse of merit, and in this, the bourgeois work as more and others work as less; this is by their design.[9]

Traces of this narrative transformation of aristocracy to meritocracy are reflected in Taylor's personal life and in the logic of scientific management. Born into a highly wealthy family, Taylor refused to attend Harvard and opted to work at a steel mill owned by his friend's father. Employed as a foreman via the forces of wealth and nepotism, he convinced the managers of the plant to allow him to conduct experiments on the workers. He began by attempting to time workers and setting up exaggerated output goals. The workers under Taylor's supervision refused to participate in any of the experiments. The results of Taylor's failed experiments—later rebranded as his managerial successes—became the founding premise of scientific management.

While the division between mind and hand was created by expropriating the knowledge of production from the proletariat, and the deunionized worker was rationalized as providing no distinctive *skill* other than bodily capacity, made replaceable via the forces of expropriation, such a configuration reified the manager's *work* as irreplaceable. Scientific management appropriated the language of work for the empowerment of managerial control and domination. If in previous historical moments the US bourgeoisie controlled the mode of production through its association with notions of European aristocracy, and proof of this came in the form of the leisure class, scientific management tracked the transformation of the discourse of aristocracy (Veblen) into that of meritocracy (Markovits). Through the invention of the category of mental work, the bourgeoisie rebrands itself as management and the exploitation of the racialized working class is carried forth via the function of the managerial class.[10]

Though scientific management was considered a new framework by business leaders and spawned the creation of planning committees throughout US corporate sectors, the creation of "mind work" reified colonially established hierarchies. Divisions between mind and body have Enlightenment roots, as they were foundational to Western philosophy. Orlando Patterson argues that this division grounded the philosophical basis for chattel slavery, and Lisa Lowe traces how the figure of the human was drawn in opposition to the colonized, enslaved figure.[11] In alignment with Lowe and interpolating Sylvia Wynter's conception of the "plantation-plot" and Braverman's labor process theory—the most comprehensive Marxist critique of scientific management—the mind-hand separation is a way to unpack the legacies of racial capitalism and colonialism in the arts.[12] Arguing that capitalism is the control and suppression of *process*, Braverman stipulated that the overemphasis on production obscured the upfolding of exploitation prefigured into divisions of labor. In his analysis, it is the divisions and processes of labor that become circulated and enforced by the global market as the most efficient systems of work.

The division between "mental" and "hand" work was about the consolidation of control narrated as efficiency, and the dispossession of production knowledge became translated as the function of management.[13] Labor historian Katherine Stone posits Taylor's *The Principles of Scientific Management* and *Shop Management* to be central ideological frameworks to the redivision process. Post-unions, steel companies installed new machinery and implemented piecework pay scales, which meant that workers would be paid for the "piece" they produced, rather than by ton or the time they worked at the company.[14] The deunionization of the previous era was a priori to the rise of scientific management. In the aftermath of Homestead and in the twentieth century, Stone locates three mutations of US labor: (1) the destruction of the "old labor system," (2) the mechanization made possible through its destruction, and (3) the system of piece-work structured through Taylorist methods.[15]

As mentioned, one of the primary caveats of the destruction of "the old labor system" was the reclassification of labor categories, which included the invention of "mental work" and the creation of the managerial class. Previously, managers at steel mills were hired through the mill, they themselves being skilled workers.[16] With the eradication of the demarcation between "skilled" and "unskilled," and the rise of "mental" and "hand" work, management became vetted through external educational measures.[17]

The objectives of the redivision are most clearly displayed in the function of the new foreman. In the old system, the foreman was "the highest position to which a blue-collar worker could aspire."[18] Post-union, the foreman was "converted" from a worker among peers to manager. In order for this to occur, the foreman was reeducated to "direct and correct the work, but never to do the work himself. His authority depended upon that."[19] And, "the re-education began with convincing them *not* to do manual work, which was no easy task."[20] This was because "foreman, as the lowest ranking 'mind' workers, had to be made distinct from the manual workers."[21] And their reeducation was, in some fashion, a deskilling of the foreman's knowledge of technique, of their impetus to know about and perform tasks related to the "hand worker."[22] In producing the new "skilled mind worker" the foreman was provided managerial knowledge, which was a position removed from techniques, skill, and craft. The manager was to be distinguished as the "skilled mind worker," a position above the "skilled hand worker."[23] These divisions are not about knowledge but about power, as divisions between "mind and hand" and "mental and physical" ossified preexisting class and racial divisions.[24]

The preservation of preexisting divisions barely found new vocabulary. Mark Bahnisch explains that pig ironing was considered "the lowest form of labour," because it was "all body"—"only workers born into the working class can stand such work: Taylor and his listeners cannot."[25] The standardization of colonial and capitalist practices became visualized in the form of work hierarchies, from the Fordist assembly line to the racialization of subcontracting processes. The effect of the category of hand work was to make the worker's "job meaningless and repetitious," to undo previous unionized categories of "skilled" to "unskilled," and to transfer all forms of production knowledge to the managerial class.[26] The redivision in Taylorism was to assuage "the bourgeois fear of undisciplined and anarchic working bodies, and [provide] the techniques for subjecting these bodies to a subjectivity not their own."[27] Once again, workers protested scientific management every step of the way, and Taylor was called to defend his methods in front of a congressional committee in 1912; in 1915, a bill prohibiting the use of scientific management was introduced to the House of Representatives.[28] Though scientific management has proven again and again to be neither science nor effective, efforts to standardize the labor process and the elevation of managerial class continued steadfast into all realms and the future.

The divisions created via colonialism aided scientific management's subsumption throughout US industries. Taylor and his compatriots believed that theorizing what the worker should be doing—irrespective of result—constituted a model for shop efficiency. And this advice was heeded. While the results of Taylor's experiments were only failures, his publications continue to be studied and taken seriously by leading business schools and the notion of centralized planning has become implemented in all spheres of work.[29]

## Chattel Slavery and Scientific Management

Scientific management must be understood as a direct descendant of the violence of colonialism and racial capitalism. In "Black Metamorphosis," Sylvia Wynter posits that the formal processes of capitalism were materialized on the slave plantation; the structure of capitalism thus retains and carries the site of the plantation, as can be witnessed all around the world.[30] Wynter's intervention into Marxist analysis and structuralist theory allows for a deeper engagement with critiques of scientific management.[31]

Critical scholarship on scientific management, while often not in conversation with Wynter, C. L. R. James, or Cedric Robinson, supports their theories. Caitlin Rosenthal explores the relationship between modern management and chattel slavery to demonstrate the direct inheritance from the "masters" of chattel slavery to the invention of Taylorist management systems. In addition to admiring the plantation site, Rosenthal describes how Taylor "justified" the existence of management by looking to the *efficiency* of slave plantations.[32] In writing about the relationship between slave plantations and scientific management, Keith Aufhauser writes, "Taylor's description of the modern factory worker resembles the accounts of slave labor that have been passed on to us by observers of the plantation."[33] Taylor's admiration of the plantation site as model management must be read through the effort to maintain the legacies of colonial hierarchies and forms. Scientific management reflects the explicit and conscious desire to extend the legacies and structures of slavery to the place of work.

This is echoed in Taylor's own conception of the workplace, which assumed an antagonistic relationship between worker and management, and his description of workers as "lazy" and "inefficient" people who "take it easy"; he writes that the worker "is so stupid [that] he must, consequently, be trained by a man more intelligent than himself into the habit of working in accordance with the laws of this science before he can be successful."[34] The worker's intellectual inferiority, however, was predicated upon their status in society. When describing why the worker cannot be part of the planning, Taylor states frankly that it is "not because the workman is not intellectually capable of developing it, but he has neither the time nor the money to do it."[35] In advocating for the suppression of the labor process, Taylor locates the very antagonisms that ground capitalism. Those uninvolved in the planning are not excluded on the basis of merit or intellectual capability—whatever this may be—but on the basis of their class and racialized positioning.

In illustrating the connections between plantations and scientific management, Aufhauser argues that both Taylor and slave plantations broke up the labor process into four similar components: (1) simple routine—labor compartmentalized supposedly devoid of thought; (2) task work design—the effort and action to reduce everything to a system; (3) job enrichment—motivations offered to the enslaved person (such as the "opportunity" for the taking of needed goods) or identification with the factory for the worker; and (4) physical coercion—the violence required to maintain these systems.[36] The parallels between scientific management to chattel slavery are most convincing with task work design and least convincing with job enrichment. The task work design devised by Taylor at Midvale Steel was as follows: "First reduce everything to system; second, introduce daily accountability in every department."[37] This parallels the language used in the "rules printed for the guidance of one planter's overseers," which stated, "Order and System must be the aim of everyone on the plantation, and the maxim strictly pursued of a time for everything and everything done in time, a place for everything and everything kept in its place, a rule for everything and everything done according to rule."[38] Maximum effort and violence was deployed to control the plantation site, and industrial management appropriated these methods.

Yet, as useful as the parallels between scientific management and slave plantations are to understanding the history of capitalism, the differences between them are inconsolable. Transnational anti-Blackness produced centuries of chattel slavery, and slavery is, in the words of poet Dionne Brand, a "tear in the world."[39] Because, to be clear, there's nothing *like* slavery, and work is not slavery; simultaneously, it is important to track—through Wynter's provocations—how twentieth-century administrative schemes were invented by admirers of slave plantations, who looked to plantations as models of efficient management. Though work is not like slavery, the architects of scientific management studied the plantation as a model and adopted its form in order to standardize the form of whole scale dispossession called modern work.

Dave Beech exemplifies the misidentification of work and slavery: "Slavery is a form of labour, of course, and therefore the Marxist analysis of social forms of surplus extraction has a legitimate contribution to make to its political discourse."[40] Slavery has never been, nor will it ever be, a form of labor, and a Marxist analysis of chattel slavery without consideration of thinkers in the Black Radical Tradition—such as W. E. B. Du Bois, C. L. R. James—serves to affirm and abstract the ongoing permutations of settler-colonial and anti-Black expansion. Critiquing how Marxism contributed to the negation of slavery and undertheorized freedom, Cedric Robinson contends that Marx himself was not a materialist but rather an idealist when it came to the abolition of slavery.[41] Moreover, Robinson's conception of capitalism as already racial capitalism is of vital importance to reiterate here, as the links from chattel slavery to scientific management are situated in the suture between capitalism and colonialism, and Robinson spoke directly of scientific management as the rationalization of expropriation, as the coding of exploitation into what was considered the rational language of management.[42]

As mentioned in the introduction, the divisions created through chattel slavery and scientific management reoccur throughout Western history. In reconsidering the origins of Marxism, Robinson situates the genesis of European socialism within heretical critiques of church and state power by those who questioned its material excess and the convenient narratives it generated of the eventual spiritual transcendence of the poor, as a way to refuse immediate wealth redistribution. Often deemed heretics and mobilized throughout peasant revolts, these figures worked to prioritize an understanding of present-day equality and justice, one that did not come with a delayed promise. By examining critiques made by heretics, peasant communities, and their antagonizers, Robinson demonstrates how the contradictory understandings of property (material) became intertwined with transcendence (immaterial): where the state/church would prescribe the rejection of property (material world) in order to offer transcendence (immaterial), through an authority rooted in property and material abundance, situating how the antagonism toward material conditions must be linked to an ongoing political continuum of state, religious, and colonial power.[43]

To reiterate, wage labor and slavery are not the same, yet the architects of scientific management admired the "management" of slavery, and in this regard, the root of industrialized racial capitalism is the conscious maintenance of the hierarchies and systems of chattel slavery. Thus, when it is said that "work is like slavery," the statement is brutally incorrect and simultaneously comments on—even if unconsciously—what Wynter posits as the foundation, the plantation *plot* across the globe and the architecture of modern work. The dispossession and propertization foundational to chattel slavery were centralized as a site of managerial *creativity*, and this site has guided modern to contemporary divisions of labor.

Predicated upon disparities and focusing on how to make the worker obey *while* acknowledging that the worker does not want to work, questions within scientific management—such as, Why is the worker uninterested in work? Why was the quit rate at the Ford factories 58 percent? Why does the worker find work to be tedious and meaningless? And why is the manager interested in getting someone else to do the work?—serve as historical signifiers and critiques to the mystification of expropriation, as they call upon its foundations.[44] Such questions, however, will never be addressed by proponents of administrative control because to do so would be to examine its foundational violence.[45]

Though perhaps it has yet to be the case that the multiracial working class and poor are united against the oppressing class, this does not negate how the owner class has remained historically consistent in its hatred of the colonized, the poor, and the working class. This hatred is reflected in the roots of colonialism, through scientific management to the rise of the managerial class, and the ideology of meritocracy with all its variants. Foucauldian approaches to critiques of scientific management have prioritized locating distributive power and complicity, theorizing at times implicitly or explicitly against class antagonisms.[46]

Labor process theory and critiques of scientific management are not studies of worker solidarity but interrogations into the efforts of the dominant class to standardize exploitation. While racial dynamics complicate strictly class-based analyses, the grand contribution of labor process theory is its deep study of managerial exploitation and antagonism. A twentieth- and twenty-first-century critique of orthodox Marxism in light of scientific management could be that it is not so much that the worker is alienated from labor, but that the worker *too* is subjected to the processes of dispossession (of skill), which remain unabolished because of the remnants and, in the words of Saidiya Hartman, "the afterlife of slavery."[47] Through the discourse of management and efficiency, the modern worker is denied the body from a mind; and the mind cannot come into consciousness from the body for individual workers any more than it could for enslaved and colonized persons because the discourse that divides the body from the mind is the matter of the system that naturalizes domination. In this light, the abolition of the systems created to uphold chattel slavery remains essential to the rupturing of racial capitalism and its mutations, be it property forms, scientific management, or another.

## Present-Day Implications

Though never a science and more a method of capitalist advocacy, Taylor's early twentieth-century framework regarding management and centralization became replicated in all industries, from factories and corporations to aesthetic forms and legal definitions of work. Critics across the spectrum highlight how, over time, the title of "manager" and the distinction between the office and the factory have become irrelevant.[48] Post Fordism, the office becomes the site of technocracy, and its separation from "the factory" does not dissolve the ideological divide between mental and hand work. Brain work becomes separated once more, revealing how this classification has been less about the worker's exemption from what is considered manual labor, but instead about the worker's approximation to control, command, and domination. In this light, Braverman notes that "management has become administration"; or, as Herbert Marcuse clarifies some years later, "domination is transfigured into administration."[49]

Taylorism invented the vocabulary central to the rationale of expropriation. Mind workers—managers—exist to uphold the deskilling of hand workers. Their primary function is to dispossess the valence of knowledge from workers, and this dispossession is mediated through the vehicle of "central planning." The question could then become, is dispossession work? Is the structural enforcement of deskilling—exploitation—*work*? Are managers workers?

The implications of these questions are multifold. In the decision *NLRB v. Yeshiva University* (1980), the US Supreme Court answered no. A case that decided the fate of tenured and tenure-track faculty in private universities across the United States, the *Yeshiva* decision legislated that professors are managers and thus ineligible for unionization. The justices ruled that while workers are a protected class eligible for unionization, managers are not workers. This decision has had wide-reaching consequences and should prompt deep inquiry into the epistemological distinctions between manager, worker, skilled, unskilled, and beyond. Thus, in the long twentieth century, exploitation becomes usurped through a division between mind and hand, which becomes bureaucratized through the vocabulary of labor that is skilled and unskilled, material and immaterial, and so on. These artificial divisions remain authoritative in all fields, be it economic, academic, or artistic.[50]

## Modernism and Divisions of Labor

Walter Benjamin's groundbreaking "The Work of Art in the Age of Mechanical Reproduction" outlines the politics and possibilities of aesthetics in commodity objects by critiquing the notion of aura, and configuring between the commodity object and the work of art. It is one of Benjamin's most highly circulated works, and the essay continues to influence contemporary scholarship. However, I believe Benjamin may have amended his formulation concerning art and film in a less-cited essay, "The Author as Producer," by destabilizing the categories of the author and worker through an interrogation of production. In this essay, Benjamin analyzes newspapers, documentaries, and photography to examine what he deems the "fruitless" and "sterile" debates around form and content. He includes photography as a useful medium for literary inspection: "What is valid for [photography] can be extended to literature. Both owe their extraordinary growth to techniques of publication."[51] Benjamin argues that in photography one can witness "a certain type of fashionable photography, which makes misery into a consumer good. . . . I must go a step further and say that it has made the *struggle against misery* into a consumer good."[52] He clarifies that this is done when the writer or author "experiences his solidarity with the proletariat ideologically and not as a producer."[53] This theorization remains most relevant today as ideological solidarity demarcates the rhetoric of modern and contemporary art.

Modernism, the avant-garde, and conceptualism depended heavily on the reclassification of the artist subject. In Taylorist terminology, artists went from understanding themselves as hand workers to occupying a position of "skilled mind worker." In order to think about the aestheticization of divisions of labor and the function of the producer, I pair Taylor's *Shop Management* manual with Sol LeWitt's "Paragraphs on Conceptual Art" (1967), considered one of the most succinct manifestos in the Duchampian-conceptual tradition. Taylor's manual states, "All possible brain work should be removed from the shop and centered in the planning or laying-out department."[54] The essence of this task is to forcefully separate the "science" of production from its supposedly manual yet necessary work. Analogously, LeWitt writes, "in conceptual art the idea of concept is the most important aspect of the work. . . . The idea becomes a machine that makes the art. . . . It is usually *free* from the dependence on the skill of the artist as a craftsman."[55] From the outset, the work of art is divided. The machine—described as "dead labor" by Marcuse and theorized by Braverman as an extension of the process of deskilling—is conjured up in place of the skill of the artist as craftsman. Even if the artist decides to become a craftsman to produce his art, the labor of making is removed from the act of the idea. Though LeWitt's hierarchical ordering of the work of art is curious, as whom must he convince of the idea's superiority?

The hierarchy formulated by LeWitt—wherein the idea is prioritized above the machine and the skill—is a doppelganger to Taylor's furor for mechanization. The general principle of Taylorism was "The man who did the work could not derive or fully understand its science," and it argued for a "radical separation of thinking from doing." Akin to LeWitt, who articulates for processes derived from the idea, in scientific management, the separation was hierarchical and organizational, with the explicit horizon where "those who understood were to plan the work and set the procedures; the workmen were simply to carry them into effect."[56] Writing on the art-historical genealogies and precursors of conceptual art, Alexander Alberro frankly describes that "the valuation of technical manual skill is largely (if not entirely) abandoned, as [is] the notion of an original, cohesive work."[57] LeWitt's "Paragraphs" clarifies that this division constituted the liberatory framework for conceptual art. Here, the artist, to take up Benjamin's language, abandons the producer function altogether, and, in the vocabulary of Taylor, takes up the location of the new foreman. The freedom *from* production, from the tedious labors of technique, craft, and skill—as provided by the historical backdrop of scientific management—is situated as the ideological position of artistic freedom.[58]

Freedom, within liberalism and in this capitalist terrain, becomes the ability to manage the labor process from the owner's perspective. LeWitt's manifesto—the direct legacy of a Duchampian avant-garde—navigates the progression from the mythology of a whole and liberal subject (artist) to the ability to instrumentalize dispossession as a triumphant new manager (artist). Whereas previously it was believed that the worker/artist might embody both the meaning and the material of their work as the knowledge of production laid with them (which did not create the conditions for freedom), evolution from this era dictates that meaning and production can and must be divided. This becomes accepted as a form of innovation; the worker is reimagined as removed and pieced, while the artist, the aspiring foreman, rearranges the commodity for better site management.

How and why do *new* artistic forms ideologically mirror *new* economic systems? And in tending to their associative *plots*, how might we better inspect the political frameworks for what becomes considered innovative capital, innovative property?[59] In thinking through this concern, I bring into the foray one other example that distills the elevation of brainwork as the function of the artist. As with scientific management, this elevation occurs in the arts through vocabulary and language; in its commitment to the aesthetics of deskilling, conceptual art moves toward a dependence on text. This approach is exemplified in 1968 by Lawrence Weiner, often noted as an artist of deep leftist leanings. First exhibited in Seth Siegelaub's exhibition of conceptual art titled "January 5–31, 1969," Wiener's piece *Declaration of Intent* states:

1. The artist may construct the piece
2. The piece may be fabricated
3. The piece need not be built

> Each being equal and consistent with the intent of the artist the decision as to condition rests with the receiver upon the occasion of receivership.[60]

The piece echoes LeWitt by exemplifying and exceptionalizing artistic intent. Abandoning the focus on the production of the object was to free the artist toward *his* true modern potential of pure, individual expression. In Weiner's work, "the piece" is ill defined; all we receive is the dialectical linkage between the "piece" and the "artist." Central to this dialectic is the authority of the artist. The artist's relegation of the "piece" becomes mythical, sacred; he decides what the "piece" is, and this intent alone is to suffice. The "intent of the artist" remains ideologically unbound. Is this because the "intent of the artist" is supposed to transcend ideology and production altogether? Is it because it is believed that the artist is neither politicized nor a worker, but outside the bounds of material frameworks altogether ("*The piece need not be built*")?

The immateriality of the artist is made possible by the material infrastructure of racial capitalism. In defiance of the past, Wiener's conclusion rejects everything but the intent of the artist. This negation is an affirmation of a colonial presence, particularly concerning the existence of the separation of mind from hand, which is rooted in the histories and presence of slavery and segregation. Modern and contemporary authorship collapses the dispossessed labor of uncredited nonartistic art persons, in the capacity of contemporary corporate commodities. When questioned about the signification of text in his art and whether "language is sculptural material" and thus, poetry, Weiner situates himself as a visual artist.[61] This marker is of interest as an articulation of property and commodity forms, as the distinction between the artistic object and the mass-produced commodity. Either way, Weiner situates his stake as the author and not the producer of the "piece."

Weiner's allegiance to the visual form is of importance in taking up production. Benjamin cautions that though the representation of the photograph may hold a revolutionary, political tendency, "it actually functions in a counterrevolutionary manner."[62] Arguing that a systematic transformation would be possible—for newspapers and for visual and literary mediums—if the laborer of their components were not fixed, Benjamin demands to tie and untie the position of the author and producer.[63] This levy differs radically from the propositions of Taylor, LeWitt, and Weiner as it asks for the unmaking of divisions of labor to destroy the position of ownership.

From scientific management to the readymade in the avant-garde, what we might be witnessing is the crossing from dispossession-as-exploitation to dispossession-as-innovation—or, more succinctly, exploitation as innovation. The indexing of innovation with exploitation was also mirrored in iterations of managerial studies. In writing about the rise of "entrepreneurial management theory," Erik Baker demonstrates that the managerial turn to the language of the entrepreneurial, charismatic leader appeased the changing liberal attitudes of the professional managerial class, yet nevertheless worked to perpetuate worker subordination.[64] In this light, it is perhaps unsurprising that the artist subjects discussed in this chapter translate the ideologies of the leisure class as innovation and freedom. Chillingly, Taylor presaged this timeline: "The writer feels that management is also destined to become more of an art. . . . Management will be studied as an art and will rest upon well recognized, clearly defined, and fixed principles."[65]

From the avant-garde to the conceptual tradition, there is a harboring of the idea and the concept *free* from materiality and, subsequently, from its laborer. Both Taylorism and avant-garde formulations of the "concept" and "intent" do not deny the existence of materiality or laborers, but they rigorously relegate the category of work and craft to a position so below and *unfree* that they, as free, are absolved of it.[66] This is most clearly witnessed in the institutional and critical overlap between the *October* school of art historians discussed below, and in Marjorie Perloff's scholarship on experimental poetry discussed in chapter 4. Both camps consider Duchamp to be, if not the protagonist, at least the central figure of modern and contemporary art.

The conflation between modern aesthetic notions of innovation and corporate notions of expansion can be connected through liberal notions of economic freedom. Each tract posits that the artist/subject cannot strive toward hand work, as work is the condition to be critiqued and subsequently and implicitly displaced. Craft, technique, skill, and knowledge of *work* was never a source of power and potential for the nameless hand worker. When labor is divided in a capitalist system, skill/craft/technique is the allocation of burden and should not be advertised as the symbol of love, achievement, or freedom. The celebration of work is not the abolition of work and, conversely, neither is the displacing, the evading, the regulation, nor the denial of work its abolition.

Though I am critical of both Taylorism and iterations of conceptualism, it should be clear that this does not lead to a romanticization of the past forms of work, previous divisions of labor, or even the elevation of craft/skill/technique *above* or below. Work has been and remains the unfree conveyor of private property. Additionally, as it has been demonstrated, the redivision of labor occurred with and through segregation: the past will never be safe. The segregation of labor and labor unions signals how previous divisions too were predicated upon violence, anti-Blackness in particular. Divisions created within capitalist systems are divisions of exploitation; we should refuse to argue that certain divisions were at one point less exploitative for specific groups of white workers.

Through aesthetic abstraction, leisure and merit become collapsed. If leisure was once the emblem of wealth, the collecting and canonization of art mutates from the ideology of art for art's sake into "concepts." By creating and then elevating the "idea" of an artwork and insisting on the separation of the idea from its material form, the avant-garde reified the hierarchies pivotal to the transition from aristocracy to meritocracy. Those who now partake in the celebration of this "new" form of the idea—be it wealthy collectors, art historians, poets, or artists—do so through their prioritization of abstract thought as the most sacred aesthetic prioritization, a notion dependent on redivisions of labor, which was actualized through the standardization of exploitation. Economic occurrences and business systems share a material infrastructure and a symbiotic relationship to aesthetics. The dialectical relationship between patron and artist, and between racial capitalism and museums, results in a shared ideology. The artist, along with the patron, is the manager, factory overseer, CEO. The brainwork of the patron CEO becomes elevated as the most important artwork—activating ideologies that maintain their positions and power.

Workers and unions understood the exploitation occurring through new forms of labor divisions and fought against the aestheticization of management.[67] In the Manifesto of 1905, announcing the IWW (Industrial Workers of the World) founding convention, the workers warned that "laborers are no longer classified by difference in trade skill, but the employer assigns them according to the machine to which they are attached. These divisions, far from representing differences in skill or interests among the laborers, are imposed by the employers that workers may be pitted against one another and spurred to greater exertion in the shop, and that all resistance to capitalist tyranny may be weakened by artificial distinctions."[68] While unsuccessful in a linear timeline, unions and workers organized against the separation of mind from hand work. They understood that what was actually being contested through artificial labor divisions was the value of a life *through* its separation from ideas. The value of the beholder of the idea is re-posited as inherently more valuable than those *without* ideas. IWW—unlike members of the avant-garde—refused identification with patrons and understood the strategies of political disenfranchisement. They saw exploitation for what it was and refused its lure.

I belabor the history and language of scientific management to materialize the ideology that separates the idea from the object in the arts and, thereby, to undo some of its romance and mystery. The conclusion both camps come to, that who makes something is inferior to who invents or thinks it—and that they must be separated—is rooted in colonial imaginaries. In scientific management, the language of exploitation manifests itself through managerial hierarchies; in the avant-garde, racial capitalism is sublimated through the discourse of innovative forms such as the readymade and the conceptual.

To exploit and be exploited is neither beside the point nor an intellectual exercise. That exploitation remains with specific racialized and colonized groups and does not disappear, that the notion of *those whose time is considered disposable* does not disappear, is critical to the notion of *new* ideas.[69] I am suggesting that conceptual formulations of the *new* within preexisting structures of capitalism reify its domination and ask for new methods, new forms, new ideas that *work* to undo the aestheticization of exploitation pivotal to the property form. In suggesting this, I understand that I am staking an antagonism toward most artists who are considered conceptual, avant-garde, and even some who may not identify as white. And in refusing the mythology of an immaterial separated from its materiality, I hope for the construction of spaces in which we can make, think, and be together.

Some will contend that contemporary class and racial antagonisms are too complicated to unravel without individuation. This attitude is reflected in contemporary art historians writing about artists who have taken up the aestheticization of exploitation as their method and object of choice, such as Santiago Sierra (discussed in chapter 6), Renzo Martens, and, I would argue, the shield of avant-garde forms and its provider of managerial permission, Marcel Duchamp.[70]

## Conceptualism and Artistic Freedom

Though art historians and artists insist on distinctions between modernist camps and the branches of the avant-garde—from the avant-garde, to concept art, conceptual art, Fluxus, post-studio, institutional-critique, and social practice, to performance, digital art, and others—in 1969, artist Joseph Kosuth clarified that "all art (after Duchamp) is conceptual (in nature) because art only exists conceptually."[71] Duchamp, as discussed in the introduction and further examined here and in chapter 3, provided the conceptual platform that has worked as a shield from materialist, labor, and racial critiques, and which modernized the positionality of the artist.[72]

Theoretical extrapolation of Duchamp's concepts has been expansive, relentless, and politically consistent, as in *October*'s 1994 issue on Duchamp. In the issue, titled "The Duchamp Effect" and eventually published as a book by MIT Press, the authors include well-known art historians and artists such as Hal Foster and Rosalind Krauss.[73] In the issue, the writers assert that Duchamp *freed them*. In a featured interview, artist Ed Ruscha, known for his pop art, explains that Duchamp "was against a kind of academic slavery that artists went through who followed a traditional path; he was for the spirit of revolt. . . . [He] discovered common objects and showed you could make art out of them. . . . He played with materials that were taboo to other artists at the time; defying convention was one of his greatest accomplishments."[74] The appropriation of critical theory is apparent both in Ruscha's exaltation of the artist and in the special issue more generally. Ruscha's statement situates the reading that many art historians and artists, including LeWitt and Weiner, have made of the readymade object and the liberatory potential of the found object form. In this mythology, Duchamp "discovered" common objects as potential art objects. Perhaps it could be argued that Duchamp legitimized "common objects as potential art objects" for recognized artists through his authority as a legible artist—a property not allotted to all. Perhaps it could be further argued that Duchamp's artistic authority was then predicated on legitimizing "common objects" into an exclusive field, performing a kind of fathering function. Further, it is interesting that the "potential art object" remains elevated above the common. What is being lauded here as *taboo* is the transmogrification from common to potential art object. The common object—which, we will have to assume, was made by someone who is not an artist or a beholder of property—does not exist as an art object. The common object becomes the potential art object, not through a transformation of its labor and materials, as that would be considered traditional, but through a discovery of its conceptual potential by a possessor of property. The discovery process in this narrative belongs to Duchamp.

Moreover, Ruscha situates the previous milieu for the artist as "academic slavery." This is a peculiar assumption, considering that at Duchamp's historical moment—which, to reiterate, occupies the same period as Taylor's experiments and the popularization of scientific management—even white women were not allowed into most art schools in Europe, degree-granting art schools in the United States were only in their nascence, and schooling was segregated nationwide. Ruscha's imagined "artist" toiling through "academic slavery" is, then, explicitly white, male, and a beneficiary of segregation. Ruscha assumes that no artist or critical thinker would enter their respective fields to follow the "traditional path" or select "academic slavery." To be an artist is to be original, and predetermined paths—conflated with the narrative of the preconceptual artist—do not lead to originality. Instrumentalizing slavery in a similar manner as the white workers and union newspapers discussed in chapter 1 did and invoking the relationship between anti-Blackness and its instrumentalization as analyzed by Christina Sharpe, Ruscha conjures up the metaphor of slavery in order to celebrate a triumphant and abstracted abolition. Is it that Duchamp rebelled against slavery and traditionalism by rejecting the tyranny of craft and the assumed labor of art (painting, sculpting, otherwise), and abolished the sanctity of predetermined paths? Unlike previous traditional forms of art that situated the artist in a position of labor (how *well* one could draw, paint, sculpt), Duchamp revealed that original artists legitimized and showcased *concepts*.

Such retellings of the readymade focus on the antibourgeois and antiestablishment potential of the avant-garde. In the same *October* issue, art historian Hal Foster offers a variation of this narrative. Though critical of Peter Burger's differentiation between Dada and neo-Dada—according to which the former was antibourgeois and attacked the market, while the latter affirmed it—Foster nevertheless confirms that "readymades and collages challenged the bourgeois principles of expressive artists and organic art work."[75] While it is true that Burger's thesis concerning Duchamp's Dadaism as singularly antimarket is not supported by material history, where only Duchamp's works hold extreme financial value and institutional presence—as examined through his letters with his patrons in chapter 3—neither critic seems unnerved by how expression holds all the political weight, and labor becomes absent from the framework. Unlike Kosuth, Foster and Burger split hairs to define the potential theoretical differences within the avant-garde tradition; but at the core of both formulations is the invention of the "anti-expressive" found object, which is recounted again and again as a once singular or no longer effective weapon against bourgeois art.[76]

To untangle the subsumed conflations of modernist and avant-garde origin myths, it is important to understand how the origin story being retold by Foster and Ruscha hinges on a politicized understanding of expression. Foster confirms that the binary dividing bourgeois art and antibourgeois art is the modality of expression, or what Duchamp's primary collector and patron Walter Arensberg describes as "taste," discussed in chapter 3. Those not involved in art spheres might be surprised to discover that *expression* has become an uneasy term in aesthetic theory, especially among artists and fanatics of the avant-garde. In this well-circulated critique of expression, the argument goes like this: one of modernism's inventions was the politicization of notions of beauty, the sublime, and with it, craft. As in, if *Art* with a capital *A* previously existed to express the immortalization of kings, queens, gods, and their commodities—usually in the form of beautiful paintings, sculptures, and the like—the expression of the artist became intertwined with the desires of its patrons and their institutions. In this triage (the artist, expression, the object/representation), expression (often associated with ideological beauty) becomes linked to the authority of the bourgeois patron, and therefore the artwork and the process of creating art is politically debased.[77] Thus, although early modernist painters who began painting nonwealthy subjects such as peasants and farmers were admired, it can be argued that such objects functioned within the bounds of the museum and the market. The antiexpressive readymade is said to interrupt this bind, as it creates the possibility of politics without the involvement of the patron's expectation of beauty (expression).

However, there is quite a puzzling jump in this triage. It is strange that "expression" alone is linked with the labor of making/craft, particularly during a historical moment where embodied hand work is being degraded. In addition, if the critique of expression was to destabilize the relationship between artist and hegemony, has it been successful? Are artists and art less compromised—is this possible? Is to be less compromised the liberatory horizon of art? Rather than this enclosed reading of expression, perhaps it is more generative to postulate a baseline Marxist understanding wherein the patron represents the bourgeoisie, and those whom they employ, subcontract, or otherwise engage *may* have differing political pursuits. Perhaps.

Further, Foster's dialectical amendment allows us to ask about the evasion of labor. In a perversion of Marxism, the artist labors to displace work. Marx's deployment of the dialectic was to serve the proletariat: "It is one of the greatest misunderstandings to talk of free, human, social work, or work without private property. 'Work' is essentially the unfree, inhuman, unsocial activity, determined by private property and creating private property. The abolition of private property becomes a reality only when it is understood as the abolition of 'work.'"[78] What, then, is the rupture that Foster's dialectic works toward, and furthermore, why are questions of labor outside the framework of this art history? The embrace of antiexpression and the readymade form, which is the aestheticization of management, is either the timeline in which artists actively remove themselves from the category of worker and the process of deproletarianization or the timeline in which a labor category unconfigured to alienation becomes invented through the artist/manager. The aestheticization of divisions of labor through the archetype of the artist makes narrative sense, as both "traditional" and avant-garde artists are intimately connected to their profession and their professions are to collapse the boundary between work and life.

Rather than through a critique of expression and racial capitalism, art and labor theorist Dave Beech examines the history of artistic deskilling. Differentiating artistic deskilling from the deskilling Braverman analyzes, Beech contends that art's "hostility to handicraft" is older and found its shape through scholarly pursuits.[79] While I agree that art has been hostile to handicraft for much longer, I would posit that its fermenting hostility paved the intellectual way for deskilling writ large; these relationships are intertwined rather than separated. Additionally, to situate the deskilling in art as separate from economic deskilling may abide by the philosophical trajectory that works to read aesthetics as removed capitalism and its mode of production, reifying the immaterial grip of aesthetics.

Moreover, antiexpressive critiques, or the hostility to handiwork, have not prevented artists from engaging with objects; such objects remain produced under the same conditions in which both a critique of work, a critique of deskilling and institutions could be forged. Though writing decades removed from "The Duchamp Effect," Beech eerily echoes the camps above, writing that the avant-garde embraced "mechanization, automation, commerce and business" in order to mount a "critique of aesthetic labor" and capital.[80] This is because the readymade opened a terrain in which, echoing Kosuth once more, "art is more abstract and general category."[81] The importance of this marking is exemplified by Thierry de Duve's argument that "you can now be an artist without being either a painter, or a sculptor, or a composer, or a writer, or an architect—an artist at large."[82] However, not *everyone* is an artist, because the space of abstraction, the ability to render abstract "has become essential in identifying the artist as the bearer of a social form of labour," which upholds the scheme wherein some perform "mental" work, or make concepts, and others (*those who cannot become artists*) labor to render this space possible. The tension in the idea that everybody is not an artist but could be, while at the same time the artist's *work* is unlike everybody else's, remains. Thus, when Kosuth states that all art after Duchamp is "conceptual in nature," this is an understanding of how the displacement of nonconceptual forms of work has become the marrow of institutionalized art, and the discourse of its freedom.

Leftist politicization of antiexpressive gestures such as the readymade is the agreed-upon convenience of a managerial system that links the politics of "non-work" and the merits of collecting the work of others to the mythos of modernism. This binary setup creates the illusion that antiexpression is affixed to *entrepreneurial inventions*, and subsumes the political differences inherent in labor divisions primary to this form. From Foster's claim of the avant-garde to the non-Marxist formulations made in de Duve's *Kant after Duchamp*, and Kenneth Goldsmith and Craig Dworkin's introduction in the polemic *Against Expression*, and even to Beech's careful study of artistic deskilling, the antagonism of expression to the evasion of labor becomes a politically expansive theme within debates concerning the importance of the avant-garde. What expression is, how it occurs, and what remains possible should be an open, not foreclosed, inquiry.

To assert that there are common objects waiting to be discovered by someone who can see their "potential" demonstrates the paradox that art historians, artists, and writers continue to make about the politics—and not the labor—of avant-garde art. The avant-garde artist is the artist against tradition, a position that is ethically and politically superior to the traditional artist, while simultaneously above the "common" and politically removed from work. His—and for Ruscha the artist is clearly a he—revolt is enacted through the appropriation of "common objects" that are assumedly foreign to established aesthetic realms. The "common objects" enter the fray, but not the laborers, the labor, or the politics of their production. The process of the readymade, of the revolt fundamental to this rebellious artist, is not about the abolition of violent structures, systems, forms, and their definitions, but about an expansion into "non-art" spaces and new objects to be claimed by the recognized, legitimized artist figure.

## Phoning It In: Post-Studio Practice and Risk Transfer

Well-known curator Hans Ulrich Obrist discusses how in 1919, "Duchamp was one of the first artists to use instructions."[83] Duchamp's sister in Paris was sent a telegram explaining how to make his *Readymade malheureux*—and she did. To this act, art historian Werner Hofmann replies, "Absolutely—just called it in. Sometimes the best solution is the easiest one—if you know what to do."[84] Duchamp's 1919 "calling it in" may be one of the first known examples of a phenomenon that is now described as post-studio practice, which provides artists with a theoretical premise for outsourcing and hiring others to make what might once have been made by the artist in their studio. While Obrist and Hofmann seem delighted by this practice for the reasons laid out by Weiner, LeWitt, Ruscha, and others, I want to push further into the ideological frameworks that give rise to the theoretical shielding of post-studio practices as "modern" and "contemporary" art. Once again, I push not in order to lament "how art was" or to place undue meaning on the notion of making, but to track how outsourcing becomes theorized as innovative, rather than exploitative, and then normalized into modern artistic production.

Hofmann reacts to Obrist's story by affirming Duchamp's exceptional position as an artist. He does not raise questions about the creative role of Duchamp's sister in fabricating his readymade or address what it might mean that Duchamp's female family members were some of the recipients of his outsourcing. Instead, he witnesses Duchamp's "calling it in" as an artist who *knows what to do*. An artist who *knows what to do* can utilize the easiest solution—which, apparently, constitutes having someone else do it for you, in this case, a family member. This implies that an artist who *doesn't know what to do* might be unable to deploy the easiest solution. Regardless, Hofmann and Obrist fixate on both Duchamp's method of phoning it in (having someone else do what you want) and his outsourcing as exceptional.

In the vicinity of the language of management, art historian Jane Blocker posits Duchamp as "the progenitor of artistic risk taking" and "the model of the artist who mimics the discourse and procedures of venture capital."[85] Blocker adopts the corporate banking term *risk transfer* to discuss artists—such as Richard Serra—who are celebrated for their dangerous ideas but are not involved in their making. Many of those executing Serra's outsourced labor have been injured, and one killed, in enacting his dangerous sculpture visions. This position of authorship, Blocker points out, is completely dependent on the celebration of displacing risk—precisely mimicking our financial and political structures. I would extend this to argue that all such phenomena—the outsourcing of risk, the entitlement to risking the lives and bodies of others, and the celebration of risk transfer—are dependent on *whiteness as property*. Whether enacted by Duchamp, Santiago Sierra (discussed in chapter 6), or in investment banking, the transfer of risk can only take place when a property-eligible subject is present to receive its gains. Throughout modernist and contemporary discourse, risk taking becomes aestheticized and risk transfer becomes "innovative and laudable."[86]

The celebration of Duchamp's "phoning it in," the theoretical delinking of object/idea from maker/artist, and the transfer of risk have spawned industries such as the Dafen Village in China. Winnie Wong materializes this contemporary phenomenon produced by the forces of conceptual art and globalization, where a group of workers/artists in Dafen produces a vast stock of masterpiece "dupes" (copies), as well as outsourced new artwork, and artists and art buyers commission and purchase their work. While Wong is careful not to compress the workers in Dafen into simplified categories of exploitation, which she argues further dehumanizes them, she presents case study after case study in which the asymmetrical power differentials between the "artists" and those hired in Dafen are made explicit. Those who commission the Dafen painters are often white and almost always established artists with forthcoming museum and gallery shows, book deals, and more. The commissioning artists not only have the capital to commission, but their claims to property and authorship are globally acknowledged. The same cannot be said of the painters in Dafen, who consistently remain unnamed as artists or workers in relation to the object, being named only occasionally when their presence is part of the artwork's conception.[87]

Wong picks up on how, in post-studio methods, authorship remains the thorniest issue. In Christian Jankowski's conceptual project *China Painters* (2008), Jankowski commissioned painters in Dafen to paint what they imagined might be displayed in the newly constructed Dafen Art Museum, and their paintings were eventually exhibited as Jankowski's series at the museum. Though Jankowski's press release states that "copyists were thus transformed into authors," the project was given a caricatural title and is listed on Jankowski's website as one of his works; he is the only named author.[88] The titles of the paintings are as follows:

> *Sexy Painting Machine*, 2007, 294.5 × 211. 5 cm
> *A Group of Naked Women*, 2007, 183 × 160 cm
> *Abstract*, 2007, 89 × 119 cm
> *Heroes*, 2007, 194 × 88 cm

Jankowski claims that the project displays the "individual tastes, interests and convictions" of the authors, who are only referred to as "copyists." Jankowski's conception of authorship precludes any name other than his own, leading one to wonder once again about the politics of modernist transformation. With regard to this method in the context of *China Painters*, Wong writes, "This transformation . . . enables the conceptual artist's purchase order to be transformed into a readymade."[89] Through the discourse of transformation and authorship—which function as modernist aesthetic buzzwords—and all the while refusing to attend to preexisting power differentials, particularly between the recognized artist and the too-often unnamed worker "copyist," Jankowski's *China Painters* exemplifies how exclusionary understandings of property as well as racial infantilization continue to function as pivotal conceptual art practices.

The painters in Dafen, their labor, and their art are treated as pieced objects that must be managed by the artist subject. The labor process normalized in these contemporary practices is rooted in an artistic tradition that centers the property-eligible subject, that works to exemplify and isolate "the concept" away from the context of its making. The contemporary neoliberal landscape is one in which workers continue to be deskilled through mechanization and the top-down forces of central management; simultaneously, Wong's research displays how the labor of acquiring a skill does not protect workers and racialized subjects from dispossession. In Dafen, it is the painters' very skills that are weaponized against their subjecthood by conceptual artists. This is because Jankowski and others animate the antagonistic relationships between property and dispossession, skill and concept, hand and mind, and artist and worker. They do so through the naturalization of a labor process that situates them above those who make *stuff*. Akin to Duchamp's phoning it in, their ease with capitalist formations of the irreplaceable manager affords them further credibility and authorship.

Wong states that the Dafen painters do not fall into the structures set up by Taylorism or Fordism. While many labor theorists have articulated that Taylorism was a failed system and was rarely enacted, its implementational failure has not decreased its ideological reach; justification for labor exploitation and dispossession is rooted in labor divisions that separate the idea from the making in all realms of production, from industrial to aesthetic.[90] Conceptual art displays how the artificial division of the idea from the object continues to be presented and aestheticized; in fact, as an unregulated, exceptionalized, and finance-driven realm, conceptual art may be the only area in which scientific management has been successfully executed. Though the term *scientific management* may have disappeared, its presence remains animated through the strictures of value and authorship.

If and when artistic labor processes parallel the capitalistic labor processes of the twentieth and twenty-first centuries, this should be examined as the mechanism of naturalization rather than dismissed as the state of naturalization. Additionally, claims that artistic production has "always been divided this way" evade how the violence of capitalism continues to metamorphize. In elevating the role of ordering other people around as the signifier of *the subject who knows what they're doing*, in producing the notion of a "found" object (a "readymade") that is theoretically destined to be made by someone else, and in exceptionalizing the idea above all else through the formation of conceptual art, modern and avant-garde art *rigorously* aestheticized preexisting divisions of labor. Artists did not create the division between mental and hand work, but they uphold and amplify it. This amplification turned a mythological division into a form and a genre, which works to maintain the illusion of art as an elite, metaphysical liberation from materiality. The artist-as-manager promulgates that the consolidation of control in the figure of an auteur who serves as the centralized figure of "command," is the marker of superior art, further legitimating capitalist divisions of labor.

Defensive arguments that posit *this is how it's always been done* are a form of denial, a way of using the past to justify the conditions of the present, or an insistence that there is no division between past and present, and thus, things will continue to exist as is either because it has always been that way or because it cannot be any other way. This prompts the question: Which is it? Are modern, postmodern, and avant-garde art forms aesthetically distinct from those of the Renaissance while, simultaneously, the labor process throughout Western art traditions has remained the same? If so, what does this reveal? Such a defense crystallizes the linkages being made on behalf of artistic labor processes.

The elimination of the "handmade" object and the glorification of the artist genius did not occur with the elimination of production or the category of artist; it simply displaced the work of production as "non-art" or not of interest and made outsourcing of theoretical importance to art theory. Inquiring into the labor process is less about the fetish of the artist's hand, or the artist breaking the illusion of the notion of a singular production, or the idea that everything has always been this way, than about the fervor with which labor processes are evaded and separated as modern art. The elimination of the "handmade" and the rise of the Duchampian tradition marks a moment in which liberal formations of freedom as predicated upon racial capitalism become aestheticized. In this sense, the artist becomes part of global managerial systems in which he remains at the apex of the production order.

* * *

Interrogation of the labor process is a gesture of good faith and a desire to understand the ways in which the object and its production interpolates and interrupts the dynamics of power. The normalized post-studio practice, in which an artist hires various assistants to do everything, speaks to the ways in which modern and contemporary art production has adopted the tenets of scientific management, wherein a designated few (those whose time is infinitely valuable) perform and become credited with the idea of the product, while others (those whose time is worth almost nothing) operate under the formal control of those select few.[91]

Consistently, the managerial function in the arts becomes swapped for the position of the proletariat, or even the lumpenproletariat. In a completely decontextualized, willful misreading of the history of modern art, theorist of immaterial labor Maurizio Lazzarato looks to Duchamp's artistic oeuvre as suggestive of the figure who refuses work.[92] Beech amends this reading by pointing to the fundamental privilege of Duchamp's position, writing, "Duchamp is not an insubordinate worker stealing time from the bosses but *an artist without a boss*. His reluctance to work [is] not a political weapon against capital but an expression of privilege and a romanticization of privilege."[93] In the following chapter, I refute the notion that Duchamp, and conceptual art writ large, is a stand-in for the maverick against work by examining Duchamp's correspondence with his primary patron, Walter Arensberg.

The separation between those who are expected to follow instructions and the expert who has ideas for what must be done is a painful, artificial creation. A critical analysis of Taylorism is not a protection of the artist, art institutions, poetry, or academia—these forms do not require protection. A critical examination of the labor (material) of aesthetics is neither protective nor celebratory. The separation of the hand from the brain, the body from the mind, is the violence upon which capitalism thrives, and Samuel Gompers reminds, "mental hunger is just as painful as physical hunger."[94]

The privileging of "brain work" and management is the hierarchical *progression* for those who are not involved in work but surrounded by the forces of wealth. Labor is what had already been removed from their realm. Labor is that which has been gendered and racialized, that which they have pushed down to the bottom of the world in achieving their own rise. Work is never the goal.[95] Those who currently escape it do so only by privatizing profit and socializing risk. Those who do not work are indebted to the labors of others. In this way, modern and avant-garde art movements that have taken up the redivision of labor as a political force consciously or unconsciously mobilize and enjoy the epistemological foundations of property, which in the United States is *whiteness as property*.

THREE

# Whiteness as Property and Found Object Art

## *Collecting and Canonizing Marcel Duchamp*

Let's bum rush a haiku party with
conceptual artists
How long can you stare at a Urinal,
for god's sake!

**Marilyn Chin, "For Mitsuye Yamada on her 90th Birthday"**

The period discussed in this chapter is often described as the segregation era, when, in the shadow of failed reconstruction, the cultural norms of Jim Crow became law. As situated in chapter 2, the early twentieth century also marked the rising influence of Fredrick Winslow Taylor's scientific management, a method invented to disempower workers, deunionize industries, and aestheticize the role of management. The segregation era is home to modernism, which coincides with the opening of prominent cultural institutions and the expansion of Carnegie's libraries across the United States. This interval also captures the dynamics between national and international colonialism and its resistance movements in publications such as *The Crisis*, established by W. E. B. Du Bois. World War I and the leadup to World War II occur at this time. This is all to state that the stakes for this moment were high. Colonial violence accrued, and, for too many, unfreedom remained.

In writing about the material history of Marcel Duchamp's artwork in permanent collections and his patronage—which reaches across the

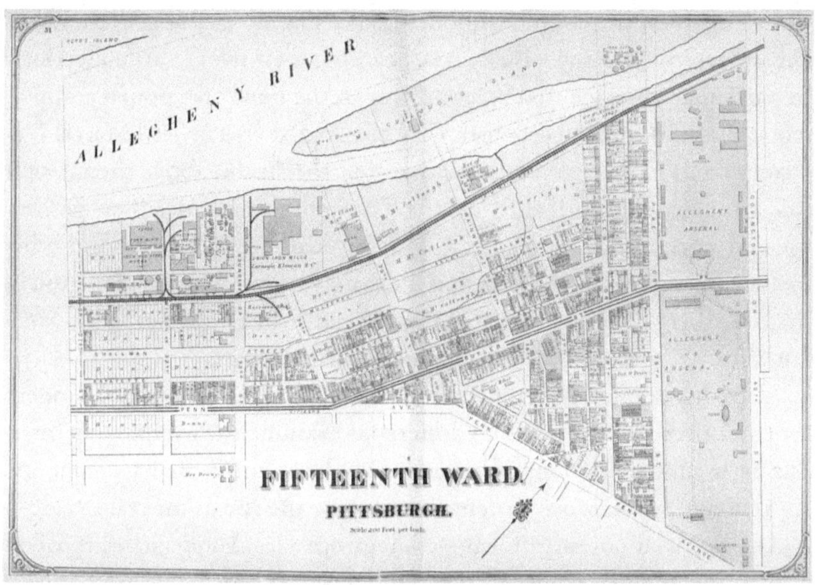


**3.1** Map of Pittsburgh's Fifteenth Ward in 1872. M. McCullough steel foundry is located on 36th Street. From *Pittsburgh Legal Journal*, vol. 55, G. M. Hopkins & Co., 1872, plate 51.

segregation era and into World War II—I was not expecting to write a chapter with direct material links to my first chapter on Pittsburgh and steel. But so is the narrative of colonialism: tangled and knotted. Duchamp's primary patrons, Walter and Louise Arensberg, were born into wealth in 1878 and 1879, respectively. Walter's inherited wealth came from his father's cofounding of the McCullough-Dalzell Crucible Company in Pittsburgh, a steel foundry. Historic maps from 1872 list the company's property as four blocks along 36th Street flanking the Allegheny Railroad, and records indicate that it remained operational until the 1930s, when it was acquired by the Crucible Company. Featured in the 1930 issue of *Prominent Families*, the Arensbergs' home address is listed in Oakmont, a town outside Pittsburgh, on Maryland Avenue, neighboring the designated National Historic Landmark of the Oakmont Country Club.[1] Louise Arensberg's family history is similar, but it is instead tied to the textile industries. Born into affluence and highly educated, neither of them worked. Their lives were supported by passive income: familial assistance, inheritance, and stocks. This arena of nonwork is an essential point to which I will return.

Together, the couple embodied what liberal sociologist Thorstein Veblen described as the leisure class, devoting their lives to art collecting.[2] In particular, they focused on collecting in the newly fashioned realm of modern art. In 1915 in New York City, the Arensbergs invited Marcel Duchamp from France to temporarily live in the studio above them. After this arrangement, until their deaths, Duchamp was under their patronage and acted as their art dealer, brokering deals between them and other modernists such as Max Ernst, and ultimately negotiating the donation of the Arensberg collection—consisting primarily of Duchamp's most well-known artworks—to the Philadelphia Museum of Art.

In this chapter, I document how avant-garde collections and modern art enter the museum space. In doing so, I examine the overlapping interests between the divisions of labor laid out by scientific management and the museum space. I seek to demonstrate how the rise of the readymade—Duchamp's well-noted art form—comes from a legal understanding of exclusionary property, rendering the found object as a form that aestheticizes preexisting racial dispossessions. While in the first chapter I examined the material processes of acquiring a personal collection and converting it into a museum, in this chapter, I delineate the process by which a personal collection becomes part of a permanent archive within an already established museum. This distinction is relevant in that the Duchamp-Arensberg collection illuminates how members of the leisure class fashion the collecting imperatives of preexisting cultural establishments, directly shaping the canon. The relationship between collector and museum remains underexamined while the notion of object merit and objective artistic value as the rationale for institutional acquisition permeates and dominates art education and the humanities. In this chapter, I demonstrate how a materialist undertaking of museum donation is required to critique the composition of artistic value, the canon, and narratives of innovation.

The arguments presented in this chapter explore the material conditions and the subsequent political dynamics in the acquisition of found object art. I examine the dominant narratives surrounding Duchamp's *Fountain*, which I argue have been the product of dehistoricized understandings removed from the context of colonialism. I offer a portrait of *Fountain*'s milieu, which is especially relevant because in the early twentieth century, segregation was present in all US sectors and visualized particularly in the space of private and public restrooms. The previous lack of such contextual examination is one way by which—as legal theorist Cheryl Harris instructs—whiteness is made neutral and yet proprietary.[3]

Conversely, literature that contests the mythology of white property—and aesthetics that intervene in its simplification, such as the sculpture of Noah Purifoy—is currently undercirculated. Through the vehicle of disparate yet entwined histories, I reexamine concepts that have since become primary in cultural production: the avant-garde, conceptualism, patronage and donation, and the properties of the found form.

With an approach similar to my methodology in chapter 1, I examine the politics of collections and the aestheticization of property through an investigation of the acquisition records for the Arensberg collection in the Philadelphia Museum of Art, including tax records and correspondences between Duchamp and the Arensbergs that occurred before the museum accepted their donation. As stated in chapter 2, the materializing of conceptual art and its property form is not an advocation of "hand work," nor am I simply pointing to the displacement of work as the end point of analysis. Rather, I engage with how property and management, how being the owner or boss and the act of ordering others around, becomes aestheticized and romanticized through the emergence and development of conceptualism. As previously delineated, I seek not to create a developmental narrative wherein aesthetics is the result of economic, legal, and social formations, but rather, I display how the relationship between aesthetics and legal formations produces cultural and canonical forms.

While my research begins in the late nineteenth century, I am interested in laying out the colonial history of immaterial/conceptual art in order to clarify the racial dynamics of the present moment. As I mentioned in the introduction, the tradition of racialized and anti-Black appropriation continues today. In the aesthetic transfiguration that becomes property, the artistic freedom afforded by the Duchampian tradition is invoked to shield artists from criticism. In my examination of the avant-garde and modernist collecting practices, I argue that what's offered by this tradition are not new forms and modes of aesthetic formation, but rather the transference of racialized objecthood becomes codified as formal innovation; simply put, it is expropriation as innovation. The formula of this transference translates material codes of property as the *new* formation of immaterialism. In pursuing the material history of immaterialism and artistic freedom, I explore the relationship between whiteness and freedom, and argue, as legal theorist Cheryl Harris has so pivotally laid out, that whiteness as property has tethered whiteness to freedom in all aspects of aesthetic culture, materializing how racialized property claims become interpolated as innovation. Extending the style of Purifoy's title *White/Colored*

(2001), for a sculpture that pairs a water fountain and a toilet bowl, Duchamp's *Fountain* might be better titled *Urinal/Fountain*. The signification of the urinal is pivotal to the imaginary of the fountain, much as *White* is predicated on *Colored*. In order to examine the relationship between whiteness and expansion in the arts, I pursue the political implications of aesthetic property claims in order to analyze their ideological implications. Through this framework, I intervene into the time-honored debate on how certain art works and literature become valued and preserved. By positioning canonical collections and forms through their colonial and legal property claims, rather than through the discourse of merit, my research inspects underexamined economic processes foundational to the arts, such as property formation, the museum space, and patronage. Investigating the aestheticization of property as a formal imperative allows for analyses of otherwise obscure political strictures and enables the possibility of variegated narratives in the arts.

My engagement with the donation of Duchamp's objects to the Philadelphia Museum of Art seeks to witness how the practices of multinational corporations and racial capitalism inhabit the acquisition policy and history of the biggest US museums, and vice versa. The parasitic relationship between artistic institutions and corporations reveals how the upholding of racial capitalism is sutured into how these institutions were and continued to be built and maintained. Additionally, my critique of Duchamp's canonization is not intended as moralistic condemnation, but rather dialogic historical materialization concerning how the "found" was and is predicated upon property formations available to whiteness in the United States.

The space of exclusion manifested as the explicit site of white freedom, and objects like *Fountain* served as its linked, transitional object. To provide a critique of property, I conclude the chapter by examining the artwork of Purifoy. Through Purifoy's *White/Colored*, it becomes clear that the myth of the original *Fountain* as a revolutionary artistic gesture, removed from racial, economic, or historical considerations, simply could not be. Investigating the urinal and drinking fountain from 1917 as objects of US segregation, and of segregated space and time, allows us to understand the stakes of what has been celebrated, immortalized, and institutionalized. And simultaneously, by examining Purifoy, I press into the ongoing presence of abstraction in radical and racial critiques of property. I conclude by wondering into the current limits of racial critiques of property—not to foreclose but to open possibilities for practices to come.

## Becoming Part of a Permanent Collection

Throughout Europe in the early twentieth century, modernist artists such as the Dadaists published their manifestos and put together independent art shows. In the 1910s, much of their work officially entered the public arena, as in the 1913 Armory Show in New York City. With mixed reception, this show introduced modern art to the New York public. Marcel Duchamp's cubist *Nude Descending a Staircase* was prominently displayed in the show and subsequently satirized in newspapers.[4] The energy surrounding the exhibition motivated New York art patrons to invite Duchamp from France. Duchamp at this time had been excused from fighting in World War I, and he entered the United States in 1915; in exchange for his art objects, he briefly took up residence in a studio owned by Walter and Louise Arensberg. Thereafter, he became a member of the infamous Arensberg salons, producing many objects to be purchased by affluent members of New York's art scene.

There are many deviations among the stories about the 1917 *Fountain*—authored by Duchamp and currently considered one of most important works of modern art—but also some clear consistencies.[5] The event takes place in New York City in 1917, with the support of Duchamp's patron Walter Arensberg. In some variations, Duchamp and his patron enter a plumbing store and purchase a urinal.[6] Others refute this account and state that Duchamp makes the urinal but provocatively tells people he found it. Others argue that Duchamp stole the work from a female friend, either Elsa von Freytag-Loringhoven or Louise Norton, and then submitted it as his.[7] All variations conclude with the "R. Mutt" signature on the urinal (one of Duchamp's artist pseudonyms), a flipping of the urinal's orientation, and the title of *Fountain*. It is agreed that the object is then submitted to an art show by the Society of Independent Artists Inc., a collective of white artists of which Duchamp and his patron were members.[8] The society, not knowing that Duchamp submitted the object in question, rejects it outright as failing to be a work of art. Duchamp decides that the rejection is an outrage and, using another pseudonym, writes a review criticizing this rejection.[9] The signed "found" urinal is lost. Decades later, during the height of the civil rights movement, reproductions authorized by Duchamp are made by Italian artisans to be sold to European and US collectors.[10]

Duchamp remains a central figure in art history and contemporary practice, often cited as the pioneer of modern art, the avant-garde, and the readymade form.[11] Through the Arensbergs' donation, the Philadelphia

Art Museum holds most of his works, while reproductions of his readymades are housed at the Centre Pompidou and other prominent museums. Both the artist and the form of found art have been fully incorporated into the narratives of art and literature and the space of the museum.

I will return to a discussion regarding the politics of the found form and theoretical readings of Duchamp, but I want to begin by discussing the procedure of Duchamp's institutionalization. Walter Arensberg wrote to Duchamp in 1945 about the possibility of donating his collection to UCLA:

> I have lived so long and so closely with your works that in some way or other they have become incorporated in my structure, but because they are so familiar and so close. I am unable to make my feelings for them articulate. *If you are the Unknown Soldier, let me be the silent guard*. . . . In a way, therefore, *the museum will be a monument to you*, and the presence of all the other things will serve as a means of defining how completely individual is your contribution to the art of the twentieth century. . . . It is hard for me to write. I feel a kind of paralysis in expressing my feeling, but I constantly think of you.[12]

Art and war have long been engaged in a chaotic relationship, a borrowing service of ill use.[13] The term *avant-garde* originated as a military term indicating a leading formation, the group sent first to "seek the enemy" and secure ground for the incoming troops. In the letter, Walter professes he has lived with the artifacts so closely that Duchamp's works have become incorporated into his "structure," and he invokes this intimacy through images of war. *The avant-garde* as an art term appears in the mid-1850s, in the writings of socialist thinker Henri de Saint-Simon. Pulling directly from the strategies of militaristic advancement, Saint-Simon theorized how artists might catalyze society into a progressive, socialist era. While Saint-Simon's vision has yet to be realized, the notion that artists remain ahead, in terms of ideas, politics, and thoughts, resides in Walter's letter to Duchamp. Duchamp is unknown and ahead; is Walter shielding his passing? This leaves us to press what was not pressed in the metonym: Who is the enemy, and what is Duchamp advancing?

The emphasis on commonality combined with rarefaction speaks to the structured process of collecting and institutionalizing art. Rather than a king, queen, or other entity of cultural importance entitled to protection, Walter identifies a soldier and a guard. Both functions—soldier and guard—operate on the level of commands. Thus, the soldier is a peculiar illumination of the *artist who advances ahead*, as it links the figure with the commands of "elsewhere." Furthermore, soldiers and guards do not usually protect one another. A guard protecting a soldier indicates an unusual circumstance, such as an injury. In the case of this soldier, the condition attributed to him is that he is *unknown*. In comparison, the customary role of the guard is to be silent. British guards famously do not speak, as speech disrupts the performance of authority. Thus, in displaying the internalization of Duchamp's structure and his commitment to protecting him, the patron utilizes the vehicle of a soldier and guard by emphasizing their very common functions: to be unknown and to remain silent.

Though the Arensbergs spent their lives acquiring art—including works by Picasso and Brancusi and what they called "Pre-Columbian art"—Walter clarifies that the collection is a Duchamp monument.[14] To forge a monument, aggression, combat, and protection are necessary. Though Duchamp's art is "completely individual," the building of a permanent monument is ritualized, so much so that there exists a vast domain of militaristic lexicon to configure the required duties. Is this because such dynamics of interpolation are common, or does the work speak to a commonness that must be protected?

Duchamp's institutional placement was no work of chance, play, or merit—it was not the trickster form of absurd and *found*, or the abrupt narrative of the "ready"—it was the result of colonial, dynastic wealth and, moreover, wealth invested in a particular kind of time, narrative, and property. Duchamp's foray into the museum space is a tale of intimate patronage and a collective commitment to seeing their property memorialized. The strategic planning and financial maneuvering that actualized the Arensberg collection (Duchamp monument) cannot be underestimated or dismissed as predictable. It is the process by which permanent collections and their canons become forged.

Moreover, Duchamp acted as an art dealer to the Arensbergs, and much of the information about their purchases, comes from the Arensbergs' California tax records.[15] The narrative of the Arensberg collection and Duchamp's dealership is described with precision in a 1951 letter sent to the California tax department. To the state's public accountant Walter writes:

> We began the formation of our art collection at the time of the Armory Show in 1914 [*sic*], and it was between this time and the time of our coming to California in 1921 that we made many of our most important purchases. They included examples by Picasso, Braque, Marcel

> Duchamp, Gleize, Derain, Rousseau, Sheeler, Brancusi, Matisse, Picabia, Stella, and Pach. It was at this time also that we made our first purchases of Pre-Columbian art, *our interest in Pre-Columbian art being very closely associated with our interest in the forms of art of the 20th century. . . . Our principal purchases of painting from that time on were made through the agency of our friend, Marcel Duchamp, rather than directly through dealers,* since he had personal relations with private persons whose pictures he was able to persuade them to sell.[16]

The collecting process is essential to understanding the finances of canonization. In the letter, Duchamp is named as a primary liaison and then as a dealer. Duchamp traveled extensively on the Arensbergs' behalf to secure a permanent US gallery space for the collection described above. As the Arensberg collection included more of Duchamp's works than any other artist, his agent-soldiering work served his future institutional placement; it would determine his canonical and archival importance.

In a financial accounting of their purchases for the California State Board of Equalization, dated November 28, 1951, the Arensbergs state that between October 1, 1943, and September 30, 1951, they acquired two oil paintings from Duchamp for $500 each in 1950, which is approximately $5,919 each today.[17] The letter vacillates between precise dates and wide ranges. For example, in 1936, Duchamp's *Boxing Match* and *Témoins oculistes* were acquired for $100 each. In April 1937, an oil painting by Duchamp was acquired through Julien Levy of Connecticut for $3,500 (approximately $74,809 today). The same year, a pencil drawing by Duchamp was acquired for $100. In 1940, the Arensbergs purchased *Boîte* for $200, and in 1950, two oil paintings for $500 each. All these purchases came directly through the artist.[18] Between July 1, 1935, and September 30, 1951, additional and earlier painting purchases are listed.[19] According to the tax records, from 1935 to 1951, the Arensbergs spent approximately $5,100 purchasing the works of Duchamp. This is not an exhaustive list, nor does the amount include Duchamp's dealer fees. As their collection displays, the Arensbergs acquired more works by Duchamp than by any other artist.

Duchamp's relationship with the Arensbergs was financially expansive, spanning patronage, dealership, and artistic support. Letters between the Arensbergs and Duchamp regularly include questions about financial assistance and welfare.[20] A folder titled "Money Sent to Marcel Duchamp" includes numerous unmarked money transfers.[21] For example, on March 12, 1931, it notes that 5,000 francs were sent, and on June 28 of the same year, Duchamp was sent $300 by draft; on December 7, Duchamp was sent $500, and so on. This intimate financial relationship is vital to examine as part of the procedure of institutionalization.

During the 1940s, Duchamp and the Arensbergs met with the Metropolitan Museum of Art, the Art Institute of Chicago, the University of Minnesota, and the University of California, Los Angeles, about a permanent home for the Arensberg collection. They received multiple offers before finalizing a deal in 1953 with the Philadelphia Museum of Art.[22] The director, Sydney Fiske-Kimball, promised the Arensbergs five times what the Metropolitan Museum offered, which was twenty-five years of permanent gallery space, with assurance the collection would be held together indefinitely. The securing of permanent museum placement for the Arensberg collection was an approximately nine-year project.

Prime location within the museum (large, connected rooms; good, high ceilings), permanency, and status were not secondary concerns but the driving force of the collection and the nine-year project. After receiving detailed notes from Duchamp's meeting with the Met's curator on the Arensbergs' behalf, Walter Arensberg writes to Duchamp describing how he believes the Met will be hostile to their collection, breaking it up as soon as it is donated.[23] In 1949, Walter informs Duchamp that the University of Minnesota is willing to build a new gallery for the collection. However, Duchamp responds with hesitation, wondering if Minneapolis receives many visitors and stating he believes the collection should be in a large city. The same year, the Philadelphia Museum of Art begins to negotiate with Duchamp and the Arensbergs about museum space. In a letter providing meeting notes and minutes with curator Fiske-Kimball, Duchamp states:

> The only problem is how to divide the space: K. agrees to divide it as you please: low and high ceilings according to size of the rooms—no too small rooms. . . . The only change I would suggest (and I did not dare propose it myself) is to try to get (instead of rm 1699) the symmetrically located rm in sect 6, immediately connected with your part of section 7 (first floor), marked A in my drawing. I did not want to ask him this change because the rm A is now occupied by things belonging to a permanent collection (I believe) but I didn't see why these things couldn't not be shifted to the rm. 1699 which is of the same size. You ought to make that proposition. . . . *All in all there is a good air of permanency in the building and in the offer.*[24]

I quote this letter at length not as an exceptional moment in the negotiation process between guard, soldier, and museum, but as a banal, undertheorized, detail. As if discussing real estate, every fissure concerning space and property were taken into consideration. As noted in this letter, the spatialization of the collection became so essential that rearrangement of other permanent collections was brought up as a negotiation factor. Duchamp meets with Fiske-Kimball again and notifies the Arensbergs of the number of years the collection would stay intact: "The period of 25 years is really comforting."[25] The Philadelphia Museum of Art has yet to break up the Arensberg-Duchamp collection; the objects, to this day, remain together.

Duchamp's thoughts were crucial to the process of securing museum placement. Tellingly, the pronouns utilized throughout the museum negotiation process are a consistent *we*, regarding all decisions. After Duchamp declares little interest in the University of Minnesota, Minnesota is never brought up again. In the final stages of the spatial negotiations with the Philadelphia Museum of Art, Walter begins to utilize first person pronouns to denote the concerns that Duchamp and the Arensbsergs have agreed upon: that the collection must be kept together. While finalizing the details of the "opening" of the Arensberg collection at the Philadelphia Museum of Art with curator Fiske-Kimball, Walter writes to Duchamp, mortified by the fact that Fiske-Kimball has no plans for a separate, exclusive opening for their collection, but would rather have a "general opening" for the Modern Art section: "In Fiske's counter-proposal he wishes to avoid altogether an opening of the collection as an independent event and to have it opened merely as a part of a general opening of what he calls the 'Modern Museum,' in which the identity of *our* collection and both its relevance and irrelevance to the Modern Museum would pass unrecognized, or at least undifferentiated. All this is not at all what we had expected."[26] Duchamp is entrusted to travel to Philadelphia not as an employee but as the partner in *their* collection, and he writes back agreeing to travel with these concerns, as such a general opening would not be *satisfying*.[27] Shortly after, Walter writes Fiske-Kimball directly, arguing for the importance of their collection, and demanding an opening that would acknowledge the collection's singularity.[28]

Within a few years, and by strategizing and creating the notion of a singular collection, almost all of Duchamp's objects were slated to be permanently housed at the Philadelphia Museum of Art. This is evidenced in a letter by Duchamp in 1953, and in two letters sent after the death of Louise Arensberg (the first sent via telegram, and the second via letter).[29] Duchamp comforts Walter Arensberg and reminds him that their collection is a shared dream. He writes: "The answer must come of itself unformulated by breathing again for her and give the final form to the work that she and you started together. When I wrote you about a month ago, I really hoped that there might be enough time to open the rooms in Philadelphia and let her know that one of her dreams had become a reality."[30] Duchamp affirms Louise and Walter's life work: the amassing of an art collection. The acquisition of this collection is a triangulated dream, as it memorializes the *work* of the patrons and the artist. Walter agrees with Duchamp and positively responds to his encouragement to open their collection.[31] He emphasizes that after the opening, he would like to bring back a few of the pieces, asserting once more his desire to live with the artifacts, while confirming with Duchamp his plans for the collection, its arrangement, and its future.

Walter's statement, "I constantly think of you," is no hyperbole. They were in each other's thoughts, lives, finances. Soldier, guard, dream worked in tandem to enshrine their lives' work of collecting art. This dream was and remains predicated upon the actualities of the segregation era.

## Canonizing Taste

In her 1994 dissertation, "Silent Guard," concerning the Arensbergs and their collection, Naomi Helen Sawelson-Gorse emphasizes the apolitical milieu of the Arensberg salon: "Indeed at the Arensberg Salon, there was an attitude of indifference and disinterest towards the world conflagration, at least to one habitee."[32] This political analysis is brought up in many different ways: "[At] the Arensbergs's duplex apt at 33 W 67th St., the intrigue was not about politics and there was intrigue enough with all the ever sexual liaisons";[33] and most plainly, "rather than social or political [issues] . . . aesthetics were discussed."[34] To really bring this discussion home, Sawelson-Gorse mentions that in Louise Arensberg's journals, she notes that she was "curiously untouched" by news of the Great War. The juxtaposition of interest in sexual liaisons and aesthetics rather than politics to Louise's journal comment is quite jarring, considering how the Arensbergs' salon and collecting efforts would have occurred through the Great War and the leadup to World War II, not to mention during Jim Crow America and the start of the civil rights movement.

Sawelson-Gorse accurately points out how a forced separation of the social and the political *from* the aesthetic is evidenced in the purchasing records and the correspondences regarding the collection. The building of the collection was apparently immune to war, injury, violence, or offense other than the occasional curatorial flippancy. However, without ever stating directly the word "politics," the collection amplifies the reach of whiteness and its desires as property. The collection does not need to pronounce its politics to be witnessed as segregated—politically, aesthetically, socially, and otherwise.

Sawelson-Gorse writes, "For them [the Arensbergs], the collection was to be seen as [a] corporeal, psychological, and emblematic representation of their selves."[35] The personalizing of the patron's objects as his own is reflected at every level of the collection and in the Arensbergs' records. The biography of Walter Arensberg, as outlined in his personal records, follows the chronological narrative provided for the California public accountants, but with more detail.[36] From moving to New York to establish an avant-garde salon, to inviting Duchamp to live in his family residence, to contributing to American Dada, Walter clearly saw his efforts as essential to the creation and curation of capital-*M Modern* capital-*A Art*. The patron sponsored Duchamp's magazine efforts and understood the readymade before all others. He contributed to modernist magazines and discourses, and even to modernist manifestos. He donated the largest collection of Duchamp's objects to a museum.

Sawelson-Gorse asserts that the objects collected and acquired by the Arensbergs were to be a faithful reflection of themselves; yet this is a strange prescription in light of what many art history books teach about how such collections and objects become canon; it simultaneously conflicts with Walter Arensberg's own artistic proclamations. In his early writings concerning art and poetry, he records: "Arriving at subconscious forms by attempting to avoid obvious and immediate associations. *Avoid Taste*. Do something contrary to taste."[37] In an undated essay, he affirms, "I objected to the sentimental character."[38] For Walter, his relationship with modern art and patronage arrives through no *obvious and immediate associations*. Contrary to Sawelson-Gorse's argument concerning the life of the Arensberg collection, the patron believes in operating *contrary to taste*. As in, though he believes he is essential to the formation of modern art, the associations of its formation should not be obvious. Does this imply he is evasive on purpose? Is this the obscuring of his involvement as patron and collector or an affirmation of estrangement from himself? Though the patron proclaims that modern art is contrary, fragmented, and antisentimental, the development of modernist collections is obviously financial, regimentally procedural, and fundamentally sentimental. While the patron mimics the sentiments of Gertrude Stein—an amplified conceptualist who sardonically debases sentiment and clarity—and insists he is operating in contradiction to *taste,* his tax records reflect otherwise. A collection does not come to an institution through disavowal of its associations; it is but another modernist fantasy to believe one's material commitment has nothing to with one's life.

## The Presence of Segregation and the Making of Property

Investigating New York City bathrooms and water fountains in Jim Crow United States requires a mixture of media. Answers to the questions I had concerning the context of *fountains* particularly—How were bathrooms segregated? What were the cultural dynamics of bathroom segregation in the North?—did not exist in the form of a singular monograph.[39] Jim Crow laws were prevalent in some states, and the absence of specific laws did not imply equal treatment, as discrimination could be practiced under many names. For example, though the 1917 Supreme Court decision *Buchanan v. Warley* protected the legal rights of Black residents to purchase property, the decision left room for interpretation regarding private agreements. Thus, throughout the United States, white businessmen and homeowners turned to racially restrictive covenants.[40] It goes without saying that New York City between 1915 and 1917 was far from neutral and remains so today. Forty percent of New York City residents at that time were former slaveholders, and today, the oldest known African burial ground, disregarded for centuries, still bears the intrusive foundations of federal buildings that house various municipal and federal agencies.[41] New York was the only state where African Americans were required to own property in order to vote.[42] Property ownership was thus a fundamental requirement to participate in political representation.

Moreover, segregation operated on multiple levels.[43] The 1925 issue of the *New York Amsterdam News* reported how, in Brooklyn, "Mr. and Mrs. Alfred D. Vaugn [were] threatened with death if they moved into a house they had purchased. N.A.A.C.P. obtained police protection." The paper stated, "Acute segregation situations in seventeen cities through the United States, ranging from New York to Los Angeles are reported by the National Association, which has just received a report adding the city of Denver, Colo., to those previously listed."[44] Throughout the early 1920s, the *New York Amsterdam News* reported on housing, education, and the cultural segregation of theater spaces. According to the reports of the paper, some New York residents were as active in the fight against segregation as their compatriots elsewhere in the nation.[45]

However, when *Fountain* is discussed, the United States and the context of segregation rarely enter the analysis or even the footnotes. In *Part Object Part Sculpture*, which may be the largest contemporary retrospective on Duchamp to date, curator Helen Molesworth offers not one word about the function, context, or history of *Fountain*. In the catalog of essays for the exhibition, every detail, every possible fissure—except the historical, the historically political, or the racial—is examined. *Part Object Part Sculpture* displayed Duchamp's work and that of seventeen artists Molesworth believed Duchamp influenced. Almost all the artists on display are white men; Yayoi Kusama, Félix González-Torres, and Gabriel Orozco are the only artists of color, and there are no Black artists. Though *Fountain* is relentlessly referenced, there is no discussion of New York (other than in reference to Duchamp's patrons), the politics of art-making in the United States, nor any interrogation of Duchamp's whiteness.[46] This decontextualization and renarrativization of *Fountain* is routine and is part of the normalizing functions of what Toni Morrison describes as the "racial unconscious."[47] The operations of the racial unconscious exemplify how white space becomes synonymous with neutrality, and race and context are unable to be configured.

David Joselit, one of the contributing writers for *Part Object Part Sculpture*, offers this illuminating reading regarding the gesture Duchamp enacted: "Language necessarily erases difference: *urinal* refers to all machines for catching the urine of men despite the fact that *every one of them is different*. Even those that came off the same assembly line, or those that stand side by side in the same lavatory, are minutely different, either through the vagaries of manufacture or through the different veils of liquid staining their surfaces."[48] Joselit begins by stating that language erases differences. Then, in a turn that anticipates neoliberal multiculturalism, he imagines the urinal as a functional object *despite* difference. The urinal cannot see difference, cannot see time, race, class, or history (though apparently it can see gender). Because Duchamp's language and performance transformed the object *urinal* into a *fountain*, one is able to grasp both the sanctity of flattening difference and the possibilities in erasing it via commodification.

Though it is stressed that the marvel of the readymade is its uplift of an everyday and ordinary object, the socioeconomic function of the toilet becomes further abstracted. The toilet and the drinking fountain occupy a space of recurrence in US history; they are banal emblems of colonial and gendered signage, interpolated by public policy, wealth, sanitation, decorum, and personalized into rituals and phobias. But Duchamp's *Fountain* does not become every urinal in the world; the act does not legislate on behalf of makers of commodities or those commoditized, democratize art-making, redistribute the function of the artist to include proletarians and those unnamed yet essential to the materials of art, nor does it demystify the function of the artist—rather, the act further cements the exceptionality of the artist, the exceptionality of the collection, and the innovation of modern art. *Fountain* is pivotal to the tradition of modern art and the museum space because it provided a formal vehicle devoid of broader liberatory possibilities. Art remains a form of exclusionary property, removed from the signifier of craft and making.

Art is closely held as a measure of white freedoms, and Duchamp's readymade marks an important turn in this enterprise. Harris argues, "Whiteness was the characteristic, the attribute, the property of free human beings."[49] Willem de Kooning illustrates this timeline in "The Renaissance and Order," a lecture given at Studio 35 in New York in 1950:

> There is a train track in the history of art that goes way back to Mesopotamia. *It skips the whole Orient, The Mayas, and American Indians. Duchamp is on it*. Cézanne is on it. Picasso and the Cubists are on it; Giacometti, Piet Mondrian, and so many. . . . I have some feeling about all these people—millions of them—on this enormous track, a way into history. They had a peculiar way of measuring. They seemed to measure with a length similar to their own height. . . . The idea that the thing that the artist is making can come to know for itself, how high it is, how wide and how deep it is, *is a historical one*—a traditional one I think. It comes from man's own image.[50]

De Kooning's attempt at historicization—an imaginary train that goes back in time to exclude particular cultures and peoples—makes its first stop to pick up Duchamp. De Kooning does not explain why his train must travel so far only to exclude, but Harris crystallizes that "whiteness shares the critical characteristics of property even as the meaning of property has changed over time. In particular, whiteness and property share a common premise—a conceptual nucleus—of a right to exclude."[51] De Kooning clarifies that Duchamp's gesture of found-and-ready is not only beholden to the date 1917, since, as according to Harris, whiteness continues to provide our current understanding of property. This is to say that while Duchamp, de Kooning, Molesworth, and the authors of almost every piece written about *Fountain* have disregarded issues of whiteness and property, it is in this omission that we can foreground their politics. De Kooning's list of passengers is telling—they are the group of white men whose objects have been most thoroughly circulated, prioritized, and continue to dominate the art market.

The found form is dependent on its origin story, which proclaims that the idea can be separated from the object; this is why I argue that conceptual art is the commodification of narrative forms and speaks to the monetization of circulation. The story is its aestheticization (its politics) and this aestheticization is dependent on its narrative circulation (how many people know and believe it). Thus, in the introduction, I describe the event of *Fountain* as mythology, as the story white artists and patrons retell to subsume the property form as the most innovative form of art. If the reading of property in "found" is unfamiliar, it is because the racial actualities of US and world history are made unfamiliar while simultaneously naturalized. To reiterate: the objects linked to these narratives do not disappear, they remain on sale and display.

The context of the readymade is 1917, in a wealthy neighborhood in New York City, in Jim Crow America. The objects selected from this moment are granted, signed, and editioned. They were, and remain, exclusive property. In the late 1990s, *Fountain* "could still be bought for less than a million dollars."[52] The art market logic has ensured that these prices have since "rocketed." For those who wish to repeat the success of this capitalist experiment, to prank the prankster, be aware: there will be legal consequences. "The Association [of Marcel Duchamp] reserves the right to take legal action against unsigned, undated, and unnumbered samples of readymades from the edition of 1964–1965."[53] Liberation from craft, from making, from labor is contingent upon property rights. The singularity and originality of readymade art is legally preserved as property and not commodity, since repetition decreases value and becomes a threat. Appropriation depends on preserving the notion of singularity by enforcing a condition of exclusion and property. The white space afforded to modernist appropriation is indicative of this.

I bring this up to say that on every level—representational, functional, political, and aesthetic—the invention of the readymade via a 1917 urinal/fountain could never be a neutral product of liberation. It is a historically telling gesture of white property relations and of whiteness made neutral. This mundane observation becomes overlooked, because museum art functions as property, and property in US and European culture functions as a vehicle of whiteness.

Commodity objects are valued according to their narrative appeal, and this is how immateriality becomes materialized as property.[54] Harris writes, "In transforming white to whiteness, the law masked the ideological content of racial definition and the exercise of power required to maintain it: It convert[ed] [an] abstract concept into [an] entity."[55] This lust for conversion is thrillingly displayed in *Fountain*. Duchamp is sponsored by his white patrons and promulgates the desire toward the signifier of segregation. The piece does not invite its making, its study, or an interrogation of its history—it aestheticizes its conquering and rewrites this narrative as an object of beauty. Portending digital commodities, fantasies for this object become fulfilled as property, and this transaction becomes the political climax for modernist art. This conversion from white abstraction to white entity is maintained tenuously, violently, culturally, legally, and monetarily. The basis of this conversion is material, historical violence—it is the conversion from white fantasies to white property. The maintenance of white space requires active concealment of the material violence required to transform fantasies into property. Colonial appropriation—as methodology and practice—is a tool that assesses and positions economic and property values. In high modernism, this was an "economic pitch"[56] made by white subject positions, and the process of conversion was one of decontextualization.

Raymond Williams's notions of the dominant, residual, and emergent are pivotal to understanding how structural violence often becomes qualified and obscured via the idealization of structural transformation or individuated metamorphoses.[57] The actuality and presence of US segregation must be read within the development of conceptual art, particularly in the narrative of Duchamp's discovery of the found object, which cannot be disassociated from the lifelong patronage he received from Walter and Louise Arensberg and their joint and successful effort to canonize his archive. During the lifetimes of Duchamp and the Arensbergs, segregation was the dominant legal structure, and therefore shaped every part of life and existence. Legal segregation and the aestheticization of segregation work in tandem, and the residual affective and intellectual protection of segregation (the leftover feelings)—in a reflection of ongoing dominance—has become interpolated as proprietary, exceptional, canonical, and innovative. The inheritance of segregation, its aesthetic and affective oeuvre, continues to structure the epistemology of property. One enduring aspect of this epistemology is the conflation between residual and emergent aesthetics, which while willfully or unconsciously deny emergence, insist that the residual *is* the emergent. This can be witnessed in the "Marxist" framing of Santiago Sierra's oeuvre, as discussed in chapter 6, and the discourse of "Newness" within the Archive for New Poetry, discussed in chapter 4. The leftover feelings and the preservation of property forms is not emergence: it is simply the maintenance of historical and material forms of domination. Additionally, emergence cannot be clearly defined, and in this, I ask for the preservation and possibility of surprise as to what emergence from segregation and property might be.

In accordance with the ontology of property rights, race is rendered invisible and denied *and* whiteness is vitalized in the permanent collection. Duchamp's whiteness (and extraordinary patronage) are not factors in the *Fountain* and his oeuvre's critical importance—they are the conditions of its existence. Such a formula may be a testament to the normalization of whiteness as property and white property as the most valuable art. Harris's extrapolation on the notion of whiteness and exclusion is particularly haunting, as high art is based on the self-exclusionary position of the artist, which was and remains primarily the white male subject. It is the exclusive and the exclusionary position of the white male artist that grants him the power to make commodity into property, and property into art. Such are the historical foundations of modern art.

## Vacancy, Abstraction, and the Materialization of Segregation

As discussed in the introduction, legal theorist Cheryl Harris foregrounds the function of vacancy in the creation of property. Harris sets up her critique of property as twofold. First, she configures how European philosophers situated an understanding of abstraction and vacancy and transferred this notion of vacancy to the land of the colonies. Though the land was not abstract, and never vacant, for the purposes of ownership it was made as such. This quality of abstraction was extended to those persons considered nonwhite, particularly those enslaved, for the making of property.[58] Second, the abstraction bestowed upon the land and persons was singular and exclusionary—it was protected from the logic of repetition, of the forces of another kind of abstraction, another sovereign. Property, then, must be understood as the combinatory forces of singular abstraction and exclusion.

Politically, vacancy and abstraction are foundational to the US composition. In writing about abstractionist African American literature,

Philip Harper explains how abstraction made the conditions of settler colonialism and chattel slavery possible. Harper demonstrates how the tool of abstraction—in the form of the surveying mechanism used in the Land Ordinances of 1785, the technocratic system used to colonize 75 percent of the United States before the passing of the 1862 Homestead Acts—allowed for the land to be imagined and claimed as vacant. Land is made abstract in the surveying system, so that settlement is understood through a grid rather than through the lives of the people, the environment—through its life. Supporting Harris's argument about the foundational function of property, if aesthetic abstraction and its assumed vacancy precedes propertization, then, as Harper deftly points out, "emptiness [is] packaged for easy consumption."[59]

The vehicle of abstraction is most clearly displayed in language. Paul de Man traces the line in Western philosophy linking metaphor to abstraction.[60] This epistemological grounding includes Locke, Condillac, and Hegel, who presented slightly varying ideas on how the function of figurative language is to allow particular ideas to travel with authority. In constructing the epistemology of metaphor, de Man highlights the accepted practice of Western, *white* poetics, which is a literature fearful of embodiment, wholly dependent on abstraction, and committed to the philosophy of authorial choice and selection concerning the symbolic order. And though de Man claimed to make an objective examination of the epistemology of metaphor, it is postcolonial and Black feminist scholars who have situated the racialized investments of such abstractions. In particular, Chandra Talpade Mohanty critiques the ways in which studies and narratives of the Global South by Western feminists produced scholarship that stabilized the subject position of the Global North.[61] Mohanty describes how in such writing, we can witness how Western feminists wrote of *the Other* as a way to write about the safety and development of themselves.[62] In *Playing in the Dark*, Toni Morrison effectively argues that, while in full contact with Black cultural production, the canonical tradition insulated white history, subject formations, and desires. In a different context, these concerns have been articulated by French philosopher Jacques Rancière, who argues for the examination of all compositions as the fictions of their *inventors*.[63]

In this vein, Grace Kyungwon Hong argues that nineteenth-century articulations of "empty, homogenous time" were replaced in the twentieth century with "its spatial equivalent: abstract space."[64] Abstract space situated the plane on which imperialism abroad would fail to be considered *real* in the United States. Through the flattening grid of abstraction, the wealth generated from the ventures of former colonies or within pockets of the Global South now situated in the Global North could be considered as profits rather than acts of devastation.[65] Recalling once again J. Kēhaulani Kauanui's provocation against the time of settler colonialism in the introduction, I would add to Hong's powerful critique that, rather than supplanting each other, empty time and abstract space operate in tandem to obscure the codependency between settler colonialism, racial capitalism, and imperialism. This is deftly demonstrated in Jodi Byrd's scholarship on how the land utilized for Japanese American internment camps were often those of tribal nations who protested their building, and this abstraction of land and colonial time operationalizes Native deterritorialization.[66] The empty time of settler colonialism coincides with the abstraction of all that it works to dispossess, from the land to its persons.

Dave Beech compellingly situates that "abstractions are separated from real history and therefore the critique of abstractions reconnects abstractions from the real histories that form them" and that the abstraction of art in general is "an effect of coloniality itself."[67] The creation of abstract space has been a purposeful, uneven political endeavor, one that works to actively negate spaces of difference, life, and injury. Dispossession is activated through the creation of abstraction, and abstract space continues to foreclose materialist, political inquiry. Rather than opposing the *real*, abstraction and the creation of abstract space can be witnessed as continuing to normalize structures of violence by forcibly creating notions of property and ownership, such as vacancy.

## Noah Purifoy: *White/Colored*

Modernist and postmodernist aesthetic projects spanning across mediums that prioritize *the idea* of the work have long been thought to expand the notion of artistic freedom. Marcel Duchamp's *Fountain* being regarded as an influential modern work should be understood as emblematic to narrative of artistic freedom in art and poetry.[68] While usually not read as such, Duchamp's *Fountain* and the readymade may be reconsidered if it is contextualized in the world of Noah Purifoy's *White/Colored* (2001), an outdoor sculpture in Joshua Tree that places a porcelain toilet next to a drinking fountain. In the slashed landscape of racial capitalism and history materialized by Purifoy, the viewer is asked to consider the historical context of US public spaces and symbols of sanitation such as the fountain and its correlate, the urinal. Through Purifoy's piece, the contexts of US segregation and the tenets of the Jim Crow North in the 1910s are undeniable, and perhaps the wordplay in Duchamp's piece is suggestive of this racial coding.[69] Rather than a signifier for emergent artistic form, the urinal/fountain prompts an inquiry into the fractured notion of space in 1917 New York City, where Duchamp and his patrons lived, a space in which the segregation of urinals in bathrooms, whether in public or private spaces, was the norm; the slash in Purifoy's title also speaks to this forced barrier.

Furthermore, the location of Duchamp's *Fountain* (Manhattan, New York City) demands investigation. There have been a hundred years of the advent of the avant-garde, a hundred years of celebrating "found objects" as an essential aesthetic rupture—why has *found* not been followed up with the questions of *where* and *how*? It has become theoretically assumed that the artist's formal innovation or contribution is in the finding, but this innovation depends on narrative leaps made away from material conditions—which, in the case of Duchamp's (and many others') discovery (the *found* form)—are the context of segregation *and* the land on which it unfolds. In *Fountain*, we can witness how aesthetic traditions have not merely participated in this violence but have actively formalized it into what are considered new aesthetic forms.

Purifoy's *White/Colored* is situated outside and within an open shed in the deserts of Joshua Tree. There is a bending wood roof, a two-tiered wall splitting at the edges, and a wooden platform. In the center of the platform is a gray drinking fountain and a toilet. Paired and titled this way, the two objects epitomize the visual markers of US racial segregation: there is a drinking fountain exclusively for whites—or, perhaps, there is a fountain for whites, and a toilet for others? The toilet is propped up by a white platform, elevated to the same height as the fountain. The objects are horizontally equalized and differentiated. Because of this, the space that separates the fountain and the toilet comes into focus. The deep space between the two materializes the punctuation occurring in the title—the slash from *white* to *colored*—as it pierces the imaginary that pronounced one from the other while simultaneously amplifying the racialized histories offered by their markings. Together, the fountain and the toilet visualize an absence in aesthetic narratives that work to disassociate: material from affect, history from memory.

The properties of segregation have made it legally possible for white art to claim institutional priority over nonwhite art.[70] As witnessed by modernism's celebration of *Fountain*, white liberation happened in isolation and through segregation. Black cultural production during this time (and since) took an entirely different approach to the question of authorship and liberation.[71] Black newspapers, and particularly Du Bois's *Crisis*, were without mention of Marcel Duchamp, found objects, or readymades.[72] From 1915 to 1917, *Crisis* featured a section for international Black news and Black resistance. Black cultural producers and periodicals witnessed a transnational Black radical activism hinged on opposing anti-Blackness and imperialism. While US politics constitutes its identity via the practice of racial segregation, Black readership and Black cultural production was not and is not formed in dialectic to this identity.[73] *Crisis* instead forged its position via a transnational articulation of Blackness, with a radically different definition of freedom. Referring to Marcel Duchamp's *Fountain* (1917) and renaming it *White/Colored* might be considered an inversion. In our current moment, we cannot escape Duchamp when bathroom objects are exhibited in isolation. However, here, the toilet is glaringly linked to the history of US segregation, and therefore, a simple reversal would collapse the vast differences between the Duchampian narrative of *found* and Purifoy's *broken, lived, found, put together*.

Purifoy's sculpture *White/Colored* exemplifies this autonomous approach, in terms of form and materiality.[74] In *Junk Art*, Purifoy and Ted Michel write: "We wish to establish more. . . . There must be a ME and a YOU, who is affected permanently. Art of itself is of no value if in its relatedness it does not effect change, a change in the behavior of human beings. And changes in behavior are effected through communication."[75] For Purifoy and Michel, art directly opposes the politics of "art for art's sake" and demands a reorienting of previously held positions. This critique does not simply describe a politics that Duchamp and his patrons were uninterested in—or situate Purifoy to be read politically in ways that Duchamp is not—but, together with his sculpture *White/Colored*, it fundamentally alters the reading possibilities for Duchamp. *White/Colored* situates the urinal and the drinking fountain as objects in a time-bound conversation, desecrating the narrative of neutral, aesthetic liberation.

Photographer Elliot Erwitt's *North Carolina, 1950 (Segregation Fountain)* is a photograph depicting an unnamed Black person leaning into the water fountain with the label "colored" above, while the fountain with the sign "white" is vacant. Widely circulated during its time, the photograph mediates the tensions actualized in Purifoy's *White/Colored*. Graphically similar in layout to the photograph—which could also simply mean graphically consistent with standard public and private segregation signage—Purifoy's sculpture weaves together the forms authorized by art history with the forms naturalized by state violence. This retelling requires their materials to be reimagined in a space called his own. Configuring the differences between Purifoy's *White/Colored* and Duchamp's *Fountain*, between Purifoy's junk art and assemblage and Duchamp's found art, could only be done if the historical forces of segregation and colonial demarcations of property were to be suspended. Purifoy encapsulates this within a critique of the adage of art for art's sake, stating, "We insisted that art speak for itself . . . it's an elitist concept to feel that art is in and of itself art. It is not in and of itself, because it interrelates with the world at large."[76]

For this reason, Roderick Ferguson places Purifoy within the lineage of the Black Radical Tradition rather than that of the avant-garde, abstract art, conceptualism, or modernism.[77] Specifically, the assemblage art practiced by Purifoy operationalizes Black people and communities into history rather than away from it. Likewise, Daniel Widener situates Purifoy's assemblage as a kind of "historical materialism" differentiated from the abstraction of depoliticized understandings of "found."[78] In Purifoy's *66 Signs of Neon* (1966), which are sixty-six separate pieces constructed from debris of the Watts riots, art becomes a "means for fostering collective responsibility and communication between individuals."[79] This communication and materialism, Widener stipulates, is expansive and specifically meaningful to Black persons in ways it may not be to others.[80] Rather than aestheticizing alienation, the objects were selected on the basis of their familiarity to Black culture. Rather than removed and isolated, the objects are incorporated into art through their intimacy with Black life. This is exemplified in their exhibition and display. While Duchamp is utilized by artists and art historians as a shield against historical materialism and context, Ferguson and Widener demonstrate how Purifoy's art must and can only be read through context—namely, the Watts Rebellion, the Black Radical Tradition, and Purifoy's changing politics.

Because Purifoy did not make art with permanency in mind, Widener argues that "*66* could return to 'the junk pile.'"[81] Purifoy's outdoor museum extends this approach. Akin to *66*, *White/Colored* may also return to "the junk pile." Outside, the fountain and the toilet cannot be cleaned; they exist forever in dust and sun. Contrary to the museum logic of preservation and care, the fate of *White/Colored* is to be slowly but surely desecrated.[82] *White/Colored* is linked to the symbols of white property, and these objects and spaces must disintegrate. In this, *White/Colored* erupts nature; it reminisces on the true function of the object and, by doing so, *exposes what empire is, what it does to its own, what it eats and shits.*[83] In this configuration, and by precise measurements, it explodes the fantasy of *Fountain* and needs none of its mythology to survive. Their cartographies have no overlap: *White/Colored* is a point of reference to a Black aesthetic practice that seeks to intervene in the properties of empire.

In speaking about how his art practice shifted upon moving to the desert, Purifoy described how he could begin to go beyond questions of what might or might not be "pleasing the public" and whether "this piece will sell and this one may not."[84] Stating that what he makes is less about "scale so much as it has to do with quality," Purifoy describes his plan for two and half acres of land, which include a fifteen-by-five-foot piece of sculpture and *The Hanging Tree*, a protest piece in the form of a "pun" that presses "Did you have to kill him after all?," as well as his approach to gardening and watering the plants which surround him.[85] Purifoy also speaks to how garbage operates differently in "pioneer country." Because residents must take their garbage to the dump, "found objects are hard to come by here unless you buy it. I have bought most of the objects that I've used for the work I've done so far."[86] The sculptures, the pieces in the desert are, in his words, "purely organic, with shapes moving in and out, having all the characteristics of a piece of sculpture, and yet it could be a painting as well, because it's a combination of canvas, wood, metal, and paint."[87]

With all of this in mind, I want to signal how Purifoy's powerful critiques and his singular outdoor museum required land, since the current backdrop and stage for his sculptures is the desert. Because if *White/Colored* and the outdoor museum successfully expose the limits of the avant-garde, other questions may be explored—such as, how does Purifoy's outdoor museum interact with the complications of land and territory in the United States?

Purifoy's 7.5-acre outdoor museum sits on unceded Yuhaviatam, Maarenga'yam (Serrano) land. The land was provided to him by his friend and patron, Debby Brewer, and the artist Ed Ruscha.[88] Ruscha was discussed in the previous chapter as emblematic of the artist who celebrates white property as new art. How then do we grapple with the fact that Purifoy's outdoor museum *too* was established via the patronage of white actors, who purchased and owned unceded land; what do we make of the ideological and material continuum of the museum form? Though Purifoy's critiques of the avant-garde and his deviations from white modernist understandings of culture are situated in the trajectory of the Black Radical Tradition—and, as such, his art deserves critical care and protection—the museum form continues to interpolate what Manu Karuka describes as "the prose of countersovereignty."[89] And though, because of the history of chattel slavery, questions of movement with regard to Black persons differ dramatically in scope and depth from those regarding white and immigrant settlement, it would be remiss to evade the function of land in critiques of property.[90]

* * *

Therefore, following the orientation provided by Harris, Harper, and Hong, I want to ask: How might critiques of property materialize land? Critical inquiry into works by Purifoy allows for an engagement with the contradictions of critique and its limitation. But the limits presented by differing radical critiques are sites of potential. These limits ask for a deeper—the deepest—critique of abstraction, whiteness, property. The expectation here is not for writers and artists to have complete and perfect critiques of settler colonialism and racial capitalism, but for thinkers, readers, and activists engaged with the politics of abolition and reparations to seek and demand the most robust critiques of the colonial world order, to take what the thinkers, artists, and writers have considered and offered before us and to ask for more possibility, just as we may ask this of ourselves. In this, the following chapters engage both the aestheticization of property through the archiving of newness and the digitization of artifacts, as well as the activists and artists fighting for their repatriation.

FOUR

# Whiteness and the New

## *Neoliberalism and the Building of the Archive for New Poetry*

I've exhausted the alphabet. But I'm not writing this for you. **Bhanu Kapil, *Humanimal: A Project for Future Children***

Resting on the coast of the Pacific Ocean, Mat Kulaaxuuy is advertised as being sunny all year round. The homeland of the Kumeyaay, Cupeño, Luiseño, and Cahuilla peoples, it is also known as the neighborhood of La Jolla. The University of California San Diego (UCSD), was developed on Mat Kulaaxuuy in 1960 on the decommissioned site of Camp Matthews, which had served as a US Marine Corps Rifle Range. In 1917 the US government leased the land from the city of San Diego, acquiring it in 1937. Soldiers deployed during World War II and in the Korean and Vietnam Wars would be trained for combat at this site. Much like 1917 New York City, the bright residential beachfronts of La Jolla were established with racially restrictive property covenants, wherein only white persons could own property, explicitly excluding Jewish and other nonwhite persons. Beloved children's book author Dr. Seuss resided in this town and, sharing its political orientation, created propaganda for the US Army corporation in favor of Japanese internment and drew anti-Semitic cartoons for various news outlets.

The previous three chapters examined the establishment of museums in New York City, the processes of canonization in Philadelphia, and the proliferation of scientific management during the height of industrialization. In this chapter, I travel from east to west and move into the 1960s to examine the establishment of the Archive for New Poetry at UCSD. This examination builds on the previous chapters, shifting the focus from private institutions to a public research university and poetry archives to inspect the function of collecting and the notion of "newness" in the derivation of more property. Like the foundations of Carnegie, Frick, and the Arenbsergs, UCSD worked within and through the structures of settler colonialism (on unceded land) and racial capitalism (through the forces of US imperial expansion and through segregated articulations of land and property) to establish the site of the university. In this context, I examine the internal rationale that prompted the establishment and function of a poetry archive and the imperative that sought to collect the papers and works of white poets post-1945.

In this chapter, I discuss how the Archive for New Poetry (ANP) began as a segregated repository through racialized scholarship on forms of "newness." I continue the materialistic undertaking of the previous chapters by looking at the financial provenance of the ANP in order to situate the politics of what becomes designated as "new" and "experimental" poetry. While the ANP has consistently compensated poets for their manuscripts, what poets were *paid* might pale in comparison to the remuneration of artists in similar professional positions. Thus poetry, and specifically experimental poetry, occupies a particular place in the morality of art in that it is the form least likely to be corrupted by the lures of finance and capitalism. The immateriality of the medium—the fact that its original documents and the objects of its creation are not necessarily held in *higher* esteem than the verse itself—precludes it from the fetish of the original object. In the case of poetry, solicitation, curation, and donation become the vehicles by which true artistic merit becomes narrated. Poetry is thus a fascinating medium to examine how *whiteness as property* operates as immaterial art. In examining the building of the ANP, I argue that poetry archives and white poetry movements have become spaces in which the most extreme avant-garde and colonial frameworks remain protected.

I continue this materialistic undertaking by looking at the financial provenance of the ANP contextualized with the poetry archives at SUNY Buffalo and Yale University, to situate the material politics of what becomes described as "new" and "experimental" poetry. For example, while the ANP and Yale have compensated poets for their manuscripts, the founding curators at Buffalo have made clear that poets received no payment. Though poets were solicited and the university supported the endeavor with a modest budget, the creation of the literary archive at Buffalo occurred via donation. That a poetry archive (and canon) of esteem can be built via purchase *and* donation, via paid curatorship *and* volunteerism, becomes a testament to the purest love of the arts.

This chapter stems from my research into the finances of artistic movements. While considering where I *wanted* to go versus where I *could* financially manage to visit, I began to see how the papers of certain poetry movements existed in concentrations, while others were dispersed. Whereas the institution in which I obtained my graduate degree (UCSD) held a comprehensive selection of papers belonging to the Language poets—housed under the umbrella of the ANP—no such archive seemed to exist for Black, Asian American, Latin American, and Native poetic movements.[1] If I had aimed to do a comparative study of the politics, aesthetics, and economies of the Black Arts movement and the Language poets, this task would have brought its own financial and political barriers, beginning with archival housing, placement, and location.[2] In examining the ANP, I argue that, akin to the rationale for conceptual and experimental art witnessed in chapter 2, the framework of "new poetry" breeds an internal and explicit logic of whiteness wherein whiteness becomes indexed to innovation.[3] These theories concerning "new poetry" motivate the creation of a physical poetry archive space.

The three frameworks this chapter addresses are: (1) How does whiteness—though visible and open in property and exclusion—remain unquestioned as a collecting practice to create institutional archives? (2) How are white archives financed and managed? And (3) in poetry, how does the politics of immateriality become understood *both* as financial investment *and* as nonincentivized management? Terry Cook poses that it is necessary to investigate "why records were created rather than what they contain . . . [and] what formal functions and mandates of the creator they supported."[4] In questioning record creation, I address how the trends of white historiography and scholarship and the logic of property underlined collection development priorities at the ANP. Without discussing white supremacy and anti-Blackness, it is unclear how various institutional actors might explain the blanket absence of nonwhite poets in the finding aid—and the lack of nonwhite poets in the collection strategy.

Though individual moments and encounters—including my own personal experience—have led me to examine the financial and racialized structures of the archive, this chapter is ultimately not about individual actions. My critique of the ANP, the politics of poetry manuscript archives, and how *whiteness as property* coagulates in the arts examined throughout the book is not about the biases or failings of individuals, or even groups of individuals, but of institutions.[5] Through my research of the planning and budgetary papers, I show how the building of the archive was not the decision of one person but a concerted effort of institutional and financial investment; I further show how this investment secured the "racial unconsciousness" of the collection development priorities.[6] While the previous chapters examined how whiteness as property becomes aestheticized as art, this chapter investigates the institutional and financial efforts to keep whiteness the norm. I argue that whiteness structured ANP's collection development priorities, and that this prioritization was institutionally justified through literary scholarship that linked innovation to whiteness.

## Archive Building, Neoliberalism, and Finance

The first US institutional archive dedicated to collecting poetry manuscripts began at the University of Buffalo in 1937 through the efforts of the late professor Charles Abbott.[7] Supplied with a $1,500 grant from the chancellor, Abbott traveled to England to solicit the manuscripts of modernists poets such as Robert Graves, Robert Bridges, and others. In describing the impetus to create the collection, Abbott recounts his meeting with Mrs. Robert Bridges: "It was . . . Sunday just after Hitler had marched into Austria."[8] And given the political uncertainty of Europe he "even suggested that in America [the manuscripts] would be safe from bombings."[9] US *safety* was cited as a primary rationale for the invention of this pre- and postwar archive. Much like the directives of ANP, Abbott was interested in twentieth-century, "contemporary" poets. Of this direction, he writes, "Worksheets have mainly been contributed by poets who, because they are themselves a part of the twentieth-century pattern, participate in the contemporary will to know."[10] "The contemporary will to know," however, carried with it a racialized understanding as, similarly to the ANP, Abbott exclusively solicited the manuscripts of white poets. Through the financial support of the Carnegie Corporation and the chancellor, Abbott was able to travel, solicit, and collect the manuscripts of some of the most well-known modernist poets.[11] The Poetry Collection at Buffalo currently houses the papers of: Robert Graves, Robert Duncan, William Carlos Williams, Dylan Thomas, and Wyndham Lewis.

Unlike the ANP and the Beinecke Library at Yale, the Poetry Collection at Buffalo did not remunerate poets or their families for their papers. This is an important point that I want to consider for a moment. Questions concerning compensation must have been pressed to Abbott throughout his tenure as the archives' curator. He writes, "The question is sometimes put: Why does the library not pay for its manuscripts? The basic answer is simple and has been inherent in the story I have just told. There has never been any money with which to pay. There has often not been enough for the project's day-to-day subsistence, never enough for its acquisition of books and other printed materials."[12] Abbott makes a clear distinction between the money required to maintain the archive (as he states in the text: money for reimbursement for his travel, solicitation, and management; the purchasing of books; the upkeep of the space; and personnel and staff) and money for the poets. He then insists that there has not been enough money for the former, thus, none for the latter. He creates a hierarchy to distinguish payment prioritization in order to justify his scale.[13] He then proceeds with the real explanation: "Our thought has necessarily assumed that, in beginning for worksheets, we are asking for something which is, sooner or later, commonly destroyed; that the giving inflicts no financial hardship on the individual."[14] Abbott reasons that poets are not paid because their worksheets—manuscripts—are essentially their garbage. Why pay poets what they were going to throw away? This makes the site of the archives a funny place where we can ask: Why does Abbott—the University of Buffalo—want garbage? And, more importantly, whose garbage becomes the archive?

In contrast, Carl Van Vechten has been discussed as pivotal to modernist literary archives. The James Weldon Johnson Collection of African American Literature at Yale was founded by Van Vechten in 1941. The impetus for the collection came from the research materials Van Vechten utilized to write the inflammatory *N——r Heaven*—a novel contested by the likes of W. E. B. Du Bois, among others. Van Vechten named the collection after his friend, civil rights activist James Weldon Johnson, so that Yale might continue to solicit manuscripts from Black writers who had previously been critical of Van Vechten's approach to Black representation. A notorious collector and a member of the leisure class, Van Vechten deployed his wealth to establish archives and collections throughout New York City libraries and at Yale. A bit of contextual insight into the political framework of Van Vechten's collecting imperatives is that while establishing the Johnson Collection at Yale, he also established the Anna Marble Pollock Memorial Library of Books about Cats.[15]

Often dismissing his anti-Blackness, contemporary literary scholars have described Van Vechten as a "librarian's dream prince"—arguing that his "sensibilities" and approach paved the way for some of the most important modernist manuscript collections.[16] In fact, that museums and literary archives arrive with this advent of modernism has often been narrated not as a plight, but its formal expression. As I discussed in the introduction to this book, individual expression remains the pinnacle of white modernism, and thus, the white individual's collection remains a true testament to his property claims.

The poetry archives at SUNY Buffalo, Yale University, and the ANP are unique in their movement-driven approach to collecting. Currently, the ANP is the only archive that boasts a "new" poetry collection. "New"—according to the definition on UCSD's finding aid—denotes postwar poetics (from 1945 on) and also, as I will argue, a particular racialized fixation. The ANP was built with the specific intention of collecting alternative, small press publications. The singularity of the ANP's collection is both its valor and its branding. The ANP's stated collection development priority was to acquire the work of alternative, nonmainstream, emerging "experimental" poets as they were writing. To provide a space in which their papers could live—along with recordings of their poetry readings—was the ANP's aim.

In a 1973 draft of a proposal titled "Notes Towards a Center for New Poetry," Kathy Woodward, then a research assistant to Roy Harvey Pearce—former dean of graduate studies and a founding member of the literature department—argued that a "Center" for new poetry at UCSD would fill the humanities void in the otherwise "science-driven" appearance of the campus.[17] The center would facilitate poetry readings—which would be recorded and archived—and would house summer workshops, a poet-in-residence program, publications, and the Archive for New Poetry. The two components of this proposal that succeeded in securing funding, and which remain on the UCSD campus, are the ANP and the poetry reading series, the latter being recorded and archived in the former.

The first and foundational acquisition for the ANP was Paul Blackburn's collection, acquired in June 1973 for $27,800. ANP would eventually pay $35,000 in total for Blackburn's "complete" papers.[18] When adjusted for inflation, $35,000 would amount to about $187,089 today.[19] In a 1980 "Paul Blackburn Preface" to the bibliography of the collection, Kathy Woodward narrates the acquisition of Blackburn's archive as a momentous event.[20] The Blackburn collection situated the shape and tone of the archive; the direction for US American "Newness" was set to a particular definition of counterculture.

The records are unclear as to what processes were involved in the appraisal of the Blackburn manuscripts, or even to what extent archivists were involved in the procedure. There are differing discussions among scholars regarding the methodologies, stakes, and politics of appraisal.[21] Cook describes several trends and histories: "First, the archivist as curator who did not do appraisal, but left that to the creator; secondly, the archivist-historian indirectly appraising based on values derived from trends in historiography; thirdly, the archivist directly appraising based on researching, analyzing, and assessing societal functionality and all related citizen-state activities; and now, fourthly, perhaps we are ready to share that appraisal function with citizens, broadly defined, where we engage our expertise with theirs in a blend of coaching, mentoring, and partnering."[22] From the acquisition records and correspondences between Pearce and research assistants and librarians, the appraisal and collections development for the ANP seem to have been executed not by archivists, but wholly by administrators and professors who situated the leanings of their scholarship as the bases for the acquisitions. Regarding the politics involved in appraising personal papers, Riva Pollard writes, "Where the question of 'value' is mentioned, it is in a vague manner, often deferred to 'experts' or 'personal knowledge.'"[23] The appraisals for the ANP seem to have been based on the tastes and values of certain figures of the literature department, particularly Roy Harvey Pearce.

The 1975 guidelines for the archive demonstrate the acquisition process.[24] The entry "I. History of the Archive for New Poetry" reads: "Ten years ago, under the direction of Roy Harvey Pearce, the central University Library began collecting books and little magazines of contemporary poetry in the English language. The aim was and still is to contain every item of such poetry published since 1945, thus serving as one of the richest sources for reading and research in its field." Regarding objectively research-driven archives, Pollard articulates, "The notion that acquisition should be researcher-centered not only promises uneven representation of a society within archives, but also leads inevitably to more questions. Which researchers, for instance, are to be considered when making such decisions?"[25] The proposal copiously outlines how the archive would keep its book collection current for this imagined researcher; in "III. Ordering Procedures," it states that there will be:

A. Blanket order. The ANP receives most of its materials through a blanket order held with Sand Dollar books in Berkeley. The terms of this blanket order are as follows:

   1. Coverage: new U.S., Canadian and Australian small press publications with emphasis on the "new poetry" published since World War II. Significant American translators may be supplied, but British imprints are to be excluded. Large presses are to be excluded as a rule.[26]

The specificity of these requirements is telling in the careful focus on white majority nation-states, the exemption of English literature from non-European regions, and the collapse of settler colonialism and English.[27] For example, English language poetry from India, Singapore, or the Caribbean is outside of the ANP's "coverage." Further, are we to conclude that Indigenous and First Nations poetry from Australia and Canada were to be included? The proposal includes the *potentially marginalized* white English poets from around the globe; its imagination is thorough in what it considers theirs and in what it cannot consider.[28]

If the aim is to "contain every item of such poetry published since 1945," it is unclear how such an aim might be achieved by placing a blanket order from one bookstore, at least not without serious flaws in its execution.[29] Surely the task of collecting "every item of such poetry published since 1945" is a limitless undertaking; the mandate could loom and loom. Depending on one bookstore to deliver all the materials is a curious approach. Regarding collecting methodologies, Anthony Dunbar writes that "archival holdings that are rich with evidential and informational value are useful in reconstructing historical moments in that they reflect the values of the individuals and historical eras in which the records were created. Examination of such records can reveal the subjective bias of the record creators or the circumstances in which records were created to document."[30] According to Dunbar's logic, the direct channel between the ANP and

Sand Dollar bookstore articulates the dynamics of a historical moment and the organizations' subjective leanings; it highlights further a blueprint of institutional gatekeeping. This blueprint is illuminated in a 1974 letter to Pearce and David Antin, in which then project coordinator Michael Davidson drafted a document entitled "Poets to be given extensive coverage in the Archive for New Poetry."[31] Out of eighty-four poets, David Henderson and Amiri Baraka are the only Black poets listed.[32] There are no other poets of color included, absolutely no women of color, and not a single Native poet, though there were many powerful such poets working at the time, such as Bob Kaufman and Gwendolyn Brooks, to name only two. According to the list of poets, "Poetry published since 1945" is filtered through a very specific racialized and gendered framework.

In the proposal, the center was imagined as what Stuart Hall described as the potential of a "living archive," what several archival theorists have described as a record continuum.[33] An updated 1974 proposal stated that the budget for three years of the poetry reading series, accounting for inflation, would be $19,363.50 per year ($93,215 today).[34] The budget included a reading and travel fees for the invited poets and an estimated cost of $4384.77 ($21,108) to record and archive all the poetry readings over the three-year period.[35] The budget for the center was proposed at $30,000 ($144,423), with $12,000 ($57,769) being the director's salary.[36]

Grace Kyungwon Hong argues that neoliberalism is "the ideological and epistemological shift that occurred with the emergence of the current stage of racial capital following the worldwide liberation movements of the post–World War II period, movements that encompassed struggles for decolonization, desegregation, and revolutionary engagements over the state."[37] Neoliberalism worked against worldwide decolonization and revolutionary movements by appropriating and manipulating the language of diversity, inclusion, and safety in exchange for accelerated state violence and neocolonial expansion. Regarding its praxis, Hong writes, "Neoliberalism is a structure of disavowal, an epistemological framing, a way of seeing and not seeing."[38]

If the "Center for New Poetry" was to symbolize a collective university appearance, one might deduce that this symbolization must at least appear inclusive, diverse—such are the operations of neoliberalism. On the last page of the 1974 proposal, Woodward writes:

> Contemporary American Voices will present nine poets and three scholars per academic year. Each quarter the three readings and one

Contemporary American Voices (5)

PROJECT DESCRIPTION

1. Poetry Series

Contemporary American Voices will present nine poets and three scholars per academic year. Each quarter the three readings and one lecture will be unified by a single theme or topic such as Black Mountain Poetry, Women's Poetry, Confessional Poetry, Ethnopoetics (Native American Poetry in Translation), Black Poetry, Poets and Science, and Inter-media Poetry. The lectures, which will be of broad appeal and serve to clarify the cultural impact of contemporary poetry, in general are planned to give critical perspective to the quarter's readings and to stimulate research in the field.

Every effort will be made to co-sponsor these events by such groups as the Black Student Union, Salk Institute, Women's Groups, etc.

4.1 Proposal for a "Center for New Poetry" at the University of California, San Diego, May 22, 1974, final page. Mss 143, box 2, folder 10, Archive for New Poetry, University of California San Diego Library.

lecture will be unified by a single theme or topic such as Black Mountain Poetry, Women's Poetry, Confessional Poetry, Ethnopoetics (Native American Poetry in Translation), Black Poetry, Poets and Sciences, and Inter-media Poetry. The lectures, which will be of broad appeal and serve to clarify the cultural impact of contemporary poetry in general, are planned to give critical perspective to the quarter's readings and to stimulate research in the field.

> Every effort will be made to co-sponsor these events by such groups as the Black Student Union, Salk Institute, Women's Groups, etc.

Next to the paragraph beginning "Every effort," there exists a handwritten question mark.[39] The gesture of inclusion in the first paragraph juxtaposed to the subsequent question mark is one way to read the collection development priorities of the ANP. The categories in the proposal—"Black Mountain Poetry, Women's Poetry, Confessional Poetry, Ethnopoetics (Native American Poetry in Translation), Black Poetry, Poets and Sciences, and Inter-media Poetry"—might represent the makeup of academic categorizations of poetry.[40] Much like the construction of ANP, they are categories of "seeing" and "not seeing." Additionally, the phrase "every effort" is revealing in that it acknowledges how expertise in these divided categories might not be held by the center and its directors alone. Lastly, the question mark shares with users and viewers the drafting process. The editor (presumably Pearce, as the papers are in his collection) might agree that the center could symbolize something for the university, and that for this reason, neoliberal inclusion would be its rhetoric—but would *outside* consultants be necessary?

"Seeing" and "not seeing" also exemplify the disavowal of Native presence by the ANP. The definition of "Ethnopoetics" in the proposal can be attributed to Jerome Rothenberg, who spearheaded the extraction and misappropriation of Native poetry. The proposal's collapsing of "Native American Poetry" and "Translation" as a category in the archive materializes the ANP's approach and vision. How can we understand the roots of the ANP, given that it *only* considered Native poetry only through the "translation" of Rothenberg, a white male poet?

The gesture of inclusion in this proposal denotes the procedures of audition. Art historian Susan Cahan describes this phenomenon as "the quality debate," as it explains the exclusion of specific actors as a quality question; the lack of quality becomes the reason that nonwhite and othered artists and writers are unable to bypass institutional gatekeeping.[41] Fundamentally eluding conversations regarding structural history and institutional policies, the quality debate reduces structural categorical segregation to the efforts of individual persons being examined by other individuals and allows institutions to remain innocent arbiters of objective value. In thinking about the inseparability of institutions, archivists, and records, Helen Samuels articulates that "individuals and institutions do not exist independently," meaning that "institutions do not stand alone, nor can their archives."[42]

To illustrate, could Pearce have worked to exclusively collect the manuscripts of poets associated with the Black Arts movement? How would the quality debate be situated in this nonhypothetical thought experiment—as the Black Arts movement too was an innovative, new poetic movement situated during the same historical moment as Language poetry? How did whiteness and its normalizing force configure what was deemed collectible? It is because of institutional policy and structures that such individual acts are not questioned.

Verne Harris argues that appraisers "assume that they can remain exterior to the processes that they are seeking to document." However, "that, of course, is not possible. They participate in those processes; they are complicit in the recording of process. The appraiser's values, quality of work, perspectives, interaction with the creators and owners of records, engagement with the policy he or she is implementing, and so on, all become markings in the appraisal and determine what becomes the archival record. The appraiser is a co-creator of the archival record."[43] Pearce was institutionally in a position to appraise, assess value, and remain unquestioned. Pearce's values, perspectives, and interactions are part of the ANP. I have examined thoroughly the correspondences of Roy Harvey Pearce in his work with the ANP, and I have yet to see any dialogue between him and the Black Student Union, Women's groups, *etc.* This is not to assert that such dialogue may not have transpired, but only that from the correspondences and acquisition endeavors, it is clear that "every effort" was only made in regard to collecting the manuscripts and inviting the figures of Language poetry and other white experimental poets.[44]

To provide a frame of reference regarding this "every effort," I turn to a correspondence between Pearce and the librarian John Haak on November 20, 1974.[45] Pearce was informed by a dealer on November 19 that while Columbia University had an original set of Allen Ginsberg's poetry collection, ANP might acquire one of the two sets of Ginsberg's archives—about "400 hours" of programming—for around $7,500 ($36,105 today).[46] One day later, Pearce wrote to Haak: "I urge you in the strongest possible terms to do all you can to acquire one of the two sets of tapes which will be produced. . . . With those tapes added to what we have in the Blackburn archives and others we are acquiring, the Archive for New Poetry will be even more a major national source of such materials."[47] Pearce's enthusiasm for one of the "sets" and the urgency with which he wrote to Haak is a clear example of "every effort." It is also an opening into the speed of the appraisal process, as well as to what manuscripts were considered valuable.

When we look at the absences in the archive, it is helpful to consider that institutional actors had focused and clear collection development priorities, which are documented in the archive.[48]

Another 1974 proposal, "Contemporary American Voices: A three-year grant to fund a San Diego New Poetry Series administered by the ANP at the University of California, San Diego, submitted to the National Endowment for the Humanities," states of the faculty at UCSD, "Prof Shirley [*sic*] Williams, [is] a specialist in Black Poetry. And what is of significant importance, most of these scholars are also practicing poets. Their expertise will be crucial in creating the context in which this project will interact with students and community."[49] If Sherley Ann Williams—emeritus professor at UCSD and a prolific writer and poet—was ever consulted about the ANP, there is no record of this in the archive. There is no correspondence between her and Pearce about this proposal or the ANP, nor between her and the curator of the archive, regarding its collection development priorities or their appraisal decisions. Of course, in a game of conjecture one might argue that communication between these figures may have been misplaced, that inquiries were made verbally, or that some other set of circumstances we cannot imagine prevented them from being preserved. But seeing as how the manuscripts of Black poets were not collected during this time nor thereafter, it is safe to deduce that her consultations were limited, though her expertise on the subject matter was advertised on behalf of potential funding for the archive. In fact, Pearce's private letters to Williams were patronizing and condescending. In a 1977 letter to Williams from Pearce regarding her essay "A Review of Onwuchekwa Jemie, LANGSTON HUGHES: AN INTRODUCTION TO THE POETRY," Pearce comments, "What I miss in such writing about Black writing as I know (admittedly not enough—but then do you know <u>all</u> of Hawthorne?) is a sense of the psycho-cultural issues involved in such matters."[50] While Pearce admits to not knowing much about Black writing, he believes he can assess its supposed shortcomings.[51] Additionally, Pearce believes his admission to a lack of knowledge of Black writing is excused by his expertise in other matters such as Hawthorne—expertise that he believes Williams surely could not possess.

I highlight this part of the letter to situate how the inclusion of Williams's expertise in the proposal for funding does not align with how her literary expertise affected the archives. Perhaps it was clear to Pearce that it would be unacceptable to describe the archive as it was actually being built: through a segregated imagination, segregated collection development priorities, and segregated appraisal decisions and acquisitions, conditions made possible by an unexamined "racial unconsciousness."[52] Perhaps it was clear to the proposal committee and the institution that such unambiguous phrasing could not be utilized in university budgets and public grant proposals.

Verne Harris continues, "Appraisal is the activity whereby archivists identify societal processes they think are worth remembering and the records that will foster such remembering."[53] The strict methodology of trusting one bookstore and ostensibly one anthology, as well as the content of the initial appraisal list, demonstrates how the architects of ANP envisioned it as quarantined and screened through a colonial framework. Whiteness is not articulated as a preference or an objective in either of the proposals, but whiteness grounds the blueprint and development of the ANP.

The discussion of *whiteness as property* is not additive nor complementary to the discussion of archives and collections but foundational. In discussing how critical race theory (CRT) must be part of the conversations regarding archives, Dunbar argues that "in the most practical sense, CRT challenges the privileges of dominant culture—particularly whiteness—as the normative benchmark of social acceptability. All whiteness theories problematize the normalization and naturalization of whiteness. Rejecting the notion of white values as a generic or colorblind norm, they point to how the very status of whiteness as a norm is a privilege."[54] The Archive for New Poetry is not white and colonial because New Poetry is white nor because poetry is colonial. The Archive for New Poetry is white because whiteness is naturalized property and exclusion via whiteness is the unexamined norm. As with previous examples in this book, the whiteness of the ANP mirrors the strategic normalization of whiteness, as first in theory, then in praxis.[55] This approach is neither objective nor reflective of just the new poetry collected by ANP. Rather, it reflects the politics of the institutions, new and old, private and public, and their collections.

* * *

Similar to what Eric Bennett charts in the case of Iowa's prominent MFA program, funding for the manuscripts and publications related to the ANP seems to have come from a mix of private donors and public funding through UCSD.[56] The funds from UCSD matched private funds or took the shape of research assistant funding.[57] To provide an example of this private-public coordination, in 1977, the ANP wished to begin a publishing press to print literary pamphlets. Pearce wrote that "its aim would be to make available documentary/archival material central to the making of poems in our time. No such enterprise, so far as I know, is presently is in operation. So that we should be pioneering." The first endeavors would be to print an interview with Ed Dorn and the archival materials of Charles Reznikoff. In securing funding for this, Pearce wrote to a frequent donor to state that the project would cost $5,000 ($19,582) and requested a $1,000 core fund.[58] On January 5, 1978, the UCSD librarian Ronald L. da Silveira informed Pearce that the library would provide $1,000, to be matched by the chancellor's office;[59] on January 20, the chancellor's office agreed to match the amount.[60]

Another example of this triangulation is the appraisal and acquisition of the archives of Jerome Rothenberg—champion of the extractive "Ethnopoetics." In a 1976 letter from Michael Davidson to Pearce, Davidson notes that Jerome Rothenberg requested $50,000 for his collection ($208,555 today).[61] The matter seems to have been resolved in 1982 with a new appraisal.[62] Pearce writes a donor asking if they could provide funds to acquire the Rothenberg collection, now set at $30,000 ($71,486). The donor agreed to provide $15,000; the other $15,000 must have been found by other means, as ANP currently holds the Rothenberg papers.[63]

Before concluding this financial and historical overview of the ANP, I want to comment that the makeup of the poetry readings series seems to have had a different approach in its curation than the acquisition of manuscripts in the ANP. Or rather, the readings do not seem like yearlong lists of whiteness and maleness, though there certainly was quite a bit of this. Regarding race relations among poets, poet and scholar Harryette Mullen states that in poetry readings and poetry circles of this time period, "these communities were not completely separate."[64] There is a glimpse of this "non-separateness" in the poetry readings.[65] As mentioned above, Amiri Baraka visited the campus in 1976; David Henderson also read in 1976, as did Wai-Lim Yip (who was a professor at UCSD). Ishmael Reed read in 1978; Wanda Coleman, in 1979; Lonny Kaneko, in 1980; Gozo Yoshimasu, in 1981; June Jordan, in 1982; and Lawson Fusao Inada, in 1983.[66] Jesús Papoleto Meléndez, a founder of the Nuyorican movement, read, as did Atukwei Okai, Alma Villanueva, Gina Valdes, and Inés Talamantez. Poets Darío Galicia, Bruno Montane, Mara Larrosa, Roberto Bolaño, Mario Santiago, Inma Marcos, Cuauhtemoc Mendez, and Rubén Medina can also be found in the curator's files.[67] This may not be an exhaustive list of nonwhite poets whose readings were sponsored by the ANP, but these are the instances currently on display in the curator's files. The point is thus not that the ANP was insulated—that is, removed from contemporary poetry. But specific politicized (and budgetary) decisions were made both in inviting poets to read and in deciding which manuscripts to then acquire.

## Rogue Counting Innovations

In "Whose New American Poetry? Anthologizing in the Nineties," the late poetry critic Marjorie Perloff linked experimentation with whiteness: "The eighties witnessed the coming of the minority communities: first women and African-Americans, then Chicano and Asian-American and Native American poets, gay and lesbian poets, and so on. In their inception, many of these poetries were, ironically, quite *conservative* so far as form, rhetoric, and the *ontology* of the poem were concerned. *But counterculture poets and critics couldn't—and still can't—say this out loud because they would have immediately been labeled racist or sexist.*"[68] With little contest, Perloff defends the dismissal of "minority" poets via the standards of formal, canonical innovation. And though according to this standard, this innovative camp is colonially exclusive, both in terms of its members and the desires it articulates—as previous members were apparently only white and not openly gay or lesbian—the genre does not wish to be labeled racist or sexist. As with the Duchampian tradition examined in chapter 3, experimental poetry will merely practice segregation as it sees fit: through its formal terms. Perloff's statements construct the ideological impetus for why certain kinds of white poetry have been structurally defined as ontologically not conservative, or new. She explicitly suggests that the exclusion of nonwhite, nonheteronormative poets in American poetry anthologies is, well, their fault: it is due to their inability or recalcitrance to embrace the formal innovation practiced by *radical white* poets. Perloff's argument situates "Other" poets as unsophisticated, outdated, lesser craftspeople more invested in an older, passé, white articulation of confession of self and identity than in the creation of new emergent white politics and white forms.[69]

Perloff remained a curious figure in literary studies. Once the president of the MLA, emerita faculty at Stanford, she was long regarded as *the* authority on poetry studies and has been credited with the rise of studies on avant-garde and experimental poetry. She also made a name for herself by defending some of the most hateful projects in contemporary art, such as Kenneth Goldsmith's anti-Black charade at Brown University and Vanessa Place's appropriation (theft) of rape testimonies.[70] Her defense of such work is consistent with her scholarship's wholesale negation of nonwhite poetry. When I was assigned her texts in graduate school, particularly *21st-Century Modernism: The New Poetics* (2002), I asked the professor why and how Black poets remained absent from the text's framework and analysis. My question was dismissed as outside the scope of Perloff's interest, which is how I began to see the canon analyzed throughout my education and notably in this book—as explicitly segregationist and formally justified.

Further, as perhaps indicated by the passage above, Perloff advocated for the Duchampian tradition of found art, wherein aesthetics is removed from the "messiness" and context of our world. She wrote countless essays on Duchamp and form, including "A Duchamp unto Myself: Writing through Marcel" (1994) and "The Conceptual Poetics of Marcel Duchamp" (2002). In her rhetorical insistence that form be witnessed outside the body, contextual and politicized narratives concerning race and colonialism become rejected as passé. Her demand that conceptual writing be affirmed as ontologically superior to nonconceptual writing situated the nonwhite poets outside her framework and understanding as "uninteresting" and "ontologically conservative"—and these postulations have not only been taken most seriously, but have been regurgitated, replicated, dangerously normalized, and practiced throughout poetic scholarship.

From the *October* school to Perloff, the shift that glorifies form (innovation) in poetry—or argues that form is in itself a category—does so by implicitly marking race and place as denigrating terms. The marking of race, land, or orientation as an epithet denounces certain work as outside the realm of experimental, conceptual, or New. Harryette Mullen has argued that aesthetic categorizations that consider race produce what she describes as "aesthetic apartheid." The marking of race and Indigeneity renders the poet, their poetry, and their poetic archive as *readily available*, readable, clear, formally uninteresting, and thus, conservative. Whether or not their work is actually available (in bookstores! in archives!) or critically examined seems to be of no concern to those who abide by the Perloff tradition.[71]

In order to read clearly how this racialized theorization of "newness" affects the ANP, I performed a kind of *rogue counting* within the archive. I call this method rogue counting because it involves using records for a purpose other than that for which they were intended. While gathering historical information in the archives, I looked through the finding aid listed under "American Poetry: Manuscript Collections" and counted how whiteness composed this collection. All sixty-nine poets listed in the finding aid for the Archive for New Poetry are white.[72] The finding aid does note that other poetry manuscripts not listed under "American Poetry: Manuscript Collections" may exist; for example, the late Sherley Ann Williams is not listed in this section, but UCSD does hold her papers, so it is possible that other entries such as hers may exist. However, other than this example, and during the immense time I have spent in the poetry section of UCSD's archives, I have not come across a significant manuscript collection belonging to a nonwhite poet other than Williams. And to repeat: she is currently not collected under the ANP collection priority.

Most of the poets listed in the finding aid are linked to Language poetry, which was a movement comprised of poets living in the San Francisco area from the 1960s to the 1970s. The name "Language" came from the title of the literary magazine *L=A=N=G=U=A=G=E*, edited by Charles Bernstein and Bruce Andrews. The magazine was a hub for the movement, publishing work by its members Michael Palmer, Lyn Hejinian, Ron Silliman, Susan Howe, Rae Armantrout, and others. The poets of the movement rejected traditional lyric and narrative poetry, as they—in the line of Perloff and with her support—argued that such forms were akin to conservative, commodity objects. They stated their poetry would dismantle language by producing what sometimes appeared to be "unreadable" language games. Unreadability and purposeful fragmentation were the defining aesthetic tropes of the Language poets.[73] Whether or not their poetry ever "dismantled" language or shifted poetry away from capitalism and commodification remains unclear. What is certain is that the movement's founding members were white, and only recently has this been critiqued.[74]

Almost since their inception, the Language poets have been theorized as direct heirs of Western avant-garde poetry and art. Much like Duchamp's instantiation into the permanent collection at the Philadelphia Museum of Art, the acquisition of the manuscripts of living Language poets by the ANP demonstrates how the Language Movement, while heralded as "radical," "new," "avant-garde," and even "marginal," received epistemological and financial institutional support from its beginning. However, this is not the way the Language poets are usually theorized.[75] In order to champion Language poetry, Timothy Yu lays out a peculiar argument regarding "ethnicization." In the second chapter of his book *Race and the Avant-Garde: Experimental and Asian American Poetry since 1965* (2009), titled "Ron Silliman: The Ethnicization of the Avant-Garde," Yu argues that Language poetry sustained the thrust of "innovation" and all that comes with the "avant-garde" by adopting a form of "ethnicization." Yu deduces this by pointing to letters in the ANP from Ron Silliman to Charles Bernstein and other Language poets. Yu cites a letter to Peter Glassgold of New Directions (a publishing house) from Silliman that reads, "I am not a language poet. I hope, in choosing your title, that you are aware of the comparability of the phrase 'language poetry' to epithets such as nigger, cunt, kike or faggot."[76] Silliman rejects the aesthetic framework his poetry received; the designation of "language poet" (he believes) is an epithet. In regard to this letter, Yu states, "Silliman's equation seems, on its face, absurd. Yet it is also true that the equation of Language writers with a racial or gender grouping flows logically out of Silliman's earlier pronouncements on poetry and politics."[77] Yu claims that this political line of reasoning can be witnessed in previous proclamations—so at least Silliman is consistent? Yu extrapolates that Silliman's positioning is avant-garde: "Silliman's *powerful, possibly offensive*, equation of 'Language poetry' with racial slurs suggests the bluntest version of this latter position: 'Language poet' is not simply an aesthetic but a social identity. Ultimately, this ethnicization of Language writing can be seen as an attempt to *reclaim* the *moral authority extended to the writing of women and minorities*—a kind of redemption of white new left discourse."[78] I am not sure how Silliman's statement could "possibly" be offensive: it is offensive. It is not offensive *and* powerful: it is offensive. It is astonishingly violent to equate racial and gendered slurs—slurs that are utilized in daily, lived experience—to a body and social position protected from the history of racialized and gendered slurs. From anti-Black images posted online to social media platforms, to the ways in which racial and ethnic slurs are hurled in public spaces, the experience of being the target of slurs is not akin to the being named into an emergent aesthetic category. Likewise, there is no parallel experience of dispossession. Clearly "Language poetry" is not an epithet—it is witnessed as an academic and formal poetic category, supported institutionally with an exclusive archive at UCSD. "Language poetry" has never been and will never be a slur.

Rather than positing a critique of whiteness and Language poetry, Yu shields the movement from *potential* critique through a formulation of "ethnicization." By suggesting that whiteness can be "ethnicized" through a false identification with racialized violence and experience, Yu's argument attempts to nuance Silliman out of structural white supremacy. Is "ethnicization" a theorem contemplating the possibilities of a different kind of ethnicity, a different kind of white, for Silliman? This argument of marginalization is supported through the personal accounts of individual members rather than through a structural examination of the collective, which is how social theories of race and ethnicity are utilized and formed.[79] In the context of the argument, the whiteness of the ANP can be appeased through this personal accounting; Yu's reading of the politics and aesthetics of the Language poets as akin to an ethnic category suggests how the composition of the "New Archive" might also be defended and justified.

Rather than a defense, both Silliman's reaction and Yu's analysis might be better expounded as the dynamics of white supremacy. Silliman's usage of racialized and gendered epithets is not a form of solidarity with "underdeveloped" writing and nonwhite writers, who in the ANP and elsewhere continue to experience ongoing erasure, absence, and marginalization. Rather, Silliman's use of racialized and gendered slurs displays the astonishment that one's superior white structural position was not immediately reflected in the manner of one's choosing.

Yu's rationale imagines ethnicization as self-righteous victimization, and this as a favorable position from which to redress wrongdoing. Does "moral authority" thus denote a sense that there are issues that women and minorities might write about, not only with *authority* but with a sense of *morality* not entrusted to white male writers?[80] To state that women and writers of color have "extended moral authority" is an argument that views racialization as a set of possessions that whiteness is deprived of—and that must be *reclaimed*.[81] This understanding is without historical premise, and is rather situated in post-racial fantasies. Yu posits, "If language-centered writing is, as Silliman argues in his earlier letters, a form of poetry just as 'underdeveloped' as the writings of women or Third World writers, and if its social origins (progressive white male writers of the 'industrialized' tradition) is just as particular and marginalized, why should a caricature of such writing not be as offensive as racist or sexist caricature, since both rely on the same logic of social marginalization?"[82] If Language poets occupied an *authentic* social position of dissent, how did their status as white men un-figure into this *new* authentic positioning?[83] Yu's reading of Silliman posits that white men—without ever having to address whiteness—were able to transcend their bodily and social positioning to create other authentic identities. The argument replicates Perloff's crass dichotomy of innovative whiteness and conservative others as it collapses the politics and positions of women and minorities as fixed, knowable, yet fungible.

Yu argues, "Silliman's utopian gamble, and the gamble of all Language writing, is that experimental techniques can render the Language poem both particular and universal."[84] The particular, we are to assume, is the extraction, the appropriation of an imagined racialized, gendered position. The universal is whiteness. Language poetry, through its "ethnicization," is able to instantiate both the absence of whiteness (as their property) and whiteness (their property).[85] It is able to swallow it whole. Since it can reach into racialized and gendered particularities while remaining universal, it needs not their flesh, their language, their presence, their forms, nor their papers and archives.[86]

## On Lived Forms

By situating the 1980s as the entry point for the "coming" of minority communities, including Native poetry, Perloff shaped a landscape in which the white male poet does everything first and everyone imitates. In her analysis, more *radical* indicates ontological experience with aesthetic forms. I want to know: How might "conceptual" poetry be defined without Perloff—a scholar who spent a lifetime negating the existence of Black and Native poets from the timeline of modernism and the avant-garde? Throughout her career Perloff dismissed writers who wrote about the body and the material weight of our world. How might we understand the framework for "conceptual" outside of this tradition—what will need to be abolished and remade once segregation is denied a formal presence as art?

For decades, Black poets have indirectly responded to those in the Perloffian tradition, be it the white scholars who have insisted on isolated "forms," the white managers of radical "ontology," or the those of the white avant-garde. Amiri Baraka's 2001 poem "The Academic Cowards of Reaction" is one such document.[87] While discussing postmodernism, Baraka skews the vocabulary of "racist" in this scholarly tradition ("We would be racist but that's been done"), following up with, "We think all struggle except to be obscure is frankly rude." Baraka, much like Noah Purifoy and others, saw the racial politics of the white avant-garde for what it was. According to the Perloffian tradition, to write about segregation while it's happening is simple, boring, formally uninteresting art—says the white critic. The enduring paradox of this claim hinges on transcendence. One cannot speak too directly about lived experience, particularly racism or sexism or homophobia, as this makes one a bad poet. This critical stance shames language that directly opposes and fights in order to uplift the language of ideological obscurity. Of this dynamic, Baraka states, "Remember post-modernism is a hip way of saying the world is rotten and must stay rotten to be metaphorically ignored though funny if you're getting paid unquote," calling such works "language without meaning without narrative." Baraka critiques the debilitating ontology of "radical" white art: art that demands silence, indifference, art of and for the status quo.

Here I would like to return to Purifoy's critique of form discussed in chapter 3. In 1971, Purifoy writes, "the symbols of west coast Black art stands in direct opposition to art for art's sake. It insists that if art is not for the sake of something it is not art. It seeks to reverse the order of art in its mundane gutless orientation and create a language through which there is a collective understanding."[88] I might insist that, like Baraka, Purifoy is addressing the scholarly tradition from which Perloff extends. Rather than dividing "conservative" from "radical" art through an artificial definition of form and collapsing form with ontology, Purifoy ruptures the definition of form. Instead of pulling art into a space of obscurity and abstraction, he asks, What does *it* stand for? And, I might add, For whom does it stand? It is not Purifoy and Baraka who take a conservative approach by asking phenomenological questions and by demanding language with orientation *toward meaning and narrative*; it is Perloff who is formally and contextually colonial in approach, and this has been, and remains, a *gutless orientation*.

Part of my education in literary studies asked me to isolate forms from content—via the lineage of Perloff and company—in order to study the *forms* of modernist innovation. Though Perloff devoted much of her life to the study of experimentation in the arts, I was never convinced by her definition of the "experiment." So what is form, and what of the experiment? As discussed, the ANP had an associated reading series. While Wanda Coleman's papers are not collected by the ANP, I was excited to see a slim curator's file for her poetry and her poetry reading.[89] Publishing throughout the 1960s to the early 2000s, Coleman resided predominately in Los Angeles and wrote forthrightly and innovatively about embodiment, politics and Black cultural production. Her ANP folio opens to the poem below, a page where the top line reads "Certificate of Death."

Opening Coleman's file, I was disoriented. Upon closer examination I realized it was, perhaps, a poem, document, or sculpture unknown. Under "Cause of Death / Primary," it lists: "CHRONIC ECONOMIC FAILURE / INHALATION OF ILLUSION / LOVE ABUSE," followed by a "Secondary" category which lists "Truth Intoxication" as one cause. The next line reads "Determination: Sufficient evidence of circumstances / to establish verdict of homicide."

Coleman's unknown object joins the formality of the death certificate with the language of confession—or accusatory intimacy? Someone, something, is being accused. Poverty, *love abuse*, and the *intoxication* of both truth and illusion has resulted in homicide. How did this happen? Who and what must be charged? And how? What is clear is that the deceased lived an untenable life. The colon after "Occupation and usual address" reads: "Poet/Unemployed." For whom does poetry make life untenable? Whose lives are made untenable via poetry? For whom is the inhalation of illusion not merely toxic, but deadly? What is the relationship between the primary cause of her death, "CHRONIC ECONOMIC FAILURE," with her occupation: poet/unemployed? And how does poetry's underemployment of this deceased interact with the abundance displayed towards the Language poets of the ANP?

I have looked for this poem in Coleman's numerous books and have yet to come across it. This leads me to surmise that it is no accident Coleman sent the ANP this particular object. I assert the term *object* not in a fetishistic sense, but in a sense that posits a site-specificity to the piece. What *truths* were intoxicated by Coleman from the ANP and its primogenitors over time? Which and what illusions? How did the ANP—and by extension, the scholars, poets, and writers who championed the terrains of "New Poetry"—perpetuate Coleman's CHRONIC ECONOMIC FAILURE / INHALATION OF ILLUSION / LOVE ABUSE? Truth Intoxication? How did they respond? And of who else? How many elses?

Coleman's folio is a testament to the failures of white "newness," white "radical" ontology, white "experimentation," and white universality. There exist institutionally constructed forms of new property—what Baraka might propel as "academic cowardice"—and then there is Coleman's untitled sculpture, which ruptures the purveyance of "New Poetry." Hers is a poetics rooted in the difficulties of the lived, uncollected, and miscollected, with stakes, dreams, charging forth.

## Conclusion

The argument that direct or indirect exclusion, neglect, and misreading have shaped historical cultural segregation and continue to do so is not new. Writers and literary scholars have written endlessly and historically on issues of race and literature, from modern American literature to British colonial works, science fiction, and avant-garde studies.[90] As I have

NO. 001313 CERTIFICATE OF DEATH

Registration County Los Angeles

Sub-district Watts-Willowbrook

Administrative Area The State of California, U.S. of A.

Date and place of Death December 17th, 1974

355 E. 120th St., Apt. 6, Los Angeles, CA. 90061

Name and Surname Wanda Coleman aka Andrew L. Tate, Editor

Maiden Name (if female) Evans

Race and Sex Black female

Date and place of Incarnation 11-13-46, Graham, L.A. County

Occupation and usual address Poet/Unemployed

Name and Surname of Informant Raymond C. Clark

Qualification Coroner for L.A. County

Date of Inquest December 27th, 1974

Cause of Death:

| Primary | Secondary |
|---|---|
| CHRONIC ECONOMIC FAILURE | Myocopulative infarction |
| INHALATION OF ILLUSION | Hyperthywordism, uncontrolled |
| LOVE ABUSE | Truth intoxication (agitationitis) |

Determination: Sufficient evidence of circumstances to establish verdict of homocide.

I hereby certify that the particulars given by me above are true to the best of my knowledge and belief.

Date signed 12-27-74 Signature Mrs. S. Grant

**4.2** Wanda Coleman, "Certificate of Death," December 17, 1974. Coleman folder, Archive for New Poetry, University of California San Diego Library.

previously discussed in the book, Toni Morrison argues that a racial "unconsciousness" structured the American literary imagination: "For reasons that should not need explanation here, until very recently, and regardless of the race of the author, the readers of virtually all of American fiction have been positioned as white. I am interested to know what that assumption has meant to the literary imagination. When does racial 'unconsciousness' or awareness of race enrich interpretive language, and when does it impoverish it?"[91] Regarding art, Susan Cahan argues that US museums have been and remain resistant, if not hostile, to racial integration, and she supports this argument through an extensive examination of museum acquisition and exhibition records.[92] Of archives, Mario Ramírez has argued that "whiteness persists as the *terra firma* of the archives profession in the United States and, in turn, informs the very formation of its praxis."[93] Cook argues that the parallel trends of exclusion, neglect, and mismanagement can be witnessed in archive development: "In many societies, certain classes, regions, ethnic groups, or races, women as a gender, and non-heterosexual people, have been de-legitimized by their relative or absolute exclusion from archives, and thus from history and mythology—sometimes unconsciously and carelessly, sometimes consciously and deliberately. Perhaps the more germane pithy assertion about appraisal should rather be: we are what we do *not* keep, what we consciously exclude, marginalize, ignore, destroy."[94] Cook's assessment of processes of appraisal and collection development corresponds to contemporary critiques made in literary, art historical, and cultural studies scholarship. Todd Honma states, "Libraries have historically served the interests of a white racial project by aiding in the construction and maintenance of a white American citizenry as well as the perpetuation of white privilege in the structures of the field itself."[95] The structures of the field—subjective appraisal methodologies and institutional collections development priorities, as well as literary scholarship—functioned in tandem to normalize the whiteness of the archive.

Archives do not need to reflect the under- and overtones of dominant narratives, and yet, in the case of the ANP, they do. How "new" was defined in the ANP's blueprint and in its original collecting efforts, as well as in its ongoing acquisitions, strictly reflects Perloff's articulation of the new in poetry. Somehow in this structural diagram, the framework of race is theorized as excluding itself out of the present, out of the future, and out of innovation, only to be stuck in a dystopic past. Though let's be honest: If they can barely be found in the archives today, which past are they so adamantly stuck in?[96] And how might we get there?

Though from the seventeenth until the mid-eighteenth century, the Spanish, British, and US colonial governments worked to take land from the Kumeyaay, Cupeño, Luiseño, and Cahuilla people; Indigenous presence and colonial violence lives in the city's language and fauna, from the name "La Jolla" to how surfing permeates its culture.[97] San Diego is also home to the largest centralization of Native reservations in the United States. Activism against forms of state violence, from immigration policies and ICE, to the building of new incarceration centers, to the militarization of the border, is spearheaded by Indigenous activists, particularly the Kumeyaay people.[98]

This Indigenous presence and activism is not reflected in the ANP. In this, the archive functions similarly to a museum, as it is situated in legal colonial and racialized terrains of exclusionary property, with the objective of accumulation. Akin to museums that situate their "care" of the objects as grounds against repatriation—as we will examine in chapter 5 through the case of Harvard and the daguerreotypes of Delia, Renty, Jem, Alfred, Fassena, Jack, and Drana—the literary archive defends its existence and growth through the merits of research. Made inherently valuable because it's been collected, the archive creates a self-fulfilling prophesy whereby collected writers receive deep scholarly attention because their manuscripts are accessible. Critical scholarly debates can occur through the examination their letters, diaries, and drafts. Thus, those who remain uncollected is a consideration made on behalf of future scholarship, and the decision to limit and erase them from historical memory apparent in this judgment.

Thus, my critique of archives is a site of contradiction, as my argument is predicated upon my extended engagement with the ANP. The attention I have paid to this endeavor means that my other pursuits—such as the examination of Wanda Coleman's archive, held by UCLA—were temporarily put on hold. Moreover, it could be argued that my critique validates the existence of the ANP, and archives writ large, as it exemplifies how archives may catalyze new analyses and how the impetus towards historical transparency makes the unimaginable possible—rendering my critique ultimately invalid. The presence of this contradiction, I would respond, does not negate my claims but materializes them, as even in my research against time, capital, access, and property, these structures are apparent. Although my research demonstrates my embeddedness in the systems I critique, this contradiction is part of a mutation I have witnessed in other arenas, one which situates the life of creators, and strives to imagine the life of their absences.

Anne J. Gilliland and Michelle Caswell examine the politics and potential of "imagined records," which they describe as spaces of potential where, in the absence of records, victims of state and structural violence desire and situate the evidence that exists in collective memories. Gilliland and Caswell argue that these imagined records harness the power of the archive and the record as legible forms of evidence.[99] What petitioners to the state and to the archive long for—this presence of longing—is the site of "impossible archival imaginaries."[100] It is the space in which what the archive could not imagine, could not fathom, could not collect, reverberates. Gillard and Caswell write, "Actual and imagined records confront each other with alternate realities, one representing 'the establishment' and the other, disaffection with or opposition to the establishment."[101] Thus, the imagined manuscripts, the manuscripts refused, burned, thrown away, uncollected, never inquired about or appraised, speak to the materialized poetry manuscripts in the archives. The imagined, unforgettable archives of nonwhite poetic movements permeate the ANP as "spectral content," "spectral context,"[102] spectral forms.

Rather than inclusion or additions to the archive, I am interested in seeing how we might grapple with its absences. Writing on the *absence* of queer sociality and nonheteronormative sexuality in the colonial archives of India, Anjali Arondekar asks, "What if the recuperative gesture returns us to a space of absence? How then does one restore absence to itself? Put simply, can an empty archive also be full?"[103] Arondekar's postcolonial project to examine the absences as "full" is powerfully applicable to the ANP. It is also a preemptive critique of neoliberal approaches to inclusion and the rhetoric of additive mending. The "solution" to the whiteness of the ANP is not the rapid addition of manuscripts belonging to nonwhite poets; this approach assumes that the structure of the archive does not need to be examined, and that the structure of the archive works to encompass more and expand endlessly. This approach also assumes that historical absences can be rectified through present-day additions. Such an approach would replicate the ANP's initial claim of "inclusion." I hope I have demonstrated that this inclusion was a gesture of public relations. And because it was limited to public relations, it could not be executed.

Regarding the Asian American social movement exhibition "Serve Your People," curator and archivist Ryan Wong states that "information regarding people of color organizing and movement history is not readily available. This information is not in textbooks, so people don't know to look for this material. And a lot of the materials are in private collections. It was a long, multi-tiered process to do just a small exhibition."[104] When absences have been institutionalized, what to look for, and even how to look, becomes an *impossible, imaginary* task. The absences in the archive rupture narratives of institutional desire, prioritization, and care. For this reason, to see what is *not there*, and to ask why, and to long that it was otherwise is imperative to interrogating what is *there*. Institutionalized absences ensure that the processes of assembling new archives, exhibitions, and histories will be an incredibly vast, laborious, directionless route.

FIVE

# Colonially *Bound*, Digitally *Free*

## *On the Distance between Object and Image*

Society must *give* them away. Unlock them from reification by giving them to slaves. Give them to trees. Give them to cows. Give them to history. Give them to rivers and rocks. . . . Flood them with the animating spirit that rights mythology fires in this country's most oppressed psyches, and wash away the shrouds of inanimate-object status, so that we may say not that we own gold but that a luminous golden spirit owns us. **Patricia Williams, *The Alchemy of Race and Rights***

In 2013, under the rubric of "open content," the Getty Museum digitized over 100,000 images from its permanent collection and made them available online. This digitization project came one year after the CEO of the Getty published a statement in *Foreign Affairs* against cultural repatriation.[1]

The Getty's digital "open content" is a familiar initiative, as similar projects have been taken up in almost all cultural institutions. In 2017, in a statement titled "Open Access," the Metropolitan Museum of Art said they would join the "digital evolution" by releasing "375,000 images of artworks from our collection to use, share, and remix—without restriction."[2] Harvard's Peabody Museum allows access to over 700,000 images. At present, most museums and cultural institutions boast some kind of digital repository: an archive that permits accessing, and sometimes downloading, its permanent collection. Digitization is an institutional gesture toward cultural heritage. As many of the objects in question are held in storage and are not on display, the tool of digitization is said to offer multiple prospects, such as public and permanent access to the objects in question. As in, while the original may reside in one place, the knowledge may be shared and held collectively across spectrums. At least, this is what is being purported.

Thus far in the book I have examined the physical spaces of the museum and the archive, from a private collection in Manhattan, to the makings of a permanent collection in a private museum in Philadelphia, to a poetry archive at a public university in California. In this chapter, I look at how these collections and archives have been colliding (a process that will accelerate), by thinking through the propertization of digitized images and archival documents. I argue that the gesture to digitize must open up questions of ownership. Open-access and open-content gestures could work to unsettle questions of property by publicly working through questions of ownership and imagining new ways to frame provenance. However, currently, ideals of *opening up access* so that *everyone can use* has not become "others can *have*"—or even, "we can share." If digitization is as powerfully vital as Western institutions claim them to be, then perhaps once-imperial and neocolonial institutions can begin repatriation of their colonially derived objects once their digitization efforts are complete. After all, why do they need both the material and digital property? Do the digital images work to transfer and displace ownership, or do they work instead to maintain it?

If digitization offers the possibility of openness and democratic access that private institutions such as the Getty and the Met—and, as we will examine in the chapter, Harvard's Peabody—claim, then conceivably, the digitization of images has the potential to affect the market value of object commodities and assuage the repatriation debate concerning colonially looted objects: the objects of empire.

Thus far, the creation of digital image databases has made no strides in the debate over objects without recognized or troubling provenance, such as the daguerreotypes of Renty and Delia examined below. Moreover, the digitization of images and objects has not decreased the value of objects or assisted in calls for abolition of property, nor has the digitization of the object been accepted as a form of a priori institutional knowledge. In this chapter, I explore the tension between the proliferation, availability, and circulation of the digital image (considered digitally *free*) and the propertization of the object (colonially bound to institutions). I find that this couplet carries the racialization of property and circulation into the present.

Additionally, the digital is material. Kate Crawford has materialized the environmental impact of machine learning to show how what occurs digitally is embodied by the earth.[3] Tremendous scholarship has labored to demonstrate how underwater cables—first laid out during British and European imperial expansion—remain essential to the internet and other forms of digital connectivity.[4] Thus, digitization projects are not removed from the colonial space of the museum; instead, they fortify and expand their property claims. Keeping these material tensions in mind, in this chapter, I explore how digitization projects like the ones pursued by the Getty, the Met, and Harvard widen the spectrum of management, curation, and enclosure of colonial objects. How does digitization evade questions of artifact repatriation, and can digitization alter—affect—the relationship between art, property, and power?

In situating the tensions between property and circulation, I examine artist Carrie Mae Weems's interaction with Harvard University, Sasha Huber's provocation of Louis Agassiz's lineage, and the Peabody's digital overview of the daguerreotypes of Delia, Renty, Jem, Alfred, Fassena, Jack, and Drana. I examine Harvard's provenance claims over the daguerreotypes of formerly enslaved persons in order to demonstrate how conversations about art objects turn into conversations about circulation privileges (exclusion) and to consider why and how the vocabulary of reparation remains absent from the archival concerns of colonial institutions.

## Provenance versus Belonging: Whose Daguerreotypes?

More than ten years ago as a graduate student, I began working on a qualifying paper about the relationship between property and art by looking at Carrie Mae Weems's *From Here I Saw What Happened and I Cried* (1995–96) and Sasha Huber's *Demounting Agassiz* (2007 to the present), and the ways in which both projects take up daguerreotypes purported to belong to Harvard via the scientist Louis Agassiz. Since then, many things have occurred, including a lawsuit brought against Harvard by Tamara Lanier, a descendant of Renty, an enslaved man photographed by Agassiz, for the restitution of the daguerreotypes—a case that remains ongoing. Here, I begin by sketching out the institutional history and provenance of the images through Weems's photograph series to situate the developing terrains of the case at Harvard, and how the implications of the case connect to the larger property concerns grappled with in this book.

Internationally renowned artist Carrie Mae Weems's *From Here I Saw What Happened and I Cried* began as an exhibition commissioned by the Getty Museum's Education Department, titled *Carrie Mae Weems Reacts to "Hidden Witness: African Americans in Early Photography."* It was to be a series of intervened photographs that responded to a show in the adjacent gallery, titled *Hidden Witness: African Americans in Early Photography*, a singular exhibit of daguerreotypes depicting chattel slavery and portraits of African Americans before the Civil War, drawn from the Getty's collection and the private collection of Jackie Napoleon Wilson.[5] Weems's 1995–96 series came specifically from the archives of two institutions: the Getty Museum, which commissioned the work and provided access, and Harvard University, which later contested Weems's use of (what they argued was) their collection.[6]

After the Getty show, Weems changed the name of the series to *From Here I Saw What Happened and I Cried*, though the majority of the included objects remained the same. The works in Weems's *From Here* appear in monochrome, with red tinting applied over the original daguerreotypes. In addition, Weems added text to each image, which sits either just below or on top of the photographed bodies. The overlaid texts, etched in glass on top of the newly colored daguerreotypes, can be read in sequence: "YOU BECAME A SCIENTIFIC PROFILE / A NEGROID TYPE / AN ANTHROPOLOGICAL DEBATE / & A PHOTOGRAPHIC SUBJECT."[7] The eyes of the unnamed, legible, yet undefined subjects inside the photographs appear right above the text, so that one reads the text alongside their gaze. The series conjoins the legacy of eugenic sciences and the politics of property relations.

In a 2009 interview for the PBS television series on contemporary art *Art21*, Weems retells the story of how she located the daguerreotypes and of the legal issues that followed her decision to utilize them. She simply refers to the images as from "the Harvard and Getty archives."[8] Weems says of the photographs, "I had been thinking about them for years and years . . . I had lectured on them." She comments that the first four images "compressed the history of photographs in African-American history," and she discusses her interest in the history of Black subjects and their images. Weems then goes on to say that Harvard, "the richest university in the world," contacted her about her art and threatened to sue her for using images that they *owned*. Her response to this threat was, "I think I maybe don't have a legal case but maybe I have a moral case that could be made that might be really useful to carry out in public."[9]

After some worry, she responded to the institution that a court case might be "a good thing," and that this was a conversation that "we" should have in court, because such a discussion "would be instructive for any number of reasons." Harvard replied to Weems that they would instead like to receive a percentage from every photograph sold. The climax comes when Weems divulges that Harvard instead decided to purchase her series. As Weems recalls the transaction, she laughs and points to the absurdity of the situation. If Harvard wants her to pay every time the images are sold, and since they would like to purchase the series, if she receives money from them, is she required to pay some of it back? In the interview her position is clear: Harvard does not own the daguerreotypes and should receive no payment or credit for their use. Harvard's position, it seems, is also clear, in that they believe they are the owners of the daguerreotypes.

It is important to discuss the context of Harvard's claim to provenance, how they came to acquire the objects, and why they believe the daguerreotypes are theirs.[10] Jackie Wilson's and the Getty's collections of daguerreotypes of enslaved persons come from myriad sources, ranging from personal archives to auctioned items.[11] This, however, is not the case for Harvard's collection, which comes from a singular source: Louis Agassiz. Agassiz was a naturalist who emigrated from Switzerland in 1846 for a position at Harvard and later became the classification consultant for natural history museums in the South and the founder of Harvard's Museum of Comparative Zoology. Before immigrating to the United States, Agassiz trained in Paris with Georges Cuvier, who has been cited as the founder of taxonomy and paleontology. Cuvier is also the figure responsible for the mutilation and display of Saartjie Baartman at the Museum of Man in Paris.[12] Like Cuvier, Agassiz became recognized professionally as an eminent scientist and marine biologist, known for his developments in species classification and polygenesis (racial separation), and was a tenacious anti-evolutionist who opposed miscegenation. According to polygenesis, only white persons are Adam's descendants, prompting Agassiz to propose that "God [separately] had created other races to fit different climates, regions, and ecosystems."[13] Hence, the relationship between eugenic sciences and the field roots of geography is rooted in polygenesis. This is to say that

Agassiz, his mentors, and much of their scientific lineage is predicated upon transnational colonialism. Their study of the world is a manifestation of colonial violence.

To support his research, which he published in articles such as "The Diversity of Origin of the Human Races," Agassiz amassed a photographic collection to be used as evidence for his theories on racial classification and was in direct collaboration with phrenologists such as Samuel Morton, who collected and purported to study the skulls of Indigenous peoples.[14] Agassiz directly participated in the contradictory politics of the mid-1800s, often refusing a public or direct political claim—but clearly having a private one.[15] Like most pre-eugenic scientists, Agassiz utilized tools of reproduction and circulation in order to legitimate anti-Blackness as a science. It has often been noted by photographic scholars such as Brian Wallis that early scientific representations such as those of Agassiz quickly became the foundation for popular anti-Black representation.[16]

In an echo that haunts museum and object ideology, Agassiz writes of his "first" encounter with a Black man in a letter to his mother in Switzerland: "I could not take my eyes off their face in order to tell them to stay far away."[17] After this encounter, Agassiz shifts to studying, theorizing, and preserving the people that he did not wish to see. This is done through the medium of photography and collecting. Instruments of reproduction echo Hortense Spillers's description of how "their New World" becomes constructed.[18] Photographs became the evidence through which racial sciences were recorded, traced, and personified.

Though Agassiz held the daguerreotypes in his archive, he was not the photographer, nor was he present when the images were procured.[19] His access was granted through his close friendship with physician and fellow polygenesis supporter Dr. Robert Gibbes, who had personal relationships with Southern plantation owners. This led him to B. F. Taylor's plantation in South Carolina, where it is understood that he "selected" the enslaved persons to be captured in daguerreotypes. While some historians have pointed to how Agassiz himself publicly endorsed the abolition of slavery, plantation owners supported Agassiz's polygenesis as a theorem consistent with Christian justifications for chattel slavery.[20] Plantation owners in South Carolina were particularly eager to be of service to Agassiz's work, in order to uphold chattel slavery.[21] Though the 1807 Act Prohibiting the Importation of Slaves made the slave trade to the United States illegal, South Carolina was notorious for continuing to partake in it.

For this reason, citations for the daguerreotypes, when reproduced, follow the format:

> Renty, Congo. Plantation of B. F. Taylor, Esq. Daguerreotype taken by J. T. Zealy, Columbia S.C., March 1850. Peabody Museum, Harvard University.[22]

In the citation, the first name of the enslaved person and their African origin is listed.[23] The owner of the plantation follows, succeeded by the photographer, then Harvard via Louis Agassiz (or vice versa), both of whom continue to hold the images through their property claims.

The fifteen daguerreotypes, which included the faces and names of Delia, Renty, Jem, Alfred, Fassena, Jack, and Drana, were supposed to be used as supporting evidence for Agassiz's academic claims on polygenesis, and their images were utilized during his public lectures. In an 1850 post in the *Tri-Weekly South Carolinian*, we discover that they were publicly displayed to support his argument:

> We notice that Professor Agassiz is still lecturing in Boston on the unity of the human race. On Friday last, in the course of the lecture, he pointed out the many differences between the forms of the negro and the white race, a large proportion of which have not been previously remarked; and in proof of his statements he exhibited a large number of daguerreotypes of individuals of various races of negroes. Many of these pictures were taken by that prince of daguerreotypists, our friend Zealy, the originals having been procured in this vicinity by a scientific friend of the learned professor.[24]

In the 1850s, the daguerreotypes were publicly exhibited and lectured on as scientific objects, while simultaneously occupying the realm of the collected "object of curiosity," the souvenir: objects from South Carolina, a plantation, "another place." In recent scholarship, Molly Rogers also categorizes the daguerreotypes as souvenirs.[25] The genre collapsing scientific object and souvenir is colonially consistent, considering how the collecting efforts of encyclopedic museums began from "Cabinets of Curiosities," which led to the establishment of the British Museum in the eighteenth century (1753), the Ashmolean Museum at Oxford in the seventeenth century, and so many other encyclopedic museums across Europe that indirectly pulled from such initiatives. Popularized during the British Empire, the cabinet of curiosities began as an individualized display of the oddities collected (taken) during one's colonial travels and studies—from cultural artifacts to pseudoscientific discoveries—and were often described as a space of wonder. The taking and displaying of objects was justified both academically and aesthetically through colonialism.

Additionally, Agassiz's collecting efforts to study the "many differences . . . between the forms of the negro and the white race" purported to taxonomize both biological *and* characteristic traits. Similar to the colonial approach of Carl Linnaeus in constructing the taxonomy of human races in *Systema naturae*, Agassiz incorrectly theorized that the African had "a proneness to imitate those among who he lives" and did not care for "civilization," existing with "peculiar apathy . . . [and] indifference."[26] The significance of Agassiz's science was not in the creativity or depth of his research—as his discoveries merely reified white supremacy and the aestheticizations of the US settler state—but rather, in its impact. With the full force of Harvard behind him, Agassiz further implanted anti-Black ideology as a science.[27] Thus, when artist Sasha Huber states in her "Agassiz Down Under" (2016) performance that "AGASSIZ TRIED TO PROVE BLACK LIVES MATTER LESS," Huber is not hyperbolizing, but rather stating a historical fact that must be rectified.

Writing on the connection between Harvard and slavery, historians Sven Beckert and Katherine Stevens describe how the "relation[ship] between Agassiz and Harvard was symbiotic."[28] As with most Ivy League universities, chattel slavery and settler colonialism grounds the presence of Harvard. Its founding leaders, faculty, and many of the students were or became slave owners.[29] The university systematically suppressed debates concerning race and slavery, and it hired and tenured professors who advocated for eugenics and racial segregation well into the late twentieth century.[30] Agassiz trained students to be professors in his and Cuvier's lineage. Students of Agassiz who became professors at Harvard—such as Nathaniel Shaler, a close friend of Theodore Roosevelt—led the scholarly charge against miscegenation.[31] Agassiz's work not only justified chattel slavery but also paved the way for segregation, eugenics, antimiscegenation laws, and global anti-Blackness.

Collecting as a method of research constituted Agassiz's academic position, one that remains legitimated to this day. In a recent biography, Agassiz's scientific work is cited as not only contemporary but also relevant. The author cites David C. Smith of the University of Maine Climate Change Institute as stating that Agassiz's work "could be consulted productively

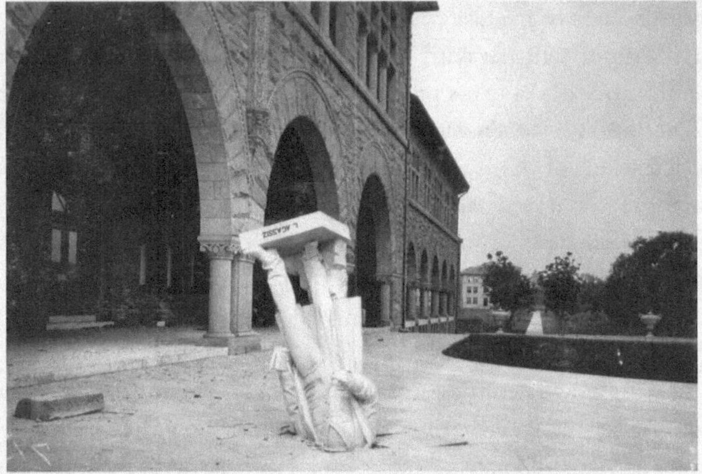




5.1 Sasha Huber, Take-away poster #1, 2015. Edition of 100, 42 × 60 cm. For *Agassiz Down Under*, Te Whare Hēra gallery, Wellington, New Zealand, July 8–22, 2015.

SASHA HUBER, TE TUHI CONTEMPORARY ART TRUST, AUCKLAND, NEW ZEALAND, AUGUST 13–OCTOBER 26, 2016

# AGASSIZ DOWN UNDER

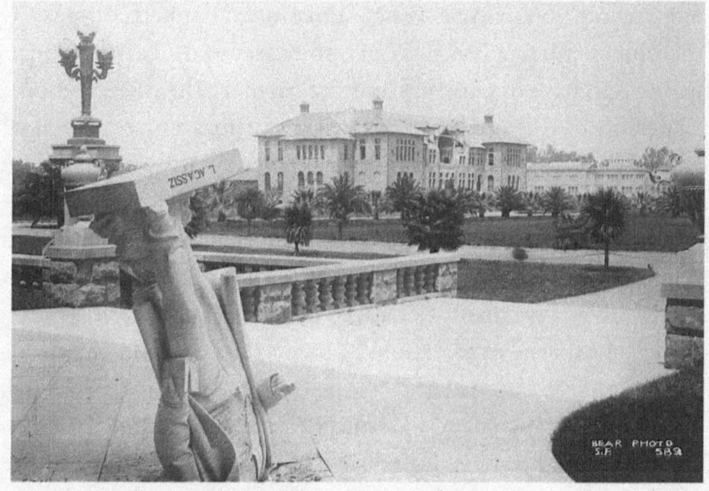


Louis Agassiz statue, fallen from pedestal. Stanford University. San Francisco earthquake of 1906. Credit: Bear Photo Co.

WHAT LOUIS AGASSIZ TRIED TO PROVE: **BLACK LIVES MATTER** LESS

IN MEMORY OF ALL AFRICAN-AMERICAN VICTIMS OF POLICE VIOLENCE IN THE USA, WHERE IN THE FIRST SEVEN MONTHS OF 2016 ALMOST 200 PERSONS HAVE BEEN KILLED.

---

"BUT RACE IS THE CHILD OF RACISM, NOT THE FATHER." TA-NEHISI COATES HAS POINTED OUT. BUT RACISM HAS ITS ANCESTORS, TOO. ONE OF THEM WAS LOUIS AGASSIZ FROM SWITZERLAND WHO IN 1847 DECLARED IN A PUBLIC LECTURE HELD IN CHARLESTON (S.C.): "THE BRAIN OF THE NEGRO IS THAT OF THE IMPERFECT BRAIN OF A SEVEN MONTHS' INFANT IN THE WOMB OF A WHITE." IN 1863, LOUIS AGASSIZ WROTE TO A US GOVERNMENT COMMISSION: "SOCIAL EQUALITY I DEEM AT ALL TIMES IMPRACTICABLE, – A NATURAL IMPOSSIBILITY, FROM THE VERY CHARACTER OF THE NEGRO RACE." SO IF IN TODAY'S UNITED STATES **BLACK LIVES MATTER** LESS THAN WHITE ONES, IT IS DUE TO MEN LIKE LOUIS AGASSIZ.

- HANS FÄSSLER, FOUNDER OF THE "DEMOUNTING LOUIS AGASSIZ" CAMPAIGN, AUGUST 2016

**5.2** Sasha Huber, Take-away poster #2, 2016. Edition of 100, 42 × 60 cm. For *Agassiz Down Under*, Te Tuhi Contemporary Art Trust, Auckland, New Zealand, August 13–October 26, 2016.

today by workers in the field," and the Museum of Comparative Zoology's web site echoes this claim.[32] The opening sentence of its "History" section reads: "The history of the Museum of Comparative Zoology begins with the vision of Louis Agassiz, a great systematist, paleontologist and renowned teacher of natural history."[33] There is no mention of polygenesis, white supremacy, anti-Blackness, eugenics, or race in the museum's "About" section. The focus remains on how his research gave *us* species classification (collection) and the natural history museum (collecting).

* * *

The generic evolution of Agassiz's commissioned daguerreotypes—from scientific objects to archival material, to museum objects, to contested art—fits the narrative of curiosity and the cabinet. The daguerreotypes of enslaved persons—collected and amassed in private archives, one of which remains unpublished—can be read both as colonial objects and as illustrations of the never-ending melancholia of racial science.[34] Agassiz's collecting imperative can be situated within the ambiguous yet clearly political transition from legally segregated to privately segregated social norms.[35] And as a private archive institutionalized in a museum space, it is protected by both the law and the expectations of ownership, as well as by the narratives foundational to the sciences.

The intellectual basis of Harvard's ownership is that Agassiz's son Alexander Agassiz gifted his father's research to Harvard in 1910; the gift included this collection together with another photographic collection of enslaved persons in Brazil, taken with the assistance of Agassiz's student William James, who would go on to become a preeminent philosopher.[36] Though never published, the photographs taken in Brazil were to be used in a paper that would argue against race mixture.[37] After the initial gift in 1910, the daguerreotype collection was said to have been forgotten within the Zoology Department's archive and then rediscovered in 1976. After its rediscovery and management, the collection transmuted from the official structures of science into art and was exhibited by Harvard's Peabody Museum in 1986.[38]

The genealogy from Agassiz's ideas for his collection to Weems's *From Here* and into this moment traces the explosion of photography and the proliferation of museum spaces—from when images could not be replicated and access was limited to those with capital and connections, to the medium's acceleration as a tool of reproduction into commercial success and then digitization. What remains constant are the property claims on the collection and its placement in the archives. The museum remains home to the object as it travels through the ownership claims made by chattel slavery—despite how these claims could have been contested through abolition—and the contemporary discourse of art-making. In this regard, and returning us to the present moment and its digital implication, what is the role of ownership and permissions after abolition, and what is the relationship between property, permissions, and circulation in light of abolition?

Harvard has systematically denied artists, researchers, and descendants access to the objects and has taken or threatened to take legal action against persons with vested ties to what Saidiya Hartman describes as the *afterlife* of slavery.[39] In pursuing the legal development of property and segregation, Cheryl Harris reveals how property remains the absolute right to exclude.[40] This is particularly visible in the management of Agassiz's archive at Harvard, as exclusion is what drives its ownership. Harvard's contemporary defense of its ownership is that the objects belong to "History."[41] And by extension, as the guardian of history, Harvard will manage and limit access to *history* through a strategy of exclusion. Situated to protect the rights and research of Agassiz, the university's current provenance claims bind enslavement to the present. When an institution retains the permission rights to objects of enslaved persons, it upholds the protection afforded to those who captured and dispossessed rather than the people whose bodies were taken, displayed, and, as Kimberly Juanita Brown has theorized, *repeated*.[42]

The conversation prompted by Weems's 1995–96 series and her subsequent interview is a contemporary display of how race, particularly anti-Blackness and chattel slavery, informs contemporary legal understandings of property. It is most useful to think back on Weems's use of a moral, rather than legal, claim. A moral claim expands not only the conversation concerning Harvard's provenance but also the possibilities of transference from the legal categorization of the object to the ethical conditioning of its existence. How might Weems's provocation prompt a reimagining of Harvard's provenance?

Since 2019, Tamara Lanier has been engaged in a legal battle with Harvard for the restitution of the daguerreotypes. The conversation Weems suggested "we" might have in court is now being pursued by Lanier. Lanier is seeking restitution, and her claims are supported by many of the university's faculty, as well as by the descendants of Agassiz.[43] Harvard opposed Lanier's claims, first on the basis that she could not prove her lineage to Renty; having since accepted her ancestry claims, they remain adamant that the daguerreotypes are their property.

In March 2021, Massachusetts judge Camille Sarrouf dismissed Lanier's case, upholding preexisting notions of property rights and citing precedents where art plundered by the Nazis from Jewish families was not be returned to their descendants due to the of statute of limitations, and where courts ruled that consent was not needed for a juvenile in custody to be photographed.[44] Sarrouf states, "Fully acknowledging the continuing impact slavery has had in the United States, the law, as it currently stands, does not confer a property interest to the subject of a photograph regardless of how objectionable the photograph's origins may be."[45] Tracing the history of property, eighteenth-century British philosopher Jeremy Bentham writes, "Property and law are born together, and die together. Before laws were made there was no property; take away laws, and property ceases."[46] Bentham argued that, rather than a material object or tangible entities, private property was a relation, an expectation, an affective structuring of ownership.[47] Contemporary legal scholar Brenna Bhadar takes up Bentham's notion to situate why property scholars such as Cheryl Harris and Ian Baucom begin with chattel slavery in order to discuss property, as chattel slavery gave rise to modern theoretical notions of private property by collapsing "the boundaries between subject and object, thing and person" in juridical form.[48] This collapsing is materialized in Judge Sarrouf's statement: What full acknowledgment of the impact of chattel slavery is afforded by classifying enslaved persons as "subject[s] of a photograph," only to refuse to contend with how they were denied subjecthood and instead made to constitute the photograph's property interest? Here Renty, Delia, and the others are not photographic subjects separate from the photos' property interests; they constitute the realm in which—in the absence of subjecthood—their objecthood was propertized, and property defined their objecthood.

Secondly, the judge writes, "it is a basic tenet of common law that the subject of a photograph has no interest in the negative or any photograph printed from the negative . . . rather, the negative and any photographs are the property of the photographer. This principle is true even where an image is taken without the subject's consent."[49] This ruling reveals how the conception of art property and artistic property are imbued within the logic of white supremacy. How property remains understood in art practices, and particularly in photography and found practices, upholds the blueprint for *whiteness as property*. The subject of the photograph—irrespective of consent—is legally considered without property claims, much as an artist's idea is believed to be above and beyond the work's materiality, maintaining a realm in which the difference between the property-eligible subject and the object (be it body, labor, or commodity) remains clearly defined.[50] Sarrouf, akin to believers in modern and conceptual art, prioritizes the rights of the artist and the property of art over the context that made its making possible.

Third, the judge writes, "Lanier alleges that although slavery was abolished in Mass in 1781, Harvard continued to advocate in favor of slavery from 1846 to 1861, through its overseers and administrators, including Agassiz. Lanier alleges that this conduct was unlawful and unconstitutional. Harvard moves to dismiss this claim, arguing that the claim is barred by the statute of limitation. The court agrees."[51] The dismissal amplifies how property continues to be defined in relation to and through the *afterlife of slavery*, in the words of Hartman. Institutions responsible for reifying and inventing ideologies pivotal to chattel slavery and white supremacy cannot be held responsible, because too much time has passed; simultaneously, the property accumulated during this time cannot belong to anyone other than those who profited from chattel slavery, because too much time has passed. The ruling implicitly affirms Richard Wright's statement that "the law is white," and inasmuch, there is no legal recourse for repatriation or restitution. Protecting the rights of property fortified through chattel slavery by excluding everything but colonial property claims, the judge refuses to intervene into the *afterlife of slavery*—though he will intervene in the afterlife of property.[52] Because the subject of the photograph was an enslaved person, the law can never recognize the subject of the photograph *as* a subject, yet the law continues to recognize and uphold the property of institutions who subjected them to the realm of objecthood.[53]

After Judge Sarrouf's dismissal, Lanier pursued her case to the Massachusetts Supreme Court for direct appellate review. On June 23, 2022, the court affirmed the lower court's dismissal with regard to property claims but vacated the dismissal of Lanier's claims for "negligent infliction of emotional distress,"[54] leaving open the possibility for Lanier to remand the case to the lower court in order to "amend her complaint to incorporate allegations of reckless infliction of emotional distress."[55] More than Judge Sarrouf did, the Massachusetts Supreme Court judges stressed the violent history of the daguerreotypes, acknowledging Harvard's lack of concern for the extended family members of those depicted, and the clear invalidity of consent, concluding that "Harvard's present obligation cannot be divorced from its past abuses." The court cited how Harvard's "horrific, historic role in the coerced creation of the degrading daguerreotypes" "triggered" a duty from Harvard to respond to Lanier's request with care.[56]

Nevertheless, the court denied Lanier restitution, citing many of the same reasons provided by Sarrouf—namely, that there is no law or precedent for the daguerreotypes to become Lanier's. In the concurrence, Judge C. J. Budd reiterates that, while Harvard's "continued retention" is "patently unjust," the court cannot grant Lanier property based on "strongly held moral belief."[57] Judge Elspeth B. Cypher's concurrence questions this line of reasoning, pointing to the absurdity of looking for a precedent that granted property to the enslaved. Speaking directly to the construction of precedent, Cypher writes with specificity that "Black Americans have long been deprived of rights and the access to the legal that others have enjoyed. . . . To rely on the premise that because we have no precedent there can be no new claims or rights does not acknowledge that the people who now assert such a claim or right previously were not recognized by the legal system."[58] The superior court judge Sarrouf ruled that Lanier is without property claims because Renty and Delia were without property claims, and the Massachusetts Supreme Court affirms Sarrouf's dismal by citing a lack of precedence as its core rationale. They argue that, while unjust, in the absence of a preexisting legal framework, the law cannot adjudicate present-day moral claims. In this charade, where historical precedent must be provided in order to fulfill the exigency of present-day justice, legal precedent works to embalm the past as present, solidifying the language that upholds chattel slavery into contemporary relations.

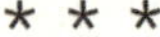

Though the subjects of the daguerreotypes were denied subjecthood, and their descendants' restitution claims were refused, artists such as Carrie Mae Weems have intervened in their imaging. My interest in Weems's work parallels many of the questions that I laid out in chapters 2 and 3. How do we read Weems's approach to the photographs in *From Here I Saw What Happened and I Cried* as *found* images, given that the images come from a myriad of sources: from the Zealy daguerreotypes discussed to images of a royal Mangbetu woman Nobosodrou, to Garry Winogrand's *Central Park Zoo* (1967), and others?[59] Is *found* an appropriate term given the archival placement and context of their finding? In order to analyze the operations of *found*, I display the full text by Weems that accompanies the photographs in the series:

From here I saw what happened
You became a scientific profile
A Negroid type
An anthropological debate
And a photographic subject

House
Yard
Field
Kitchen[60]

You became Mammie, Mama, Mother
and then Yes, Confident—ha
Descending the throne you became Foot Soldier & Cook

Rider
And Men of Letters
Drivers

Black and tanned your whipped wind of change howled low
Blowing itself—ha—smack into the middle of Ellington's orchestra
Billie heard it too and cried Strange Fruit tears

Born with a veil you became Root Worker
Ju-Ju Mama Voodoo Queen Hoodoo Doctor
For your names you took Hope and Humble

Your resistance was found in the food you placed on the master's
    table—HA
You became playmate to the patriarch
And their daughter

Some said you were the spitting image of evil
You became an accomplice
Out of the deep rivers mixed-marched mulattos
A variety of types mind you—HA—sprang up everywhere

. . . Yes the strong gets more while the weak one fade
empty pockets don't ever(y) make the grade
Mama may have, Papa may have,
but God Bless the Child thats got his own
—thats got his own

You became the jokers joke and anything but what you were
Some laughed long & hard & loud
Others said "only thing a niggah could do was shine my shoes"

You became Boots, Spades and Coons.
Restless after the longest winter you marched and marched and
    marched
In your sing song prayer you asked, "Didn't my Lord deliver
    Daniel?"

And I Cried[61]

As previously discussed, the notion of "found object" purports to isolate ideas from the materiality of the object. Weems's text traces the history of photography within the history of pre-eugenic propaganda and the development of colonial somatology and takes from anti-Black photographic history to situate a critique of representation. In contrast to found art, her series is rooted, amalgamated, and contextualizing.

To home in on the text, in stanza eight, the lines "Some said you were the spitting image of evil / You became an accomplice" come together separated only by the enjambment. The proximity of "some said" and "evil" near "accomplice" shakes the positioning of the latter. The word *accomplice* comes in heavily, perhaps gesturing to the legacies of violent and compulsory assimilation. "Evil" is an exploding word within the lineage of chattel slavery and early African American history. Since it is clear that the "you" in the text is speaking to Black representation and histories, it can be deemed that the "some" refers to the pre-eugenic scientists and plantation owners infatuated with early eugenics and to their power in preforming early anti-Black representation. "Evil," then, is the prescription for countergestures. This is why "accomplice" is thrown, unstable, and ready for interpretation. The line immediately asks of itself, "accomplice" to whom? To the "some" or to the "image of evil?" Accomplice to the replicating reproductions of what has already been made and said, or to their direct opposition? Or perhaps more accurately, and more complicatedly, both?

The line "You became an accomplice" amalgamates and fractures the operations between text and image. In the art object, "YOU BECAME AN ACCOMPLICE" sits below the face of an unidentified Black woman.[62] Her eyes do not meet the camera; they are positioned as looking down at her clasped hands. She is in formal attire: a dark evening gown with what looks to be a headpiece and makeup. She reads as feminine and alone, supported only by a chair. The photograph mimics her as an entertainer—someone beautiful, positioned, and accustomed to the camera yet looking away. In the object, we get to meet the subject accused of being an accomplice; the accomplice is gendered, alone—she cannot deny this accusation because this is her only frame. Within Weems's sequence of photographs, the text reads: "YOU BECAME PLAYMATE TO THE PATRIARCH / AND THEIR DAUGHTER / YOU BECAME AN ACCOMPLICE."[63] The first line of text accompanies a photograph of a Black woman who is posed in the nude; the next line accompanies a closeup of another Black woman's face, who is holding close a white child; the final line accompanies the woman with hands clasped. In the objects, the image of the Black woman reappears as the signifier of coconspirator, traitor.

This accusation has historical standing. In discussing the memoir of Condoleezza Rice and narratives that place Black women as agents of US empire (rather than its insurgents), Erica Edwards analyzes the function of "imperial grammars" as "the codes of cultural production and public discourse linking the rationalization of US imperial violence in the late— and post–Cold War years to the US public sphere's manipulation and incorporation of Blackness as the sign of multicultural beneficence."[64] Thus, Edwards's contemporary scholarship reads how cultural texts in particular have incorporated Black women into the marrow of US Empire, from state agents to its fictionalized counterpart.[65]

Though it tenuously suggests frameworks without resolve, Weems's series practices something different than the appropriation prescribed by the modernists. Rather than effacing time and place, Weems's series amplifies history, context, and more. Additionally, she takes from photographic history because it is her history. This cannot be read as mere appropriation art. It must be read as something more.

Furthermore, while Weems was commissioned by the Getty to interpret a particular photo collection and was given blanket permission to take their images, her interaction with Harvard indicates how for her, appropriation—that is, the act of repropertizing—remains repudiated. Thus, the threat of a lawsuit against Weems—as well as Lanier's current lawsuit—displays the ways in which white scientists and artists and their institutions appropriate objects according to their laws and colonial history. The form of appropriation is their legal technique. This has yet to transfer across color lines; when it does, will it travel in the form of neoliberal appropriation for all, or via reparation and restitution? Or will it mutate as a both and nothing?

In situating Weems's work in the tradition of modernist appropriation art, Cherise Smith foregrounds the politics of circulation. She writes, "Clearly, Weems appropriated documentary images from several archives as an attempt to critique the representations and the recirculation of them. Yet, by using them in her work, she does the same thing: recirculates the images."[66] In this, Smith emphasizes the recurring concern, which is amplified in the digital, that circulation does not foreclose questions of ethics, colonialism, or repatriation, but rather eludes them in order to exacerbate them.

In her latest reading of Weems's 1995–96 series, Smith does something that we rarely see from scholars: she revises an argument she once made about an artwork and disagrees with her previous position. She goes from a previously critical appraisal of a Black artist reimagining the past to situating Weems as a Black artist who takes up conceptualism, appropriation, and its politics, and in so doing, perpetuates the harm carried forth through its forms. Smith asks, "Should images like J. T. Zealy's daguerreotypes of slaves from a South Carolina plantation continue to be circulated? Or should they, like the people they represent, be put to rest, allowed their peace?"[67] She places the artist and her intention secondary to the unresolved context of the images, which is intensified through their circulation. As in, as objects created to uphold chattel slavery—considering that they remain objects confined as institutional property—their appropriation and use cannot easily, or ever, be actualized as merely triumphant. I might push further to state: as long as their ownership remains within the strictures of white property, their inversion is neither materially nor immaterially unbound.

Tacking onto this debate in a strange yet perhaps predictable turn, art historian Claire Raymond attempted to intervene into Smith's rereadings by refuting them. Raymond states that, because the persons in the daguerreotypes are no longer alive, the images cannot perpetuate harm. Positioning herself as a feminist (in the tradition of white feminism), Raymond inserts herself into a critical Black dialogue, with language affirmative to Harvard's legal ownership.[68] She writes, "The Peabody Museum daguerreotypes on which I place emphasis were taken some 150 years before Weems's installation piece was created, and the enslaved Americans whose images the Peabody Museum kept in its files are no longer available to be re-victimized in a straightforward sense. In a strictly physical sense, those who suffered the humiliation of Agassiz's 'study' are now beyond further harm."[69] In addition to fundamentally misinterpreting Smith's critique as having been concerned with Weems's potential *sadism* rather than the politics of circulation and property, Raymond's "rebuttal" mimics Judge

Sarrouf's ruling. In Raymond's understanding, the object could have only harmed the subjects during their lifetime. One is to infer from this statement, as she does not extrapolate, that because the subjects—as enslaved persons—could not have offered consent, the existence of the daguerreotypes is a reminder of their enslavement. Raymond's limited reading admits to this much. And based on this logic, the death of Renty, Delia, and others, frees the object from harming them, rendering the object *harmless*. This is rapacious rhetoric, rooted in the institutional normalization of anti-Black violence. According to this logic, the deaths of those enslaved persons resolve questions of harm unresolved during their lifetime. As in, though they were never compensated, nor did they receive reparation or justice from the institutions that enslaved them, the end of their lives releases institutions, persons, and the world from the depths of justice they were denied. This line of argumentation has been refuted by scholars such as Daina Ramey Berry and is cited in Judge Cypher's concurrence.[70] Contrary to pivotal Black studies scholarship, Raymond situates harm as individualistic, and foreclosable through the life and death of those enslaved. This logic expounds endless questions: How does the lifespan of an object fortified by chattel slavery become neutral through the death of the enslaved person? And what of their descendants, whose connection to their image remains fortified through the *afterlife of slavery* and *whiteness as property*? Considering how the objects remain confined to the very institutions that procured their making and inflicted harm, exactly which questions have their deaths resolved? Death does not ameliorate the existence of the daguerreotypes. Rather, death here exacerbates them. That no justice was served in their lifetime does not alleviate our burden to provide justice, abolition in the present.[71]

Moreover, Raymond's art historical analysis contradicts the 2022 ruling, which states, "Even long after the deaths of Renty and Delia Taylor, the degrading and dehumanizing daguerreotypes that Agassiz arranged to have made of them retained their capacity to wound."[72] Noting how the researcher who discovered the objects in 1976 registered this concern, and how Harvard disregarded their concern in the pursuit of property, the writing of the court displays a nuance and criticality missing from Raymond's defense of artistic rights.[73]

Raymond's scholarship reproduces many of the talking points held up by colonial institutions and museums. It emphasizes the singular life of one individual, or some individuals, rather than the collective, transgenerational lives of communities. It exceptionalizes the image as but *one* object, and concludes that through death, the object can remain collected or appropriated without harm.[74] Defensive institutional arguments such as Raymond's break down if and when we refuse the bounds of the object. Inside of the daguerreotype there is a person who is part of a community and a lineage that have grieved, and are grieving, have fought, and are fighting for abolition, liberation. Their lives are not foreclosed by the object—nor is their death the opportunity for a colonial institution to retain their objecthood. The harm remains as dispossession remains. Restitution and the transfer of ownership is but one step.

Smith's revised critique is pivotal, in that she takes up the history of conceptualism and the politics of circulation in her reengagement with Weems's series. Raymond's counter is predictable in that she repeats the arguments that institutions have made about the past (its death) as feminist politics, revealing the relationship between white feminism and the maintenance of institutional status quos. Lanier's suit against Harvard and the language of ancestry contextualizes the lives and communities at stake in these debates. The arguments are, here and always, theoretical and material.

The ethics of circulation raised by Smith enter into a longer, wider debate in Black studies regarding the representation of violence. In *Scenes of Subjection*, Hartman powerfully writes against the re-presentation of violence:

> I have chosen not to reproduce Douglass's account of the beating of Aunt Hester in order to call attention to the ease with which such scenes are usually reiterated, the casualness with which they are circulated, and the consequences of this routine display of the slave's ravaged body. Rather than inciting indignation, too often they immure us to pain by virtue of their familiarity—the oft-repeated or restored character of these accounts and our distance from them are signaled by the theatrical language usually resorted to in describing these instances—and especially because they reinforce the spectacular character of black suffering. What interests me are the ways we are called upon to participate in such scenes.[75]

Hartman's refusal has prompted many scholars across Black studies, cultural studies, and history to reconsider the site and power of refusal, and to take seriously the material infrastructure of the supply chain that maintains violence. In contrast, Fred Moten has responded to Hartman, writing, "The decision not to reproduce the account of Aunt Hester's beating is, in some sense, illusory," in that even the mere reference to the scene represents it, and, thus, Hartman's "refusal" perpetuates a repression where "Douglass passes on a repression that Hartman's critical suppression extends."[76] In Moten's reading, Hartman participates in the circulation of the object but by a different name.

Moten's argument refutes the foreclosure of circulation so long as it remains an object of importance. Following Smith and Hartman, I want to carefully advance the idea that property and commodity cannot be exchanged for the other, insofar as one remains proprietary, and the other exists exclusively through the form of circulation. Judge Cypher raises this point in the concurrence, noting how a daguerreotype is "fundamentally distinct from a photograph: photography results in an image designed [to be] easily reproduced ad infinitum," while the daguerreotype was not made to be reproduced.[77] This point is raised to question whether photography precedence can be applied to this case, and it creates a basis on which to question the ways in which Harvard has digitally reproduced images of Renty, Delia, and others at will and for its own benefit and profit. This contemporary form of circulation allows for property holders to commodify through their ownership claims. Objects fortified in chattel slavery—which remain property—create protected networks of circulation.[78] This reveals the power differentials between property (the right to exclude) and commodity (circulation).

In her insistence, Hartman makes a fundamental critique of property by invoking the discourse of refusal and exclusion. Moten's insistence that Hartman cannot refuse speaks to the contradictions that abound in commodification and the expectations allotted (or denied) to her authority, but it does not tend to her powerful a priori critique besieged in property. Some images that have been constructed must be deconstructed (abolished); their circulation need not be accommodated as inevitable and immortalized.

This is ever more apparent in the distance between object and image in the case of Harvard and the digitization that makes their endless circulation possible. Returning to the function of property in the case of the Peabody Museum, it is unclear what the notion of "public commons" means for the daguerreotypes displayed online. A loss of copyright for an object does not mean that the public owns the object, that it is a part of the commons, or that one can distribute the work without explicit permission by the owners of the object.[79] For example, when the image in question becomes part of an "open access" program, how does this affect the nondigital artifact? Moreover, copyright is only one part of object ownership, one that readily monitors image-sharing and circulation. An examination of copyright alone does not begin to address the estrangement of object ownership.

To illustrate further, one daguerreotype from Agassiz's archive—which became part of Weems's 1995–96 series and is at the center of Lanier's lawsuit—depicts a man referred to as Renty. Online, at the Peabody Museum's website, the image is available for download, making it essentially open access.[80] This downloadablility speaks to the problems raised by Hartman about the circulation of anti-Black violence. As, what is open access for this image? The image available on Harvard's site is not at high resolution: How would one obtain this image in a format for use? I have often worked in copyright clearing projects where clearing copyright does not equate to access. That is, even if I have paid for the license (or if it is in the public domain and I do not have to pay), the payment does not equate to access to the usable image file itself—and the file does not constitute the permissions for the object. I must obtain the file through some other means, direct or indirect.

Moreover, in the case of the daguerreotypes, the realm of the "digital" is the actualization of the *immaterial*, as the objects will soon cease to exist. Current museum policy dictates that the daguerreotypes can only be exposed to ten hours of sunlight each year.[81] These ten hours are broken up into thirty-minute appointment slots. Additionally, the daguerreotypes have undergone at least two restorations, to little avail. The objects in the daguerreotypes are fading and will soon be black squares inside red velvet frames. They have already faded so dramatically that, among the few visitors allowed, viewers with lighter skin tones must stand at specific angles to view what remains of the object, as the light reflecting from lighter skin tones refracts onto the image, making it impossible for the viewer to see. Given all of this, it is not inconceivable that the objects will soon live exclusively as digital images in the databases at Harvard, or as thumbnails on the Peabody's website.

Relatedly, both court decisions consider the daguerreotype as object that's intact, and not as one that's fading and in disrepair. Perhaps because of the limitations of the viewing possibilities, neither the judges, the artists, nor the critics speak of the degradation of the object, and the life and possible death of the object. Instead, all parties speak of the object as photography; the judges cite photography precedents to speak of the daguerreotype and the art historians speak of the history of photo appropriation and its critiques to discuss Weems' series. The metamorphosis of the daguerreotype as photograph is through its digitized form, which is delivered via Harvard. The object is not on view and, I might add, the object onto itself is rarely discussed. The *copy* is what has spurred all facets of discourse, from ownership to art project and archive. This case clearly instructs that the object's contestation is a fight over its circulation and control, which exists and will continue to exist in digital form. Irrespective of condition, the material authorizes the immaterial. And the immaterial affords the material narrative power.

Harvard wields exclusionary powers over the afterlives of the enslaved persons depicted in the daguerreotypes: Delia, Renty, Jem, Alfred, Fassena, Jack, Drana, and others. The physical existence of the daguerreotypes provided the institution with its primary property claims, *and* the degradation of the object does not sever its bonds; it is immateriality rooted in material deaths—most specifically, in the afterlives of chattel slavery.[82] Rather than destroying them, the digital circulatory protection continues property claims. The immaterial, the digital, has been unable to resolve material concerns. Violence remains so long as property, as it is currently understood, remains. US object permissions are constructed to protect the maintenance of Agassiz's "living laboratory"[83] and Harvard's claim to the daguerreotypes of enslaved persons. The theoretical forging of property happens with and through chattel slavery and segregation, situating how the antithesis to the moral claim is not exceptional to arguments for reparation, against private property, but foundational.

As a different kind of thought experiment, with different stakes but still housed in the law, let's go back to 1975, when Agassiz's collection was "rediscovered" by Harvard. Museum laws, and in particular the 1970 UNESCO Convention on the Means of Prohibiting and Preventing the Illicit Import, Export, and Transfer of Ownership of Cultural Property, are of importance to this exercise.[84] While 1970 is too late a date to prevent the legacy of chattel slavery, colonization, and the centuries of cultural object theft, the UNESCO convention predates Harvard's 1975 rediscovery of their own lost archives and questions this provenance.

Judge Cypher points to the need for new common laws that can provide justice for descendants of enslaved persons. A vital argument should be made that objects and images of enslaved persons cannot belong to colonizers, that the photographs of enslaved persons taken to perpetuate chattel slavery as scientific or aesthetic property cannot be owned by any person or scientific and artistic community or institution that sponsored such efforts, that the documentation of eugenic sciences is not protected private property, and that the subjects presented in the object cannot be aligned with cultural positions adjudicated by the US nation-state.[85] These are some of the arguments that could be made for the daguerreotypes to chart a new provenance.[86]

## Everlasting Accumulation

There are two things I want to discuss before ending: the first is how institutions discuss reparations, and the second is how contemporary artists have been dematerializing the process of restitution through the channels of art.

As mentioned in the prelude to this book, James Cuno, CEO of the Getty from 2011 to 2022, was an opponent of almost all object protection laws that attempt to address archeological looting concerns.[87] Echoing Raymond's claim that the deaths of those enslaved renders the objects harmless, Cuno reaches for an abstracted notion of cultural sharing that authorizes preexisting claims to property made by museums. Rather than repatriation, Cuno argues that we should embrace a notion of global heritage and work to problematize the linearity of legacy. His arguments critique nationalism but do not extend to anticolonial or decolonial critiques. In a 2015 interview, Gideon Rose, the editor of *Foreign Affairs*, pressed him to define his position: "The cultural theorists might argue that kind of [encyclopedic] gaze is a kind of a proprietary, imperial, penetrating gaze that the artifact was ripped by colonial masters from its original context and taken to the Metropol and that therefore . . . what you were doing is engaging in and perpetuating a kind of a narrative of domination, and an act of domination against the sort of subaltern people whose art it was. . . . You just don't buy that at all?"[88]

Rose references what many cultural theorists would be familiar with—we are trained to critique decontextualization and dehistorization against imperial narratives. His comments readily suggest the critique that cultural theorists might offer regarding colonially looted objects, or objects made by enslaved persons. To Rose's question regarding the potential critique, Cuno provides a peculiar response: "I don't buy that at all. . . . *If you're looking for evidence of empire in museums, you'll see it everywhere because it's a historical fact.* We can embrace that history, look beyond that history, be critical of that history, but—and include it as part of our own history, but I don't think it's matter of just trying to read, retrace, and correct the imbalances of power of the past.'[89] I want to grapple with the tension in this exchange. First, Rose comments on Cuno's arguments against repatriation by extending what he believes to be the work of a cultural theorist: to contextualize and analyze cultural production. Cuno is asked to respond to cultural theory, cultural criticism, as a museum director. Though no theorists are cited or named, the mere reference to the cultural theorist offers the opportunity of what Walter Benjamin described as "the task to brush history against the grain"—it opens up the narrative as ripe for inspection. Cuno acknowledges that materialist histories are undeniable: "You'll see it everywhere because it's a historical fact," as in, historical facts are colonial cabinets of curiosities becoming national museums. Reading, retracing, and compositing may challenge the imbalances of power in the past, as reading, retracting, and rewriting are about confronting the powers of the past in the present—namely, the very space in which the debate occurs. An institution predicated on preserving our cultural histories will always be (not merely, or just) about the powers of the past; it is a fight that concerns the powers of the present.

In June 2017, it was announced that the Getty Museum would be returning one sculpture to Italy, and in 2018, it was announced that it would be working with the government of Greece in an objects loan program. The French government recently announced that it would be returning twenty-six objects to Benin.[90] Though the British Museum exhibits only 1 percent of its eight million objects, it has refused all restitution claims. In 2010, it was reported that the Met returned nineteen objects from its permanent collection to Egypt; the Boston Museum of Fine Arts returned thirteen to Italy; and the Getty returned forty-six to Italy.

Irrespective of the vigor of the debate, artifact repatriation and reparations seem to have no bearing on museum presentations and archives. Claire Lyons, Getty's senior curator of antiquities, stated, "A significant number of those objects were in storage, so their return didn't dramatically affect our presentation."[91] Due to the rarity of such exchanges, the return of each object makes the art news circuit. The material loss and return of the object (even when held in storage, even when the curator cannot comment one way or another about the impact of its stay or return) spurs a debate about rights, property, and globality. Compared to the digitization of objects, which is occurring in the hundreds of thousands, repatriation seems to be happening only in the double digits, perhaps even in the single digits for most institutions, if at all. If an art object accrues value through its rarity, singularity, and aesthetic value—and its loss would be an unrecoverable loss and must be protected against—then digitization, as a vehicle that accelerates reproduction, functions as its gift shop counterpart: a fine commodity.

Is digitization the metaphorical opening up of the collection—a way to show what it has in store? Could digitization then lead us to ask, how do museums and institutions acquire what they acquire? The transition from an object in storage to a digital commodity is a process imbued with political and economic implications.[92] It constructs a map of the past in the present and performs computations of denial. Curators have lamented that this process "seem[s] endless. You wonder, 'When will it end?'"[93] As of now, restitution and repatriation remain unmoved by digitization. And Weems's 1995–96 series delineates how appropriation does not become the process of repatriation. Thus, I close by looking at two distinct examples where the artist works to actively repatriate objects, or takes part in what archival studies scholars describe as record continuum.

## Art as and against Record Continuum

### There Is Nothing I Can Possess Which You Cannot Take Away

For her show *From India to Canada and Back to India (There is nothing I can possess which you cannot take away)* (2020) at the Mackenzie Art Gallery at the University of Regina, Saskatchewan, Divya Mehra examined the gallery's archives. Upon discovering that various sculptures in the collection had been looted from India during British imperialism by the founder of the gallery, Norman Mackenzie, and miscataloged for over a hundred years, Mehra proposed repatriating an object to the place from which it was looted, in exchange for her sculpture. The gallery agreed, and thus a sculpture of Annapurna was returned; in its stead, Mehra placed *There is nothing you can possess which I cannot take away (Not Vishnu: New ways of Darsána)* (2020) a sculpture in the form of a bag of sand, in the manner of Indiana Jones, the colonialist hero who left a bag of sand in place of his loot (a gold Chachapoyan fertility idol—a fictitious artifact).

For Mehra, the process of repatriation was pursued outside of the law and within her practice as an artist, which included deep institutional archival research. Mehra investigated the veracity of Mackenzie's claims through the gallery's archives and consulted multiple sources before determining that the statue in question was of Annapurna, not Vishnu as cataloged. This correction is key, as proper naming is foundational when speaking of the gods, especially in the case of Annapurna. It is believed that Annapurna is the avatar of the Hindu Goddess Parvati. The abridged story goes that in response to the mockery from her partner (Shiva) of her care for the material world as akin to illusion, Parvati abandons the world, leaving it unattended and famished, but then becomes sympathetic to the world's situation, eventually returning in a new form as the avatar Annapurna, the goddess of nourishment, who offers a reprieve from starvation.

Mackenzie's looting of a statue of the goddess of nourishment from colonial India to be held captive under a different name in Canada, existing merely as an object of wealth accumulation for the gallery, parallels the trodden narrative of the enforced migratory routes and systems that colonialism depended upon to uphold its existence, and this parallel is commented upon in Mehra's work. *There is nothing you can possess which I cannot take away* materializes the dynamics of colonization in order to address its harms. Mehra's practice must be situated in a lineage of artists, writers, and activists who remain committed to anticolonial pursuits, irrespective of fashion or comprehension.

Mehra homes in on the importance of ethics and methods in the processes of repatriation, posing questions such as: What happens to stolen idols? Where do they go in the absence of devotees? She echoes the concerns of Stuart Hall, who writes, "Migration is a one way trip. There is no 'home' to go back to. There never was."[94] The processes of forced removal, forced migration, enforced archive—for the colonial object and subject—disturb the beloved dialectic of return. The actualities of the colonized could not be made adventurous by Indiana Jones, and this is what the artist will now declare: *they can take everything from you*, and even when you return it to where it was found, do you know how to make up for the time, the centuries, in which the return was denied?

The artist explains, "When Hindus go to temples, we don't say we're going to worship, but that we're going to do darsána, as in we're going to 'see' the divine, and have the divine 'see' us," emphasizing how darsána means "to see," and that this sight refers to the seeing of truth. Within this context, Mehra poses two key questions: "1. How is Annapurna's return complicated by the fact that it hasn't been seen for over a century? 2. Have these sacred objects become polluted as a result of the fact that no one has done any darśan?"[95] The return of a god without its devotees is both a necessity and a kind of sacrilegious sanctimony. Because even though colonialism changes everything so much that there isn't anything to return to, surrender to colonial dictums must be refused. Just because the return cannot be romanticized doesn't mean things can remain as is, foreclosed and suppressed in glass in Canada, far from fears, fantasies, language, and sight. It will be uncomfortable and difficult for Annapurna to leave, to be elsewhere, to be accepted, to be seen; over a hundred years have passed and everything has changed, including and especially memories. Yet such are the tenuous methods and feelings required of intervening into colonial presence.

Though Mehra's project is nestled in a history differentiated from US colonialism and chattel slavery—as it grapples with the context of British colonialism, the Canadian settler state, and the occupation of India—her project reveals several key points of relevance. First, institutional agreement is pivotal to the expediency of restitution. The Mackenzie Art Gallery recognized Mehra's intervention as one that the institution would participate in, rather than oppose. Second, for better or worse, the call grew and shifted; Mehra's intervention has been taken up by Indian nationalists, to the point in which the artist's initial intervention has almost disappeared. The current narrative has become about the supposed good relationship between the two nation-states rather than the artist's imagination. This renarrativization is of importance as it clarifies how structural and systemic violence surpasses individual pursuits, which become situated within political terrains unfamiliar or in disagreement with the artist's initial vision. Lastly, Mehra's aim to repatriate, rather than to appropriate or recirculate, is of deep importance, as it speaks to how the circulation process is not inevitable but can and must be interrupted.

Mehra's art intervenes in a modernist appropriation fantasy that promises remedies by displacing them. Her process of utilizing the institution's own database to gather information and then taking up prized forms of contemporary art such as performance to enact the process of repatriation opens up a space in which the thing they say cannot happen, could, and does.

## Demounting Agassiz

To continue looking outside of the law—but remaining within its praxis—I lastly turn to debates within recent archivist scholarship. Archivists working with colonial and postcolonial documentation of archives' subjects and their histories have argued for the fundamental overhaul of the definition of provenance. Propositions such as "parallel provenance" have been put forth by scholars such as Chris Hurley to mitigate the dogmas of origin, and to recognize the subjects of the archive as "co-creators" of the records.[96] In *Archiving the Unspeakable: Silence, Memory, and the Photographic Record in Cambodia*, archivist Michelle Caswell refutes this suggestion, arguing that notions such as parallel provenance and cocreatorship are not enough for the subjects of atrocity.[97] Caswell questions the validity of labeling the subject of the document as its creator.[98] What does the shifting of positions—from object to creator—produce? Caswell posits an alternative for archivists: rather than "reinterpreting victims as co-creators" within the archives, we should instead create "new records [that] repurpose the old, transforming them from objects of mass murder to agents of witnessing."[99] But what would records that centralized "agents of witnessing" look like? How would they differ from the old records? Could records ever be new if their institutional housing remains fixed?

Patricia Hill Collins has argued that Black women found and find "alternative ways of producing and validating knowledge itself."[100] Collins's argument and work centers around the idea that interrogating interpretations of knowledge does not suffice. Instead, one must labor to create new forms of knowledge so that interpretation and knowledge are not always severed from or in competition with each other. Such are the undertakings of *(T)races of Louis Agassiz: Photography, Body, and Science, Yesterday and Today*. *(T)races* is an exhibition catalog composed of writings by transatlantic historians, anthropologists, activists, artists, curators, and art critics for the twenty-ninth São Paulo Biennial. *(T)races* examines Agassiz's South Carolina daguerreotypes and interrogates his 1865 and 1866 photographic "Thayer Expedition" to Brazil. The book explains that not only did Agassiz utilize his relationships with plantation owners to document slavery in South Carolina, but, as mentioned earlier, he traveled to Rio de Janeiro and Manaus with a team of photographers and Harvard students to test out his pre-eugenic theories and to collect evidence against miscegenation.[101]

The catalog addresses the contexts involved in Agassiz's photographic collection and proposes a militant renaming campaign alongside performative interventions. The authors propose new ways of reading and addressing the history of the daguerreotypes—as subjects who must take the place of the scientist and artist.[102] In order to fulfill this aim, the book does four things:

1 It displays Agassiz's photo collection in full, including his insertion of an image of the statue of Apollo Belvedere, which marked for him the difference between enslaved persons and Western ideals of beauty;[103]

2 It provides historical and contemporary context for the photographs, which is used to critically analyze Agassiz's representations;
3 It interweaves Sasha Huber's performances in Rio de Janeiro and Manaus into its project;
4 It challenges photographic law and memory by taking on an international renaming campaign that calls for sites named after Agassiz to be named in honor of those he exploited—such as a stretch of the Swiss Alps to be renamed "Rentyhorn," after the given name of one of the enslaved persons in Agassiz's South Carolina daguerreotypes and ancestor to Tamara Lanier.[104]

The book is part art experiment and part direct activism, and takes on Agassiz and the protectors of his name as the antagonists of its project. For the contributors to the book, the opposition is clear: Agassiz, sites with Agassiz's name, and Swiss bureaucrats. There is also a clear and better direction for the future: for the subjects of chattel slavery to be remembered in place of the scientist.

Haitian-Swiss artist Sasha Huber participates in the book on multiple fronts: scholarly, politically, and performatively. The photographic documentation of her performances in *Agassiz: The Mixed Traces Series* includes *Somatological Triptych of Sasha Huber I* (2010), which displays Huber's body, nude, against the backdrop of Agassiz's site, the so-called Furnas de Agassiz, in the Tijuca Forest in Rio de Janeiro, Brazil. Huber inserts her body both as a subject of Agassiz's somatology and within the site of Agassiz's name. Huber poses her body the way Agassiz's subjects were posed: nude and from the front, back, and side. The documentation of this performance is part of a decades-long and ongoing series by Huber titled *Demounting Agassiz*, and it pulls from the practices of Black feminist photography—where the site of one's body is centered as the political grounds from which to explode the existing dialectic. Huber says of the performance that, as a descendant of the Caribbean diaspora, she is the "product of what Agassiz would not approve" of, and that this was a way for her to show "solidarity with the people in the photographs."[105]

In defining provenance and "new records," Caswell writes, "In the view from the continuum, all of these activations—past, present, and future—form the never-ending provenance of these records, each adding a new layer of meaning to a constantly evolving collection of records that open out into the future."[106] Caswell's description of the archive continuum applies to Huber's performance and the project of *T(races)*. Huber participates to redirect Agassiz's continuum. Huber's work actively alters the provenance of the records by inserting her body into the naming space of Agassiz and positioning herself as the subject of his gaze. Her project is situated by the records, through naming, and their contexts. Rather than obscuring or abstracting the context and the object, Huber and the members of the transatlantic committee recenter questions of naming and provenance in what becomes transformed.

Perhaps in parallel to the absolute measures concerning "the imbalances of power of the past," and perhaps even in contrast to the notion of continuum, writing on archival absences, Saidiya Hartman asks, "How does one recuperate lives entangled with and impossible to differentiate from the terrible utterances that condemned them to death, the account books that identified them as units of value, the invoices that claimed them as property, and the banal chronicles that stripped them of human features?"[107] Speaking to that which will never be found, which was never stored, Hartman writes of the impossibilities of recuperation, not merely because the collection is incomplete, but because it was made without completion.

The managerial function ascribed to enforced practices of artistic "completion" and easy representational solutions to structural injustice will be further explored in the last chapter, which is on neoliberal aesthetics and the contemporary permutations of property, appropriation, and contemporary found practices.

SIX

# Neoliberal Aesthetics

## *The Legacies of White Modernism*

We should have the theoretical courage not to identify the violence of liberation with the violence of repression, all subsumed under the general category of dictatorship. Terrible as it is, the Vietnamese peasant who shoots his landlord who has tortured and exploited him for decades is not doing the same thing as the landlord who shoots the rebelling slaves. **Herbert Marcuse, letter to Theodor Adorno, July 21, 1969**

In *250 cm Line Tattooed on 6 Paid People*, six men entered a private commercial gallery space in Cuba, to be tattooed in a continuous line across their backs for thirty dollars each, or their expected daily income as migrant laborers. Organized in December 1999 by Spanish artist Santiago Sierra, the event was documented in photographs later editioned as a set of four and sold through the Lisson Gallery in London, and then again anonymously on the auction market. While Sierra is purported by some art historians and contemporary writers to be an exemplary Marxist artist with "better" politics, I contextualize his work in this final chapter to situate a working definition of neoliberal aesthetics. Without the shield of previously discussed art forms—such as modernist and avant-garde art, found object and conceptualism, scientific management style divisions of labor, post-studio practices, the normalization of institutional racism, patronage, and exceptionalist applications of theory—Sierra's projects and the responses to them may be viewed merely as another example of racial capitalism and the legacies of transnational colonialism. In this chapter, I argue that *250 cm Line* is not a critique of white supremacy and capitalism, but rather, the work demonstrates the absolute limits of the tradition of colonial aesthetics. As a descendant of the Duchampian tradition where the artist is a manager, in his project, Sierra attempts to develop this thesis further by outsourcing the making or finding of the object entirely to persons in the most precarious situations. Instead of aestheticizing an object such as a urinal, Sierra travels around the world to document the dispossession of migrants, day laborers, and homeless women and children as his art. Here, I situate how the avant-garde thesis concerning the *idea* of the artwork and the separation between the idea and object (subjects) must be entirely destroyed.

In previous chapters, I have noted the Indigenous presence and land that institutions and archives exist upon. Akin to the complications of place posed by digitization, as discussed in chapter 5, the tracking of Sierra's practice is a transnational pursuit that follows an old imperial route. He lives in Spain and travels around the world via commission. His most infamous "works"—from the hiring of migrant workers to the use of homeless children—occur mostly in formerly colonized nation-states and exemplify, as Fatima El-Tayeb has theorized, the need to decolonize Europe in order to decolonize the world.[1]

This final chapter, which concerns the work of Sierra and the affirmative writing that surrounds it, investigates how neoliberal capitalism has magnified previous forms of modernist, conceptual art. As previously analyzed, the modernist timeline falls within the timeline of racial capitalism and settler colonialism, and it is here that the division of labor—particularly the role of the artist—becomes resituated. The difference between Marcel Duchamp's and Sierra's practices is reflected in the shifts that take place in racial capitalism. From the beginning of the twentieth century to the start of the twenty-first, we have seen gradual to accelerated breakdowns in social structures, social institutions, and state services. Racial capitalism begets racial neoliberal financial capitalism.[2] Neoliberalism, as Jodi Melamed discusses in *Represent and Destroy*, "remains a form of racial capitalism" that produces and then codifies and commodifies "difference."[3] Wendy Brown situates neoliberalism as the transformation toward a hyperrationality which collapses the *homo politicus* into the *homo economicus*.[4] And Roderick Ferguson adds that neoliberalism differentiates, abstracts, and distills so that hegemonic structures may remain fixed; neoliberalism not only identifies the market use of difference (of sex, gender, race, politics), but also manages and organizes difference, finding a placement for it within capital's imagination.[5]

The gallery space is the economic sphere that facilitates the exchange between political and economic capital. Here, aesthetics become a forceful shield in managing the economic and institutional processes of neoliberal capitalism. While poverty exists everywhere, only in the commercial and finance-driven gallery space is it codified as exceptionalist, critical art. In order to interrogate the gallery's aesthetic shield and examine the possibility of decentering Sierra's narrative, I reposition his work as/within timelines of exploitation and Global North dominance. I argue that the "exclusion by homage"[6]—another form of the aestheticization of property—presented in Sierra's gallery performances and photographs is a primary function of neoliberal aesthetics.[7]

Regarding imagination (and by extension, representation), Max Haiven writes, "Neoliberalism is hostile to the radical imagination in unprecedented ways," because "the expansion of the financial imaginary must necessarily come at the expense of the radical imagination."[8] The aesthetic manifestation of neoliberalism abides by this logic. Because neoliberalism is opposed to forms of imagination that refute or negate its existence, neoliberal aestheticians insist that representing the actualities of neoliberal capitalism must be achieved by replicating it. If neoliberal capitalism is the permanent condition of the alienation of some for the ongoing wealth management of others, neoliberal aesthetics is the philosophy, predicated on a foundational commitment to the affirmation of bodily alienation, whereby a few managers produce nothing but their own financial and economic replication.

The process of this replication is expropriated from laborers. As discussed in chapter 2, Jane Blocker has examined the celebration of risk within art and art criticism and drawn parallels to contemporary US banking and war culture. She adopts the corporate banking term *risk transfer* to discuss artists who are celebrated for their dangerous/innovative ideas but who are not directly involved in the making/destruction of art objects, nor held accountable for the damage they purport to be tending to. This position of authorship, Blocker points out, is dependent on dissociating risk from damage and converting it into profit through the transfer of risk—mimicking our current financial and political systems. I would further argue here that the right to transfer risk is dependent on racial capitalism. In Sierra's work, the risk lands on the skin of Black and Brown persons via the tattoo instrument, and the tattoo line exists to symbolize the permanence of the worker's poverty. Sierra uses bodies as material for his financial and social gain, and he profits as the artist. The questions of what damage the risk might cause and whom it might wound remain irrelevant in the banking world as well as in the arts.

Taking Melamed's and Ferguson's articulations of neoliberalism, Brown's analysis of neoliberalism as a project of exclusive economic evaluation, Haiven's insight into the quarantined conditions of capital's financial imagination, and Blocker's thesis of how success and creativity are defined as risk transfer in both finance and the arts, I define neoliberal aesthetics as the commitment to reifying the imagination of financial capitalism by denying all other forms of imagination, via the replication of preexisting structures in aesthetic representation. In addition, I argue that in neoliberal aesthetics, the body of the other is represented to make the process of violence visible, and the circulation of this racialized hypervisibility exists to normalize and surveil this violence. I examine Sierra's methodology as a model of neoliberal aesthetics in order to construct a genealogy intertwining Western modernist aesthetics and contemporary neoliberal capitalism, so that it may, one day, be abolished.

After reading the surface of what Sierra offers ideologically, I examine arguments made by contemporary art historians that uphold Sierra's work as instructive and effective. I argue that most of the writing surrounding Sierra's work has become an extension of his commercial gallery's press statements—the structural shield for this production. Contemporary writing concerning Sierra validates and celebrates his management. The scholars discussed in this chapter deploy critical theory and Marxism to decorate Sierra's enactments as interesting, radical, and ultimately acceptable. In line with the *October* issue examined in chapter 2 and the new poetry scholarship examined in chapter 4, this scholarship serves to uplift and legitimize neoliberal aesthetics. I interrogate the field's unaddressed tensions and propose that it may be fruitful to abandon gestures operating under the logic and imagination of destructive neoliberal capitalism.[9]

My model in investigating the ecology of neoliberal aesthetics is Saidiya Hartman's decree against the ease of circulation of the representation of slavery. As examined in chapter 5, in *Scenes of Subjection*, Hartman explains why she has directed her inquiry toward the politics and power of circulation.[10] Rather than displaying and replicating the representation of anti-Black violence, Hartman questions the mode of circulation in place. This critique is the basis for my questions concerning performance, representation, and circulation. It is important to note, however, that Hartman's language is specific to the milieu of chattel slavery, and that this particularity does not transfer and cannot be effaced. In this sense, Hartman's articulation concerning the circulation of slavery is not just the center of my argument, but, as situated in chapter 2, it is the center of all representation and circulation made possible via chattel slavery. The circulation of the "ravaged slave body" is not the backdrop but the foreground in which representations of suffering and neoliberal aesthetics continue to flourish.

Hartman cautions against the consumption of Black suffering that enables our current circulation practices. In this light, questions raised in Black studies become the most useful methodology for foregrounding and examining neoliberal aesthetics. The resulting process for evaluating an aesthetic work is:

1 To measure its position and investigate the politics of representation and circulation.
2 To analyze the rhetoric enabling its circulation and replication.
3 To problematize, in each instance, the dynamics of neoliberal aesthetics and the audience that engages with them.
4 To press the questions: For whom is such material useful? Who does it discipline? Who does it mimic? Who is its subject? Who is the object?
5 Whenever necessary, to halt its circulation.

This is the framework that will guide me in reading the desire for circulation. Framing *250 cm Line* as neoliberal aesthetics, I ask, for whom must poverty and racialized violence be *aesthetic*? For whom is the circulation made pleasurable?

The use of bodies as material has roots in all forms of dance, theater, and *tableaux vivants*; my investigation of Sierra is thus a case study not of the absurd or the new, but of a recalcitrant candidate in the exceptionalized space called the arts. Additionally, my investigation of Sierra is not aimed to make aberrant Sierra's business practice or to suggest he is singular in his approach, but to fatigue all other possible readings of his work, and in so doing, to develop a form with which to critique neoliberal aesthetics. The art criticism discussed in this chapter that surrounds Sierra takes great pains to avoid addressing race, ethics, labor, or even class. Though I would not like to participate in further developing what Jacques Rancière calls "the drama of the universal victim," I try with great care to position myself, Sierra, and the laborers who are connected to this project—who have been purposefully made disparate in every way possible—so that I may locate but not intrude into spaces of silence and their potential.[11]

## Scientific Management and Capital's Imagination

Santiago Sierra has been producing art prolifically since the 1990s. His work for the last two decades consists of subcontracting people to perform his "pointless tasks," his readymades. As a policy, Sierra has never involved his own body in his works, and when giving interviews he keeps his face hidden, rendering his physical presence nearly absent.[12] A brief and telling list of a decade of his output includes:

> *Line of 30 cm Tattooed on a Remunerated Person*, May 1998
> *250 cm Line Tattooed on 6 Paid People*, December 1999
> *8 People Paid to Remain inside Cardboard Boxes*, August 1999
> *24 Blocks of Concrete Constantly Moved During a Day's Work by Paid Workers*, July 1999
> *3 People Paid to Lay Still inside 3 Boxes during a Party*, November 2000
> *Ten People Paid to Masturbate*, November 2000
> *160 cm Line Tattooed on 4 People*, December 2000
> *Group of Persons Facing a Wall*, 2002
> *The Penetrated*, October 2008

Sierra's works are unironically titled; the titles to his pieces are the explanations.

Viewing a black-and-white photograph from *250 cm Line Tattooed on 6 Paid People*, I notice how the tattooed line travels straight but lands at a different place on each body.[13] The line is fresh—almost leveled, fake, and prank-like. In the documentation, some of the men wear caps and almost all of them have belts. They are all facing the wall, backs bare, away from the camera. There is one image of a man being tattooed in which the side of his face is lined—so he can either be grinning or grimacing. All the heads appear to be "bowed in submission," except one.[14] In the first image, there is a young man in a cap who looks to his side, almost as if he is looking at the people adjacent to him. He could be speaking to the man next to him, as their heads are down but slightly tilted. In the second image, the one head not facing down is that of the man on the far right. He looks up. He is the sixth person in line so there is no one to his right—though he looks. Everybody in the photograph appears to be young, thin, and Black and Brown.

Much like the scholarship surrounding Duchamp, art criticism of Sierra has heralded him as a radical artist involved in institutional critique, one who antagonizes relational aesthetics. Sierra's own interviews and public letters are laced with critiques of capitalism, exploitation, colonialism, and empire.[15] Sierra explains his commitment to this fixity: "I do not use any methods distinct from capitalism, since there is no such alternative methodology, and I do not caricature capitalism for I consider it a kind of 'eternal damnation' inflicted on humankind. . . . I agree with you when you define them [the bodies he seeks] as those 'who are already victims.'"[16] The tattoo line, according to Sierra and his catalog text, oscillates between the representation of aesthetic production and the representation of social constraints. Of the line and his commitment to replicating and upholding the logic of financial capitalism, Sierra comments, "A person without money has no dignity. . . . The tattoo is not the problem. . . . The problem is the existence of social conditions that allow me to make this work."[17] In a catalog for one of Sierra's gallery shows, Eckhard Schneider writes, "He does not use some literary or decorative motif but the symbol of modern art, the unrepresentational line."[18] The line serves as its own shield, as it is a creation with so many origins: the line is created by modern art; the line is created because of social conditions; the line is created inside the gallery; the line exists according to the blueprint of the present. The line was constructed as an act of permanence. The line can be constructed inside the gallery but cannot be removed by it.

Sierra's citation of Marxism is ornamental. The workers, much like the hand workers and artisans theorized against by managers (as discussed in chapter 2), are deliberately not compensated as artists and performers. For their minimum necessities (a day's wage, a place to sleep), his subcontractors carry Sierra's risk and become rebranded as his art. In *Group of Persons Facing a Wall* (2002), homeless women in London were paid eighteen pounds—the amount they might pay for a night at a hostel—in exchange for standing facing a wall at the Tate Modern. In another, substance-reliant sex workers were paid the price of their heroin fix to be tattooed in a gallery. A life of destitution and abject marginality is the price required to *participate* as material in Sierra's art. He makes the narrative of this exchange value part of his oeuvre: the migrant laborer will make thirty dollars for the photograph, but Sierra the artist will collect 20,000 to 60,000 euros from its sale. Though the worker's body must be displayed, offered, and reproduced ad nauseum, Sierra's photographs are limited-edition sets.[19] As mentioned previously, many of them enter the secondary market to fetch even higher fees. Sierra does not shield the fact that only he may be compensated as the artist, or, more accurately, as the CEO of his gallery production. In the economic structure of art, Sierra elucidates—both as his critique and as the premise of his artistic production—that only he is selected to receive the artist commissions and paycheck.[20] With every new idea and commissioned performance he further establishes his brand and career, stabilizing his future commissions and projects.

Grace Kyungwon Hong's investigation of US migrant labor and the problem of visibility offers a useful framework for thinking about the labor and spatial logic of the Global North gallery system. Hong and Saskia Sassen have argued that the trend in post-Ford US labor practices is to maintain "pockets" of the Global South within the Global North. This spatial positioning of the Global South can be recast as a way to view *250 cm Line*. The unnamed "unemployed men" enter the "pocket" of gallery space (situated by the Global North gallery system) and remain arrested as such. As with neocolonial and neoliberal labor routes and the supply chain, *250 cm Line* asserts that wherever "they" go, the labor logic applied to the economic south must follow. The placement of our bodies imposes our economic value even when moving through space. The production of pockets of the Global South, captured as aesthetic objects for the consumption of the Global North, reveals the artifice of Sierra's installation, in particular, its use of the surveillance pivotal to contemporary commercial art making—as well as its hostility to radical imaginations.

The tattoo line in *250 cm Line* and the neoliberal economic logic of this performance insist that the people within the frame are interchangeable. Whether they are in the gallery or "outside," they are migrant, they are laborers. The workers are without names, without particularity—they were hired because they were the six that could not find employment that day. They are fixed yet interchangeable. Sierra hires them to re-represent this reality for the unspecified yet clearly classed gallery viewer. And in the gallery space, the visuality of neoliberal aesthetics is treated as the remedy to global injustice. This logic says *it is because we cannot see* that injustice exists, and presents the viewer with the opportunity to surveil the people in the gallery performance and in the photograph of it—and then commodify them through purchase.

Visibility, however, is as fraught as invisibility. Hong has argued that women of color feminist frameworks do not suggest visibility "as an easy remedy for the condition of invisibility, but imply a dialectical relationship between the two. In other words, for women of color feminist practice, visibility is a rupture, an impossible articulation."[21] In *250 cm Line*, Sierra visually replicates the conditions of economic devastation, but each attempt only clarifies the distance between the recognized subject and his chosen objects. Hong argues against mediated and immediate visibility as a solution to the problems of conditioned and practiced invisibility. Hong cites Mitsuye Yamada, who argues that while "invisibility is an unnatural disaster . . . so too, is visibility unnatural; it is also a kind of violence . . . visibility is not inclusion, but surveillance."[22] The unnamed bodies in the image of *250 cm Line* amplify the invisible visibility maintained through the surveillance of commodified gallery representation.

Sierra's understanding of capitalism is dehistoricizing and defensive. For Sierra, surveillance, policing, exploitation, oppression, and exclusion are essential strains of neoliberal capitalism because they are the only methods of art available. Sierra repeats his commitment to upholding neoliberalism's financial imagination and its current market values: "There is no alternative to this systems [*sic*], or way to dodge it, change it, or question it."[23] Sierra argues again and again against anything other than the imagination, procedures, and structures of neoliberal capitalism. As a producer of neoliberal aesthetics, he insists that the role of an artist is to uphold and replicate its violence. Capitalism is eternal, and there is no need or reason to remember history otherwise or to imagine future impossibilities—a convenient interpretation for a successful, contemporary capitalist.

## The Ecology of the Market

Andrea Fraser describes the landscape of museum/gallery board members and owners—those with purchasing powers and vested interests. She writes,

> We all know that the art field is the site of enormous concentrations of wealth and power. Museums are the wealthiest institutions in the world if we calculate their assets. *Art objects are far and away the most highly valued objects in the world, rendering the art market a kind of economic freak show*. . . . Museums are also directly linked to powerful political interests. And at this point there can be no doubt that the art market and museum building boom of the past decade was fueled by the very same individuals who drove the stock and real estate markets to dizzy heights with unsustainable if not fraudulent financial tactics—tactics that contributed to dramatic increases in social inequality in the past ten years and have now resulted in global economic collapse. *These are our patrons*.[24]

Fraser concludes that institutional critique—the aesthetic form with which she is most closely associated—is not possible. What is critique (and how effective could it be) if it's what the patron has ordered? What is institutional critique to the patrons of the global economic collapse? Fraser, Chin-Tao Wu, and Gregory Sholette have pointed to how fluidity exists between stock portfolios and art portfolios; museums are sites of old, colonial power. Purchasing power readily applies to the arts—as witnessed in phenomena ranging from Frick's and Carnegie's profits from the steel industry going into philanthropy and museums, to Duchamp's placement in the Philadelphia Museum of Art, to the current position of Chinese buyers at the top of the art and antiquities market.[25] The relationship between the finance sector and aesthetic production is not the product of accidental, unfortunate circumstance but a procedural relationship.

Linking the affective directly to the financial, Haiven suggests that it may be more fruitful to configure the most recent financial meltdown not as a catastrophe of events, but as a crisis in the imagination of capital.[26] If we configure finance as capital's imagination (where it mutates, disseminates, and circulates most expediently), then a crisis within finance is the manifestation of a limit—however momentarily—being reached. In an abstract thought experiment, the Marxist potential of the failure of finance is provocative and alluring. Mirroring the financial sector, the deregulated art market becomes the site of pure freedom and the secondary site of the imagination of capital where Sierra actualizes his replication of neoliberal capitalism. Perhaps part of the implicit aim in Sierra's works is that deregulation will lead to its own imaginative crisis: the replication of violence and further deregulation will ultimately crush capitalism. Sierra's practice in *250 cm Line* is loyal to reproducing the imagination of capital alone. What does it mean when the limit can be reached, yet nothing but repetitions follow? What does it mean when this replication is the one most desired by galleries, museums, and their patrons?

Blocker posits that performance art in the 1960s was particularly mobilized to shift away from the dominating presence of the market. She argues that the crisis of the market in art, of art's fixation on the market, pressed the minds of artists and art historians alike, and that this anxiety pushed performance away "from the tired tradition of painting."[27] Performances did not, however, constitute a radical break. They replicated the market dynamics that previous mediums, such as photography and painting, had embodied. In extending the presence of the visual art market, Blocker argues that the performers—such as Vito Acconci, Yves Klein, and Gary Hill—enacted a "feminized position" and worked through and represented a "hoped-for" body, a normatively desired body.[28] The desire to move away from the market did not produce a space away from the gendered, sexualized, and bodily constraints of market desires. In this narrative of performance art, Sierra goes against traditional strains of performance by refusing to display his body—what Blocker might identify as a rejection of the feminized position—and by refusing to display the "hoped-for body." It is in this terrain that commentators and gallerists have lauded Sierra's gestures; they read Sierra as working against the traditions of performance art, and this opposition, his "against," becomes read as subversive.

*250 cm Line* attempts to demonstrate that the body removed from hope is the racialized suffering body. Much like segregation as the pivotal signifier in the Duchampian tradition of aesthetic liberation, race becomes the material in constructing the contrarian performance. The racialized body is surveilled, excluded, anonymized, and at the same time made to serve as the site of value from which the artist creates, peddles, and profits. And here, the fissures of neoliberal aesthetics are found: to be additive via humiliation (especially within the terrains of the market) is the very definition of multiculturalism in the service of white supremacy. To be additive means that difference will quickly or eventually be commodified, and so, by the logic of neoliberalism, to be additive is most laudatory.

As Sierra's body is outside the performance but he profits from the documentation, Sierra's role in these enactments is as the manager of dispossession and terror. Who is at the receiving end of this management? Art historian Grant Kester, like Hartman, calls for scholars to examine the circulation processes in place. He writes, "The writing on Sierra's work continues to focus on its reception in the gallery by an imaginary viewer, while neglecting entirely the actual forms of reception and performative interaction set in motion during its commercial after-life."[29] Utilizing an interview of Sierra's New York–based art dealer, Kester argues that performance within the self-legitimized "high art" institutions can never be removed from the market. The performance of visual art—in both earlier forms of performance art and its neoliberal rendition in Sierra's oeuvre—falls in line with the same market logic of production and circulation.

## Lessons for Whom?

It is not the laborer who is unaware of the processes of labor extraction. If Sierra's work attempts to elucidate the material realities of capitalism, for whom is the process of exploitation alien? When probed on his practice of labor extraction, Sierra responded, "Paying more than what they expect, or in a way that suits my conscience, is useless.... That would suggest that I'm a good guy and that I did my bit towards saving these souls. Ridiculous! If I can find someone prepared to hold up a wall for 65 Euros, *I'd be showing you a true fact*. If I pay double that, I'd be showing my *generosity*."[30] Fiction, rather than fact, is an accurate word to describe our wage system, neoliberal capitalism, and Sierra's oeuvre. Are the ideological relations of capitalism (meritocracy, the moral righteousness of bourgeois paternalism) not also fiction? Based on the fiction of wage negotiations and the terms of the subcontract, the wealthy and the Global North consumer are provided with ways to imagine the end of capitalism—and a central role in this scenario. The enactments of Sierra's wage scheme offer the customer: (1) revolution as fiction, and (2) the abjection of the present. Both functions exist to confirm the power of the artist.

*250 cm Line* homes in on the commodification of orthodox Marxism, as well as a neoliberal understanding of revolution. In "Rent of Land," Marx writes, "Eventually wages, which have already been reduced to a minimum, must be reduced yet further, to meet the new competition. This then necessarily leads to revolution."[31] While wage negotiations are vital, essential, and ongoing, neoliberal capitalism displays the limits of wage-based revolutions. The narrative of *250 cm Line* is that the only role capitalists (Sierra, art-gallery culture) can play is to reveal/enforce/replicate the bare minimum in order to trigger the revolution. This scenario privileges the bourgeois subject, the exceptional artist manager, as the instigator of new and better things to come. Additionally, as wages are controlled by multinational corporations that both maintain global poverty and keep the high art market sector alive, the formula of exploitation-to-lead-to-revolution is one that is devoted to privileging the wealthy customer.[32] This wage-based critique is neither the end of white supremacy nor the destruction of capitalism but is the material for the re-representation and replication of neoliberal capitalism. This revolution fantasy focuses on the awareness of the wealthy patron and the vision of the artist—it prioritizes their consciousness and existence as *liberators*.

Sierra's notion of "true fact" and the pejorative placement of "generosity" regarding labor relations is also revealing. Is it truly generous to "pay more"? How and why does this particular affect erupt at the site of economic negotiations?[33] Payment for labor power is not an issue of generosity and expectation, but one that acknowledges the mode of production. Marx argues that the extraction and exploitation of capitalism reside in the vulnerability of the contract to the affective whims of capitalists. It is in making the discourse of payment affective that the value of labor power and value of the work can be denied; the affective conditions of the contract are fundamentally exploitative and violent.[34] The violence is the ability to privilege one's affect over the work and life of another; the contract stipulates that the worker labors for three days, but the capitalist may pay for one. Marxism works to destroy the artifice of this relationship—to halt the continuation of fictitious capital as everlasting and true.

In addition, Marx argues that money does not represent value. Haiven points out that for Marx, "money is not a measure of actually existing labor power, but a measure of *anticipated* labor power to yet be mobilized toward the production of commodities."[35] Money symbolizes that which is "already anticipatory and speculative"—negotiations for money are not about the exchange of labor power, but are about the exchange of projected value.[36] Sierra's lump sums for his subcontracts (30 dollars, 120,000 lire, 18 pounds, 65 euros) assess value by symbolizing poverty.

To insist that wages rest in the affective whims of some and that money symbolizes only exchange value is the logic of capitalism. Sierra insists that his sum is purposefully base to reveal how the workers, those subcontracted but not employed, operate as the excesses of capital and outside of the symbolic activity of anticipation, as they are unable to demand *money* or are unable to be conceived of as *deserving* more. And in this line of reasoning, Sierra's price points of 20,000 to 120,000 euros exist because he is not exploited by the affective whims of the speculative economy but is a manager within their regimes. Sierra does not receive payment in the form of symbolic sums (one mortgage payment, a weekly food stipend, a year's clothing allowance), as his exchange value is *desired* and *anticipated*. The amount of money he will be paid secures his managerial excess.

Haiven argues that money "colonizes the future, replacing the limitless potential of social cooperation with the limitless accumulation of capital."[37] Sierra's use of money in his project has only one function: to quarantine poverty into the future. His provided working conditions conclude that the status quo of exploitation must persist as representation. The status quo must be represented ad infinitum to highlight this claim. For Sierra, commercial art objects and their transactions are the best mirror of the power dynamics of capitalism—even as fiction, they cannot distort, rupture, reverse, splinter, create, or process. Sierra does not believe in change or possibility, because art is a representation of reality, without "possibility of change."[38] One can deduce from this rationale that serious art is the advertisement of the status quo.

Princeton University Art Museum's first curator of modern and contemporary art, Kelly Baum, agrees that it is the crystallization of the status quo that makes Sierra's work interesting. She describes the *Submission* series, displayed at the university, as a performance of the speech act: "These subject positions (whether as perpetrator or victims), are not given beforehand, but are constituted in the very act of enunciation."[39] Baum writes that Sierra's works are filled with "incisive exploration," legitimizing his configuration of the bodies of others as raw material, while confirming that Sierra, just like the institutions and structures he supposedly critiques, produces nothing other than exploitation.

The critical focus brought by Baum and others emphasizes that Sierra's exploitations are valuable because they are interesting and educational, that he is teaching about the violence of capitalism.[40] But then why not marvel at other acts that similarly demonstrate the violence of capitalism, like the brutality of the prison industrial complex or the ways in which privatized military corporations have yet to answer for their countless mass murders? Additionally, what is the point of further exploiting abjection as a performance? Why not just pass out copies of *Capital*, or another insightful text of choice? What is the pleasure of replication? A more critical and accountable focus might be: What does the interest in Sierra's performances tell us about highbrow gallery and museum culture? How has art continued to remain a site of exception—particularly a site permitted to enact exploitation and violence?

Kester argues that there is a long fetishistic history of instructionally shocking aesthetic representation. Tracing a tradition spanning from nineteenth-century documentary photographers such as Jacob Riis to Sierra, Kester argues that these artists deploy the old methodology of shock representation—as though it were new—to visualize/materialize the oppressed in order to *teach* the middle to upper class (the museum class, the leisure class) a *lesson*. Kester asserts that artists such as Sierra believe they "can shock (implicitly bourgeois) viewers out of their complacency and into the correct critical consciousness of both the Other's suffering and their own privilege."[41] The shock of this representation serves as a reminder to remain in the confines of one's economic positioning. *250 cm Line* affirms that our value is immovable and must be maintained. In interrogating artistic exceptionalism, Kester furthers that "Sierra conflates a critique of aesthetic autonomy with a critique of bourgeois complacency. . . . The conflation is further complicated by his tendency to project his own guilt as a 'white, Caucasian, male' on to the implied viewer or audience of his work."[42] The viewer assumes the "white, Caucasian male" subject position, and the laborers in Sierra's projects become objects for this gaze. The premise of Sierra's artwork thus fixes the white male gaze—an oppressive gaze that needs no further practice or circulation.

*250 cm Line* works to turn economic desperation and devastation into a performance for the Global North consumer. Utilizing the language of wage and choice, it asks subjects of economic devastation to display the depths of their abjection for the dominator's pleasure. Violence here is sanctioned, enforced, and installed. The title, the scenario, and the replication exist to reinforce for consumers that we are not that performer, that Sierra is the political artist, and that neoliberal capitalism can be contained in a photograph, a gallery space. The explicit argument of *250 cm Line* for the viewer is *you would never stand in this line, you would never be tattooed for thirty dollars, you would never take off your shirt, turn your head away to admit how little power you really have. You are not my commodity—feel the distance from the poor to enjoy and purchase the photograph. 250 cm Line* reasons that art too is where neoliberalism must be perpetuated. Art is the extension of neoliberal capitalism—and to affirm this thesis, its managers reject even the possibility of imagining and constructing otherwise.

## The Aesthetic Shield: Normalizing Risk Transfer via Marxist Public Relations

Institutionalized commentary on Sierra's works has served to normalize the processes of risk transfer without examining the desire for circulation. The critiques offered by contemporary art historians defend Sierra. Art historian Claire Bishop writes, "The work of Hirschhorn and Sierra is *better art* not simply for *being better politics. . . . Their work* acknowledges the limitations of what is possible as art . . . and subjects to scrutiny all easy claims for a transitive relationship between art and society."[43] Bishop reads Sierra's enactments as endowed with superior politics. However, the politics of the pieces, if we are to take Sierra's rhetoric at face value, is the recapitulation of capitalist methodology as art—a practice that I have described as the tenet of neoliberal aesthetics.

In this configuration, Bishop subsumes the workers Sierra solicits as his art—their labor becomes his ingenuity, their alterity his material.

Continuing her discussion of Thomas Hirschhorn and Sierra in *October*, Bishop explains, "These artists set up '*relationships*' that *emphasize the role of dialogue and negotiation* in their art, but do so *without collapsing these relationships into the work's content*. The relations produced by their performances and installations are marked by sensations of unease and discomfort rather than belonging. . . . An integral part of this tension is the introduction of *collaborators from diverse economic backgrounds*, which in turn serves to challenge contemporary art's self-perception as a domain that embraces other social and political structures."[44] There is much rhetorical fluidity in this passage, and it is important to configure and connect Bishop's subject-object-verb usage in order to explore the relations and ideas that she is at risk of collapsing here. To gauge the possibilities and their connections, I will attempt to define Bishop's description of Sierra's work and practice:

#### "RELATIONSHIPS"

≈ The financial relationships between Sierra and those he "subcontracts"

≈ The financial and cultural relationships between Sierra (extensions of his persona) and gallery viewers

≈ The financial relationships and connections between Sierra and his gallery team

≈ The financial relationships between the gallery and its collectors

#### "EMPHASIZE THE ROLE OF DIALOGUE AND NEGOTIATION"

≈ *Between Sierra and his subcontractors*. Sierra proclaims that he will pay thirty dollars each for six bare backs. Viewers are not provided with a transcription of the dialogue, the exchange, or any notion of a verbal response; we are to assume that, since documentation of the event exists, Sierra's command was executed and the negotiation worked in his favor.

≈ *Between Sierra and gallery viewers*. Sierra remains absent, so it is unclear what the dialogue or negotiation between his viewers and his labor could be.

≈ *Between Sierra and his gallery*. Sierra states that he only uses methodologies found in capitalism. His gallery and art historians consistently inform us how to understand the Marxist potential in his work and his "better" politics.

≈ *Between the gallery and collectors.* Gallery statements utilize the language provided by art historians to discuss the work with collectors.

### "COLLABORATORS FROM DIVERSE ECONOMIC BACKGROUNDS"

≈ Exploitation to create unease as a form of belonging?
≈ The rich subcontracting the poor as the new standard for art diversity?
≈ The dynamics of oppression aestheticized as collaboration?

It's unclear why Sierra's unnamed workers are consistently called "collaborators," "participants," and "volunteers," and at the same time, this vocabulary crystallizes the marriage between neoliberal rhetoric and neoliberal capitalism."[45] I am interested to know how collaboration and volunteering are defined. Are the men in *250 cm Line* collaborators, as their bodies have been forcefully made to offer and authenticate the signifier of abjection in a documented "performance" about poverty conceived by a Global North manager? Are they collaborators in the sense that neoliberal capitalism has so effectively extracted their power to negotiate their labor that they are *free* only to be *objects* in the management of base value?[46] Are they collaborators because they have become uniformed as "material"? Are the women in *Group of Persons Facing a Wall* collaborators because they needed a place to sleep? Are these women collaborators because Sierra saw in them the value of replicating and representing the failures of the state, the excesses and triumphs of neoliberal capitalism? Or are they collaborators because their economic and racial positions could be used as material by an artist?

How do the poor collaborate with the wealthy, in Marxian terms? What are collaborators from diverse economic backgrounds, again, in Marxian terms? The status of the worker is vital to the analysis of this kind of art. *If* they are volunteers, then what Marxist frameworks are being tested? *If* they are workers, what will be the analysis? *If* they are art enthusiasts who do not feel like they've been exploited—as his critics insist—then what forms of power are being analyzed? Is Sierra an enactor of brute force, forcefully tattooing a line on the backs of day laborers? Surely it is not being argued that the line is akin to a commemorative tattoo. The tension between exploitation and volunteerism is the titillation crucial to the narrative of *250 cm Line*. That so many Marxist scholars seem unable to state that this is exploitation is part of the work's ability to enthrall. That so many want to imply that the workers are in fact volunteers in an art project is the slippage, the sublimation of politics and aesthetics into power. How do homeless women volunteer their homelessness, how do they volunteer their subjugation? If they are volunteering—why? If they are not—what is happening instead? I do not ask such questions to remove subjecthood from those inside the frame but to suggest that such depictions—in both the performance and the circulation of their reproductions—require the workers to be without names, life, and subjecthood. They are required to be without particularity yet remain racially and colonially marked.

* * *

Artist and writer Coco Fusco's description of Sierra's project is similar to Bishop's. Fusco details Mexico's post-NAFTA landscape: in an economy drenched in the corruption of neoliberal capitalism, a cultural milieu populated by artists who are "vampires of misery," Fusco elevates the works of Sierra as "stand[ing] out as countervailing forces."[47] In this Mexican context, she compares his work to that of SEMEFO (a group that creates installations under the acronym for the Servicio Medico Forense [Forensic Medical Service]) and the Electronic Disturbance Theater as "offer(ing) key critical visions of the social and political situation of the country."[48] Fusco explains that Sierra "calls upon the services of others and makes a public display of their work."[49] She writes, "His pieces have taken place in alternative spaces, galleries, and museums. He purposely selects or offers employment to individuals from the most marginalized sectors of the cities in which he works. . . . The actions Sierra requests others to perform are repetitive, often nonsensical, and even humiliating."[50] Once again, there is obfuscation between work, labor, and exploitation. To "offer employment" is quite a euphemism. Sierra's pay system is structured only to humiliate those who accept its terms. Even if one is to account for the notion that all work under management is tedious and humiliating, employment suggests a contractual exchange, with the notion of ongoing terms and agreements recognized both by the employer, the laborer, and the state. In this way, Fusco's euphemism "offer employment" is similar to Bishop's usage of "collaborator," which evades the violence of the working conditions. These conditions most resemble an outsourced subcontract: the economic terms furthest removed from corporate and institutional accountability, which are exempt from considering the ongoing life of the subject.

Similarly to Bishop, Fusco states that "Sierra seeks to shock, not as a flip gesture but as a form of institutional critique detonated by the breaking of social taboos"—a claim that effectively excuses Sierra from ethics or responsibility for his business practices.[51] Fusco then goes on to state that while Sierra is white, those who have called him exploitative are usually from Mexico's wealthiest families, implying that his critics have no ethos to critique his work. The juxtaposition between Sierra's whiteness and the wealth of Sierra's critics suggests that the two forces are mutually exclusive: Sierra might not belong in the wealth bracket of this "critical" class, or the critical class is exempt from the privileges of whiteness.

After silencing potential criticism surrounding his work, Fusco repeats that "Sierra's work, on the other hand, foregrounds desperation and futility, the gap between rich and poor, the constant humiliation to which the needy are subjected, and the discretionary power of those with even a modicum of wealth."[52] Fusco describes *Person Remunerated for Cleaning Shoes of Attendees to an Opening without Their Consent*, a "performance" where an eleven-year-old boy who cleaned shoes at the subway station was brought into a gallery to perform this task for attending gallerygoers; *Santiago Sierra Invites You for a Drink*, where "international art tourists" were invited to sit on wooden benches that functioned as temporary coffins for sex workers who were paid thirty dollars to remain hidden inside of them; and *250 cm Line*. Of these acts, she asserts, "Having had the opportunity to speak to the participants, I do not come away with the impression that they see themselves as exploited."[53] Yet the word "participants" is unspecified. In this construction, "participants" could refer either to the subcontracted, the gallerygoers, the gallerists, or Sierra. Moreover, Fusco's insertion is a deep paradox. If the "participants" who are being paid thirty dollars each to be tattooed, concealed, and humiliated, as well as the "participants" attending the galleries, parties, and festivities, all proclaim not to feel exploited, then for whom does "Sierra bring the power dynamics into focus?"[54] The witnesses of the photographic documentation of the event, the buyers, the audiences we have yet to hear from? If no one feels the weight of exploitation, how is "desperation" "foregrounded"? Isn't the function of Sierra's enactments to replicate humiliation, desperation, and exploitation so that the gallerygoer might be faced with Sierra's understanding of "true facts?" If exploitation is not felt, critiqued, and rectified on-site, how else is power transmitted? Fusco defends Sierra's project as unexploitative for the participants and, in the process, deflates her own theory about how Sierra's works deal with desperation, power dynamics, and institutional critique. In defending Sierra's critical project (his artistic rights), Fusco ultimately demonstrates that the dynamics of power could not effectively be played out at all. Such a conclusion raises serious questions as to why these projects need to exist in the first place, and the ferocity with which their failures are defended.[55]

## Subcontract with Marxist Public Relations

For many of the scholars who write affirmatively about Sierra's work, the lack of clarity surrounding the status of his workers implicitly imbues it with more possibility. After having studied the language of his projects, my assessment is that the term *subcontractor* seems to most accurately describe the labor conditions Sierra creates. As in, the agreement between artist and worker seems to be, at best, tertiary. Sierra pays the workers the amount advertised in the art project, and they do not remain on his payroll to receive sick days, vacation hours, health insurance, and royalties for taking part in the actualization of his art. He hunts people living in abject poverty, barters with them (one day's wages, a place to sleep, cocaine), and denounces all rationales as to why he should pay more. Sierra, artist, inc., is not liable for anything, he says.

Bishop and Fusco enact a critical function traced throughout this book. In the same way that triumphant writings on Duchamp worked to naturalize his radicality and Marjorie Perloff's scholarship racialized the terms of experimentalism in poetry, Bishop and Fusco extend their critical authority not only to legitimate Sierra as an artist, but also to affirm his exploitative working conditions as *better art*. Tellingly, this kind of criticism cannot differentiate itself from the public relations (PR) statements meant to sell the work. For example, in the exhibition catalog *Santiago Sierra: 300 Tons and Previous Works* (2004), Eckhard Schneider affirms, "We see no active representation of the horror of social accusation or political metaphor in front of us, but rather the work relates directly to the individual in his role within society and art."[56] Gallery PR statements have consistently labeled Sierra's works as radical explorations of power. His 2012 Lisson Gallery retrospective was titled *Santiago Sierra: Dedicated to the Workers and Unemployed*. Part of the PR statement for the retrospective reads, "Eschewing notions of the politically correct, Sierra forces us to question the commodification of life, exposing and challenging the structures of power that operate in society."[57] Such statements—from art historians and gallerists alike—represent the general tenor with which his projects circulate.

Santiago Sierra is the cutting edge of institutional critique—this is the PR message. Sierra's own rhetoric reflects this sentiment. When interviewed about his projects, he states, "We First-Worlders and, above all, the world of culture, have no idea how grim and deep this issue [global poverty] is. We usually think it has been settled or mitigated. . . . But all you need to do is take a flight to Manila or Medellin to see the collateral damage of our option. When you migrate the other way around, the feeling of being a dominator—as you put it—never leaves your mind."[58] The artist acknowledges his position as the dominator—he makes art from this space. And when awarded for these gestures, he is lauded for rejecting the prizes. When it was announced in 2010 that Sierra would receive Spain's highest aesthetic award, the Premio Nacional de Artes Plásticas (National Prize for Plastic Arts), Sierra promptly released a statement rejecting the prize and announcing his "NO" campaign, which was documented with photography and video and then sold via his gallery, Lisson (see figures 6.1 and 6.2). He declared,

> I wish to make clear, now, that art has given me freedom, which I am not ready to give up. Consequently, my common sense obliges me to reject this prize. This prize exploits the prestige of its winner for the benefit of the state. A state that is desperate for legitimacy, given its contempt for its mandate to work for the common good no matter which party occupies the office. A state that participates in crazy wars in alliance with a criminal empire. A state that happily gives away public money to the banks. A state committed to dismantling the welfare state for the benefit of a local and international minority. The state is not for all of us. The state is for you and your friends. Therefore, do not count me among them, for I am a serious artist. No, sirs, No, Global Tour.[59]

Sierra has stated of this project, "People who are actively fighting against the system need images, and we, artists, must provide them with them. This 'NO' is made for all who are fed up with injustice, domination, censorship, and oppression."[60]

Sierra's ethos of demonizing the public state while in collaboration with privately operated cultural institutions and their wealthy benefactors is illuminating. In his statement, is Sierra implying that the function of a serious artist is to be working with private galleries instead of the state? And how will Sierra provide the images we need to fight empire, utilizing only the tools given to him by capitalism? I believe Sierra is stating that he will give us images, replicated through the violence of capitalism, in hopes that capitalism will be demolished at some point by such representations: such is trademark neoliberal aesthetics.

Santiago Sierra
NO
LUCCA, ITALY. JULY 2009. 2010
Lambda print on aluminium
125 x 167cm
ed. unique
SIER100002

EUR 25,000.00

Santiago Sierra
NO Global Tour, Tbc 2009-2010
B&W Photograph, lambda print on dibond, + Wooden Frame and Plexiglass
100 x 177 cm (unframed)
ed. unique
SIER100007

EUR 25,000.00

**6.1 & 6.2** Price sheet, Lisson Gallery, New York, showing information for two photographs from Santiago Sierra's "NO, Global Tour" (2009–10), in which a large sculpture of the word *NO* was documented in locations around the globe. Price: 25,000 euros each.

This is one among many examples that reveal the layers to neoliberal aesthetics: to insistently reproduce neoliberal capitalism; to replicate the violence of capitalism, particularly through the abjection of its subcontractors in private commercial spaces; to appropriate Marxist and revolutionary rhetoric, in this case, in order to normalize the processes of subcontracting and risk transfer; to affectively sell the documentation of neoliberalism to patrons of the global economic collapse; and to successfully define those subcontracted, particularly those most subjected to racial capitalism, as raw material. While aiming to dismantle "criminal empires" and capitalism, Sierra reenacts the terror and violence of neoliberal capitalism—all while making a profit. If Sierra does show us one thing, it is the limits of Marxist rhetoric within gallery spaces and the possibility for Marxist critique to become co-opted by neoliberalism to further justify exploitation.

## The Artist and His Object

Jacques Rancière's reading of Marx is particularly helpful in understanding why Sierra and his critics deploy Marxism as public relations—theirs is a Marxism that instructs from an exclusive position of power. Rancière argues that there is a historical, philosophical, and leftist tradition of requiring silence from the poor.[61] The inspection of a higher truth/art/idea becomes solidified only through the author's objectification of others, be it in the service of a revolution, an artistic shift, or a philosophical undertaking. The subject position and, more importantly, the ideas (the intellectual, immaterial labor) come only through the work, the lived experience, and the material labor of those unnamed. This division of power is maintained through the preestablished divisions of labor examined throughout this book.

Rancière provides reasons why Marx required the poor to be distant, calling this practice "exclusion by homage."[62] Using the fable of the shoemaker-poet repudiated by Marx, Rancière elucidates Marx's need for the proletariat to stay as such. For Marx, participation in aesthetics is a feature of submission to the ways of the bourgeois, which would follow submission to capitalism, when the correct path for the proletariat is revolution. The function of the proletarian was to see the virtue of one's chosen labor and to remain militantly protective of its value. The function of the proletarian was to remain in place, while the function of the philosopher was to behold that placement.[63] This dynamic, Rancière posits, reveals the distance and desires of the philosopher. Of this power play, he states, "It does not have written on it that it is the 'sign of the division of labor that marks it as the property of capital' except in the form of hieroglyphics *that cannot be read* by workers who wear on their brows the sign of a people both *chosen and condemned*."[64] The philosopher utilizes languages, media, and genres that the worker is never meant to have access to; the artist deals in artifacts the worker cannot afford; the worker is purposefully alienated. The processes of such critiques require the existence of an object that can be transformed into a subject if the precise instructions are followed. The transition from object to subject is the condition of being both chosen and condemned, excluded yet represented. Thus, Rancière goes so far as to say that while it is through the *Communist Manifesto* that proletarians are granted subjecthood, such conditions of subject making encompass the power that continues to divide the world.[65]

The curse of being "chosen and condemned" echoes Sierra's convenient inscription of capitalism as "eternal damnation." In this repeating cycle, Sierra is tasked as the artist who waits with his objects. He instructs them to perform meaningless tasks again and again, waiting. This endless re-presentation is delivered as a reminder that the conditions under which the poor live, though exhibitable, cannot ever be changed. The six men in *250 cm Line* are worthy of homage because they can never be financially included; they do not say "NO" and thus cannot be compensated as performers or as artists. Further, *250 cm Line* highlights the tradition and desire to distill the poor, the other, as objects. It encapsulates the dominator's fear of them as anything other than objects.

In this formulation, the unknown desires of others—the subaltern, those dispossessed—are associated with aesthetic formations through the philosopher's and artist's propertizing understanding of aesthetics. The laborers must remain the laborers and can only be compensated as such. Their fixed placement, their suffering, is the homage—exclusion from the realm of aesthetic desire and subjecthood is the only way for them to remain pure and uncompromised. In the events designed by Sierra, aesthetics become the proletariat's expulsion from revolutionary purity. The proletariat in abject poverty must remain pure by suffering as the artist CEO wills—this is what Sierra's artistic oeuvre offers their world.

## Death of the Author, Rise of the CEO: Race and Divisions of Labor

Sierra's most important projects are the ones that that never happened; they are direct threats against neoliberal aesthetics. Dean Kenning writes of Sierra's practices that he "does not represent this reality from a distance, but presents it in operation as the participation of the remunerated persons becomes a site-specific index of the existence of poverty and inequality."[66] Who is the site? As Kenning describes, "Sierra's proposal to line up the gallery staff, bare backed in order of salary, from the director at one end to the cleaners and caterers at the other was rejected by both [MoMA] PS1 and the Kunsthalle Vienna. . . . What this means in effect is that those with power and money are obviously not compelled to move out of their comfort zone and risk potential humiliation."[67] In an interview with Gerald Matt, Sierra explains that one of these projects actually did come to fruition, and one was rejected. At the Project Space of Kunsthalle Vienna, he had thirty men arranged via skin color from lightest to darkest.[68] He then wanted to install the same performance at MoMA PS1 in New York City, but according to museum staff, including curators and the director, his request was denied. Sierra articulated that he wanted to show the "widespread" acceptance of racialized labor.[69] He believed the results with the PS1 museum staff would have been the same as in Vienna.

The artist articulates a reading that acknowledges that labor and power are racialized, but this critique leads him to reproduce its dynamics. Echoing Fredrick Winslow Taylor's admission that the only reason hand workers do not perform "mind-work" is that they lack social standing, Sierra admits that his managerial reach does not extend beyond poor, racialized persons. He either does not have enough money to negotiate with the museum director, or he is unwilling to use *force* (what else is poverty but structurally imposed force?) to control museum curators—in reality, his subcontract is without incentive for those with more power. What might the contract have to be for the dominators—for those in positions to say *no*—to be defined, identified, staged, and exhibited? This would be an exchange in which Sierra the manager would have to negotiate with someone like him.

What tools of capitalism would need to be utilized to complete Sierra's PS1 performance? How much would Sierra have to give up, how devastated would his accounts be, if he were to pay six prominent museum curators and directors to take off their clothes and line up according to rank to be gawked at and photographed, and for those photographs to be sold on secondary markets? Would payment be enough? Rather than the bodies most marginalized, could art visualize and denigrate men in positions of power, members and directors of the museum class?

Some contemporary critics have already prepared a rationale against visually locating the dominator, or the "enemy": we are all complicit. In the catalog for the exhibition *Police*, a 2005 show in Linz, Austria, in which Sierra was prominently included, Oliver Marchart explains, "If one is always operating on the same terrain as the adversary ('the enemy') then the traditional accusation that one has been 'recuperated,' [*sic*] that one has 'sold out!' or been 'assimilated!' loses its meaning. It presupposes, in fact, that there can be a clear distinction between the instance of power or the State on one hand and that of the resistance or refusal on the other."[70] It is inaccurate to insinuate that we are all complicit when the police exist to protect some and slaughter others. In acts ranging from anti-Black violence, Indigenous dispossession, and neocolonial expansion to the ways extractive capitalism exploits members of the most impoverished communities, the position of the "enemy" and the war staged against the enemy are not abstractions. This defensive rhetoric—while comforting for curators, gallerists, writers, artists, and patrons who congregate between high art and philanthropic ecologies—is in service of neoliberal capitalism, environmental destruction, and the maintenance of global white supremacy. And to miss the dynamics of oppression—particularly within a gallery show about "the police"—is baffling, but not surprising. The gallery or museum is, as I have shown throughout this book, an economic space that profits from naturalizing the ideologies of the ruling class and aestheticizing their property formations.

In the context of defining the enemy, we can see the importance of Sierra's own "NO." According to his methodology, there are no "other ways" than the eternal damnation of capitalism. However, there are those who can utter "NO." Thus far, those subjects include museum curators and himself. In this sense, Sierra is fully capable of addressing, humiliating, mocking, and subverting the enemy, which for him at one point was the Spanish state. Contrary to Marchart's claim that we are all complicit and the enemy is obscure, Sierra's "NO" campaign and his rejection of awards display how—in full disagreement with Fusco, Bishop, Kenning, Baum, and other theorists—some are able to identify the enemy and address him accordingly. The enemy is unified. They will not reveal their symbolic price. They will not abide by the instructions of another manager, they will say "NO." They are shielded from humiliation, from its circulation and propertizing forces. The performance of wealth is the lived reality of their "NO." For these reasons and others, Sierra makes the critique of capitalism into its advertisement, filled with persons he has stated he does not need to negotiate with but, under the rhetoric and tutelage of capitalism, can exploit to fulfill his will.

## Art against the Artist

Kenning posits that Sierra is ultimately interested in a "new" kind of aesthetic practice, situating "the artist as a present absence rather than an absent presence."[71] This practice, as demonstrated in chapter 2 and throughout this book, is an old one in which ideas prevail over materials—as in the case of the found object. In our contemporary moment, the artist is analogous to the head of a company, removed from both the notion of the object and its material laborer. In contemporary finance, the creation of financialized products and the transfer of risk for profit are the most highly prized forms of immaterial labor and must be valued as such; the same logic applies to the arts.[72] The artist, while compensated as such, now exists as the beholder of immateriality. Regardless of the artist's material presence, his ideas will be manifested. Kenning continues, about Sierra's work, "In displacing the action from the artist's own body to the bodies of others, Sierra thereby takes part in the more general move away from individual interiority as embodied by the artist—the authenticity of the artist's suffering flesh—*towards the elimination of the physical presence of the artist who now becomes an absent director or organizer, operating 'behind the scenes.'*"[73] After the death of the author rises his omnipresence. This is the aestheticization of displacement—the corporate and state practices of dispossession aestheticized—and it displays the commitment of the arts to capital's imagination and financial logic.

The death of the author before the death of copyright, patrons, galleries, and agents is not a useful contradiction; it is not one that can be struggled with and against to reach a more open and socialist future. Rather, this death is a capitalist fallacy grounded in white supremacist denials of property formations. As long as there is an author collecting payments as the author, depositing it into an account labeled with that author's name, building a career under that author's name, why must we continue to pretend there is no author? But more pivotal than mere payment, as long as the author remains separated from and above the producer, the "death" of the author is simply the rise of the CEO.

In 2010, Iraqi American artist Wafaa Bilal performed . . . *and Counting*, a work in which the artist's body was tattooed in a gallery in New York City. Scholar Ronak Kapadia describes the performance: "The artist transforms his body into a canvas by tattooing the names of Iraqi cities on his back, and then, during a twenty-four-hour live performance, tattooing 105,000 dots onto this borderless map as audience members stand as witnesses while a select few solemnly recite the names of Iraqis and Americans killed in the U.S. occupation since 2003. Five thousand dots are marked first in red ink to represent dead American soldiers. The remaining 100,000 dots, meant to memorialize the 'official' Iraqi death toll from the war, are in ultraviolet ink, invisible unless viewed under a black light. . . . Bilal's piece asks its audience whose death 'counts' in times of war."[74] Through his body, Bilal's work confronts the ongoing violence of US imperialism. His work also prompts a question that has yet to be asked about *250 cm Line*: What is the difference between the bodies of others and the body of the artist, and specifically, what is the difference between a forced tattoo (branding) and self-marking?

In . . . *and Counting*, the body of the artist is to serve as the site of suffering and revelation. The title references the impossibility of counting the victims of war, and yet the artist attempts one account. Part of the shock—the scandal, the risk—of *250 cm Line* is the element of tattooing. Tattoos signify a permanency. *250 cm Line* is not only an installation, a performance—it will remain permanently on the bodies of those who have been tattooed unless surgically removed. The tattoo represents Sierra's fetish and their risk, Sierra's ideas and their bodies, Sierra's vision and its potential permanency. This is also the awe of . . . *and Counting*. Through the form of the tattoo, Bilal asks viewers to consider most intimately the possibilities of living amid war, the materiality of the death count, the pain of remembering the dead, and more. Bilal's performance takes up commemorative tattooing, and situates his body as the archive. In contrast, how would one describe the tattooing in *250 cm Line*?

Forced tattooing is often most associated with Nazi concentration camps and with branding as practiced by enslavers. Numbers were placed onto prisoners and enslaved persons to mark their dispossession and objecthood. As the reification of dispossession, to brand a person is the marking of genocide. In contrast, commemorative and ritual tattooing is often associated with memorialization and particularity. The individual partakes in the memorialization of life, death, and love as permanently as we know how. From survivors of cancer or domestic violence to young lovers, the commemorative tattoo carries a deep sense of importance for the individual and the community, as well as potentially for everyone who sees the marking.[75] The individual self-wounds to self-mark their body as an act of reclamation, insight, or collective belonging. Commemorative tattoos situate an individuated manifestation of the desire to possess one's body. The overlapping quality between enforced branding or tattooing and commemorative tattoos is, as Andreas Kitzmann writes, that the latter are "wounds nevertheless."[76]

The historical context and politics of tattooing is vital to discussing *250 cm Line*. The six day laborers have been systematically and violently cornered into the framework in which Sierra seeks to exploit them. Explaining that they had a choice to be *wounded* is akin to reasoning that living in abject poverty is their doing. The absence of a *no* is not the presence of a *yes*. Additionally, Sierra's refusal to barter and negotiate with anyone who has said no to him must always be remembered; he will not fight with museum curators or directors—a recurring theme for white artists. How then do we analyze the marking, the wounding, of someone else's body?

The *250 cm Line* tattoo was not a self-wound. It was Sierra's wound, which is what he considers his art, and is circulated and sold as such.

In Sierra's oeuvre, we can trace the colonial logic of whiteness as property, scientific management, and the avant-garde. From a distance Sierra manages his "workers." His ideas and his brand—not his body, not the object—are prized morsels in the operations. In . . . *and Counting*, the body of the artist does not fall into avant-garde divisions of "mind" and "hand." The artist is not the manager of outsourced labor; the work of art is not naturalized as being removed from ideas. Bilal utilizes his body to clarify his commitment to his practice. This, too, can be interpreted within the fold of modernism, as modernist art has highly acclaimed individuated acts of suffering and expression, but I would assert that Bilal's work spills outside of modernist notions of individual sacrifice. Bilal does not usurp the position of power and authority in this manifestation of his art. Unlike Sierra, Bilal does not *become* the colonialist in his efforts to critique US imperialism. Bilal's back demonstrates how he is neither colonialist nor victim. His body is a cartography of all that remains unspoken, forsaken, and forgotten. On him, the dead will remain commemorated. They are made into him and, in him, unforgettable. Kapadia emphasizes how it is Bilal's body that situates the power of the work. He writes, "The source of this affective connection is the artist's own skin. . . . While this performance is surely a visual experience for his audience, it is only through the tactile—where we are asked to confront Bilal's body in pain—that this affective relation to past histories is drawn."[77] Bilal's body becomes the portal into the histories and presents conjured up by his performance. He is there, and thus we are asked to be there. His body does not serve as the conclusion, as the site of *better art, better politics*, but as the space from which we might imagine other questions, other frameworks, other emotions, the shard in which we might consider something other than that which we already know.

The people in *250 cm Line*—unnamed and made invisible yet marked and priced—become the reasons I cannot move beyond them to witness Sierra's vision. If Santiago Sierra chooses bodies as material because he feels they are the truest material to work with, he fails because their presence could never create an absence. Their surveilled presence becomes the antithesis to aestheticized property, which is to say, their abstractions.[78]

Sierra's oeuvre is part of the tradition of the white avant-garde examined throughout this book. Currently, he is one of many commercial artists, such as Vanessa Beecroft, Thomas Hirschhorn, Francis Alÿs, and

Renzo Martens, whose practice revolves around exploiting others. Sierra, however, more so than his contemporaries, and with the aid of prominent art historians, has refined his rhetorical defense of exploitation. After almost three decades of subcontracted pointless tasks and a global "NO" tour, together with the history of similar approaches, we can conclude that neoliberal aesthetics cannot shock the viewer into a critique of capitalism or a refined understanding of exploitation, much less into revolution—at most, it succeeds in keeping its own subgenre alive. Perhaps it is time to take seriously Sierra's insistence that he is not capable of producing anything other than capitalism by rejecting his work and his approach, along with all celebrations of neoliberal aesthetics and their predecessor forms.

CODA

# On Inoperation and Glory

Mother, they write poems. **Paul Celan, *Wolfsbohne/Wolf's Bean,* translated by Michael Hamburger**

In an interview with Ezra Klein, Facebook's former artist-in-residence Jenny Odell explains recent efforts to collect contemporary art by touching lightly on cofounder and former CEO of Gap Inc. Don Fisher's donation of his personal collection to the San Francisco Museum of Modern Art (SFMOMA).[1] With no critical commentary, Odell celebrates the processes by which contemporary art becomes amassed. Noting that, before SFMOMA, much of Fisher's collection lived at Gap's corporate headquarters in San Francisco,[2] Odell uses Fisher as an example of a contemporary enthusiast and educated patron and of how art continues to be protected during our times.[3] Odell does not discuss how Fisher came to be a collector, how he financed his collection, or the various ways in which Gap unmakes communities and lives in the name of profit.[4] It is assumed that collecting and showcasing art is inherently a gesture of public good will.[5] It is even implied that this gesture should be admired and, whenever possible, duplicated.

It is, however, the case that Fisher's donation follows the formula of racial capitalism traced throughout this book: through primitive accumulation, a wealth transfer occurs from the public to a private individual or enterprise; with this wealth, he or the enterprise begins a collection of objects. I utilize the term *personal collection museum* throughout this book to be explicitly clear that certain objects *end up* in the museum (or become one themselves) through the euphemisms *patronage* (dispossession) and *donation* (expropriation). As an individual's collection grows, so do his plans for its immortalization and the immortalization of his name—

results that are seen as interchangeable. Through his stature and wealth, his personal collection enters permanently into a preexisting museum archive (in the case of Fisher, the Arensbergs, the Sacklers, and many others), or he builds a space called the museum for its maintenance (in the case of Henry Clay Frick, Gertrude Vanderbilt Whitney, Eli Broad, and many others).[6] *We* are to be grateful to him and his relatives for leaving us with his accumulation of art things. His ideas for aesthetics are to remain.

In analyzing the remnants of transition, the things that continue from one European dynasty to the other, Giorgio Agamben presses upon the notion of "the kingdom and the glory." He states that what continues to persist in the dynamics of power is the desire for something *even more*. Of their transference, Agamben asks, "Why does power need glory? . . . What is the relation between economy and Glory?"[7] This is the framework I have turned to in order to question the shifts between aesthetic styles and tastes and to understand the relationship between forms of desired aesthetics and power.

In this vein, I turn to a line from the poet Paul Celan. Celan lived in a German-speaking region of Romania, which, when he was born in 1920, was part of the Austro-Hungarian Empire. He spent his formative years in Nazi-enforced ghettos and then in labor camps. As the sole survivor of his family, he wrote often about the tensions of a mother tongue. Though German was the language he would publish in throughout his life, Celan noted that it was the language of his family's murderers. It was the language he wrote in, and it was an alienated language, an alienating language.

It wasn't simply that he and his mother shared a language with her executioners; Celan ruminated on aesthetic planes. In the long poem *Wolfsbohne* (translated as *Wolf's Bean*), he states, "Mother, no one / interrupts when the murderers talk. / Mother, they write poems."[8] *They write poems* encapsulates much that has been woven through this book. *They*, the enemy, the colonizers, the fascists, *write*, share, partake, build, make *poems*, art forms that seem so primary and, perhaps, sacred. *They write poems* is both matter of fact and full of surprise, discovery, and surrender. In *Anarchism Is Not Enough*, Laura Riding considers that people often write poetry to feel upper class or exceptional.[9] Celan besieges this exceptionalist narrative concerning art. Art is not sacred, exclusive—it does not make one better or human. It certainly cannot make one antifascist. Art is not a straightforward entrance into liberation, but a pathway into usurped and enforced forms of power. This is both devastation and a matter of fact: *They write poems*.

In the discourse of liberal humanism, aesthetics is often gestured toward as the signification of humanity. Hence, anthropologists and art historians look at cave drawings, sculptures, and pottery as markers of civilization. In science fiction, art becomes the test of the human against the potential other: clones and artificial intelligences are asked to *make art* to prove their worth. This gesture spans into colonization. On the one hand, art and poetry are proof of *humanity*—how many films, stories, are there about the marginalized individual who is secretly a great poet and is thus able to elevate her life? And in these stories, what of everyone who remains not a poet, by selection or structural design? On the other hand, *they write poems.* Thus, what would it be to take most seriously the politics of art institutions, aesthetic forms, and their ideologies? And what would it take to consider art and poetry not as inherent goods but as forms recognized in power?

The architecture of Celan's work presents us with the complexities and possibilities of aesthetics. It simultaneously asks whether people who practice art can do so as an extension of preestablished ideologies *and* whether poetry has ever been enclosure.

## Artist: Manager, Worker, Traitor

To return to the underexamined and overdetermined realm considered outside of "art" and "the artist," I turn once more to the function of the worker. In theorizing the relationship between artist and worker, Julia Bryan-Wilson opens her book *Art Workers: Radical Practice in the Vietnam Era* with an anonymous letter from 1969.[10] The letter powerfully states, "We must support the Revolution by bringing down our part of the system and clearing the way for change. This action implies total dissociation of art making from capitalism. . . . Signed 'An art worker.'" Bryan-Wilson writes that the group that penned the letter advocated for a system where "*art work* is no longer confined to describing aesthetic methods, acts of making, or art objects—the traditional referents of the term—but is implicated in artists' collective working conditions, the demolition of the capitalist art market, and even revolution."[11] And in this vein, she concludes the book by describing a performance that I wish to analyze with a contemporary comparison. She writes:

> On November 14, 1969, the day of a nationwide anti-Vietnam War moratorium, members of GAAG [Guerilla Art Action Group] dumped

> red liquid on the lobby floor of the Whitney. The artists then produced sponges and mops and began furiously to scrub the bloodied floors, intentionally spreading the crimson pigment as far as possible. GAAG's laborers were accompanied by two scripted lines of dialogue, which they muttered as their hands became stained with fake blood: "We've got to clean this place up. This place is a mess from the war." In so doing, they castigated the museum for its failure to respect a nationwide anti-war moratorium. . . .
>
> By making a mockery of cleaning, they visibly *worked* at dirtying the floors. It was a performance inflected with gendered labor, to be sure . . . but their alignment with labor only went so far. When a Whitney worker approached them to ask what their demands were and identified himself as part of the repair and maintenance team, someone in GAAG replied, "That's not enough, we want to see an official representative of the museum." They waited until the director of public relations came to take their leaflet, and then they abandoned their buckets and rags and left the museum, leaving a wide swath of shiny, slippery liquid for the cleanup crew. This refusal to deal with the worker who would be responsible for cleaning up their mess exemplifies the frequently tense affiliation between the artists' identifications as art workers and the "actual" working class. Such a contradiction demonstrates the vexed nature of artistic labor *as labor* in this moment.[12]

While I admire in many respects the art workers' manifesto and believe we need more legible critiques of museums, war, and capitalism, theirs is a liberal idealization of radical politics. The differentiation between them and the worker is one that they did not create, yet which, through stratification, they embody, as their interaction with "nonofficial representatives" replicates the hierarchies of the systems they publicly claimed to have opposed.

In connection with this protest, I quote the comments of Naeem Mohaiemen and Hans Haacke on their attempt to negotiate the working conditions at Guggenheim Abu Dhabi in 2011 on behalf of the Gulf Labor Coalition:

> One of the radical moves artists can make is to challenge the conditions under which institutions exhibit their work. But why do such tangible demands get bracketed as posturing, while *metaphoric confrontations* are celebrated? Defiance is welcomed when it is sanctioned and staged as art. Drill a crater in the floor, flood a gallery, embalm an animal, smash

> an object, stage a pitiful death—critics hail these gestures as having the power to "shape worlds." But when artists sit down at a conference table with museum administrators and read from a list of demands for labor rights, this work—involving conversation, negotiation, research, protest—suddenly becomes illegible to the same museum. The artists whose projects were previously praised as stretching boundaries are now tagged as maverick spoilers.[13]

Mohaiemen and Haacke illustrate the ongoing contradiction highlighted by the GAAG artists and their refusal to engage with a maintenance worker. I would counter that defiance is welcomed in the museum space because defiance has been the narrative of artistic development; defiance is the sheen of capital-*A* art. The museum space is a concentrated vacuum for metaphoric defiances—such acts have never been gestures of radical violence, worker solidarity, or even critique of the artist subject.

Similarly to GAAG's "performance," yet more subtly, Mohaiemen and Haacke confirm a tradition of museum art and institutional critique that has collapsed performance and protest. They seem to be surprised that their protest was not accepted as part of their aesthetic oeuvre. In the GAAG "protest," we can see how a protest that fundamentally affirms a division of labor that's been historically accepted as part of art history is recorded subsequently as art. In the case of the Guggenheim, we see how protesting the working conditions and the context of racial violence affirmed in erecting the structure of the museum space is not only derelict, but illegible as an "artistic" claim. Strikes that contest property, that defy the space being constructed as the "owners" see fit, will not be accepted as aesthetic, as they threaten the very ideological foundations of its existence.

Depending on their stratification, the artist often occupies a range of hazy functions. As in, unbeknownst to anyone, they could be the sole laborer, the sole manager, audience, and patron. Equally, the artist could also be the laborer of another artist as a wage worker, in the form of artist assistants. The artist could also be the manager, the CEO. Because work and labor continue to be mystified in the realm of aesthetic production, and aesthetic creation, the work, worker, and property remain mystified.

Additionally, Mohaiemen and Haacke's commentary illuminates how the category of artist becomes incapacitated when the protest is no longer metaphorical. When artists identify not with the museum director and managers—no longer speaking and interacting only with them—but instead collaborate against them and with others, then artists are no longer afforded the protection of the museum space. To address labor conditions, to work through the dynamics of exploitation as they unfold—these are the concerns of illegible nonsubjects, not the artist subject. I would argue that artists who partake in such protests are not merely witnessed as "maverick spoilers" but as traitors to the agreed upon limits of their critique. Institutional critique as grounded in liberalist discourse may offer only metaphorical gestures—paint on the ground—and must exit before *others* show up to clean up its mess.

## Those Inoperative—

Suppose that, instead of the "art workers" and their dumping of paint onto museum floors as antiwar art, it is the museum worker's inquiry that's examined as an experiment in rupture. Suppose that, instead of the artists' appearance and disappearance from the museum as the scene of emphasis, it is the bodies of those who appear after, to clean the space, that situate something more powerful than the "art workers" imagined. Suppose their bodies, their lives, span from workers, unrecorded, illegible, into something else. Suppose the project is not an expansion of the category of art, still preserved for the artist, but the expansion of art for those outside the artist subject—and more.

Instead of artists engaging in a memorialized protest for art documentation, suppose that illegible impressions become an aesthetics we have yet to fathom. Aesthetic categorizations would not absolve such actions from an analysis of race and land relations, as aesthetic categorizations are not shields against politics or analyses. They are, however, forms of categorizations cultivated as deserving protection and care. Even when the artifacts (their performances) disappear or are destroyed—as with the art workers and their performance strikes—we seemingly work to preserve their version of the narrative.

So suppose we tend to that which remains unconsidered, theorized as an aesthetic commons.[14] Suppose, too, such aims are not sanctified; it is an ideal in need of protection and inquiry. Publics from all over the universe arrive to tend to and preserve this manifestation; how else might it grow? The aesthetic collection then is not one room, one building, one space, but the unforgettable lives impressed and submerged so deep within us that we have forgotten—and below that. How can we but remember?[15]

Rather than glorifying the invention of the Bessemer process and the Whitney cotton gin, the formation of Carnegie Steel, and the innovation of profit, this project looks in the direction of Aimé Césaire:

> Eia for those who never invented anything
> for those who never explored anything
> for those who never conquered anything
> but yield, captivated, to the essence of things . . .
> indifferent to conquering, but playing the game of the world.[16]

While the things we have been given reflect all that has and continues to be lost, the absence of those who never invented or conquered anything remains. Because of this and from here, *eia*. To those inoperative, who make nothing but the world.

# NOTES

## Prelude. On Motivations

1 For historical analyses of the trajectory and systems of neoliberalism, see Wendy Brown's *Undoing the Demos: Neoliberalism's Stealth Revolution* (2015) and *In the Ruins of Neoliberalism: The Rise of Antidemocratic Politics in the West* (2019); Melinda Cooper's *Family Values: Between Neoliberalism and the New Social Conservatism* (2019); and Quinn Slobodian's *Globalists: The End of Empire and the Birth of Neoliberalism* (2018).

2 For example, venture capitalist Eli Broad (of the Broad museum, opened in 2015) worked to dismantle the teachers' union in Los Angeles. Peter James Hudson commented on this phenomenon at the Common Field conference in 2017; see Hudson, *Bankers and Empire.*

## Introduction

1 Websites such as artprice.com, artmarket.com, and liveart.io provide uninterrupted updates on price points and market trends to whoever is interested. Critics such as Gregory Sholette and Chin-tao Wu have devoted their work and practice to interrogating the function of finance within museum and gallery spaces. For an introduction to a list of artists and writers engaged in this critique, see Sholette, *Dark Matter.* Sholette examines the genealogy of artists and scholars who trace and critique finance and capital within their practice.

2 News organizations will often report the sale of an expensive artwork or cover the scandals of auction houses. However, most careful inspections of the art market are aimed at people who are already part of niche circles, and are often disregarded by the larger public.

3 This was not Safer's first review or criticism of contemporary art; a similar piece titled "Yes . . . But Is It Art?" aired on CBS in 1993, which was followed by responses by prominent art critics. See Carol Vogel, "Art World Is Not Amused by Critique," *New York Times,* October 4, 1993.

4 "Even in Tough Times, Contemporary Art Sells," *60 Minutes*, CBS News, produced by Morley Safer. For a full transcript, see https://www.cbsnews.com/news/even-in-tough-times-contemporary-art-sells/.

5 Jerry Saltz, "Jerry Saltz on Morley Safer's Facile *60 Minutes* Art-World Screed," *New York Magazine*, April 1, 2012, https://www.vulture.com/2012/04/jerry-saltz-on-morley-safer-60-minutes-art-world.html; and Roberta Smith, "Safer Looks at Art but Only Hears the Cash Register," *New York Times*, April 2, 2012, https://artsbeat.blogs.nytimes.com/2012/04/02/morley-safer-launches-a-halfhearted-salvo-in-his-war-on-the-art-world/.

6 Smith, "Safer Looks at Art."

7 "Even in Tough Times, Contemporary Art Sells."

8 I thank Doreen Lee for a conversation that led to clarifying the terms of this trajectory.

9 See Robinson, *Anthropology of Marxism*.

10 For linear historical accounts of art collecting that naturalize empire and capital in the development of the museum space, see Alsop, *Rare Art Traditions*; Pearce, *Interpreting Objects and Collections*; and Muensterberger, *Collecting*.

11 For more on this, see Bourdieu, *Distinction*.

12 Authors in INCITE! Women of Color Against Violence, *The Revolution Will Not Be Funded*, demonstrate how this phenomenon works throughout the nonprofit industrial complex.

13 Armed with this new wealth, the foundation now hosts annual prizes, from the "discovery" award for young poets to the Ruth Lilly Poetry Prize for established writers. The legend of this donation goes that Ruth Lilly—heir to Lilly pharmaceutical company—spent her life writing and trying to publish poetry. Though never published, she submitted often to *Poetry*, a magazine established in 1912 in Chicago, with a long history and modest operations budget. And for whatever reason—be it *Poetry*'s polite rejection letter or its stature in US poetry—Lilly decided to write the magazine into her will.

14 See Julia M. Klein, "A Windfall Illuminates the Poetry Field, and Its Fights," *New York Times*, November 12, 2007.

15 I thank the poet Cassandra Gillig for doing pivotal research into the history of Lilly. See Cassandra Gillig, "The Poetry Foundation, Eli Lilly, and the PIC," Out 2 Pasture (blog), February 9, 2021, https://orlandogillig.blogspot.com/2021/02/the-poetry-foundation-eli-lilly-pic.html.

16 Although the Poetry Foundation is the most powerful center for poetry in the United States, due to its endowment from Lilly pharmaceutical profits, which configures into paying more for published poetry and more prize money to emerging poets than any other organization, it turns out that this giving is arguably ungenerous, as it constitutes less than 4.5–5.5 percent of the organization's net asset value, or the precise minimum outlay required

by the government to maintain its not-for-profit status. Moreover, as documented by tax filings, the majority of its funds are invested back into the market. This phenomenon—the absolute dependence on preexisting property forms, the absolute minimal expenditure on the arts, and the absolute maximum spending on financial services—is routine for museums and literary foundations, and marks the colonial continuum in which the world resides. Thus, rather than deference toward organizations such as the Poetry Foundation for annually gifting the public with 4.5–5.5 percent of its funds, might we suggest anything but gratitude? Nothing they have is theirs. And they are barely giving. See Foundations must meet the "The Five Percent Minimum Payout Requirement" within the 12 month fiscal calendar. For the Poetry Foundation's language on its 4.5–5.5 percent giving, see *The Poetry Foundation, Financial Report, December 31, 2019*, https://assets.poetryfoundation.org/uploads/documents/128178-The-Poetry-Foundation-1219-FS-Final.pdf.

17 In thinking about the function of anti-Blackness, I particularly looked to Vargas, *Denial of Antiblackness*; Roediger, *Working Toward Whiteness*; and Kim, *Bitter Fruit*.

18 This endeavor hopes to follow the scholarship of theorists Lisa Lowe and David Lloyd's collection *The Politics of Culture in the Shadow of Culture*. They distill, "If the tendency of transnational capitalism is to commodify everything and therefore to collapse the cultural into the economic, it is precisely where labor, differentiated rather than 'abstract' is being commodified that the cultural becomes political again. . . . Culture becomes politically important where a cultural formation comes into contraction with an economic or political logic that tries to refunction it for exploitation or domination" (24). The work of materializing abstracted labor, and abstraction writ large, remains my theoretical and political aim.

19 Harris, "Whiteness as Property," 1716, 1736.

20 See Mullen, *Cracks between What We Are and What We Are Supposed to Be*, 210.

21 Jodi Kim's *Settler Garrison* and Iyko Day's *Alien Capital* are indispensable examinations of the enmeshment of racial capitalism, settler colonialism, and cultural production. Their approach to the entanglements of structures and systems has been an important guide for this project.

22 Cahan, *Mounting Frustration*.

23 Peter Monaghan, "Bloodletting over an Anthology," *Chronicle of Higher Education*, December 20, 2011, https://www.chronicle.com/blogs/pageview/bloodletting-over-an-anthology/29876.

24 Spillers, "Mama's Baby, Papa's Maybe," 60.

25 I thank Carrie Nakamura for this insight.

26 Britain's Tate Museum depended heavily on Joseph Duveen for its collection and financing. For more on Duveen and his life as an art dealer see S. N. Behrman's "The Days of Duveen," *New Yorker*, September 22, 1951;

and *Duveen: The Story of the Most Spectacular Art Dealer of All Time*. See also Brewer, *American Leonardo*.

27 In his archive, Duveen kept an exhaustive list of established and emerging personal collection museums. See Joseph Duveen Files, 2007.D.1, Box 733, Getty Research Institute, Los Angeles.

28 Foucault, "Of Other Spaces."

29 Foucault, *Archaeology of Knowledge* 1972, 129.

30 In *Transit of Empire*, Jodi Byrd delineates how "racialization and colonization should thus be understood as concomitant global systems that secure white dominance through time, property, and notions of self" (xxiii); and Goeman, in *Mark My Words*, compellingly argues, "Though the current liberal state disavows violence, both temporally, in ways that render the former as an unfortunate remnant of a violent past, and spatially, in which unjust spatial practices construct a racial and colonial distribution of property that in turn is normalized in settler cartographic languages, the material reality of these patterns nonetheless remains part of dispossessed peoples' everyday existence" (188). For Native critiques of progress and time, see Carpio, "(Un)disturbing Exhibitions"; Deloria, *God Is Red*; and Simpson's "Consent's Revenge."

31 Kauanui, "A Structure, Not an Event"; see also Ferguson, *Reorder of Things*.

32 "Yasmine knows in her hardest heart / that truth is worked and organized by some, / and she's on the wrong side always." Brand, *Ossuaries*, 53.

33 "A mild narcotic" is Freud's description of art in *Civilization and Its Discontents*, 35.

34 "So many dreams were full of prisons, / mine were without relief." Brand, *Ossuaries*, 10.

35 For critiques of the legitimations of property, see Nichols, *Theft Is Property!* For the historicization of debates and definitions of property, see Park, "History Wars and Property Law."

36 Joe Zadeh writes, "Colonialism was not just a conquest of land, and therefore space, but also a conquest of time. From South Asia to Africa to Oceania, imperialists assaulted alternative forms of timekeeping." Zadeh, "Tyranny of Time." For critical engagements with the construction of how time is understood, see Canales, *The Physicist and the Philosopher*; and Birth, *Objects of Time*.

37 DuBois, *Slaves and Other Objects*, 23.

38 Benjamin, "Theses on the Philosophy of History," 256. I thank Luis Martin-Cabrera for bringing this quote up with me during a meeting at the Getty in 2012, as it helped shape the possibility of this project.

39 Too often, coffee shop galleries, youth-run art spaces, and even the walls in homes and offices reference and mirror the space naturalized by museums and collections. Such mirroring prompts questions yet is not the focus of this chapter or book. Here, I provoke that which has been crimi-

nalized, outlawed, and almost disappeared because of the hegemonic notions of artistic expression.

40 This concern is amplified by Brian Wallis's thoughts on the work of Carrie Mae Weems, whom I discuss in this book. He writes, "If colonialism and ethnographic exploitation depend on appropriation, one must acknowledge that what is taken can always be taken back"; Wallis, "Black Bodies," 59. I find intensely seductive this notion that objects and symbols can be taken back and forth, and wonder if it is from this place that an abolitionist continuum might take shape.

41 Harris, "Whiteness as Property," 1725.

42 Kenneth Goldsmith, "I Look to Theory Only When I Realize That Somebody Has Dedicated Their Entire Life to a Question I Have Only Fleetingly Considered," Poetry Foundation, https://www.poetryfoundation.org/poetrymagazine/articles/70209/i-look-to-theory-only-when-i-realize-that-somebody-has-dedicated-their-entire-life-to-a-question-i-have-only-fleetingly-considered.

43 See Alec Wilkinson, "The Poet Who Went Too Far," *New Yorker*, July 9, 2019, http://www.newyorker.com/magazine/2015/10/05/something-borrowed-wilkinson.

44 I thank Theo Davis for this provocative question.

45 Joy James's "Womb of Western Theory" lays out how pivotal European philosophers, such as Foucault and Arendt, evaded the lives and intellectual pursuits of thinkers such as Frantz Fanon while fundamentally dependent on them, rendering them "captive maternal." James's scholarship consistently delineates how anti-Black violence becomes architecturally important to liberal democracy. Relatedly, the collection Koshy et al., *Colonial Racial Capitalism*, critically examines the dynamics between settler colonialism and racial capitalism.

46 For the colonial continuum of the financial industries, see Hudson, *Bankers and Empire*.

47 Negri and Hardt, *Multitude*.

48 Barker, "Territory as Analytic," 27.

49 Barker, "Territory as Analytic," 28.

50 I am critically taking up the understanding of "excess" put forth by Georges Bataille in *The Accursed Share: An Essay on General Economy*, which prioritizes the site of consumption as the formation of society.

51 For a contemporary study of this phenomenon, see Brown, "Logic of Settler Accumulation."

52 Harris writes, "To the conquerors, the land was 'vacant'"; and further, "the notion of vacant land belongs to Locke: the right to acquire property through labor as long as there was some 'good left in common for others' applied to the 'inland vacant places of America' (Locke, *supra* note 46, at 130, 134). Neither of these two premises is tenable." Harris, "Whiteness as Property," 1716, 1727.

53 For a searing discussion concerning the lives considered property, see Patricia Williams, "On Being the Object of Property," in Williams, *Alchemy of Race and Rights*, 216–38.

54 For Indigenous critiques of Marx and political economy, see Coulthard, "From Wards of the State to Subjects of Recognition?" See also Barker, "Corporation and the Tribe"; and Grande, "Accumulation of the Primitive."

55 For a historical discussion of this, see Rancière, *Philosopher and His Poor*.

56 Robinson, *Black Marxism*.

57 Peter James Hudson traces the ways in which the term *racial capitalism* was deployed earlier by South African scholars. This is to note that the analytic of racial capitalism remains robust and unsettled, its origins and mutations ongoing. See Peter James Hudson, "Racial Capitalism and the Dark Proletariat," *Boston Review*, February 20, 2018, https://www.bostonreview.net/forum_response/peter-james-hudson-racial-capitalism-and/

58 Du Bois, *Black Reconstruction in America*.

59 For historical and theoretical discussions of this phenomenon and trajectory, see Kelley, *Hammer and Hoe*; and Hunter, *To 'Joy My Freedom*.

60 Braverman, *Labor and Monopoly Capital*.

61 Gordon, "Disciplining as a Human Science."

62 Nazish Brohi, "Herald Exclusive: In Conversation with Gayatri Spivak," *Herald Exclusive*, December 23, 2014, https://www.dawn.com/news/1152482.

63 There is a body of work that has foregrounded the relationship between race, class, and art institutions. This includes Lawrence Levine's *Highbrow/Lowbrow: The Emergence of Cultural Hierarchy in America*; Bridget Cooks's *Exhibiting Blackness: African Americans and the American Art Museum*; Mary Ann Calo's *Distinction & Denial: Race, Nation, and the Critical Construction of the African American Artist, 1920–40*; and artist Martha Rosler's pivotal "Lookers, Buyers, Dealers, and Makers: Thoughts on Audience," which addresses the politics of artistic patronage.

64 This is Claire Bishop's framing of Santiago Sierra; see Bishop, "Antagonism and Relational Aesthetics," 79. I also discuss this framing in chapter 6.

65 See El-Tayeb, *European Others*.

66 Lowe, *Intimacies of Four Continents*, 7.

67 Lowe, *Intimacies of Four Continents*, 7.

68 Pamela Lee's groundbreaking analysis on the symptomatic relationship between modernism and the space of the militarized laboratory is most instructive in moving towards critical understandings of modernism. See Lee, *Think Tank Aesthetics*.

69 For a full accounting of the liberal history between the categories of human and freedom as constructed against the non-human and enslavement, see Lowe, *Intimacies of Four Continents*.

70 See Mullen, *Cracks Between What We Are and What We Are Supposed to Be*, 210.

71 For some literature examining racial segregation in New York, see Finkleman, *Age of Jim Crow*; Kelley, *Right to Ride*; Massey and Denton, "Dimensions of Residential Segregation"; Gellman and Quigley, *Jim Crow New York*; Bellush and David, *Race and Politics in New York City*; Kantrowitz, *Ethnic and Racial Segregation in the New York Metropolis*; Daily, *Age of Jim Crow*; Sokol, *All Eyes Are Upon Us*; L. Harris, *In the Shadow of Slavery*; and Rothstein, *Color of Law*.

72 See Lowe, *Intimacies of Four Continents*.

73 The Language poets were a group who, beginning in the 1970s, argued militantly against lyricism, in another attempt to create abstracted, whitened spaces for poetry. Members included Lyn Hejinian, Ron Silliman, Bruce Andrews, and others.

74 In "Signs Taken for Signifiers," David Marriott argues an orthodox Marxist analysis to language as production will no longer suffice when examining contemporary finance and poetics. He writes, "The speed of financial speculation, which has transformed the world into a single global day, is fundamentally based on communication and not on production" (340).

75 Quoted in Férez Kuri, *Brion Gysin*, 153.

76 This isn't to suggest that poetry spheres are without funding sources, as the poetry market could consist of the operations of prizes and residencies (witness the Poetry Foundation's inheritance of Lilly pharmaceutical company stock, and how this funding source altered twenty-first-century poetry organizations).

77 For example, and perhaps in a different vein, Tristan Tzara advocated for the "found poem" in the early 1910s.

78 See "Signs Taken for Signifiers," 340.

79 I derive "killjoys" from Ahmed, "Feminist Killjoys (And Other Willful Subjects)."

80 See the arguments made in Spieker, *Big Archive*; and Buchloh, "Conceptual Art 1962–1969."

81 I draw the concept of the aestheticization of politics from Walter Benjamin's statement, "This is the situation of politics which Fascism is rendering aesthetic." Benjamin, "Work of Art in the Age of Mechanical Reproduction," in *Illuminations*, 244.

82 For a discussion of the "dark matter" of the art industry, see Sholette, *Dark Matter*.

83 Portending a 2004 survey for the Turner Prize that named Duchamp's urinal as the most influential work of modern art, in 2001, *The Principles of Scientific Management* was voted as the most influential management book of the twentieth century by the Academy of Management.

84 In *Playing in the Dark*, Toni Morrison argues powerfully that race is central, and not tertiary, to literature and literary analysis. In *The Other Side of Terror*, Erica Edwards demonstrates how Black feminist writers pushed back and against the strictures of both US literary formation and US empire.

85 Vora and Atanasoski, *Surrogate Humanity*.

86 Joselit, "NFTS, or The Readymade Reversed," 3.

87 Joselit, "NFTS, or The Readymade Reversed," 4.

88 See Lowe, *Intimacies of Four Continents*.

89 Those analyzed in chapter 6 include Claire Bishop's and Coco Fusco's affirmative scholarship of Sierra's practice.

90 See Brown, *Repeating Body*.

91 Spivak, "Can the Subaltern Speak?"

92 Grace Kyungwon Hong uses "messiness" in *Ruptures of American Capital* to describe how theorists often treat racial dynamics.

93 Angela Davis articulates that *radical* means "grasping things at the roots." Davis, *Women, Race and Class*, 14.

## Chapter 1. Personal Collection and the Museum Form: Racial Capitalism, Settler Colonialism, and the Legacies of the Homestead Strike of 1892

1 Crawford, *Atlas of AI*.

2 Barker, "Territory as Analytic," 28. For translations of the river names, see *The Lenape Talking Dictionary*, https://www.talk-lenape.org/. Settler and missionary accounts also described "Allegheny" as coming from the Lenape language; see Heckewelder and Reichel, "Names Which the Lennie Lennape or Delaware Indians Gave to Rivers, Streams and Localities."

3 Stewart, *Names on the Land*.

4 See *The Lenape Talking Dictionary*.

5 Jeannette Bastian writes about the webpage "Flowers for Homestead" at the website Practical History (accessed in 2008 and no longer available), which displayed a photograph of flowers placed outside Dulwich Picture Gallery in London in July 2000, when a talk on Henry Clay Frick's art collection was scheduled to take place there; the website stated: "How easy it is to buy a place in posterity, so long as you can pay the asking price. The stories of the great cultural benefactors—the Fricks, Carnegies and Tates—rarely ask about the origins of their wealth. . . . But our memories are not for sale. For us Frick will always be remembered for his role in the Homestead strike in 1892 when he employed armed company

goons to shoot workers at the Carnegie Steel Company." Bastian, "Flowers for Homestead," 114.

6 Burgoyne, *Homestead Strike of 1892*.

7 In 1882, Carnegie "bought a half interest in the Frick Coke Company for $1.5 million." Burgoyne, *Homestead Strike of 1892*, 8. This would be more than $47 million today.

8 There are 35,000 active museums in the United States. See Christopher Ingraham, "There Are More Museums in the U.S. than There Are Starbucks and McDonalds—Combined," *Washington Post*, June 13, 2014, https://www.washingtonpost.com/news/wonk/wp/2014/06/13/there-are-more-museums-in-the-us-than-there-are-starbucks-and-mcdonalds-combined/.

9 While writing fairly critically about the ways in which previous labor historians have centralized the strike, Jonathan Rees concludes that "even though the fate of unionism in this industry was already sealed, Carnegie's reversal of his earlier policy towards the Amalgamated Association still made the Homestead lockout a major turning point in American labor history." Rees, "Homestead in Context," 530.

10 Braddock, *Collecting as Modernist Practice*, 2.

11 Stone, "Origins of Job Structures," 27–28; Krause, *Battle for Homestead*. Paul Krause writes, "The lockout crushed the largest trade union in America, the AAISW [Amalgamated Association of Iron and Steel Workers], and it wrecked the lives of its most devoted members. Marking the end to what John Fitch described in the Pittsburgh Survey as a decades-long struggle for control of the city's steel mills, the victory at Homestead gave Carnegie and his fellow steelmasters carte blanche in the administration of their works. The lockout put 'the employers in the saddle'-precisely where they would remain, without union interference, for four decades" (13).

12 See Stone, "Origins of Job Structures": "Frick was already notorious for his brutal treatment of strikers in the Connellsville coke regions" (27).

13 There were limited laws concerning insider trading at this moment. Thus, his rags to riches narrative needs to be revised. See Standiford, *Meet You in Hell*.

14 In *The Gospel of Wealth*, published in 1889, Carnegie argued for the redistribution of wealth, made pro-business arguments for unions, and remained consistent in public interviews by stating that socialism was the inevitable future. And Carnegie told the *New York Times*, "I believe that socialism is the grandest theory ever presented, and I am sure some day it will rule the world. Then we will have attained the millennium." Quoted in Krause, *Battle for Homestead*, 235.

15 "Carnegie had the greater concern—a passionate concern—for his public image, which he was willing to maintain through duplicity, if necessary." Burgoyne, *Homestead Strike of 1892*, 314.

16 Stone, "Origins of Job Structures," 61.

17 Tremendous work by historians has been devoted to prying open Frick and Carnegie's economic rationale against unions as unjust and contradictory. Yes, steel prices had been and were in flux, as with all other metals and extracted goods. However, Carnegie's strategy thus far had been predicated on the economics of the depression, as he seized the steel industry through depressed steel prices. Because of the Depression, steel prices had been low, but they could not remain this way forever. Additionally, for all discussions regarding profitability and the loss of profits that might occur due to the set minimum, the Carnegie Steel company had netted an average profit of $4 million (approximately $110 million today) throughout 1889–92.

18 Much has been written about written about how the ruse of meritocracy, or the ethic of "hard work," is antithetical to economic precarity, such as in Weber's *The Protestant Ethic and the Spirit of Capitalism* and Markovits's *The Meritocracy Trap.*

19 What Carnegie and Frick sought to break had actually been their previous doing. In 1888, during negotiations with Amalgamated Steel, Carnegie demanded that the wage system be pegged to the market price of steel, arguing that such a dynamic would ensure better investment from all involved parties and grow the "partnership." Thus the backdrop of the 1892 strike was the successful strike of 1889. The central contentions of the 1882 strike were the wage system and shift duration. On those points, the striking union reached an amicable agreement. By 1892, Carnegie and Frick had decided to eliminate the previously agreed upon union contract and break the union at the mill in its entirety. Contracts made during 1882 were to expire by June of 1892, and by April 30 of that year, Frick, as part of the new terms, demanded that all of the workers sign individual contracts, effectively deunionizing the plant. The workers at Homestead did not foresee this development of bad faith. When the workers realized their negotiations for wages were part of a scheme to wholly shut down the union, they organized a strike, which began on June 30, 1892. See Krause, *Battle for Homestead*, 232.

20 In the summer of 1892 Carnegie left for his vacation home in Scotland amid contract negotiations with the workers, which had begun earlier that year in January. Carnegie and Frick were in correspondence and agreement about their plans to break the union. See Krause, *Battle for Homestead*, 302–6.

21 "10:30, three hundred employees of the Pinkerton National Detective Agency hired by the Carnegie Steel Company arrived by rail in Bellevue, near Davis Island Dam, about five miles down the Ohio River from Pittsburgh." Krause, *Battle for Homestead*, 15. For a history of the hiring of Pinkertons, see also Danver, *Revolts, Protests, Demonstrations, and Rebellions.*

22 Krause, *Battle for Homestead*, 27. There's much to say on the historical strike suppression deployed by Frick and Carnegie before Homestead. Burgoyne discusses that "Mr. Frick had several serious strikes to contend with. His plan of campaign was always the same—to crush the strikers by main force and make no concessions. The Coal and Iron police, an organization of watchmen maintained under a state law, the drilled and armed watchmen of the Pinkerton detective agency, and the state militia were pressed into service as the occasion demanded, and the shedding of blood and sacrifice of human life resulted on more than one occasion." Burgoyne, *Homestead Strike of 1892*, 9. Refusing to negotiate with workers and the deployment of violence had been part of Frick and Carnegie's practices in the past.

23 Krause, *Battle for Homestead*, 357.

24 See Krause, *Battle for Homestead*, 162, 353.

25 Krause, *Battle for Homestead*, 157. Note that the sale of bad steel to the US Navy came out through the hearing, and the Carnegie Company was charged a fine, not with treason.

Strikes had been adjudicated as criminal conspiracies as early as the 1870s. As Krause recounts, "Employers grounded their attack against the right to organize in a series of judicial rulings based on Pennsylvania's anticonspiracy laws and the common law tradition that defined a conspiracy as any combination of two or more persons who sought to accomplish a criminal purpose. . . . Largely because of this tradition, unions in Pennsylvania found themselves without formal legal sanction into the 1870s" (*Battle for Homestead*, 157). Krause elaborates, "As the *Journal of United Labor* put it: 'The fact remains that working men in Pennsylvania are . . . liable to arrest and trial for simply organizing.' The *Journal*'s point captured the essential meaning of the anticonspiracy law: it was a vehicle for defenders of corporate rights, and of the state, which privileged these rights, for solving the problem of coercion in the most efficient way, that is, by minimizing its use" (159). This legal precedent was pushed by Carnegie and Frick's lawyer, Knox; see Krause, *Battle for Homestead*, 26.

26 Krause, *Battle for Homestead*, 12. Emphasis mine.

27 Veblen, *Theory of the Leisure Class.*

28 Veblen, *Theory of the Leisure Class.*

29 Williams, *Marxism and Literature.*

30 Davis, *Life in the Iron Mills*, 12.

31 Henry Clay Frick, letter to Andrew Carnegie, July 4 1892, University of Pittsburgh, Henry Clay Frick Business Records, 1862–1987, 701, AIS.2002.06. Emphasis mine.

32 Benjamin, "Critique of Violence."

33 Benjamin, "Critique of Violence," 279.

34 Benjamin," Critique of Violence," 281.

35 Three men died at Homestead from machine injuries between September 19, 1891, and September 26, 1891, and another died in April 1892. All incidents were reported in issue no. 16, of the *National Labor Tribune*, April 9, 1892.

36 Davis, *Life in the Iron Mills*, 50.

37 Davis, *Life in the Iron Mills*, 50

38 Davis, *Life in the Iron Mills*, 50.

39 "The battle for Homestead had thus become a battle over conflicting property rights." Krause, *Battle for Homestead*, 313.

40 See Krause, *Battle for Homestead*, 162, 353.

41 For the note to Sheriff McCleary, see Krause, *Battle for Homestead*, 313.

42 In particular, many of the sources I consulted did not discuss Black workers nor the anti-Black riots. As pivotal as Katherine Stone's work on the 1892 strike and union has been to my understanding of union busting, she does not mention the anti-Black riots. Neither does Jeannette Bastian's pivotal work "Flowers for Homestead," nor Jonathan Rees's "Homestead in Context," nor the encyclopedia edited by Steven Laurence Danver, *Revolts, Protests, Demonstrations, and Rebellions*. And in Edward Baptist's podcast *American Capitalism: A History*, in the episode titled "Henry Frick and the Homestead Strike," Black workers and anti-Black riots are not mentioned. The first time I learned of this was in Paul Krause's *Battle for Homestead*. In the subsequent sources that I have come across that mention anti-Blackness or Black workers, Krause is cited.

43 After the event, Hugh O'Donnell, first chairman of the advisory committee for the Homestead Workers, recommended surrender. O'Donnell stated to his colleagues, "This attempted assassination of Mr. Frick, you know, has created a bad impression all over the country, and for the sake of the men, I would recommend an almost unconditional surrender." Krause, *Battle for Homestead*, 355–56.

44 The only visible and legible support of the assassination was from a member of the National Guard. See Krause, *Battle for Homestead*, 3.

45 Beverly Gage writes, "Especially for anarchists, this was one of the goals of political violence: to dramatize the deep conflicts at work in American society, to make it impossible for the nation to avoid questions of social and industrial justice.... They understood radical violence as an important factor in American class relations, even if historians have not always done the same." Gage, "Why Violence Matters," 107. While it would be a mistake to claim simple solutions to structural injustice, it would also be a mistake to continually obscure the process in which class disparities flourish. Narrative clarification concerning capitalist violence is indispensable, as too often they are obscured for the maintenance of ongoing exploitation. While even the suggestion of Frick's assassination (or any) may leave some with a bitter taste—such is the very purpose of mythic violence—such reactions would not negate Gage's argument. Berkman's political

violence is a moment of dramatization: it demands society reckon with the distance between owner and worker; it questions the fallacy of singular ownership; it wonders how easy or how difficult it would be to unravel the fiction of capitalist hierarchies and confronts one possible conclusion.

46 In terms of the contradictions between radical violence and union strikes, Gage has posited that while US union strikes have been distinctly violent—most often in the form of violence against workers or workers protecting themselves from the violence of state and private militia—unions have refused association and participation with radical violence. Such tendencies have led historians to argue that US unions have disengaged from ideological conflicts. Gage writes, "Within these conflicts, violence on the part of employers and police far outnumbered any sort of violence committed by workers or union members." Gage, "Why Violence Matters," 104; see also 99.

47 Gage, "Why Violence Matters," 107.

48 Krause discusses the intra-ethnic solidarity among immigrant groups at Homestead.

49 In a speech at the 1927 National Interracial Conference calling for the integration of Black laborers into unions, Philip Randolph openly spoke on this issue, stating that a desegregated union policy was the only way "the superstition and belief in the mind of the white worker that the Negro is a natural scab, a strikebreaker, and that he is trying to pull down the standards of life built up by organized labor" could be eradicated. Quoted in Magat, *Unlikely Partners*, 80–81. From the 1890s well into the 1920s, Black workers were viewed as the "enemy of unionized workers." Relatedly, on the historical labor segregation of Black workers, Richard Magat writes, "Barred from crafts, trade unions, and apprenticeships by the hostility of southern white workers, steered away from industrial employment, reliant on cotton plantation culture and its farm tenancy and peonage, blacks in large numbers began to move north. Although an 1890 resolution of the American Federation of Labor (AFL) opposed exclusion of persons from unions because of race and color, exclusion was a fact. Ten years later the AFL endorsed organizing blacks in separate unions, which the organization would then admit." Magat, *Unlikely Partners*, 78. It is important to note that by 1885 Asians were also excluded, and the organization supported the Chinese Exclusion Act of 1882.

50 Magat writes, "However, by the 1890s, the ascendant AFL, led by the narrow Gompers, focused on the need to protect skilled jobs and generally saw poor Blacks, whom corporations occasionally recruited as scabs, as the enemies of unionized workers." Magat, *Unlikely Partners*, 80.

51 I thank archivist Ryan Henderson at Rivers of Steel in Pittsburgh for pointing me to this vital historical context. See Dickerson, *Out of the Crucible*; Bodnar, Simon, and Weber, *Lives of Their Own*; and Hinshaw, *Steel and Steelworkers*.

52 Davis, *Life in the Iron Mills*, 28.

53 Krause, *Battle for Homestead*, 346.

54 See Benjamin, "Critique of Violence," 295.

55 Krause, *Battle for Homestead*, 250.

56 Krause writes, "O'Donnell, never one for rhetorical bluff, said as much: 'We can't fight the state of Pennsylvania, and even if we could, we cannot fight the United States government.'" Krause, *Battle for Homestead*, 334.

57 "The employment of black workers by Carnegie Steel effectively marked a new era in the labor practices of the steel industry. In their effort to defeat the Sons of Vulcan in the lockout of 1874–75, owners had hired black puddlers from Richmond, Virginia. But it was not until July 1892, in Homestead, that large numbers of black workers began to enter the steel mills of the industrial North. And the violence that greeted them there was the beginning of a pattern that would endure across the country for decades. Superintendent Potter, in an immediate attempt to lessen tensions among the new workers, promised to build separate housing facilities for the 'coloreds.'" Krause, *Battle for Homestead*, 346.

58 See Robinson, *Black Marxism*; and Du Bois, *Black Reconstruction in America*. Krause discusses how some of the Homestead strikers would go on to organizing against immigrants and would work on anti-immigrant legislation for politicians—odd, as there were no immigrant aggressors in the Homestead strike, other than Carnegie, the Scottish immigrant. Krause, *Battle for Homestead*, 297.

59 With regards to this dynamic, Magat refers to the prescient words of the AFL's Randolph in 1927: "As long as you have great masses of people competing in the industrial field for jobs, in the relationship of organized and unorganized, there will naturally grow up bitterness; it would be inevitable even if both groups were white, but when you have one group black and the other group white, there is the additional element of color and race which makes it all the more intense and antagonistic and hostile. So that by way of remedying this whole question of race relations, if we are able to bring the Negro workers into the general field of organized labor and break down the superstition and belief in the mind of the white worker that the Negro is a natural scab, a strikebreaker, and that he is trying to pull down the standards of life built up by organized labor, then you are going to remove that feeling of antagonism in the mind of the white worker toward the Negro worker, and he is going to feel that here we have a common interest, common struggle, a common cause." Quoted in Magat, *Unlikely Partners*, 80–81.

60 In *Hammer and Hoe: Alabama Communists during the Great Depression*, Robin D. G. Kelley tracks Black communist and labor organizing during the 1930s and 1940s, the period after the Wagner Act and the deunionization of Carnegie and Frick plants. Suffice it to say that the narrative of

Black labor and Black work remains open and ongoing, and cannot be controlled by the forces of white hegemonic forms.

61 During this time, some European immigrants, particularly from Ireland, Italy, and Eastern Europe, would not have been seen as white. For a discussion of how the workers at Homestead organized intraethnically, see Krause's chapters on European immigrant workers in *Battle for Homestead.*

62 Magat, *Unlikely Partners*, 78.

63 Quoted in Krause, *Battle for Homestead*, 174.

64 Sharpe, *In the Wake*, 21.

65 Du Bois, *Black Reconstruction in America*, 16.

66 Du Bois, *Black Reconstruction in America*, 18. For more on the history of race riots, see Johnson, *Broken Heart of America.*

67 Harris, "Whiteness as Property," 1722.

68 Harris, "Whiteness as Property," 1741.

69 "John Chinaman," *National Labor Tribune*, Saturday April 9 1892, 5; "Excessive Immigration," *National Labor Tribune*, May 23 1892, 1; "Wholesale Immigration," *National Labor Tribune*, June 6 1891, 2.

70 Harris, "Whiteness as Property," 1725.

71 Gage writes, "In the extremely small number of cases when workers used violence, that violence was rarely ideological—which is to say it was rarely carried out by anarchists, syndicalists, or other political radicals in the name of either revolution or class war." Gage, "Why Violence Matters," 105.

72 "Without the encumbrance of the union, Carnegie was able to slash wages, impose twelve-hour workdays, eliminate five hundred jobs, and suitably assuage his republican conscience with the endowment of a library." Krause, *Battle for Homestead*, 361.

73 Krause, *Battle for Homestead*, 361.

74 Aufhauser writes, "Although it is possible to argue that these developments were an inevitable consequence of the existence of a free market in labor, it is also possible to imagine another history which would have preserved the structure of the economy before the coming of Carnegie and Rockefeller." Aufhauser, "Slavery and Scientific Management," 823.

75 Stone, "Origins of Job Structures," 21. By the 1890s the Carnegie Steel Company had "captured 25 per cent of the nation's steel market" and by 1901, U.S. Steel Corporation controlled 80 percent.

76 As of 2021, there are six companies valued at over one trillion. Four are US-based companies: Apple passed $1.37 trillion on August 4, 2018; Amazon passed $1 trillion on September 4, 2018; Microsoft exceeded the $1 trillion mark on June 7, 2019; and Alphabet, Google's parent company, went to $1 trillion on January 16, 2020. While it is difficult to accurately contextualize inflation and globalization over a hundred-and-twenty-year

period, US Steel, and Carnegie's wealth, is commensurate with that of many corporations and individuals today.

77 Chris Arsenault, "Only 60 Years of Farming Left If Soil Degradation Continues," *Scientific American*, December 5, 2014, https://www.scientificamerican.com/article/only-60-years-of-farming-left-if-soil-degradation-continues/. See also ITPS, *Report of the Fourth Working Session of the Intergovernmental Technical Panel on Soils*; and "Global Symposium on Soil Erosion," Food and Agriculture Organization of the United Nations, https://www.fao.org/about/meetings/soil-erosion-symposium/key-messages/en.

78 Arsenault, "Only 60 Years of Farming Left."

79 On the transcontinental railroad, see Karuka, *Empire's Tracks*.

80 Tess Riley, "Just 100 Companies Responsible for 71% of Global Emissions, Study Says," *Guardian*, July 10, 2017, https://www.theguardian.com/sustainable-business/2017/jul/10/100-fossil-fuel-companies-investors-responsible-71-global-emissions-cdp-study-climate-change.

81 Krause, *Battle for Homestead*, 361.

82 Du Bois, *Black Reconstruction in America*, 15–16.

83 The law fairly acknowledges the property of devoted, successful capitalists. See "Henry Clay Frick," The Frick Collection, https://www.frick.org/about/history/henry_clay_frick.

84 See Magat, *Unlikely Partners*.

85 See Lowe, *Intimacies of Four Continents*.

86 Krause, *Battle for Homestead*, 230.

87 David P. Demarest Jr., "Afterword," in Burgoyne, *Homestead Strike of 1892*, 315.

88 Andrew Carnegie, "The Common Interest of Labour and Capital: Address to Workingmen, Braddock, 1889," in Carnegie, *Empire of Business*, 77, 80. I first found this speech cited in Krause, *Battle for Homestead*, 232.

89 Carnegie, "Common Interest of Labour and Capital," in *Empire of Business* , 82. After these remarks, Carnegie tempers his recommendations with slight exceptions: "Then, far less important, but still important, to bring sweetness and light into your life, be sure to read promiscuously, and know a little about as many things as you have time to read about" (83); "I trust that you will not forget the importance of amusements. Life must not be taken too seriously" (88). Given his disregard for Native languages and reading literature writ large just one moment before, and with the now twelve-to-eighteen-hour workday, the recipe for additive promiscuity and sweetness seems, at best, mendacious.

90 Krause, *Battle for Homestead*, 233.

91 Krause, *Battle for Homestead*, 232.

92 There is a deep irony here, as this chapter works to link the acquisition of art with the wealth derived through the denial of the worker. Here, it seems that irrespective of the sale potential, the abstracted worker is

denied access to art and literature. There are people who have written on this; see, in particular, Rancière, *Nights of Labor.*

93 See Rancière, *Philosopher and His Poor.*

94 Krause, *Battle for Homestead*, 231. Emphasis mine.

95 "Indeed, in the thirty-three years during which Carnegie bestowed libraries, 225 communities turned down his offer. Not surprisingly, this sentiment was especially strong in Pennsylvania: 20 of the 46 towns Carnegie solicited said no." Krause, *Battle for Homestead*, 238. Another worker stated, "I would sooner enter a building built with the dirty silver Judas received for betraying Christ than enter a Carnegie library" (239).

96 Krause, *Battle for Homestead*, 230.

97 See Burgoyne, *Homestead Strike of 1892*, 6.

98 For museum architecture, see Duncan and Wallach, "Museum of Modern Art as Late Capitalist Ritual." For Marxist and social critiques of the museums, see Clark, *Farewell to an Idea*; Mainardi, *Art and Politics of the Second Empire*; and especially Duncan, *Civilizing Rituals*; and Wallach *Exhibiting Contradiction.*

99 August 10, 1792. Quoted in Spalding, *Poetic Museum*, 14.

100 From the 1798 banner for the exhibition of the Laocoon, Horses of St. Mark's, and Apollo Belvedere. Spalding, *Poetic Museum*, 15.

101 Quoted in Spalding, *Poetic Museum*, 15.

102 I found one example in the Knoedler Gallery sale book for January 1897 suggesting they purchased art objects together, or at least a painting by the same artist, in the same month. Sales book 7, July 1892–October 1900, 173, box 67, Knoedler Gallery Archive, Getty Research Center, Los Angeles (hereafter Knoedler Gallery Archive).

103 It is important to note that in my analysis, I have been without the acquisition records for purchases made through Joseph Duveen, Frick's personal art dealer, which have been noted as some of his largest purchases. So this accounting, while far from small, is but one fragment of the document of wealth accumulation and museum building. I examined the Getty Research Institute's vast collection of the Duveen Brothers records, but the sales to Frick are not part of that collection. As Duveen's records are spread out throughout the United States, I have focused my efforts on the Knoedler Gallery Archive.

104 For the language of corporate governance in his will, see Henry Clay Frick, Will, Article 4 Section 2: "I HEREBY GIVE AND BEQUEATH, all of the said trust fund unto the said corporation hereinbefore directed to be formed and to be known as 'THE FRICK COLLECTION,' . . . the income of such endowment fund to be used for the maintenance, care, protection and support of said gallery of art and the personal property therein contained. . . . It is my wish that said corporation shall, in respect to its said endowment fund, have the like broad powers and discretion of investment." Henry Clay Frick Papers, series V: subject files, Frick Art Reference Library, Frick Collection, New York.

105 Here I am paraphrasing former New York City mayor Michael Bloomberg, who in 2010 stated that "the reality of great wealth is that you can't spend it and you can't take it with you." Quoted in Callahan, *Givers*, 12.

106 Sales book 5, November 1881–November 1885, 1883, box 65, Knoedler Gallery Archive.

107 Sales book 6, December 1885–June 1892, box 66, Knoedler Gallery Archive. There's no record of Frick purchasing at this time.

108 Sales book 7, July 1892–October 1900, box 67, Knoedler Gallery Archive. Frick is noted on pages (in the order reflected in the records): 158, 160, 161, 164, 173, 182, 197, 198, 200, 202, 203, 205, 210, 72, 104, 109, 114, 116, 117, 120, 127, 134, 140, 146, 147, 253, 254 258, 267, 268, 279, 283, 289, 290, 296, 213, 220, 223, 229, 234, 236, 241, 243, 246, 307, 308, 319, 337.

109 Sales book 7, July 1892–October 1900, 104, box 67, Knoedler Gallery Archive.

110 Sales book 7, July 1892–October 1900, box 67, Knoedler Gallery Archive.

111 One was a painting by Sir Joshua Reynolds, for $24,000 ($728,700 today), and the other, a painting by J. B. Corot, *Ville D'Avray*, for $25,000 ($760,000 today), totaling $49,000 ($1,488,700 today).

112 Sales book 7, July 1892–October 1900, box 67, Knoedler Gallery Archive.

113 Sales book 8, November 1900–April 1907, box 68, Knoedler Gallery Archive.

114 Sales book 8, November 1900–April 1907, box 68, Knoedler Gallery Archive. These are the pages in which Frick appears: 9, 21, 23, 26, 39, 42,47, 49, 50, 59, 65, 69, 73, 77, 91, 96, 101, 120, 132, 143, 144, 145, 147, 149, 179, 182, 208, 210, 222, 228, 229, 231, 254, 273, 291, 292, 297, 300, 311 328, 335, 352, 373, 374, 379, 405.

115 Some of the bigger purchases were Millet's *How the Gossip Grew* for $14,649.65 (approximately $430,000 today) in June 1901, and $87,000 (approximately $2.455 million today) during September 1901. The year 1903 is distinctive, as previous amounts double, if not triple. During January 1903, Frick acquires four paintings for $138,000 ($3.9 million today); three paintings for $145,000 ($4.15 million today) in February; and then, at the end of the month, on February 28, nine paintings for $76,000 ($2.2 million today). His acquisitions persist in this range until December 1905 when his purchases jump to $150,000 and then $229,000. From there on, the prices he paid remain consistently astronomical: in February 1906 there is a purchase of $100,000; on September 29, 1906, one of $230,000; on December 31, 1906, one of a $275,000 painting by Sir Joshua Reynolds. On January 18, 1907, he purchases Rembrandt's *Rembrandt with a Stick in His Left Hand* for $225,000, and on April 30, 1907, two paintings by Van Dyck are purchased for $120,000 (that is: $1.3 million and $37 million today, respectively).

116 Though not listed in the sales books, from 1908 to 1910 he acquired at least seven paintings by George Romney, Diego Velasquez, Anthony Van

Dyck, and Thomas Gainsborough documented by the inventory card listings. Frick is credited with having acquired: *Countess of Warwick & 2 Children* by Romney, August 1908, 11668, card 50; *Salisbury Cathedral* by Constable, September 1908, 11684, card 51; *Queen Marianne of Austria* by Velasquez, November 1908, 11706, card 52; *Mrs. Snyder's* by Van Dyck, April 1909, 11789, card 54; *Mrs. Watson* by Gainsborough, May 1909, 11788, card 53; *Mr. Snyder's* by Van Dyck, November 1909, 11873, card 55; *Portrait of a Lady* by Hals, April 1910, 12022, card 59. All cards, Knoedler Gallery Archive. Titles and names have been recorded as they appear in the cards, which may differ slightly from today's accepted versions.

117 In 1911, he acquired one work by Rembrandt in January for $175,000; another by Velasquez, *Portrait of Philip the Fourth*, for $475,000 in February; and then *The Soldier and the Laughing Girl* by Vermeer for $225,000, and another by M. Hobbema for $135,000, both in November. Sales book 9, May 1907–January 1912, box 69, Knoedler Gallery Archive.

118 The *Allegory of Wisdom & Strength* by Paul Veronese is acquired for $200,000 in 1912, a Van Dyck and Velasquez for $350,000 and $75,000 respectively in February 1913, and Peter Paul Rubens's *Ambrogio de Spinola* in February 1916 for $90,000.

119 Sales book 10, February 1912–April 1916, box 70, Knoedler Gallery Archive.

120 Krause writes that by July 1, 1892, the mill had contracts for "797,286 tons of steel ingots. . . . The 110-acre Homestead plant alone boasted sixteen open-hearth furnaces with an annual capacity of 250,00 tons of steel ingots," Krause, *Battle for Homestead*, 286.

121 During this time Frick spent: $213,420 in 1912; $562,156 in 1913; $901,000 in 1914; $468,000 in 1915; and $179,000 in 1916. This is a total of $2,323,582, or $53 million today. As the inventory cards indicate, other paintings were purchased in these years, and it's unclear if $457,500 has to be added to this total. All in all, it's a lot. Sales book 10, February 1912–April 1916, box 70, Knoedler Gallery Archive.

122 Sales book 11, May 1919–December 1920, box 71, Knoedler Gallery Archive. "Frick H. C. 1 East 70th St" appears on pages: 3, 33, 34, 138, 192, 246.

123 The purchase is recorded in sales book 10, March 1919, 14595, card 98, page 246, Knoedler Gallery Archive: "New York, March 1919, H. C. Frick 1 East 70 st, Painting by Gilbert Stuart 'Portrait of George Washington,' Earl of Camperdown Collection Payable 30 days, $65,000 paid."

124 Careful analyses have been performed regarding Whistler's work in particular. It should be clear that I am not stating the opposite (that the artworks present a politics unlike Frick) as much as I am stating that the politics of the paintings cannot be consumed by Frick. Additionally, I am not forgetting that some of the workers refused Carnegie's library.

125 Spivak, "Scattered Speculations on the Question of Value," 85.

126 Diane di Prima, "Revolutionary Letter #31," in *Revolutionary Letters*, 43. I thank the poet Cassandra Gillig for reminding me of this line.

127 "Frick Gallery Gets Two Art Treasures: Paintings by Duccio and Berna Purchased for the Public for about $500,000," *New York Times*, November 19, 1927. The acquisition is recorded as: "Barna da Siena and Duccion," 1927, Acquisitions–Benson Collection, Board of Trustees Files, 1920–1931, Frick Art Reference Library, Frick Collection, New York (hereafter Board of Trustees Files, 1920–1931).

128 At this time, the board was operating without an official acquisitions policy.

129 "Coronation of the Virgin," 1930, Acquisitions–Veneziano, Board of Trustees Files, 1920–1931.

130 Rare was the occurrence where price became the reason to shy away from the acquisition for the board.

131 "Coronation of the Virgin," 1930, Acquisitions–Veneziano, Board of Trustees Files, 1920–1931. Emphasis mine.

132 Robinson, *Black Marxism*, 29.

## Chapter 2. Scientific Management and Conceptual Art: The Invention of the Artist Manager

1 I take the "battle between capital and labor" from Katherine Stone, who writes, "The strongest lodge of the Amalgamated Association was at Carnegie's Homestead mill; it is no wonder that the battle between capital and labor was shaped there." Stone, "Origins of Job Structures," 27.

2 The implementation of Taylorism was the result of union-busting. Stone writes, "The steel masters needed to replace men with machines, which meant changing the methods of production. To do that, they needed to control production, unilaterally. The social relations of cooperation and partnership had to go if capitalist steel production was going to progress. The steel companies understood this well, and decided to break the union." Stone, "Origins of Job Structures," 27. Tiffany Willoughby-Herard examines how the Carnegie Corporation was pivotal to South African Apartheid. Suffice it to say that the legacies of philanthropy and U.S. Steel have had and have international implications. See Willoughby-Herard, *Waste of a White Skin*.

3 See Delaware Nation v. Pennsylvania, 446 F.3d 410 (3rd Cir. 2006).

4 Lenin was critical of Taylorism but then worked to implement this system in factories across the Soviet Union. See Scoville, "Taylorization of Vladimir Ilich Lenin"; Devinatz, "Lenin as Scientific"; and Lenin, "Scientific Management and Dictatorship of the Proletariat."

5 Braverman, *Labor and Monopoly Capital*, 87.

6 Braverman, *Labor and Monopoly Capital*, 55.

7 Braverman, *Labor and Monopoly Capital*, 17.

8 Braverman, *Labor and Monopoly Capital*, 15.

9 Markovits, *Meritocracy Trap.*

10 For a historical critique of the managerial class, see Ehrenreich and Ehrenreich, "New Left and the Professional-Managerial Class." See also Merkle, *Management and Ideology.*

11 See Lowe, *Intimacies of Four Continents.*

12 See Wynter, "Novel and History, Plot and Plantation."

13 See Kanigel, *One Best Way*; and Burawoy, *Manufacturing Consent.*

14 Stone, "Origins of Job Structures," 43.

15 Stone writes, "This mechanization would not have been possible without the employers' victory over the workers at Homestead." Stone, "Origins of Job Structures," 30. And regarding piece work: "With the defeat of the Amalgamated Association, the entire complex traditional system of wage payments collapsed. The sliding scale of wages for paying skilled workers and the contract system for paying their helpers rapidly declined. Employers considered them a vestige of worker power and rooted them out of shop after shop. Thus, the employers had the opportunity to unilaterally establish a new system of wage payment. Initially, they began to pay the new semi-skilled men day wages, as they had paid the unskilled workers. Soon, however, they switched *to the system of piece work*, paying a fixed sum for each unit the worker produced" (35).

16 According to Stone, "Before 1900, most managers in the steel industry were men who had begun at the bottom and worked their way all the way up." Stone, "Origins of Job Structures," 50.

17 Stone writes that the bird's eye design of wanting to eradicate the category of skilled merely complicated the notion of skilled. Stone, "Origins of Job Structures," 45. She extrapolates that by 1905 this was understood from all angles, and "employers' associations began to complain about the shortage of skilled men" (46). However, this shortage was by their own design, since "when the employers destroyed the unions and the old social relations, they destroyed at the same time the mechanism through which men had received their training" (46).

18 Stone, "Origins of Job Structures," 48.

19 Stone, "Origins of Job Structures," 48.

20 See Stone, "Origins of Job Structures," 52, 48.

21 Stone, "Origins of Job Structures," 48.

22 Stone, "Origins of Job Structures," 49. I want to note that Taylor's manual provides no adequate definition of the mind. Additionally, scientists have debated the term *mind* for decades and, in fact, are moving towards a definition that refuses to separate the mind from movement and the body. See Siegel, *Mind.*

23 Stone, "Origins of Job Structures," 49.

24 Stone discusses how scientific management destroyed and replaced the labor system that worked against identification, writing that "employers were creating a new labor system to replace the one they had destroyed. . . . All of the methods used to solve this problem were aimed at altering workers' ways of thinking and feeling. . . . The polices were supposed to prevent workers from identifying with each other across company and industry lines, thus preventing the widening of strike movements into mass strikes." Stone, "Origins of Job Structures," 56.

25 See Bahnisch, "Embodied Work," 10, 15, 63.

26 Stone, "Origins of Job Structures," 52. "The effect of this redivision of labor on the worker was to make his job meaningless and repetitious. He was left with no official right to direct his own actions or his own thinking. In this way, skilled workers lost their status as partners, and became true workers, selling their labor and taking orders for all of their working hours."

27 Bahnisch, "Embodied Work," 55.

28 Bahnisch, "Embodied Work," 55, 53. For Taylor's 1912 testimony, see Taylor, "Taylor's Famous Testimony,"

29 Braverman, *Labor and Monopoly Capital*, 60. "[Taylor's] fundamental teachings have become the bedrock of all work design." For more on Taylor's impact, see Waring, *Taylorism Transformed.*

30 Wynter, "Black Metamorphosis."

31 I thank Bedour Alagraa for pointing me to Wynter's critique of scientific management.

32 Rosenthal, *Accounting for Slavery*, 5.

33 Aufhauser, "Slavery and Scientific Management," 813.

34 Taylor, *Scientific Management*, 44–46, 59.

35 Cited in Braverman, *Labor and Monopoly Capital*, 80.

36 Aufhauser, "Slavery and Scientific Management," 815.

37 Aufhauser, "Slavery and Scientific Management," 816.

38 Starobin, *Industrial Slavery in the Old South*, 91; see also Phillips, *American Negro Slavery*, 262.

39 Brand, *Map to the Door of No Return*, 4.

40 Beech, *Art and Labour*, 12.

41 See Robinson, *Anthropology of Marxism*, chapter 4.

42 Robinson, *Terms of Order*, 56–57.

43 Robinson, *Anthropology of Marxism,* chapter 2.

44 See Braverman, *Labor and Monopoly Capital*, for a larger analysis of race and the Ford factory; see also Esch, *Color Line and the Assembly Line*; Roediger and Esch, *Production of Difference*; and Hong, *Ruptures of American Capital*, ch. 3.

45 Yet surprisingly, critics of labor process theory often fixate on worker subjectivity, performing sociological studies on job satisfaction.

46 I pull this argument from Spencer, "Braverman and the Contribution of Labour Process Analysis to the Critique of Capitalist Production."

47 Hartman, *Lose Your Mother*, 6.

48 Hanlon, *Dark Side of Management.*

49 Braverman, *Labor and Monopoly Capital*, 186; Marcuse, *One-Dimensional Man*, 35.

50 See Klare, "Bitter and the Sweet."

51 Benjamin, "Author as Producer," 5.

52 Benjamin, "Author as Producer," 5. Emphasis mine.

53 Benjamin, "Author as Producer," 3.

54 Stone, "Origins of Job Structures," 49.

55 LeWitt, "Paragraphs on Conceptual Art," 12. Emphasis mine.

56 Stone, "Origins of Job Structures," 50.

57 Alberro and Stimson, *Conceptual Art*, xvi.

58 Blake Stimson touches on this point in "The Promise of Conceptual Art" (xliii), as does Robert Smithson, who in "Production for Production's Sake" writes, "Because galleries and museums have been victims of 'cutbacks' they need a cheaper product—objects are thus reduced to 'ideas,' and as a result we get 'Conceptual Art.' Compared to isolated objects, isolated ideas in the metaphysical context of a gallery offer . . . an aesthetic bargain" (284). Both texts in Alberro and Stimson, *Conceptual Art.*

59 I derive this question from Sylvia Wynter; see Wynter, "Novel and History, Plot and Plantation."

60 See "LAWRENCE WEINER (1942–2021)," *Artforum*, December 2, 2021, https://www.artforum.com/news/lawrence-weiner-1942-2021-251172/.

61 "'Art Is Not about Skill': Benjamin Buchloh Interviews Lawrence Weiner on His Sensual Approach to Conceptual Art," *Artspace*, February 16, 2017, https://www.artspace.com/magazine/art_101/book_report/art-is-not-about-skill-benjamin-buchloh-interviews-lawrence-weiner-on-his-sensual-approach-to-54588.

62 Benjamin, "Author as Producer," 3.

63 Benjamin, "Author as Producer," 5.

64 See Baker, "Rise of Entrepreneurial Management Theory in the United States." Erik Baker generously shared with me a draft of his dissertation chapter on management history and offered his critiques of scientific management—for which I am indebted and grateful.

65 Taylor, *Scientific Management*, 63.

66 Thus, and relatedly, Sidney Pollard likens the function of management to ideals of incarceration: "There were few areas of the country in which modern industries, particularly the textiles, if carried on in large buildings, were not associated with prisons, workhouses, and orphanages. This connection is usually underrated, particularly by those historians who assume that the new works recruited free labour only . . . the modern industrial proletariat was introduced to its role not so much by attraction or monetary reward, but by compulsion, force and fear." Pollard, *Genesis of Modern Management*, 45–46. Thus, there is much to be said

about the colonial and imperial history that situates the normalization of centralized management. I thank Carrie Nakamura for pointing me to this passage.

67 Stone, "Origins of Job Structures," 59.

68 Industrial Workers of the World, "Industrial Union Manifesto," issued by the Conference of Industrial Unionists at Chicago, January 2–4, 1905, quoted in Stone, "Origins of Job Structures," 71.

69 See Braverman, *Labor and Monopoly Capital.*

70 In *Systems We Have Loved: Conceptual Art, Affect, and the Antihumanist Turn*, Eve Meltzer describes Robert Morris's *Blind Time II* (1976), in which Morris hired a blind person (identified as A.A.) to make drawings for him, and how the series ended because, "A.A. began to resist Morris' direction." Meltzer, *Systems We Have Loved*, 115. Meltzer's description of Morris's practice colliding with the desires of A.A. (who, it is assumed, was not supposed to have desire) is something to consider in the *longue durée* of the aestheticization of exploitation.

71 Kosuth, *Art after Philosophy and After*, 18.

72 For scholarship that tends to dominant configurations of Duchamp, see Naumann, *New York Dada 1915–1923*; and Dezayas and Naumann, *How, When, and Why Modern Art Came to New York.*

73 Buskirk and Nixon, *Duchamp Effect.*

74 Armstrong, "Interviews with Ed Ruscha and Bruce Conner," 55–56.

75 Foster, "What Is Neo about the Neo-Avant Garde?," 13.

76 This is the argument made in Martha Buskirk's "Thoroughly Modern Marcel" and in the roundtable "Conceptual Art and the Reception of Duchamp," in Buskirk and Nixon, *Duchamp Effect*, 113–26 and 127–46, which reprints the articles in *October*'s 1994 special issue on Duchamp. These arguments have also been made in Dworkin and Goldsmith, *Against Expression.*

77 For affirmative retellings of this justification, see the editor's note in Dworkin and Goldsmith, *Against Expression*; and see Perloff, *Unoriginal Genius.*

78 Karl Marx, "Friedrich List's Book *Das Nationale System der Politischen Oekonomie*," quoted in Thoburn, *Deleuze, Marx, and Politics*, 65.

79 Beech, *Art and Labour*, 267.

80 Beech, *Art and Labour*, 274.

81 Beech, *Art and Labour*, 44.

82 De Duve, *Pictorial Nominalism*, 154.

83 Obrist, *Brief History of Curating*, 38

84 Quoted in Obrist, *Brief History of Curating*, 38. *Readymade malheureux* consisted of a geometry textbook hung outdoors on a string, exposed to the elements.

85 Blocker, "Aestheticizing Risk in Wartime," 195.

86 Blocker, "Aestheticizing Risk in Wartime," 195.

87 See Wong, *Van Gogh on Demand.*

88 Christian Jankowski, "China Painters: Concept, 2008," Christian Jankowski, https://christianjankowski.com/works/2008-2/china-painters/.

89 Wong, *Van Gogh on Demand*, 194.

90 See Baker, "Rise of Entrepreneurial Management Theory in the United States." Baker delineates how the function of management is less ideologically varied than managers and scholars of managerial studies would have us believe.

91 Several former studio assistants have spoken about the conditions of their labor; see John Powers, "I Was Jeff Koons' Studio Serf," *New York Times*, August 19, 2012, https://www.nytimes.com/2012/08/19/magazine/i-was-jeff-koonss-studio-serf.html?_r=1; and Tim Schneider, "Who Needs Assistants When You Have Robots? Jeff Koons Lays Off Dozens in a Move toward a Decentralized, Automated Studio Practice," *Artnet*, January 17, 2019, https://news.artnet.com/art-world/jeff-koons-downsizing-1442788. On the reporting of assistants, see Henri Neuendorf, "Art Demystified: Why Do Contemporary Artists Use So Many Studio Assistants?," *Artnet*, July 14, 2016, https://news.artnet.com/art-world/art-demystified-the-use-of-assistants-549284.

92 Lazzarato, *Marcel Duchamp et le refus du travail.*

93 Beech, *Art and Labour*, 255.

94 Samuel Gompers was a cigarmaker living on New York's Lower East Side in the 1860s. This line is from his *Seventy Years of Life and Labor: An Autobiography*, 57. I first came across his book in Braverman, *Labor and Monopoly Capital.*

95 For a critique of work, see Weeks, *Problem with Work.*

### Chapter 3. Whiteness as Property and Found Object Art: Collecting and Canonizing Marcel Duchamp

1 Another linking note of interest is that, in 1889, the owners of Carry Furnaces in Homestead sold the plant to Carnegie to begin the Oakmont Country Club.

2 Veblen, *Theory of the Leisure Class.*

3 See Harris, "Whiteness as Property."

4 Marcel Duchamp, *Nude Descending a Staircase*, 1912, was shown at the Armory Show in 1913. For an example of the newspaper comic, see J. F. Griswold's "The Rude Descending a Staircase (Rush Hour at the Subway)," which first appeared in the *New York Evening Sun*, March 20, 1913.

5 As described in this book's introduction, Duchamp's *Fountain* has been labeled by art historians as one of the most influential works of modern art. This claim has been affirmed by the likes of de Duve, *Kant after Duchamp*; Lazzarato, *Marcel Duchamp et le refus du travail*; and the scholar-

ship discussed in chapter 2, among others. I am not, however, arguing affirmatively that Duchamp's artwork should be recognized as the most influential, or that current narratives about *Fountain* should be circulated without its material history. I certainly hope that categories such as "the most influential" become problematized and fragmented in the future.

6 Art historians have been looking for the exact urinal. The fact that commercial replicas have not been found has been utilized to support claims that Duchamp, in fact, "made" the urinal.

7 Research contesting Duchamp's authorship is robust. Siri Hustvedt writes of the evidence found connecting Baroness Elsa von Freytag-Loringhoven to *Fountain*, to no avail. Siri Hustvedt, "A Woman in the Men's Room: When Will the Art World Recognise the Real Artist behind Duchamp's Fountain?" *Guardian*, March 29, 2019, https://www.theguardian.com/books/2019/mar/29/marcel-duchamp-fountain-women-art-history; and Dalya Alberge, "'This Was His Revenge on Art': Is Marcel Duchamp's Greatest Work a Fake?" *Guardian*, October 15, 2023, https://www.theguardian.com/artanddesign/2023/oct/15/conceptualist-art-fountain-is-fake-say-historians-marcel-duchamp.

8 Duchamp and Walter Arensberg quit the society after the incident.

9 The review appeared in Duchamp's magazine, the *Blind Man*, which was sponsored by the Arensbergs.

10 See Molesworth, *Part Object Part Sculpture*.

11 For scholarship on the artistic configuring of Duchamp see Naumann, *New York Dada 1915–1923*, and the 2019 exhibition at the gallery Francis M. Naumann Fine Art, *New York Dada: The Arensberg Circle of Artists*. See also Dezayas and Naumann, *How, When, and Why Modern Art Came to New York*; and Richter, *Dada*.

12 Walter C. Arensberg to Marcel Duchamp, January 11, 1945, Walter and Louise Arensberg Papers, box 6 F 29, Arensberg Archives, Philadelphia Museum of Art, Philadelphia (hereafter Arensberg Archives). Emphasis mine.

13 For a critical analysis of the ways critics continue to write about art as akin to war, see Sahakian, "What We Are Fighting For."

14 The Arensbergs' collection of Indigenous art in relation to and toward the Duchamp monument must be critically examined.

15 See Walter C. Arensberg to Marcel Duchamp, August 11, 1951, box 6 F 34, Arensberg Archives. Duchamp responds to this news of a tax report with, "What a nuisance!" (Marcel Duchamp to Walter Arensberg, 8 Sept 1951, box 6 F 35, Arensberg Archives); to which I must respond: thank the heavens for tax nuisances.

16 Another book could and should be written on the impact of patrons such as the Arensbergs collecting and narrating modern art through the lens of "Pre-Columbian art." See, in particular, the note concerning the Arensbergs' "289 indigenous materials" in Arensberg, CA Use Tax, December 1, 1951, box 30 F 25, Arensberg Archives. This quoted excerpt comes

from Arensberg, CA Use Tax, October 29, 1951, box 30 F 18, Arensberg Archives. Their detailed narration is denied exemption. Emphasis mine.

17 See the document Arensberg, "Schedule A Out-of-State Purchases, State Board of Equalization, Sales Tax Divisions" CA Use Tax, November 28, 1951r, box 30 F 6, Arensberg Archives. I utilized the inflation calculator provided by the United States Department of Labor to arrive at the figures; "CPI Inflation Calculator," U.S. Bureau of Labor Statistics, https://www.bls.gov/data/inflation_calculator.htm.

18 From the document "Art Collection," Arensberg, CA Use Tax, undated, box 30 F 6, Arensberg Archives.

19 See the document "Complete List of Purchases from Out-of-State Retailers," Arensberg, Walter C., CA Use Tax Undated, box 30 F 6, Arensberg Archives.

20 On August 5, 1941, Walter Arensberg asks Duchamp, "Dear Marcel . . . Do you need financial assistance?" Walter C. Arensberg to Marcel Duchamp, August 5, 1941, box 6 F 27, Arensberg Archives. This is one of many such moments.

21 Arensberg, Personal Records, Notes Re: Money Sent to Marcel Duchamp, December 1931–June 1932, box 46 F 5, Arensberg Archives.

22 See Walter C. Arensberg to Marcel Duchamp, May 11, 1949, box 6 F 31, Arensberg Archives. Duchamp responds on August 8, 1949, expressing a disinterest in Minnesota.

23 Walter C. Arensberg to Marcel Duchamp, March 31, 1950, box 6 F 32, Arensberg Archives.

24 Marcel Duchamp to Walter C. Arensberg, May 8, 1949, box 6 F 31, Arensberg Archives. Emphasis mine.

25 Marcel Duchamp to Walter C. Arensberg, January 16, 1951, box 6 F 34, Arensberg Archives.

26 Walter C. Arensberg to Marcel Duchamp, January 9, 1954, box 6 F 38, Arensberg Archives. Emphasis mine.

27 Duchamp's response was immediate. On January 13, 1954, he writes, "Dear Walter . . . I will of course go to Philadelphia when you ask me and follow your instructions in my interviews with Fiske. . . . I agree with you that the project of mixing your collection with a general opening of a Modern Museum is not at all satisfying. Give me your definite views and instructions as soon as you can." Duchamp to Walter C. Arensberg, January 13, 1954, box 6 F 38, Arensberg Archives.

28 In objecting to a general opening, Walter writes to Sidney Fiske-Kimball (January 11, 1954, box 6 F38, Arensberg Archives),

> To force our collection with its highly individual character into the Procrustes bed of a "Modern Museum" suppresses the individuality of the collection and the individuality of the gift and reduces the whole thing to a mere "also-ran." In suppressing the individuality of the collection, I mean the suppressing of its unique combination

> of twentieth century works with pre-Columbian and other primitive works . . . as a compromise alternative to your total postponement of a showing of our collection until you open your "Modern Museum," to a prior showing of the outstanding portion of the 20th Century portion of the collection, including all the Brancusis, all the Duchamps, Legers, Chagalls, Picassos, Klees, etc., etc., and that you would show them in the galleries prepared for them and so described long before any mention whatever of your "Modern Museum" had ever been made? I would like to have the foregoing conditions fulfilled primarily for Lou's sake, as the final justification for all that she sacrificed in making the collection possible and as a confirmation of all the faith that she had in its unique character. Her interest in the presentation of the collection was the latest interest that she maintained in the outside world up to the day of her death.

29 Marcel Duchamp to Walter C. Arensberg, telegram, November 26, 1953, box 6 F 38, Arensberg Archives.

30 Marcel Duchamp to Walter C. Arensberg, December 3, 1953, box 6 F 37, Arensberg Archives.

31 Walter writes to Duchamp (January 9, 1954, box 6 F 38, Arensberg Archives),

> The project in which Lou kept her interest the longest . . . was the opening of the collection at Philadelphia as soon as possible, in accordance with the suggestion that you made in a letter of November 2. . . . It was because Lou was so interested in the idea suggested in your letter that I have been shipping to Philadelphia all of the more important paintings remaining in the house, together with a few Pre-Columbian pieces that were not sent before the Before Columbus Exhibition. The material for the opening would therefore be in Philadelphia in a plenty of time and I could have the right, after the opening itself, to bring just a few—and only a very few—of the less important paintings back to the house here so as not to have it completely denuded until my death.

32 Sawelson-Gorse, "Marcel Duchamp's 'Silent Guard,'" 119. Sawelson-Gorse's dissertation is full of interesting financial information, such as, "The second of three children, the only daughter born to Harriet Louisa Stevens and John Edwards Stevens enjoyed a pedigree the Arensberg clan could only aspire to through marriage" (22).

33 Sawelson-Gorse, "Marcel Duchamp's 'Silent Guard,'" 121.

34 Sawelson-Gorse, "Marcel Duchamp's 'Silent Guard,'" 122.

35 Sawelson-Gorse, "Marcel Duchamp's 'Silent Guard,'" 3.

36 Arensberg, Personal Records, Biographical Chronology: Walter C. Arensberg. undated, box 47 F 1, Arensberg Archives.

37 Arensberg, Writings, 1916, Arensberg Papers, Box 43 F 9, Arensberg Archives. Emphasis mine.

38 Arensberg, Writings, Untitled Essay, Re: Conversations with Marcel Duchamp, February 1916, Arensberg Papers, box 43 F 17, Arensberg Archives.

39 There is something to be said about the ways in which academia continues to discourage dissertations and book projects that require research into subject matters that remain underproduced due to anti-Black racism.

40 Zhang Juguo writes, "Whites in New York City signed restrictive covenants, swearing not to rent or sell their houses to African Americans." Juguo, *W. E. B. Du Bois*, 80.

41 See McKittrick, "Plantation Futures."

42 Wood, Budnitz, and Malhotra, *Jim Crow in New York*, 4. As Harris articulates, such laws manifest that "the origins of property rights in the United States are rooted in racial domination." Harris, "Whiteness as Property," 1716.

43 For formative legal analysis of Jim Crow history and laws see, Burnham, *By Hands Now Known*.

44 "Segregation Fight on in 17 Cities: Denver, Colorado, Is Latest Addition to Growing List," *New York Amsterdam News*, October 4, 1925.

45 See "Separated Colored and White at Negro Show: Well Known Author and Newspaperman Writes Hudtig and Seamen of Discrimination," *New York Amsterdam News*, February 25, 1925; "Segregation Fight Spreads North," *New York Amsterdam News*, September 30, 1925; and Edgar M. Grey, "Close Ranks or Perish," *New York Amsterdam News*, June 10, 1925, 16.

46 Just because whiteness is not articulated does not mean it is not being deployed. See Harris, "Whiteness as Property," 1734.

47 Morrison, *Playing in the Dark*, xiii.

48 David Joselit, "Molds and Swarms," 161. Emphasis mine.

49 Harris, "Whiteness as Property," 1721.

50 De Kooning, "Renaissance and Order," 86–87. Emphasis mine. This lecture is from a series on modern art presented at Studio 35 on 8th Street in New York. The book *Artists' Sessions at Studio 35 (1950)*, edited by Robert Goodnough, gives an overview of the conversations taking place at Studio 35 among Janice Biala, Willem de Kooning, Hans Hofmann, Richard Pousette-Dart, Ad Reinhardt, and others. *Artists' Sessions* provides a transcript of the salon session that took place April 21–23, 1950, when artists were invited to discuss art, community, the avant-garde, and more. De Kooning's lecture "The Renaissance and Order" would have been presented to a similar audience.

51 Harris, "Whiteness as Property," 1714.

52 Girst, *Duchamp Dictionary*, 22.

53 Girst, *Duchamp Dictionary*, 23.

54 Cheryl Harris notes, "Property is thus said to be a right, not a thing, characterized as metaphysical, not physical." Harris, "Whiteness as Property," 1725.

55 Harris, "Whiteness as Property," 1741.

56 In *Apparitions of Asia*, Josephine Nock-Hee Park uses this phrase to analyze what figures such as Ernest F. Fenollosa practice in their orientalism (10).

57 See Williams, *Marxism and Literature.*

58 Phillip Brian Harper writes that, in order to structure systems of enslavement, Black persons were "reduced to a lowest-level commonality in which their very humanity was annulled, black people assumed a condition of abstraction whose import was wholly negative." Harper, *Abstractionist Aesthetics*, 31. See also Harris's articulations of legal vacancy in "Whiteness as Property," 1716, 1727.

59 Harper, *Abstractionist Aesthetics*, 42.

60 De Man, "Epistemology of Metaphor," 15.

61 See Mohanty, "Under Western Eyes."

62 Mohanty, "Under Western Eyes," 71.

63 "This trial is trickier than the other, since the judge and the executioner are the same person as the inventor of the character." Rancière, *Philosopher and His Poor*, 236.

64 Hong, *Ruptures of American Capital*, 110.

65 Sassen, *Global Networks, Linked Cities.*

66 Byrd, *Transit of Empire*, 186.

67 Beech, *Art and Labour*, 31, 32.

68 In 2004, Duchamp's *Fountain* was voted "the most influential modern art work of all time" in a survey conducted with 500 art experts in the run-up to the prestigious Turner Prize. See "Duchamp's Urinal Tops Art Survey," BBC, December 1, 2004, http://news.bbc.co.uk/2/hi/entertainment/4059997.stm. Furthermore, reproductions of *Fountain* have been acquired by prestigious museums such as the Tate Modern, SFMOMA, and the Centre Pompidou. The form of the readymade and the figure of Duchamp have been theorized as both radical and iconic by many outlets, including numerous retrospective shows and countless books. Through the canonization of the work, Duchamp has been granted generous titles, from the father of institutional critique, to the inventor of appropriation art and conceptualism, and the original antibourgeois antiartist. In chapter 2, I discuss as the arguments made in the collection *Duchamp Effect.*

69 For literature on segregation in New York, see Gellman and Quigley, *Jim Crow New York*; Bellush and David, *Race and Politics in New York City*; Kantrowitz, *Ethnic and Racial Segregation in the New York Metropolis*; Daily, *Age of Jim Crow*; Sokol, *All Eyes Are upon Us*; and Adelman and Mele, *Race, Space, and Exclusion.*

70 This is not to say that there have not been pivotal, groundbreaking Black artists throughout US history—only that their contributions, according to canonical placement, collection holdings, and circulation, are almost always at the periphery and significantly less valued. See

Susan E. Cahan's demonstration in *Mounting Frustration* of how even when museums purchased Black art, they have limited its circulation and exhibition.

71 For an in-depth analysis of this, see Huggins, *Voices from the Harlem Renaissance.*

72 *Crisis* was a monthly New York City publication produced by W. E. B. Du Bois. This insight is based on the issues from 1915 to 1917.

73 Here, I am thinking about the political orientations presented in Du Bois's *Souls of Black Folk* and Hartman's *Lose Your Mother.*

74 Special and many thanks to Grace Kyungwon Hong, who pointed me to this work.

75 Purifoy and Michel, *Junk Art.*

76 Purifoy, "African American Artists."

77 Ferguson, "Purifoy," 450.

78 Widener, *Black Arts West*, 166.

79 Widener, *Black Arts West*, 170.

80 Visual artists working principally in the mixed-media assemblage form sought to develop an expansive, open-ended, yet socially committed abstract art, which, in the words of John Outterbridge, while "open to anyone," was first and foremost "always relevant to us black people." Outterbridge, quoted in Widener, *Black Arts West*, 175.

81 Widener, *Black Arts West*, 171.

82 The rhetoric of preservation is reiterated in James Cuno's writings, most recently in "The Case against Repatriating Artifacts," *Foreign Affairs*, November/December 2014, https://www.foreignaffairs.com/articles/africa/culture-war.

83 This line is derived from Don Mee Choi's text, *Freely Frayed*, where she writes, "I am not transnationally equal. My intent is to expose what a neocolony is, what it does to its own, what it eats and shits." Choi, *Freely Frayed*, 10.

84 Purifoy, "African American Artists," 169.

85 Purifoy, "African American Artists," 170, 167.

86 Purifoy, "African American Artists," 165.

87 Purifoy, "African American Artists," 168.

88 Suzanne Muchnic, "To Protect and Preserve and Desert Legacy," *Los Angeles Times*, January, 14, 2001, https://www.latimes.com/archives/la-xpm-2001-jan-14-ca-12054-story.html.

89 Manu Karuka develops the vital argument that the US nation state is situated through countersovereignty and is reactionary to the sovereignty of Native peoples. For his historical charting of this framework, see Karuka, *Empire's Tracks.*

90 For critical analyses of how land and place intersect with Black and Native communities, see King, *Black Shoals.*

## Chapter 4. Whiteness and the New: Neoliberalism and the Building of the Archive for New Poetry

An earlier version of this chapter appeared as "Appraising Newness: Whiteness, Neoliberalism, and the Building of the Archive for New Poetry," in "Critical Archival Studies," ed. Michelle Caswell, Ricardo Punzalan, and T-Kay Sangwand. Special issue, *Journal of Critical Library and Information Studies* 1, no. 2 (2017). https://doi.org/10.24242/jclis.v1i2.38.

1 In 2015, I was informed that Tony Seymour's papers had been acquired by the ANP in 2012. I assumed that Seymour's papers would be under the ANP, making him the sole nonwhite poet linked to the ANP's collection. As of 2023, when this chapter was being finalized, Seymour's papers can be found through UCSD's website but are not linked to the ANP's manuscript finding aid (for American Poetry), meaning that, unless a researcher knows exactly what they are looking for, they will not find his papers. Moreover, there are collections and libraries devoted to Black, Asian American, Latin American, and Native poetic movements. The Schomburg Center for Research in Black Culture, a part of the New York Public Libraries, collects works and manuscripts belonging to cultural producers documenting and researching the African American, African Diaspora, and African experiences. Centers such as the Museum of Chinese in America, the Smithsonian's National Museum of the American Indian, and the Beinecke Rare Book and Manuscript Library at Yale University have also worked to collect the papers and documents of cultural producers documenting immigrant and Native communities. The work of libraries, centers and museums committed to this approach is indispensable and essential. However, the labor performed at centers, archives, and museums such as these does not eradicate the responsibility of public archives across the United States to develop and manage desegregated collections.

2 The Schomburg Center for Research in Black Culture holds the papers of members of the Black Arts movement, including Bill Gunn, Julian Mayfield, Michele Wallace, and others. However, additional archival research on the founding Black Arts movement poets would be require extensive travel.

Amiri Baraka's papers from 1945–2014 are housed at Columbia University, while the University of California, Los Angeles, holds select correspondence from 1958. Nikki Giovanni's manuscripts from 1943 are currently at Boston University, while Gwendolyn Brooks's papers are situated at the University of California, Berkeley, and the University of Illinois Urbana-Champaign. Etheridge Knight's papers are held at the University of Toledo, Butler University, and Indiana Historical Society. Sonia Sanchez's published writings and photographs are held at Boston

University, though in May 2016 and 2023, I could not find information regarding her poetry manuscripts.

3 "New Poetry" is defined by the ANP as English-language US poetry after 1945. See Kathleen M. Woodward for Roy Harvey Pearce, Proposal, February 1, 1974, box 2, folder 10, coll. MSS 0143, Roy Harvey Pearce Papers, Archive for New Poetry, Special Collections and Archives, University of California San Diego Library, University of California San Diego (hereafter ANP). That such definitions are implicitly linked to whiteness is a point being taken up by contemporary figures in poetry studies; see, in particular, Wang, *Thinking Its Presence.*

4 Cook, "Mind over Matter," 47.

5 Archive-building—particularly in the case of ANP—was a collaboration between university faculty and archivists. A defense of previous and current acquisition practices might be that there were no faculty at the university interested in setting up a "Black Arts archive" or Latinx experimental poetry archive. This defense, however, would not be a defense of current or previous archiving practices but a statement as to how institutionalized racism (faculty hiring, course listings) is expressed in the archives, and how the archives are not immune to the formations of institutionalized racism. This is especially important as these formations are disseminated into the larger culture of the medium. In a letter of May 30, 1975, Michael Davidson informed Roy Harvey Pearce of the various publications that had received a résumé of ANP. These were: "APR, Boundary 2, Journal of Modern Literature, 20th Century Lit., PMLA, Antaeus, Paris Review, Poetry Chicago, Poetry Review, Tri-Quarterly, Contemporary Literature and the St. Marks Poetry Project." The archive's objectives were not to be insulated or obscured from the literature community. I cite this note as visualizing a structural problem: where whiteness can be seen again and again, distributed and circulated without question or inquiry. Michael Davidson to Roy Harvey Pearce, May 30, 1975, box 2, folder 11, coll. MSS 0143, Roy Harvey Pearce Papers, ANP.

6 See Morrison, *Playing in the Dark*, xiii.

7 Abbott et al., *Poets at Work.*

8 Abbott et al., *Poets at Work*, 21.

9 Abbott et al., *Poets at Work*, 22.

10 Abbott et al., *Poets at Work*, 32.

11 The Buffalo archive also received funding from the Carnegie Corporation. Charles Abbott writes, "Once again the Carnegie Corporation had given us a life, this time with a grant that captious management could make do for three or four years." Abbott et al., *Poets at Work*, 25.

12 Abbott et al., *Poets at Work*, 33.

13 Abbott writes, "But there is a deeper moral problem in all this. Once or twice an indigent struggling poet has put the question, Will the library

pay me for manuscripts? And I have felt guilty—not because we cannot pay, but because the world denies him a satisfactory return for his work. . . . He may be creating something that is right and honest and true. . . . But when I say No to such a poet, shame wells inside me nonetheless, and I am sick with guilt." Abbott et al., *Poets at Work*, 35.

14 Abbott et al., *Poets at Work*, 34.

15 "Van Vechten's research collection of music materials, for example, initiated the Gershwin collection at Fisk; his research materials for *N—r Heaven* represented the origins of the Johnson Collection of African American Literature at Yale; and sources for his books on cats, *The Tiger in the House* (1920) and *Lords of the Housetops* (1921), helped establish the Anna Marble Pollock Memorial Library of Books about Cats at Yale." MacLeod, "The 'Librarian's Dream-Prince,'" 368.

16 MacLeod, "The 'Librarian's Dream-Prince.'"

17 There are several drafts of this proposal, dating from September 1973 to late 1974. See Kathleen M. Woodward for Roy Harvey Pearce, Proposal, September 1973, coll. MSS 143, box 2, folder 10, Roy Harvey Pearce Papers, ANP.

18 Additional funds were needed for the Blackburn archives, as the papers from 1950–55 had not been acquired in 1973. Pearce looked first to private donors, writing, "The collection is a paramount one, both intrinsically and in relation to our possession of the rest of the Blackburn materials." Roy Harvey Pearce to Charles Taubaum, October 11, 1979, Roy Harvey Pearce subject file, box 5, folder 24, Curator's Correspondence and Subject Files, 1974–1989 (RSS 1034), ANP.

19 To calculate inflation rates, I used http://www.usinflationcalculator.com. The acquisition prices for the Blackburn and Rothenberg papers are similar to previous sale points for highly noted writers. See Sutton, "Destinies of Literary Manuscripts." Sutton notes that Gabriel García Márquez's papers were auctioned at Christie's with a price guide "between $80,000 and $120,000" (289).

20 Woodward writes, "In the summer of 1973, the Archive for New Poetry at the University of California at San Diego was fortunate to acquire the Paul Blackburn Archive. Consisting of poetry manuscripts, personal journals, over 650 books, a vast correspondence with other poets and publishers, some 350 reels of tapes of poetry readings, 1150 little magazines, and memorabilia of all kinds, it is a magnificent collection of research materials for both Blackburn studies and American poetry." Kathleen M. Woodward, "Paul Blackburn Preface," January 17, 1980, Documents for New Poetry II, box 6, folder 7, Curator's Correspondence and Subject Files, 1974–1989 (RSS 1034), ANP.

21 See Couture, "Archival Appraisal"; Samuels, "Who Controls the Past"; and Cook, "Mind Over Matter."

22 Cook, "We Are What We Keep," 182.

23 Pollard, "Appraisal of Personal Papers."

24 See Michael Davidson to Roy Harvey Pearce, June 18, 1975, coll. MSS 143, box 2, folder 11, Roy Harvey Pearce Papers, ANP.

25 Pollard, "Appraisal of Personal Papers," 136–50.

26 Kathleen M. Woodward for Roy Harvey Pearce, Proposal, May 22, 1974, box 2, folder 10, coll. MSS 0143, Roy Harvey Pearce Papers, ANP.

27 The proposal states: "The archive for New Poetry at the University California, San Diego, represents an attempt to collect all poetry written in the English Language since World War II." Kathleen M. Woodward for Roy Harvey Pearce, Proposal, May 22, 1974, box 2, folder 10, coll. MSS 0143, Roy Harvey Pearce Papers, ANP.

28 I wish to thank Dorothy Wang for a conversation in which these questions were raised.

29 The Sand Dollar bookstore was run by Jack Shoemaker. Discussions regarding the "blanket order" began as early as fall of 1974. In a September 25, 1974, letter to Pearce, Davidson outlines the guidelines. See Michael Davidson to Roy Harvey Pearce, September 25, 1974, coll. MSS 143, box 2, folder 10, Roy Harvey Pearce Papers, ANP.

30 Dunbar, "Introducing Critical Race Theory to Archival Discourse," 117.

31 Michael Davidson to Roy Harvey Pearce, September 25, 1974, Roy Harvey Pearce Papers, ANP.

32 The eighty-four poets listed in this document overlap with the poets from *The New American Poetry 1945–1960*, edited by Donald Allen (whose papers are in the ANP), which was considered a canonical anthology. The Spring 1978 "Archive Newsletter" announcing the acquisition of the Donald Allen archive states, "If the names O'Hara, Ginsberg, Olson, Snyder, Creeley, Kyger, Whalen and Welch mean anything to us today, it is largely through the efforts of Donald Allen, the editor of the landmark anthology, *The New American Poetry*. When it came out in 1960, the book virtually defined the field of contemporary poetry in its most progressive stage by presenting poets such as those mentioned above along with prose statements in the back of the book which articulated poetic stances." Newsletter, Spring 1978, coll. MSS 143, box 2, folder 12, Roy Harvey Pearce Papers, ANP. The book, it seems, also defined the archive.

33 Hall, "Constituting and Archive," 89. See also Upward, "Continuum Mechanics and Memory Banks"; McKemmish, "Placing Records Continuum Theory and Practice"; and Caswell, *Archiving the Unspeakable*. Caswell writes, "In the view from the continuum, all of these activations—past, present, and future—form the never-ending provenance of these records, each adding a new layer of meaning to a constantly evolving collection of records that open out into the future" (159).

34 The May 22, 1974, proposal prefaces that it is for a "three-year grant San Diego New Poetry Series administered by the Archive for New Poetry

at the University of California, San Diego." The proposal seems to have been written for a broad and unspecified audience, as it reads, "We are therefore requesting ________ for the following . . ." What is clear is that the university is part of the dialogue. At the end of the first page, it reads, "The University of California, San Diego, is ready to finance this proposal with matching funds representing one-fourth of the total." See Kathleen M. Woodward for Roy Harvey Pearce, Proposal, May 22, 1974, coll. MSS 0143, box 2, folder 10, Roy Harvey Pearce Papers, ANP.

35 The budget indicated that acquisitions for the Archive for New Poetry, as imagined under the "Center for New Poetry," would be handled by the libraries' budget. Later in the chapter, I discuss how the manuscript acquisition for the archive seems to have occurred through the assistance of private donors, friends of the library committee, and funds matched through the chancellor's office.

36 See "Proposal for: Contemporary American Voices," Kathy Woodward for Roy Harvey Pearce, May 22, 1974, coll. MSS 143, box 10, folder 2, Roy Harvey Papers, ANP.

37 Hong, *Death beyond Disavowal*, 17.

38 Hong, *Death beyond Disavowal*, 17.

39 An early reader of this chapter contested my reading of the question mark. I acknowledge that this reading is my critical speculation and cannot be confirmed. I would also state that the ANP acquired no poetry from the aforementioned groups.

40 The formal definition of *Ethnopoetics* given in the proposal, as well as the term writ large, is deserving of much longer critique and critical attention.

41 Cahan, *Mounting Frustrations*, 6.

42 Samuels, "Who Controls the Past," 111, 112.

43 Harris, "Postmodernism and Archival Appraisal," 48–50.

44 I have spent some time looking through the chancellor's office papers, but I have been unable to procure the final draft proposal sent. However, in a correspondence addressed to Pearce, John L. Stewart, and Andrew H. Wright from Paul Saltman of the Office of the Vice Chancellor, Saltman states, "The possibility of moving towards such a program or center, within the context of the University. Obviously, outside funding will necessarily have to be sought. It should be done in the context of a total understanding of the role of the center in the education and research plan before the campus as a whole and the department in particular. We also have to put it into the priorities of our fund-raising activities." The proposal received positive interest and initial institutional support. Saltman to Roy Harvey Pearce, John L. Stewart, Andrew H. Wright, Letter, October 2, 1973, coll. MSS 143, box 2, folder 10, Roy Harvey Pearce Papers, ANP.

45 Roy Harvey Pearce to John Haak, November 20, 1974, coll. MSS 143, box 2, folder 10, Roy Harvey Pearce Papers, ANP.

46 Laurence McGilvery to Roy Harvey Pearce, November 19, 1974, coll. MSS 143, box 2, folder 10, Roy Harvey Pearce Papers, ANP.

47 Roy Harvey Pearce to John Haak, November 20, 1974, coll. MSS 143, box 2, folder 10, Roy Harvey Pearce Papers, ANP.

48 I should note that for reasons unknown, the Ginsberg set was not acquired by the institution.

49 Roger Rosenblatt to Roy Harvey Pearce, October 21, 1974, coll. MSS 143, box 2, folder 10, Roy Harvey Pearce Papers, ANP. This version of the proposal was not approved for funding, and it is unclear whether the proposal was resubmitted. In the proposal, Sherley Ann Williams's name is clearly misspelled.

50 Roy Harvey Pearce to Sherley Ann Williams, May 28, 1977, MSS 492, box 2, folder 32, Papers of Sherley Ann Williams, ANP. The essay referred to is Essay, draft by Sherley Ann Williams, May 28, 1977, titled: "A Review of Onwuchekwa Jemie, LANGSTON HUGHES: AN INTRODUCTION TO THE POETRY," MSS 493, box 2, folder 32, Papers of Sherley Ann Williams, ANP. I am preserving the punctuation of the original letter (Pearce underlines "all").

51 Toni Morrison remarked that such confessions of "lack" are often made with a sense of pride. In fact, Pearce, after confessing his lack, proceeds to list book recommendations for Williams, trusting that while he lacks knowledge of Black writing, he has the knowledge to mend the critical framing in Williams's essay. Morrison writes: "It is interesting, not surprising, that the arbiters of critical power in American literature seem to take pleasure in, indeed relish, their ignorance of African-American texts. What is surprising is that their refusal to read black texts—a refusal that makes no disturbance in their intellectual life—repeats itself when they reread the traditional, established works of literature worthy of their attention." Morrison, *Playing in the Dark*, 13.

52 See Morrison, *Playing in the Dark*, xiii. I use the term *segregated* not as an abstraction. While the Civil Rights Act of 1964 and *Brown v. Board of Education* in 1954 were implemented to overturn federal segregation, scholars have long argued that desegregation did not happen immediately. *Alexander v. Holmes County of Education* in 1969 exemplifies the ossified pace of desegregation. The historical context of the 1974 proposal for the ANP is a period when desegregation was supposed to take place, but instead, as Michelle Alexander argues, segregation simply transformed into our current system of mass incarceration. See Alexander, *New Jim Crow*.

53 Harris, "Postmodernism and Archival Appraisal," 48–50.

54 Dunbar, "Introducing Critical Race Theory," 113.

55 See Lipsitz, *Possessive Investment in Whiteness*.

56 Today, the University of Iowa's MFA writing program is considered to be one of the best such programs in the country; it has produced a slew of

well-known writers and poets. However, Bennett argues that this was not the case when the program began. For more on Iowa's accounting history see, Bennett, *Workshops of Empire*.

57 Starting in 1976, there is consistent correspondence to renew a twelve-month research assistant (RA) stipend for the ANP. Financial discussion regarding the RA occurred on January 11, 1977, and February 28, 1979. On February 25, 1982, Pearce wrote to Manuel Rotenberg requesting that the RA period remain at twelve months rather than be shortened to nine, as the ANP "now constitutes one of the three or four major collections of its sort in the world. It is the most used of the division of Special Collections. It attracts researchers not only from the United States but from abroad." It is unclear if his request was met, but RA position continued at least until 1982. See coll. MSS 143, box 2, folder 12, Roy Harvey Pearce Papers, ANP.

58 To Kenneth Hill from Roy Harvey Pearce, November 7, 1977, coll. MSS 143, box 2, folder 12, Roy Harvey Pearce Papers, ANP.

59 Ronald L. da Silveira to Roy Harvey Pearce, January 5, 1978, coll. MSS 143, box 2, folder 12, Roy Harvey Pearce Papers, ANP.

60 William D. McElroy, Chancellor, to Ronald L. da Silveira, January 20, 1978, coll. MSS 143, box 2, folder 12, Roy Harvey Pearce Papers, ANP.

61 Michael Davidson to Roy Harvey Pearce, October 13, 1976, coll. MSS 143, box 2, bolder 11, Roy Harvey Pearce Papers, ANP.

62 Roy Harvey Pearce to Charles Taubman, March 4, 1982, Roy Harvey Pearce subject file, box 5, folder 24, Curator's Correspondence and Subject Files, 1974–1989 (RSS 1034), ANP.

63 Roy Harvey Pearce to Kenneth Hill, April 16, 1982, Roy Harvey Pearce subject file, box 5, folder 24, Curator's Correspondence and Subject Files, 1974–1989 (RSS 1034), ANP.

64 Harryette Mullen, in discussion with the author, January 2016.

65 The majority of the reading dates come from: Curator's Correspondence and Subject Files, 1974–1989 (RSS 1034), ANP.

66 The subject files for these poets can be found in Curator's Correspondence and Subject Files, 1974–1989 (RSS 1034), ANP, as follows: David Henderson (box 4, folder 48); Wai-Lim Yip (box 6, folder 2); Wanda Coleman (box 4, folder 11); Gozo Yoshimasu (box 6, folder 3); Lonny Kaneko (box 4, folder 55); June Jordan (box 4, folder 54); and Lawson Fusao Inada (box 4, folder 51). There is no file for Ishmael Reed, so this date is from the Archive's Newsletter, Winter 1978, MSS 143, box 2, folder 12, Roy Harvey Pearce Papers, ANP.

67 Darío Calicia, Bruno Montane, Mara Larrosa, Roberto Bolaño, Mario Santiago, Inma Marcos, Cuauhtemoc Mendez, and Ruben Medina are grouped under "Latin American Poets," and the subject file indicates "n.d.," or no date. It is unclear whether this means the date for the reading was not recorded, or if a planned event did not come to fruition. Latin

American Poets subject file, box 4, folder 61, Curator's Correspondence and Subject Files, 1974–1989 (RSS 1034), ANP.

68 Perloff, "Whose New American Poetry?," 118. Emphasis mine. Perloff implies here that counterculture experimenters of ontology and form were polite enough not to label "Other" poetry as conservative, though clearly Perloff was unafraid of being labeled racist and sexist. So. Let's call it what it is.

69 For critiques of how poets such as Anne Sexton and Sylvia Plath became reduced to caricatures, and the implications of their flatlining see White, *Lyric Shame*. Also note that, in such reductive arguments, the forms that "Other" poets are engaging with are not their "own"; they are simply the old (white) forms that new white poets no longer wish to engage with. For a full reading of Perloff's approach to race and poetry, see Wang, *Thinking Its Presence*.

70 See Jen Hofer, "If You Hear Something Say Something, or If You're Not at the Table You're on the Menu," *Entropy*, December 18, 2015, https://entropymag.org/if-you-hear-something-say-something-or-if-youre-not-at-the-table-youre-on-the-menu/.

71 I am inclined to argue that the "Perloff tradition" is the one in which the ANP operated at its inception, in its design, and in its curatorial and acquisition practices. From February 9 to 11, 1982, the ANP held a conference titled "San Francisco Renaissance Conference" in which Perloff, and an all-white speaking list, discussed the innovation of "San Francisco Poetry." Whose San Francisco, whose new, whose poetry? See San Francisco Renaissance Conference files, box 7, folders 12 and 13, Curator's Correspondence and Subject Files, 1974–1989 (RSS 1034), ANP.

72 At times there were two different finding-aid links separating correspondence and papers for the same poet. Though there are two links, I counted this as a single poet. I did not count press materials (Momentum Press Archive, Moramarco and Zolynas Editorial Files, Sun & Moon Press Archives, United Artists Records) nor did I count the curator files. My decision not to count the press and curator files comes not out of a desire to exclude their narrative or politics, but out of a decision to examine the papers of poets in the archive. In addition, the press papers reflect the correspondences that occurred between the poets in the archive and their publishing endeavors. For this reason I did not count them twice.

73 For a full synthesis of their practices, see Marriott, "Signs Taken for Signifiers."

74 See Wang, *Thinking Its Presence*.

75 There have been meaningful critiques of Language poetry. In particular, see Marriott, "Signs Taken for Signifiers."

76 Ron Silliman to Peter Glassgold, June 9, 1986, quoted in Yu, *Race and the Avant-Garde*, 64.

77 Yu, *Race and the Avant-Garde*, 58–59.

78 Yu, *Race and the Avant-Garde*, 60. Emphasis mine.

79 Many scholars have written on the construction of race. Though not an exhaustive list, see Bonilla-Silva, *Racism without Racists*; Davis, *Women, Race and Class*; Lipsitz, *Possessive Investment in Whiteness*; and Omi and Winant, *Racial Formation in the United States*.

80 Moral authority shares the logic of "playing the race card." For an accounting of how moral authority is not entrusted, how race is rarely a playing "card," how women and minorities are negated and unbelieved, and how systematic and institutionalized gendered and racialized violence permeates writing and academia, see Gutiérrez y Muhs et al., *Presumed Incompetent*.

81 For whiteness studies that critique this position, see Cacho, "'People of California Are Suffering.'"

82 Yu, *Race and the Avant-Garde*, 59. Being racist and sexist as a white male is still racist and sexist. Because to "use" racist and sexist caricatures is not a "privilege" that white men are denied, that "women and minorities" practice in their writing.

83 Yu does not shy away from the positioning of Language poetry. He writes, "There can be no doubt that Silliman is making an analogy between such categories as 'women's writing' 'black writing' and 'Language writing'—understood as "white male heterosexual writing." Yu, *Race and the Avant-Garde*, 50.

84 Yu, *Race and the Avant-Garde*, 70.

85 See Harris, "Whiteness as Property."

86 The notion of a poetic presence comes from Wang, *Thinking Its Presence*.

87 Amiri Baraka, "Academic Cowards of Reaction."

88 Noah Purifoy, "Eleven from California."

89 Some of Wanda Coleman's papers are held at University of California, Los Angeles.

90 On US literature, see Morrison, *Playing in the Dark*; and Trinh, *Woman Native Other*. On British colonial works, see Spivak, "Three Women's Texts and a Critique of Imperialism." On science fiction, see Carrington, *Speculative Blackness*. See also Lowe, *Immigrant Acts*; Hong, *Ruptures of American Capital*; and Wang, *Thinking Its Presence*.

91 Morrison, *Playing in the Dark*, xiii.

92 See Cahan, *Mounting Frustrations*. The Whitney Biennial of 2014 is further evidence of this; see Eunsong Kim and Maya Mackrandilal, "The Whitney Biennial for Angry Women," *New Inquiry*, April 4, 2014, http://thenewinquiry.com/essays/the-whitney-biennial-for-angry-women/.

93 Ramírez, "Being Assumed Not to Be," 340.

94 Cook, "We Are What We Keep," 174.

95 Honma, "Trippin' over the Color Line," 4.

96 A footnote cannot suffice to cover the current absences in what might constitute the new in US American poetry. And *absence* is a failing word,

as though their absence in the ANP is in any way an indicator of their lives elsewhere.

97 For critical analyses of settler colonialism and the university, see Stewart-Ambo, "The Future Is in the Past"; and Prodanovich, "Whose Coast Are You Surfing in San Diego?"

98 For a critical analysis of the land history of UCSD and critique of the limitations of land acknowledgements, see Stewart-Ambo and Yang, "Beyond Land Acknowledgment in Settler Institutions." See also "Kumeyaay Timeline," *Kumeyaay*, https://www.kumeyaay.com/kumeyaay-timeline.html.

99 Gilliland and Caswell, "Records and Their Imaginaries."

100 Gilliland and Caswell, "Records and Their Imaginaries," 16.

101 Gilliland and Caswell, "Records and Their Imaginaries," 16.

102 See Harris, "Hauntology, Archivy and Banditry." Regarding the "unforgettable," Giorgio Agamben writes, "The exigency of the lost does not entail being remembered and commemorated; rather, it entails remaining in us and with us as forgotten, and in this way and only in this way, remaining unforgettable." Agamben, *Time That Remains*, 40.

103 Arondekar, *For the Record*, 1.

104 Ryan Wong (curator, writer), in discussion with the author, December 2015.

## Chapter 5. Colonially *Bound*, Digitally *Free*: On the Distance between Object and Image

1 See Rose, "James Cuno on Museums."

2 See Tallon, "Introducing Open Access at The Met."

3 Crawford, *Atlas of AI*.

4 For more on this, see Starosielski, *Undersea Network*; Vatanparast, "Infrastructures of the Global Data Economy"; and Parikka, *A Geology of Media*.

5 The show came largely from the private collection of daguerreotypes amassed by the collector and lawyer Jackie Napoleon Wilson, who had assembled a specialized and singular photographic series of pre– and post–Civil War era portraits of Black persons. His collection garnered interest, and in the early nineties, he was invited to the Getty Museum by the founding curator of photographs, Weston Naef, to look through the Getty's photo archives. Getty's late nineteenth-century photo collection had approximately 1,500 photographs, and among them, Wilson was able to locate thirty daguerreotypes, tintypes, and ambrotypes similar to his current collection; these were included in the exhibition. See Wilson, *Hidden Witness*.

6 Though the Getty commissioned the series, they did not acquire it. As noted by Getty curator Weston Naef, through a donor the Museum of Modern Art in New York received a complete set of the series. Many years

after the show, top US art collectors Daniel Greenberg and Susan Steinhauser donated eight works from Weems's series to the Getty.

7 Though from the series *From Here I Saw What Happened and I Cried*, this sequence of four photographs is titled *Scientific Profile, 1995*.

8 Carrie May Weems, in "Compassion," *Art21*, October 7, 2009, https://art21.org/watch/art-in-the-twenty-first-century/s5/carrie-mae-weems-in-compassion-segment/.

9 Weems, in "Compassion," *Art21*.

10 I use *provenance* here in the most traditional sense of "history of ownership" in order to display Harvard and the Peabody's ties to the daguerreotypes.

11 See note 5 above.

12 Baartman was a Khoikhoi woman from southwestern Africa who resided in Paris in abject poverty until her death. Her remains were on display for over a hundred years. After decades of criticism and protest, they were returned in 2002 to the Eastern Cape of South Africa. See Young, *Illegible Will*.

13 Quoted in Beckert and Stevens, *Harvard and Slavery*, 20. See also Agassiz, *Diversity of Origin of the Human Races*, 138; and Agassiz, "Natural Provinces of the Animal World," xxvi.

14 On Agassiz, see Huber and Saarikko, "Louis Who?," 131; on Morton, see Wallis, "Black Bodies, White Science," 42, 53.

15 Wallis, "Black Bodies, White Science," 42.

16 Wallis, "Black Bodies, White Science," 53.

17 Quoted in Wallis, "Black Bodies, White Science," 43.

18 Spillers, "Mama's Baby, Papa's Maybe," 60.

19 Since writing this paper in 2012, updating it as my book chapter in 2018, and then visiting the Peabody on April 25, 2019, it has come to my attention that there is a new controversy around whether Agassiz himself directly procured the daguerreotypes. Curators at the Peabody are now suggesting that Agassiz's "involvement" in procuring the images may have been "ambivalent." Some of the archivists at the Peabody are claiming that there is no record of Agassiz's purchase of the images, and that they may have been "gifts" from friends of his research. As in, he may not have commissioned them or wanted them, as there is no correspondence between Agassiz and Dr. Gibbes or J. T. Zealy (the daguerreotypist) regarding the daguerreotypes. Yet, considering that Agassiz explicitly pursued the gathering of "photographic evidence" for his "scientific" research, I do not believe this detail depoliticizes Agassiz's and Harvard's treatment of the daguerreotypes. I learned of this new development during my appointment to visit the Peabody archives to examine the daguerreotypes on April 25, 2019, from 10:45–11:15 a.m. This thirty-minute slot was what the Peabody allowed me. I shared the appointment with a white male curator who had traveled from Switzerland and a white woman from

England, and was the only nonwhite person in the room and apparently the only nonwhite person provided permission to view the images that morning. This is not a small detail, as it was impressed upon me several times before my appointment that, due to the sensitivity of the daguerreotypes, and because the images must be "protected from light sources," the Peabody only grants a few appointments a year to view the images. Furthermore, it was immediately stated that the curators would not be "discussing the pending lawsuit," and that we were only allowed to keep our appointments because we had made them before the lawsuit was announced—translation: we were not seen as a threat to the institution. And I would agree that the other two persons at the appointment were not a threat. The Swiss curator told us that he was at the appointment in order to put together an exhibition of Swiss photographers. And, though Agassiz did not photograph the enslaved persons personally, it was for his scientific ideals, so de facto, is he not a Swiss photographer? He shared this information as if he was sharing a revolutionary idea, a truly new approach to art while continuously remarking that the daguerreotypes were "beautiful" and that this attention to "lighting" is something one cannot find today. He also remarked how difficult it would have been to "light" the "bodies," as the contrast is so sharp. He did all of this after the curator provided an introduction as to how the images in question were procured to support Agassiz's thesis on polygenesis, and his theory of white supremacy. Dear Reader: I felt so violent toward him. The other viewer in the room, the woman from England, who came late to the appointment, seemed relatively nonplussed, and left shortly after. As for myself, I tried to ask questions in a nonthreatening and abstract manner, a privilege that I can access as an Asian American woman. I tried to collect as much information as possible and made an appointment to discuss my questions further with the archivists. My exchange with them, and my threat status, is pending.

20 Beckert and Stevens, *Harvard and Slavery*, 20. See also Agassiz, "Diversity of Origin of the Human Races," 138; and Agassiz, "Natural Provinces of the Animal World and Their Relation to the Different Types of Man," ixxvi. In polygenesis, the biblical story of God and creation was resituated as a narrative concerning freedom and whiteness.

21 Huber and Saarikko. "Louis Who?," 131.

22 This citation appears in Wallis, "Black Bodies, White Science." At the Harvard Peabody site the information with this image reads, "Mounted daguerreotype in case, black male, nude to waist, front view. Photographer: J. T. Zealy. Paper label reads: 'Renty, Congo, on plantation of B. F. Taylor, Columbia, S.C.'"; https://collections.peabody.harvard.edu/objects/details/82212.

23 Contrary to new claims made by the archivists, previous scholars have suggested that this was done at Agassiz's request. See Machado, "Traces of Agassiz on Brazilian Races," 20–28.

24 "Daguerreotypes and Anatomy," *Tri-Weekly South Carolinian*, October 10, 1850, 2.

25 See Rogers, *Delia's Tears.*

26 Louis Agassiz to Samuel G. Howe, August 9, 1863, in Agassiz and Agassiz, *Louis Agassiz*, 597–98; Weinberg, "The Incalculable Legacy," 10–11. Akin to Agassiz, pivotal taxonomist Linnaeus wrote of male Homo sapiens asiaticus as "yellowish, melancholy, endowed with black hair and brown eyes . . . severe, conceited, and stingy. He puts on loose clothing. He is governed by opinion." Carl Linnaeus, quoted in Benton and Gomez, *Chinese in Britain*, 287. See also Dain, *Hideous Monster of the Mind*, 7. I found these references in Chun, "Introduction: Race and/as Technology," 11n8.

27 Many of the grants Harvard received at the time were directed to or for Agassiz's "research." See Beckert and Stevens, *Harvard and Slavery.*

28 Beckert and Stevens, *Harvard and Slavery*, 21.

29 See Wilder, *Ebony and Ivy.*

30 For example, see "Harvard Professor is for Segregation," *New York Amsterdam News*, August 29, 1923. I found this article while doing research for chapter 2.

31 See Shaler, "Negro Problem," 698; and Weinberg, "Incalculable Legacy," 16.

32 See Irmscher, *Louis Agassiz.* Christoph Irmscher writes that Agassiz began building the Museum of Comparative Zoology at Harvard University in 1859. A few years later, in a meeting of the American Association for the Advancement of Science, he argued that races are "zoologically distinct" (354, 355). Note that the building of the museum coincides with his development of polygenesis.

33 "History," Museum of Comparative Zoology, Harvard, accessed January 13, 2020, https://mcz.harvard.edu/history.

34 As witnessed by UNESCO laws and the rhetoric of encyclopedic and universal museums. See Cuno, *Who Owns Antiquity?* Machado explains why the South Carolina and Brazil daguerreotypes alone remained unpublished: "The Brazilian collection never reached the public eye. The delicate political climate of post-bellum new English, along with Louis Agassiz's own loss of scientific credibility following the publication of Charles Darwin's *Origin of Species* prevented him from making public what was to be his definitive work in establishing the inferiority of blacks and the ills of hybridism." Machado, "Traces of Agassiz on Brazilian Races," 26.

35 See Hartman, *Scenes of Subjection*, 202.

36 Both the donation and the dates of the photographs suggest that their copyright should have lapsed. Though, as I will discuss later, Harvard makes legal claims for these photographs to be controlled as their own.

37 Machado, "Traces of Agassiz on Brazilian Races," 26.

38 It should be noted that the current manufactured rarity of daguerreotypes exists in the photographic continuum of what David Marriott

describes as "the process, another form of racist slur which can travel through time to do its work." Marriott, *On Black Men*, 9. Marriott has argued that the possibility of endless circulation was foundational to photographs of lynching. He writes, "The technological moment which gives us the Kodak—the first turn-of-the-century mass-produced roll-film camera—also gives us a way of venturing into some dark places . . . the photograph represents the climax of an unfolding drama" (9). While the daguerreotype is singular in its production, it exists within the continuum of representational technologies that exist to carefully archive the proliferation of anti-Blackness.

39 Hartman, *Scenes of Subjection*.

40 Harris, "Whiteness as Property."

41 I thank Jarrett Drake for pointing me to this quote. When asked about Tamara Lanier's lawsuit, current Harvard president Lawrence S. Bacow responded, "Those images belong to history." Quoted in Harvard Prison Divestment Campaign, "PRESS RELEASE: Harvard President Claims without Evidence That Investments in Prisons Total Only $18,000, Still Refuses to Divest," April 18, 2019, https://harvardprisondivest.org/press-release-harvard-president-claims-without-evidence-that-investments-in-prisons-total-only-18000-still-refuses-to-divest/.

42 Brown, *Repeating Body*.

43 See Eamon Whalen, "A Lawsuit at Harvard Pries Open Debates About Science and Reparations," *Nation*, November 26, 2019, https://www.thenation.com/article/harvard-slavery-racism/; Joey Garrison, "Fight over Renty and Delia, Earliest Photos of US Slaves Sees Agassiz Descendants Team up against Harvard," *USA Today*, June 20, 2019, https://www.usatoday.com/story/news/nation/2019/06/20/agassiz-descendants-urge-harvard-give-up-renty-delia-slave-photos/1508475001/); and Associated Press, "Woman Suing Harvard over Slave Portraits Gets Key Support," *Chicago Sun-Times*, June 20, 2019, https://chicago.suntimes.com/2019/6/20/18693068/woman-suing-harvard-slave-portraits-images-tamara-lanier-louis-agassiz. In addition to an amicus brief from the descendants, see Lanier's appeal of the March 2021 decision in her suit, Tamara Lanier v. President and Fellows of Harvard College, No. SJC-13138, Mass. Appeals Ct. (2021), Mass. Supreme Ct. (2022).

44 These two cases, *Museum of Fine Arts v. Seger-Thomschitz*, 562 U.S. 1271 (2011) and *United States v. Jiles*, 658 F. 2d 194, 200 (1981), among others cited in the decision, demonstrate the depth to which fascism, mass incarceration, and the history and presence of chattel slavery have and remain concomitant in the law. In Lanier's case, the refusal to redress Nazi plunder and the denial of consent to juveniles in police custody were conjured as pivotal facts to the denial of her restitution. These interlinkages are echoes of the independence too often denied by the sheen of neoliberal individualism.

45 Mem. Dec. and Ord. on Defs.' Mot. Dis. 2d Am. Compl. at 11–12, Tamara Lanier v. President and Fellows of Harvard College, No. 1981CV00784, Mass. Superior Ct. (March 1, 2021) (hereafter Sarrouf decision).

46 Bentham, *Theory of Legislation*, 113.

47 See Bhadar, *Colonial Lives of Property*.

48 Bhadar, *Colonial Lives of Property*, 22.

49 Sarrouf decision at 11.

50 For texts that grapple with the alliance between photography and settler colonialism, see Tsinhnahjinnie, "When Is a Photograph Worth a Thousand Words?"; Faris, *Navajo and Photography*; Azoulay, *From Palestine to Israel*; and Dowie, *Conservation Refugees*.

51 Sarrouf decision at 11.

52 In an earlier draft of this chapter, poet and writer Justin Hogg asked about "abolishing slavery without property" and how this couplet remains in all facets of society today.

53 See an earlier version of this argument in "Eunsong Kim: An Endorsement of an Amicus Brief for Lanier v. Harvard," *Hyperallergic*, October 27, 2021, https://hyperallergic.com/686937/eunsong-kim-an-endorsement-of-an-amicus-brief-for-lanier-v-harvard/; a revision of it appears in Kim, "On the Depth of Fakeness."

54 *Lanier v. Harvard*, No. SJC-13138 at 3. Mass. Supreme Ct. (June 23, 2022) (hereafter Mass. Supreme Ct. decision).

55 "We separate claims for emotional distress from property-related claims." Mass. Supreme Ct. decision at 11.

56 See Mass. Supreme Ct. decision at 6, 21, 12, and 13.

57 Mass. Supreme Ct. decision (Budd concurring) at 11.

58 Mass. Supreme Ct. decision (Cypher concurring) at 13, footnote 8.

59 For writers and researchers who have worked to identify the various sources of the series, see Sasha Bonét, "Carrie Mae Weems Confronts the Fraught History of American Photography," *Aperture*, April 9, 2021, https://aperture.org/editorial/carrie-mae-weems-confronts-the-fraught-history-of-american-photography/; and Barbash, Rogers, and Willis, *To Make Their Own Way in the World*.

60 This stanza represents the part of Weems's original selection for the series, which took from Robert Frank's and Robert Mapplethorpe's photography. This part was subsequently removed during Weems's show at the Getty at the request of their trustees.

61 This is the full text of *Carrie Mae Weems Reacts to Hidden Witness*, from the Getty Museum's photography department. I have transcribed the text according to the department's archival documentation. The text above replicates, to the best of my abilities, the original spacing, enjambments, and style configurations. This text differs slightly in arrangement and length from *Here I Saw What Happened and I Cried*.

62 I have asked and interviewed a plethora of photo curators and educators familiar with Weems's work, including Weston Naef, to see if they could identify the subject in this photograph. I have also looked at the 1995 exhibition notes to see if there might be some clues. I have been unable to locate the photographer or the subject of this image, which speaks to my limitations.

63 This sequencing is gathered from Weems's website. It is unclear if there is an official order to the photographs. Institutions such as the Getty hold eight pieces from the series and have displayed a small selection of them.

64 See Edwards, *Other Side of Terror*, 39

65 Edwards also inspects what she calls "insurgent grammars" and analyzes the work of June Jordan and others to demonstrate the ways in which Black women intimately worked through and against the variegated forces of US empire.

66 Smith, "Carrie Mae Weems," 50.

67 Smith, "Carrie Mae Weems," 38.

68 For historical critiques of white feminism, see Jones, *They Were Her Property*; Gruber, *Feminist War on Crime*; and Zakaria, *Against White Feminism*.

69 Raymond, "Crucible of Witnessing," 31.

70 Specifically, the line "Death did not end the . . . commodification [of the enslaved]" was cited from Berry, *Price for Their Pound of Flesh*.

71 Part of this section of my chapter was drafted in support of Tamara Lanier's case, particularly the amicus brief.

72 Mass. Supreme Ct. decision at 22.

73 Court rulings and legal documents are rarely the place where exploratory analyses are found, as the law attempts to uphold an image of objectivity and science. That in order to protect the absolute rights of an artist this art historian's writing is more racially conservative than the Massachusetts Supreme Court speaks to the defensive milieu of the foundations of modernism.

74 During a 2021 talk I gave on this case and on Raymond's position, Tamara Lanier was in attendance and responded against Raymond's thesis that Renty's death foreclosed harm, that no one can be harmed. It was a moment that clarified for me the material stakes of the theoretical debates.

75 Hartman, *Scenes of Subjection*, 3.

76 Moten, *In the Break*, 4, 5.

77 Mass. Supreme Ct. decision (Cypher concurring) at 30.

78 For a historical discussion on the function of images of slavery, see Fox-Amato, *Exposing Slavery*.

79 These are concepts and arguments from the "Legal Issues in Museum Administration" handbook of the American Law Institute–American Bar Association, 2012 version, given to me by an image permissions expert at the Getty Center.

80 See "Daguerreotype, Renty, frontal," Peabody Museum of Archaeology and Ethnology, Harvard, accessed November 11 2023, https://collections.peabody.harvard.edu/objects/details/82212.

81 "Daguerreotype FAQs," Peabody Museum of Archeology and Ethnology, Harvard, accessed August 30, 2019, https://www.peabody.harvard.edu/sites/default/files/Daguerreotype%20FAQs%2C%2030%20August%202019_1.pdf.

82 See Hartman, *Scenes of Subjection.*

83 I am pulling "living laboratory" from Hortense Spillers, who writes, "This profitable 'atomizing' of the captive body provides another angle of the divided flesh: we lose any hint of suggestion of a dimension of ethics, of relatedness between human personality and its anatomical features, between one human personality and another, between human personality and cultural institutions. To that extent, the procedures adopted for the captive flesh demarcate a total objectification, as the entire captive community becomes a living laboratory." Spillers, "Mama's Baby, Papa's Maybe," 63.

84 Some US museums have set 1983 as the date after which anything wrongly acquired must be returned; France has set 1997. UNESCO and other museums have set the date of November 20, 2004, as an exception for the Iraq war and the publication of cuneiform tablets that were likely looted during the war. I began writing a version of this chapter as my qualifying exam paper in 2011. A couple of years later, I came across Yxta Maya Murray's "From Here I Saw What Happened and I Cried: Carrie Mae Weems's Challenge to the Harvard Archive," published in 2013. In the essay, Murray considers the UNESCO Convention as a possible justification for the images to be returned to the descendants of those depicted in the daguerreotypes. My argument, while not in conflict with her suggestion, pushes for the images to be resituated entirely, as the procedure of finding descendants may be difficult, and if descendants are not easily accessible, this process may seriously deter the process. The removal of the daguerreotypes from Harvard must happen regardless of found or unfound descendants. See Murray, "From Here I Saw What Happened and I Cried."

85 I do not bring up the "end" of slavery to situate illusions about this. However, as consent laws are essential to photography copyright, the "end" of US slavery and the rhetoric of consent before and after is crucial to situating photographic permissions today.

86 Or, the vocabulary used to distinguish what can belong to a nation-state, culture.

87 For more on his arguments against all kinds of repatriation, see Cuno, *Who Owns Antiquity?*

88 Rose, "James Cuno on Museums."

89 Rose, "James Cuno on Museums." In this section of the interview, Cuno also discusses the colonially legal: "If the things have been removed legally and the circumstances—a circumstance of the time which they were removed, and we know from the Parthenon Marbles, they were in fact removed legally because the Ottoman authorities gave Elgin permission to remove them." It is important to note here that it was Joseph Duveen—personal art dealer to Henry Clay Frick (discussed in detail in chapter 1), Andrew Carnegie, Andrew Mellon, J. P. Morgan, and others—who brokered the "permission" deal for the Parthenon marbles. Many, if not all, of his art dealings have come under serious scrutiny today, ranging from the selling of fakes to dubious provenance concerns. I bring this up to state that Cuno cannot use the Parthenon Marbles as an example of "legal" removal or "permission," unless what he is really trying to point to is the impossibility of permission.

90 For ongoing discourse regarding the return of these objects, see Philip Oltermann "Germany Returns 21 Benin Bronzes to Nigeria—Amid Frustration at Britain," *Guardian,* December 20, 2022, https://www.theguardian.com/world/2022/dec/20/germany-returns-21-benin-bronzes-to-nigeria-amid-frustration-at-britain; and Douglas Bloom, "Stolen Colonial-Era Objects Will be 'Unconditionally' Returned, Says the Netherlands," *World Economic Forum,* February 23, 2021, https://www.weforum.org/agenda/2021/02/all-stolen-colonial-era-artefacts-will-be-returned-says-netherlands/. Additionally, the damage to the artifacts being returned is most concerning; see Philip Oltermann, "Toxic Dilemma Faced by German Museums Repatriating Artefacts," *Guardian,* January 17, 2023, https://www.theguardian.com/world/2023/jan/17/toxic-dilemma-german-museums-repatriating-artefacts-pesticides-objects-contaminated.

91 Daniel Grant et al., "What Happens When Museums Return Antiquities?," *Hyperallergic,* March 21, 2014, https://hyperallergic.com/115015/what-happens-when-museums-return-antiquities/.

92 I am taking up Jane Blocker's "Aestheticization of Risk in Wartime" in my analysis here.

93 See Grant et al., "What Happens When Museums Return Antiquities?"

94 Hall, "Minimal Selves," 44.

95 Divya Mehra, interview with the author, May 2021. This discussion draws on my essay on Mehra's exhibition, Kim, "We Hope You Can See Your Way Home."

96 See Hurley, "Parallel Provenance."

97 Caswell, *Archiving the Unspeakable,* 255.

98 Caswell, *Archiving the Unspeakable,* 255.

99 Caswell, *Archiving the Unspeakable,* 258.

100 Collins, "Social Constructions of Black Feminist Thought," 183.

101 Interesting to note: philosopher William James volunteered to assist Agassiz on this trip when he was a student at Harvard University. See Machado, *Brazil through the Eyes of William James.*

102 See Machado, *(T)Races of Louis Agassiz.* This project was the first time the Peabody Museum granted permission for the reproduction of Agassiz's images. At first, the group was denied permission, but after a series of inflammatory articles questioning the Peabody's position, the museum changed its mind (13). Suzanne Schneider also comments on how difficult it was for her to gain access to these daguerreotypes. In footnote 7 of the chapter "Louis Agassiz and the American School of Ethnoeroticism," Schneider comments on how she has been denied access to the daguerreotypes since 2000.

103 Machado, *(T)Races of Louis Agassiz*, 24. As the catalog explains, in building a racialized and pre-eugenic classification system, Agassiz "went so far as to insert postcards of Greek Statues (such as Apollo Belvedere) in his Brazilian collection, intending to contrast the purportedly brutish features of Africans and mestizos with the delicate Greek physiognomy" (23).

104 See Fassler, "What's in a Name?" The artists' online petition generated over 2,712 signatures and prompted international discussion. See "RENTYHORN PETITION," accessed January 14, 2020, http://www.rentyhorn.ch/.

105 Sasha Huber, interview with the author, April 3, 2013.

106 Caswell, *Archiving the Unspeakable*, 257.

107 Hartman, "Venus in Two Acts," 3.

## Chapter 6. Neoliberal Aesthetics: The Legacies of White Modernism

An earlier version of this chapter appeared in *Lateral: Journal of the Cultural Studies Association*, no. 4 (2015).

1 For Fatima El-Tayeb's articulation toward this idea, see "Digital Lecture with Prof. Fatima El-Tayeb on Decolonizing Europe," YouTube, September 21, 2020, posted by the Schwarzkopf Foundation, https://www.youtube.com/watch?v=uXVyHb-glbY&ab_channel=SchwarzkopfFoundation; and El-Tayeb, "The Universal Museum."

2 For historical analyses on the trajectory of neoliberalism, see Fraser, *Old Is Dying*; and Slobodian, *Globalists.*

3 Melamed, *Represent and Destroy*, 42.

4 Brown, *Undoing the Demos.* The transformation Brown describes can be seen in "theory of the firm" scholarship; see, among others, Williamson, "Theory of the Firm as Governance Structure"; and Kantarelis, *Theories of the Firm.*

5 For a historical analysis on the institutional management and appropriation of difference, see Ferguson, *Reorder of Things*. "Capital's imagination" is Max Haiven's term; see Haiven, "Finance as Capital's Imagination?"

6 Rancière, *Philosopher and His Poor*, xxvi.

7 See Walter Benn Michaels, "Neoliberal Aesthetics: Fried, Rancière and the Form of the Photograph," nonsite.org, January 25, 2011, https://nonsite.org/neoliberal-aesthetics-fried-ranciere-and-the-form-of-the-photograph/; and Jeon, "Neoliberal Forms." These writers situate "neoliberal forms/aesthetics" as forms of refusal, or forms of potential unveiling. While I find their investigations to be rich, my definition of the term takes a different focus.

8 Haiven, "Finance as Capital's Imagination?," 104, 117.

9 See Blocker, "Aestheticizing Risk in Wartime."

10 Hartman, *Scenes of Subjection*, 3.

11 Rancière, *Disagreement*, 50.

12 In the Tate Modern museum's video documentation for *Group of Person Facing a Wall*, Sierra articulates that he is against the artist-brand regime and therefore will not reveal his face. As rhetoric devoid of the context of his aesthetic approach to subcontracting, this is an interesting notion. In capitalist economies, value is linked most closely to the fiction of the brand rather than to the quality of or the labor invested in the object in question. However, the Santiago Sierra brand is not dependent on his face or body—it is linked to his name and the repetitive enactments of using other people's bodies. Once again, tedious contradictions are introduced; is Sierra resisting, then, the function of branding in capitalism by hiding his face, even though, as this chapter discusses later, he purports to stay within the confines of capitalist methodologies? It should be noted, however, that he is not anonymous. He is present at his gallery openings and other such events. I would argue that it is an act of immense cowardice to be the manager of brutality but remain anonymous, ensuring that he will never be met with detailed and focused protest himself. For the video, see "Tateshots Issue 13—Santiago Sierra," November 25, 2019, Sternthal Books, Vimeo, https://vimeo.com/35787572.

13 I am reminded of Rancière's quip: "I forgot that I had never known how to draw a straight line." *Philosopher and His Poor*, xxvii.

14 Kenning, "Art Relations and the Presence of Absence," 438.

15 In an interview, Sierra states, "You are of the opinion that it is wrong to say that people work for money and sell their time and that somebody who says so is a great liar, and this in fact suggests some priggishness in dealing with these issues." Matt, *Interviews*, 152.

16 Matt, *Interviews*, 153.

17 As quoted in Nelson, *Art of Cruelty*, 127.

18 Schneider, *Santiago Sierra*, 28.

19 Currently the *250 cm Line* photographs have all been sold. Price and information obtained from Lisson Gallery in 2012 and 2014.

20 Bishop, "Antagonism and Relational Aesthetics," 70.

21 Hong, *Ruptures of American Capital*, xxviii.

22 Hong, *Ruptures of American Capital*, xxviii.

23 Quoted in Echeverría, "Santiago Sierra Minimum Wages," 103.

24 Fraser, "'I Am Going to Tell You What I Am Not.'" Emphasis mine.

25 See "China Tops Art and Antiques League," BBC News, March 20, 2012, https://www.bbc.com/news/entertainment-arts-17442619. See also Alexandra Bregman, "China's Billionaires Set to Dominate the World's Art Market," *Nikkei Asia,* December 4, 2020, https://asia.nikkei.com/Opinion/China-s-billionaires-set-to-dominate-the-world-s-art-market; and Eileen Kinsella, "Demonstrating Resilience during the Pandemic, the Market for Chinese Art and Antiques Reaped $5.7 Billion Last Year, Our Report Found," *Artnet,* November 22, 2021, https://news.artnet.com/market/the-market-for-chinese-art-and-antiques-caa-report-2020-2035623.

26 Haiven, "Finance as Capital's Imagination?," 112.

27 Blocker, *What the Body Costs*, 14.

28 Blocker, *What the Body Costs*, 15.

29 Kester, "Device Laid Bare."

30 Quoted in Kester, *One and the Many*, 169. Emphasis mine. Kester also has an incisive reading of this passage.

31 Marx, *Economic and Philosophic Manuscripts of 1844*, 105.

32 A contemporary example of this is Hyundai Corporation's eleven-year sponsorship of Tate's Turbine Hall—the longest corporate sponsorship in museum and gallery history. For a full diagnosis of this phenomena, see Wu, *Privatising Culture*.

33 For a compelling analysis on the function of aesthetic realms and their political economies, see Ngai, *Our Aesthetic Categories*.

34 See Marx, *Economic and Philosophic Manuscripts of 1844*, 255, especially the passage (emphasis mine):

> You pay me for one day's labour-power, whilst you use that of 3 days. That is against our contract and the law of exchanges. I demand, therefore, a working-day of normal length, and *I demand it without any appeal to your heart, for in money matters sentiment is out of place.* You may be a model citizen . . . but the thing that you represent face to face with me has no heart in its breast. That which seems to throb there is my own heart-beating. I demand the normal working-day because I, like every other seller, demand the value of my commodity.

35 Haiven, "Finance as Capital's Imagination?," 111.

36 Haiven, "Finance as Capital's Imagination?," 111.

37 Haiven, "Finance as Capital's Imagination?," 101.

38 Sierra, *Santiago Sierra: Works 2002–1990*, 15. The full quote is: "I can't change anything. There is no possibility that we can change anything

with our artistic work. We do our work because we are making art, and because we believe art should be something, something that follows reality. But I don't believe in the possibility of change."

39 Baum, "Santiago Sierra: How to Do Things with Words."

40 There could be a longer discussion here as to how class and taste contribute to what is acceptable and desirable in high gallery economies. In *Privatising Culture*, Chin Tao Wu pulls from Pierre Bourdieu's *Distinction: A Social Critique of the Judgment of Taste* to display how cultural capital functions as museum culture and how museum culture becomes an "instrument of domination." The shared agreement between gallerists, critics, and patrons on Sierra's enactment might be an indicator of their class standing. See Wu, *Privatising Culture*.

41 Kester, *One and the Many*, 163.

42 Kester, *One and the Many*, 166.

43 Bishop, "Antagonism and Relational Aesthetics," 79. Emphasis mine.

44 Bishop, "Antagonism and Relational Aesthetics," 70. Emphasis mine.

45 In her video-recorded lecture "The General Strike," art historian Jaleh Mansoor describes Sierra's subcontractors as "paid volunteers." She does so when discussing his *133 Persons Paid to Have Their Hair Dyed Blonde* (2001), an enactment that bleached 133 persons' hair for 120,000 lire ($60) per person at the Venice Biennale. In this work, Sierra specifically subcontracted refugees or immigrants of African, East European, Asian, and Middle Eastern descent. Mansoor says that Sierra "collected them." See Jaleh Mansoor, "The General Strike," YouTube, October 30, 2012, https://www.youtube.com/watch?v=kHjnUivdqzc.

46 It is important to remember here the creation of free time in capitalism. Marx writes, "In capitalist society, free time is produced for one class by the conversion of the whole lifetime of the masses into labour-time." Marx, *Capital*, 667.

47 Fusco, *Bodies That Were Not Ours*, 64.

48 Fusco, *Bodies That Were Not Ours*, 64.

49 Fusco, *Bodies That Were Not Ours*, 65.

50 Fusco, *Bodies That Were Not Ours*, 65.

51 Fusco, *Bodies That Were Not Ours*, 66.

52 Fusco, *Bodies That Were Not Ours*, 67.

53 Fusco, *Bodies That Were Not Ours*, 69.

54 Fusco, *Bodies That Were Not Ours*, 67.

55 Here, I want to quote Jane Blocker, who asks what "an artist boycott of risk might look like, and whether our refusal to participate in that game would help productively to change its rules." What might it look like if museums, art historians, artists, economists and so forth, boycotted risk transfers rather than celebrated them? See Blocker, "Aestheticizing Risk in Wartime."

56 Schneider, *Santiago Sierra*, 166. This is a crude subpoint, but is Sierra a qualified commentator concerning the devastating and violent conditions

of structural and economic injustice? Why his desires as a wealthy and successful artist must be taken above those of his subcontractors has yet to be addressed.

57 "Santiago Sierra: Dedicated to the Workers and Unemployed," Lisson Gallery, https://www.lissongallery.com/exhibitions/santiago-sierra-dedicated-to-the-workers-and-unemployed.

58 Martinez, "Interview with Santiago Sierra," 189, 197.

59 For Sierra's statement, see "Santiago Sierra Says No," *Monthly Review,* November 6, 2010, https://mronline.org/2010/11/06/santiago-sierra-says-no/, translated by Yoshie Furuhashi. This article first appeared as "Se puede decir más alto pero no más claro: 'NO,'" *Ciudad Futura,* November 6, 2010, https://ciudad-futura.net/2010/11/06/se-puede-decir-mas-alto-pero-no-mas-claro-no/.

Sierra's "NO, Global Tour" was his 2009–12 installation campaign, in which a truck carrying a large sculptural sign "NO" stopped at various locations throughout Europe, where the sculpture was then photographed. The "NO" is meant to represent a rejection of the state and capitalism. See Sierra's website, NO, GLOBAL TOUR, accessed January 15, 2020, http://www.noglobaltour.com.

60 Quoted in "Santiago Sierra Says No."

61 In an interview with Fulvia Carnevale, Rancière makes a strange statement about Sierra: "I don't have a lot of sympathy for Santiago Sierra's actions, but when he pays immigrant workers minimum wage to dig their own graves or to get tattoos that signify their condition, he reminds us at least that the 'equivalence' of an hour of work and its effect on the body is not the so-called equivalence of everything that slides across a screen." Rancière, quoted in Carnevale and Kelsey, "Art of the Possible." This statement differs vastly from Rancière's own critique of Marx's fraught position of power as teacher, writer, and revolutionary. In *The One and the Many*, Grant Kester has an in-depth critique of Rancière's approach to contemporary visual arts. While I agree with Kester's assessment of Rancière's nonmaterialist approach to the field of contemporary art, I find Rancière's political philosophy to be a different matter.

62 Rancière, *Philosopher and His Poor*, xxvi, 104, 68.

63 Of this Rancière writes, "The proletarian is someone *who has only one thing to do*—they make the revolution—and who *cannot not do that* because of what [s]he is." *Philosopher and His Poor*, 80. Emphasis mine.

64 Rancière, *Philosopher and His Poor*, 75. Emphasis mine.

65 Rancière, *Philosopher and His Poor*, 81.

66 Kenning, "Art Relations and the Presence of Absence," 438.

67 Kenning, "Art Relations and the Presence of Absence," 441.

68 When asked why he selected Vienna for this project, Sierra responds, "In Vienna, just like in the rest of the European Union, a strange discussion is going on that is all about race but without ever using the term. But

they are only getting adjusted to something that is a common practice in places such as New York." Matt, *Interviews*, 316.

69 Denise Ferreira da Silva has described this as "global raciality." See Ferreira da Silva, *Toward a Global Idea of Race*.

70 Marchart, "Art Institutions between Politics and the Police," 73.

71 Kenning, "Art Relations and the Presence of Absence," 442.

72 See Michael Maiello, "Yes—You Deserve a Fat Bonus," *Forbes Magazine*, July 16, 2012, http://www.forbes.com/forbes/2009/0316/028_deserve_fat_bonus.html.

73 Kenning, "Art Relations and the Presence of Absence," 442. Emphasis mine.

74 Kapadia, "Up in the Air and On the Skin," 362.

75 See, for example, Jenny Kutner, "This Woman Is Covering Up Domestic Violence Survivors' Scars With Beautiful Free Tattoos," *Mic*, September 8, 2015, https://www.mic.com/articles/124964/flavia-carvalho-is-covering-up-domestic-violence-survivors-scars-with-free-tattoos.

76 Kitzmann, "Between the Inside and the Outside."

77 Kapadia, "Up in the Air and On the Skin," 368.

78 In 2011, the young artist Gerry Duran reconfigured Sierra's work in a short film titled "Art Talks." Duran, sticking to Sierra's form and methods, subcontracted friends from his community with gummy bears and subcontracted another friend to paint rainbows on their backs. By using friends and those closest to him, Duran critiques Sierra's labor narrative: how Sierra is able to objectify his laborers within his art project and situate people as "raw material," as objects of exploitation. When describing the project, Duran writes that he does not understand how Sierra was able to capitulate to his performance at all, as Duran "got this weird heinous feeling inside" participating in his friends being painted for his art—even if they were just painted with rainbows. When Duran describes the relationship between subjects, he sympathizes with and relates to those who participate in his filmmaking. For the video, see Gerry Duran, "Art Talks," Vimeo, 02:36, https://vimeo.com/26689613#at=2.

## Coda. On Inoperation and Glory

1 Ezra Klein, "Jenny Odell and the Art of Attention," interview, *Vox*, May 23, 2019, https://www.vox.com/ezra-klein-show-podcast/2019/5/23/18636332/jenny-odell-how-to-do-nothing.

2 While works of art have been housed in the safety of Gap Inc. headquarters, there have been numerous reports of Gap's deathly labor abuses abroad, including a 2021 incident where fifty-two workers were killed in a fire in Bangladesh, unable to escape a factory because the door was illegally locked from the outside. See "At Least 52 Killed in Bangladesh Factory Fire as Workers Trapped inside by an Illegally Locked Door," CBS

News, July 9, 2021, https://www.cbsnews.com/news/bangladesh-factory-fire-dozens-dead/; and Kristine Wong, "Bangladesh Factory Collapse: Can Gap and Others Pin Down Worker Safety?," *Guardian,* September 10, 2013, https://www.theguardian.com/sustainable-business/rana-plaza-gap-worker-safety.

Concomitantly, the dispossession of Native communities has been historical and ongoing. For research focused on the San Francisco Bay Area, see Bay Area Equity Atlas, https://bayareaequityatlas.org/; and Moore, Montojo, and Mauri, *Roots, Race, and Place.*

3 It is important to note that Fisher's donation came after he failed to build a museum of his own. SFMOMA agreed to the donation because it came with the funds to expand its galleries; in exchange, the donation stipulates a one-hundred-year term, and includes conditions such as that 60 percent of what is publicly on display in the galleries must be from the Fisher collection at all times. Lastly, Don Fisher's son Robert Fisher is the president of the museum board. For more on this, see Charles Desmarais, "Unraveling SFMOMA's deal for the Fisher collection," *SFGATE,* August 31, 2016, https://www.sfgate.com/art/article/Unraveling-SFMOMA-s-deal-for-the-Fisher-9175280.php; and Cy Musiker, "Shiny, New SFMOMA a 'Who's Who' of 20th Century Art: So What's Missing?" KQED, May 13, 2016, https://www.kqed.org/arts/11574512/shiny-new-sfmoma-a-whos-who-of-20th-century-art-so-whats-missing.

4 Reports of abuses by Gap have been ongoing for some time. See Bhattacharjee, *Gender Based Violence in the GAP Garment Supply Chain*; and Kate Hodal. "Abuse Is Daily Reality for Female Garment Workers for Gap and H&M, Says Report," *Guardian,* June 5, 2018, https://www.theguardian.com/global-development/2018/jun/05/female-garment-workers-gap-hm-south-asia.

5 Contrary to the wishful thinking that some patronage and philanthropy could be put to good use, W. E. B. Du Bois had a foundational critique of philanthropy in Black education: "Led on by British capitalism, founded on Negro slavery, we assumed that income from a given batch of invested capital would if rightly administered continue forever. This we now realize is false and evil. Wealth for consumption or future use is no more eternal than the muscle or brain which created it and can only last forever by continuing to take from wages and giving to profit an absolutely unjustifiable share. It is on this fact that the whole argument for more equitable distribution of production rests." Du Bois insisted against the good capitalist narrative that would justify present dispossession for the potential gains of some future. Du Bois, "Future and Function of the Private Negro College," 184.

6 Louise and Walter Arensberg's collection was integrated into the Philadelphia Museum of Art; see chapter 3. The Sackler family donated art to numerous museums in Britain and the United States, often establish-

ing galleries or wings named for them (many since unnamed, in the aftermath of the opioid crisis attributed to the family's company, Purdue Pharma). Henry Clay Frick's personal collection formed the Frick Collection, New York; Gertrude Vanderbilt Whitney's collection formed the Whitney Museum of American Art, New York (her wealth came from both the Vanderbilt and Whitney fortunes); and Eli Broad's collection formed the Broad, Los Angeles.

7 Agamben, *Kingdom and Glory*, trans. Lorenzo Chiesa and Matteo Mandarini, xii.

8 Celan, *Wolfsbohne/Wolf's Bean*, trans. Michael Hamburger, 340–45.

9 Riding, *Anarchism Is Not Enough*.

10 Bryan-Wilson begins the book by describing the self-described "art workers" and the antiwar artists of the 1960s and 1970s. She concentrates on Carl Andre, Hans Haacke, Lucy Lippard, and Robert Morris as artists reaching for a utopian ideal while reinventing how art is transcribed. While I believe in the importance of Bryan-Wilson's research, I have always wondered about the implicit and explicit whiteness of *art workers*. Much is lost or subsumed in the focus on only white, mostly male artists. How do critiques of capitalism and war occur without a reckoning with whiteness, anti-Blackness, race? And what should one make of the gendered violence situated by this framing of art workers? Carl Andre *killed* Ana Mendieta.

11 Bryan-Wilson, *Art Workers*, 1.

12 Bryan-Wilson, *Art Workers*, 221.

13 Naeem Mohaiemen and Hans Haacke, "The Loneliness of the Long-Distance Campaign," *Sightlines*, December 7, 2016, https://walkerart.org/magazine/gulf-labor-hans-haacke-naeem-mohaiemen.

14 I am pulling here from Fred Moten's definition of the *commons*; see Harney and Moten, *Undercommons*.

15 I am expanding Giorgio Agamben's notion of the *unforgettable* here. *Time That Remains*, 40.

16 Césaire, *Notebook of a Return to the Native Land*, 43–44.

# BIBLIOGRAPHY

## Archives

Archive for New Poetry, University of California San Diego Library, University of California San Diego.

CURATOR FILES.

ROY HARVEY PEARCE PAPERS.

Walter and Louise Arensberg Papers. Arensberg Archives, Philadelphia Museum of Art.

Frick Art Reference Library, Frick Collection, New York.

BOARD OF TRUSTEES FILES, 1920–1931.

HENRY CLAY FRICK PAPERS.

Henry Clay Frick Business Records. University of Pittsburgh, Pittsburg, PA.

Getty Research Institute, Los Angeles.

JOSEPH DUVEEN FILES.

KNOEDLER GALLERY ARCHIVE.

Rivers of Steel, Pittsburgh, PA.

## Books, Articles, and Other Sources

Abbott, Charles, Rudolf Arnheim, Karl Shapiro, and Donald A. Stauffer. *Poets at Work: Essays Based on the Modern Poetry Collection at the Lockwood Memorial Library, University of Buffalo*. New York: Harcourt, Brace, 1948.

Adelman, Robert M., and Christopher Mele, eds. *Race, Space, and Exclusion: Segregation and Beyond in Metropolitan America*. Abingdon: Routledge, 2014.

Adorno, Theodor, and Herbert Marcuse. "Correspondence on the German Student Movement." Translated by Esther Leslie. *New Left Review*, no. 233 (January/February 1999): 134.

Agamben, Giorgio. *Kingdom and the Glory: For a Theological Genealogy of Economy and Government*. Translated by Lorenzo Chiesa and Matteo Mandarini. Stanford, CA: Stanford University Press, 2011.

Agamben, Giorgio. *The Time That Remains*. Translated by Patricia Dailey. Stanford, CA: Stanford University Press, 2005.

Agassiz, Louis. *Diversity of Origin of the Human Races: From the Christian Examiner for July, 1850*. London: Forgotten Books, 2018.

Agassiz, Louis. "Natural Provinces of the Animal World and Their Relation to the Different Types of Man." In *Types of Mankind: Or, Ethnological Researches, Based Upon the Ancient Monuments, Paintings, Sculptures, and Crania of Races, and Upon Their Natural, Geographical, Philological and Biblical History*, edited by J. D. Nott and Geo Gliddon, lvii–lxxvi. Philadelphia: Lippincott, Grambo, 1854.

Ahmed, Sara. "Feminist Killjoys (And Other Willful Subjects)." *Scholar and Feminist Online* 8, no. 3 (2010). https://sfonline.barnard.edu/polyphonic/print_ahmed.htm.

Alberro, Alexander, and Blake Stimson. *Conceptual Art: A Critical Anthology*. Cambridge, MA: MIT Press, 1999.

Alexander, Michelle. *The New Jim Crow: Mass Incarceration in the Age of Colorblindness*. New York: New Press, 2010.

Alsop, Joseph. *The Rare Art Traditions: The History of Art Collecting and Its Linked Phenomena Wherever These Have Appeared*. New York: Harper and Row, 1987.

Armstrong, Elizabeth. "Interviews with Ed Ruscha and Bruce Conner." *October* 70 (1994): 55–59.

Arondekar, Anjali. *For the Record: On Sexuality and the Colonial Archive in India*. Durham, NC: Duke University Press, 2009.

Aufhauser, Keith. "Slavery and Scientific Management." *Journal of Economic History* 33, no. 4 (1973): 811–24.

Azoulay, Ariella. *From Palestine to Israel: A Photographic Record of Destruction and State Formation, 1947–1950*. London: Pluto, 2011.

Bahnisch, Mark. "Embodied Work, Divided Labour: Subjectivity and the Scientific Management of the Body in Frederick W. Taylor's 1907 'Lecture on Management.'" *Body and Society* 6, no. 1 (2000): 51–68.

Baker, Erik. "The Rise of Entrepreneurial Management Theory in the United States." *Modern Intellectual History* (2021): 1–25. https://doi.org/10.1017/S1479244321000597.

Baraka, Amiri. "The Academic Cowards of Reaction." *Blacklisted Journalist*, March 1, 2002. https://www.blacklistedjournalist.com/column69k1.html.

Barbash, Ilisa, Molly Rogers, and Deborah Willis, eds. *To Make Their Own Way in the World: The Enduring Legacy of the Zealy Daguerreotypes*. New York: Aperture, 2020.

Barker, Joanne. "The Corporation and the Tribe." *American Indian Quarterly* 39, no. 3 (2015): 243–70.

Barker, Joanne. "Territory as Analytic: The Dispossession of Lenapehoking and the Subprime Crisis." *Social Text* 36, no. 2 (2018): 19–39.

Bastian, Jeannette A. "Flowers for Homestead: A Case Study in Archives and Collective Memory." *American Archivist* 72, no. 1 (2009): 113–32.

Bataille, Georges. *The Accursed Share: An Essay on General Economy*. New York: Zone, 1949.

Baum, Kelly. "Santiago Sierra: How to Do Things with Words." *Art Journal* 69, no. 4 (2010): 7–13.

Beckert, Sven, Balraj Gill, Jim Henle, and Katherine Stevens. "Harvard and Slavery." *Transition*, no. 122 (2017): 201–5.

Beckert, Sven, Katherine Stevens, and the Harvard and Slavery Research Seminar. *Harvard and Slavery: Seeking a Forgotten History*. Cambridge, MA: Harvard University, 2011. https://www.harvardandslavery.com/wp-content/uploads/2011/11/Harvard-Slavery-Book-111110.pdf.

Beech, Dave. *Art and Labour: On the Hostility to Handicraft, Aesthetic Labour and the Politics of Work in Art*. Chicago: Haymarket, 2021.

Behrman, S. N. *Duveen: The Story of the Most Spectacular Art Dealer of All Time.* New York: Little Bookroom, 2003.

Bellush, Jewel, and Stephen M. David, eds. *Race and Politics in New York City: Five Studies in Policy*. New York: Praeger, 1971.

Benjamin, Walter. "The Author as Producer." Translated by John Heckman. *New Left Review* 1, no. 62 (1970): 83–96.

Benjamin, Walter. "Critique of Violence." In *Reflections: Essays, Aphorisms, Autobiographical Writings*, edited by Peter Demetz, 277–300. Boston: Mariner, 2019.

Benjamin, Walter. "Theses on the Philosophy of History." In *Illuminations*, edited by Hannah Arendt, 253–64. New York: Schocken, 1969.

Benjamin, Walter. "The Work of Art in the Age of Mechanical Reproduction." In *Illuminations*, edited by Hannah Arendt, 217–52. New York: Schocken, 1969.

Bennett, Eric. *Workshops of Empire: Stegner, Engle, and American Creative Writing during the Cold War*. Iowa City: University of Iowa Press, 2015.

Bentham, Jeremy. *Theory of Legislation*. London: Trübner, 1871.

Benton, Gregor, and Edmund Terence Gomez. *The Chinese in Britain, 1800–Present: Economy, Transnationalism, Identity*. London: Palgrave Macmillan, 2008.

Berry, Daina Ramey. *The Price for Their Pound of Flesh: The Value of the Enslaved, from Womb to Grave, in the Building of Nation*. Boston: Beacon, 2017.

Bhadar, Brenna. *Colonial Lives of Property: Law, Land, and Racial Regimes of Ownership*. Durham, NC: Duke University Press, 2018.

Bhattacharjee, Shikha Silliman. *Gender Based Violence in the GAP Garment Supply Chain—Workers Voices from the Global Supply Chain: A Report to the ILO 2018*. Geneva: International Labour Organization, 2018. https://www.globallaborjustice.org/wp-content/uploads/2018/06/GBV-Gap-May-2018.pdf.

Birth, Kevin. *Objects of Time: How Things Shape Temporality*. New York: Palgrave, 2012.

Bishop, Claire. "Antagonism and Relational Aesthetics." *October* 110 (2004): 51–79.

Blocker, Jane. "Aestheticizing Risk in Wartime: The SLA to Iraq." In *The Aesthetics of Risk*, edited by John C. Welchman, 191–223. Zurich: JRP Ringier, 2008.

Blocker, Jane. *What the Body Costs: Desire, History and Performance*. Minneapolis: University of Minnesota Press, 2004.

Bodnar, John, Roger Simon, and Michael P. Weber. *Lives of Their Own: Blacks, Italians, and Poles in Pittsburgh, 1900–1960*. Urbana: University of Illinois Press, 1983.

Bonilla-Silva, Eduardo. *Racism without Racists: Color-Blind Racism and the Persistence of Racial Inequality in America*. Lanham, MD: Rowman and Littlefield, 2003.

Bourdieu, Pierre. *Distinction: A Social Critique of the Judgement of Taste*. Translated by Richard Nice. Cambridge, MA: Harvard University Press, 1987.

Braddock, Jeremy. *Collecting as Modernist Practice*. Baltimore, MD: Johns Hopkins University Press, 2013.

Brand, Dionne. *A Map to the Door of No Return: Notes to Belonging*. Toronto: Vintage Canada, 2002.

Brand, Dionne. *Ossuaries*. Toronto: McClelland and Stewart, 2010.

Braverman, Harry. *Labor and Monopoly Capital: The Degradation of Work in the Twentieth Century*. New York: New York University Press, 1998.

Brewer, John. *The American Leonardo: A Tale of Obsession, Art, and Money*. Oxford: Oxford University Press, 2009.

Brown, Kimberly Juanita. *The Repeating Body: Slavery's Visual Resonance in the Contemporary*. Durham, NC: Duke University Press, 2015.

Brown, Nicholas A. "The Logic of Settler Accumulation in a Landscape of Perpetual Vanishing." *Settler Colonial Studies* 4, no. 1 (2014): 1–26.

Brown, Wendy. *Undoing the Demos: Neoliberalism's Stealth Revolution*. Princeton, NJ: Princeton University Press, 2015.

Brown, Wendy. *In the Ruins of Neoliberalism: The Rise of Antidemocratic Politics in the West*. New York: Columbia University Press, 2019.

Bryan-Wilson, Julia. *Art Workers: Radical Practice in the Vietnam War Era*. Berkeley: University of California Press, 2011.

Buchloh, Benjamin H. D. "Conceptual Art 1962–1969: From the Aesthetic of Administration to the Critique of Institutions." *October* 55 (1990): 105–43.

Burawoy, Michael. *Manufacturing Consent: Changes in the Labor Process under Monopoly Capitalism*. Chicago: University of Chicago Press, 1979.

Burgoyne, Arthur. *The Homestead Strike of 1892*. Pittsburgh, PA: University of Pittsburgh Press, 2014.

Burnham, Margaret A. *By Hands Now Known: Jim Crow's Legal Executioners*. New York: W. W. Norton, 2022.

Buskirk, Martha, and Mignon Nixon, eds. *The Duchamp Effect*. Cambridge, MA: MIT Press, 1996.

Byrd, Jodi. *The Transit of Empire: Indigenous Critiques of Colonialism*. Minneapolis: University of Minnesota Press, 2011.

Cacho, Lisa. "'The People of California Are Suffering': The Ideology of White Injury in Discourses of Immigration." *Cultural Values* 4, no. 4 (2000): 389–418.

Callahan, David. *The Givers: Wealth, Power, and Philanthropy in a New Gilded Age*. New York: Knopf, 2017.

Cahan, Susan E. *Mounting Frustration: The Art Museum in the Age of Black Power*. Durham, NC: Duke University Press, 2016.

Calo, Mary Ann. *Distinction and Denial : Race, Nation, and the Critical Construction of the African American Artist, 1920–40*. Ann Arbor: University of Michigan Press, 2007.

Canales, Jimena. *The Physicist and the Philosopher: Einstein, Bergson, and the Debate That Changed Our Understanding of Time*. Princeton, NJ: Princeton University Press, 2015.

Carnegie, Andrew. *The Empire of Business*. New York: Doubleday, 1902.

Carpio, Myla Vicenti. "(Un)disturbing Exhibitions: Indigenous Historical Memory at the National Museum of the American Indian." *American Indian Quarterly* 30, no. 4 (2006): 619–31.

Carrington, Andre M. *Speculative Blackness: The Future of Race in Science Fiction*. Minneapolis: University of Minnesota Press, 2016.

Caswell, Michelle. *Archiving the Unspeakable: Silence, Memory and the Photographic Record in Cambodia*. Madison: University of Wisconsin Press, 2014.

Celan, Paul. *Wolfsbohne/Wolf's Bean*. Translated by Michael Hamburger. New York: Persea, 2002.

Césaire, Aimé. *Notebook of a Return to the Native Land*. Middletown, CT: Wesleyan University Press, 2001.

Chin, Marilyn. "For Mitsuye Yamada on Her 90th Birthday." In *A Portrait of the Self as Nation: New and Selected Poems*, 173–76. New York: W. W. Norton, 2018.

Choi, Don Mee. *Freely Frayed, ㅋ=q, and Race=Nation*. Seattle: Wave, 2014.

Clark, T. J. *Farewell to an Idea: Episodes from a History of Modernism*. New Haven, CT: Yale University Press, 1999.

Chun, Wendy Hui Kyong. "Introduction: Race and/as Technology; or, How to Do Things to Race." *Camera Obscura* 24, no. 1 (2009): 7–35.

Collins, Patricia Hill. "The Social Constructions of Black Feminist Thought." In *The Black Feminist Reader*, edited by Joy James and T. Denean Sharpley-Whiting, 183–208. Malden, MA: Blackwell, 2000.

Cook, Terry. "Mind over Matter: Towards a New Theory of Archival Appraisal." In *The Archival Imagination: Essays in Honour of Hugh A. Taylor*, edited by Barbara L. Craig, 38–70. Ottawa: Association of Canadian Archivists, 1992.

Cook, Terry. "We Are What We Keep; We Keep What We Are: Archival Appraisal Past, Present, and Future." *Journal of the Society of Archivists* 32, no. 2 (2011): 173–89.

Cooks, Bridget R. *Exhibiting Blackness: African Americans and the American Art Museum*. Amherst: University of Massachusetts Press, 2011.

Cooper, Melinda. *Family Values: Between Neoliberalism and the New Social Conservatism*. New York: Zone, 2019.

Coulthard, Glen. "From Wards of the State to Subjects of Recognition? Marx, Indigenous Peoples, and the Politics of Dispossession in Denendeh." In *Theorizing Native Studies*, edited by Audra Simpson and Andrea Smith, 56–98. Durham, NC: Duke University Press, 2014.

Couture, Carol. "Archival Appraisal: A Status Report." *Archivaria* 59 (2005): 83–108.

Crawford, Kate. *Atlas of AI: Power, Politics, and the Planetary Costs of Artificial Intelligence*. New Haven, CT: Yale University Press, 2021.

Cuno, James. *Who Owns Antiquity? Museums and the Battle over Our Ancient Heritage*. Princeton, NJ: Princeton University Press, 2011.

Daily, Jane. *The Age of Jim Crow: A Norton Casebook History*. New York: W. W. Norton, 2009.

Dain, Bruce. *A Hideous Monster of the Mind: American Race Theory in the Early Republic*. Cambridge, MA: Harvard University Press, 2003.

Danver, Steven Laurence, ed. *Revolts, Protests, Demonstrations, and Rebellions in American History: An Encyclopedia*. Vol. 1. Santa Barbara, CA: ABC-CLIO, 2011.

Davidson, Deborah, ed. "Between the Inside and the Outside: Memorial Tattoos and the Externalization of Loss." *The Tattoo Project: Commemorative Tattoos, Visual Culture, and the Digital Archive*. Toronto: Canadian Scholars' Press, 2016.

Davis, Angela Y. *Women, Race and Class*. New York: Vintage, 1983.

Davis, Rebecca Harding. *Life in the Iron Mills: And Other Stories*. London: Ward, Lock, and Tyler, 1868.

Day, Iyko. *Alien Capital: Asian Racialization and the Logic of Settler Colonial Capitalism*. Durham, NC: Duke University Press, 2016.
de Duve, Thierry. *Kant after Duchamp*. Cambridge, MA: MIT Press, 1998.
de Duve, Thierry. *Pictorial Nominalism: On Marcel Duchamp's Passage from Painting to the Readymade*. Minneapolis: University of Minnesota Press, 1984.
de Kooning, Willem. "The Renaissance and Order." *Trans/formation* 1, no. 2 (1951): 85–87.
Deloria, Vine, Jr. *God Is Red: A Native View of Religion*. 2nd ed. Golden, CO: Fulcrum, 1994.
de Man, Paul. "The Epistemology of Metaphor." *Critical Inquiry* 5, no. 1 (1978): 13–30.
Devinatz, Victor G. "Lenin as Scientific Manager under Monopoly Capitalism, State Capitalism, and Socialism: A Response to Scoville." *Industrial Relations* 42, no. 3 (2003): 513–20.
Dezayas, Marius, and Francis M. Naumann. *How, When, and Why Modern Art Came to New York*. Cambridge, MA: MIT Press, 1998.
Dickerson, Dennis C. *Out of the Crucible: Black Steel Workers in Western Pennsylvania*. Albany, NY: SUNY Press, 1986.
di Prima, Diane. *Revolutionary Letters*. San Francisco: City Lights, 1971.
Dowie, Mark. *Conservation Refugees: The Hundred-Year Conflict between Global Conservation and Native Peoples*. Cambridge, MA: MIT Press, 2011.
Du Bois, W. E. B. *Black Reconstruction in America: An Essay toward a History of the Part Which Black Folk Played in the Attempt to Reconstruct Democracy in America, 1860–1880*. Edited by Henry Louis Gates Jr. Oxford: Oxford University Press, 2007.
Du Bois, W. E. B. "The Future and Function of the Private Negro College." In *The Education of Black People: Ten Critiques, 1906–1960*, 139–48. New York: Monthly Review, 1973.
DuBois, Page. *Slaves and Other Objects*. Chicago: University of Chicago Press, 2003.
Dunbar, Anthony. "Introducing Critical Race Theory to Archival Discourse: Getting the Conversation Started." *Archival Science* 6 (2006): 106–29.
Duncan, Carol. *Civilizing Rituals: Inside Public Art Museums*. New York: Routledge, 1995.
Duncan, Carol, and Alan Wallach. "The Museum of Modern Art as Late Capitalist Ritual: An Iconographic Analysis (1978)." *Marxist Perspectives* (1978): 28–51.
Dworkin, Craig, and Kenneth Goldsmith. *Against Expression: An Anthology of Conceptual Writing*. Evanston, IL: Northwestern University Press, 2011.
Echeverría, Pamela. "Santiago Sierra Minimum Wages." *Flash Art* 34, no. 225 (2002): 100–104.

Edwards, Erica R. *The Other Side of Terror: Black Women and the Culture of US Empire*. New York: New York University Press, 2021.

Ehrenreich, Barbara, and John Ehrenreich. "The New Left and the Professional-Managerial Class." *Radical America* 11, no. 3 (1977): 7–24.

El-Tayeb, Fatima. *European Others: Queering Ethnicity in Postnational Europe*. Minneapolis: University of Minnesota Press, 2011.

El-Tayeb, Fatima. "'The Universal Museum': How the New Germany Built Its Future on Colonial Amnesia." *Nka: Journal for Contemporary African Art* 46 (2020): 72–82.

Esch, Elizabeth D. *The Color Line and the Assembly Line: Managing Race in the Ford Empire*. Berkeley: University of California Press, 2018.

Faris, James C. *Navajo and Photography: A Critical History of the Representation of an American People*. Albuquerque: University of New Mexico Press, 1996.

Fassler, Hans. "What's in a Name? Louis Agassiz, His Mountain, and the Politics of Remembrance." In *Rentyhorn*, edited by Sasha Huber, 8–21. Helsinki: Kiasma, 2010.

Férez Kuri, José. *Brion Gysin: Tuning in to the Multimedia Age*. London: Thames and Hudson, 2003.

Ferguson, Roderick A. "Purifoy: The Shit, the World, and Their Remaking." *South Atlantic Quarterly* 119, no. 3 (2020): 447–60.

Ferguson, Roderick A. *The Reorder of Things: The University and Its Pedagogies of Minority Difference*. Minneapolis: University of Minnesota Press, 2012.

Ferreira da Silva, Denise. *Toward a Global Idea of Race*. Minneapolis: University of Minnesota Press, 2007.

Finkleman, Paul, ed. *The Age of Jim Crow: Segregation from the End of Reconstruction to the Great Depression*. New York: Garland, 1992.

Finkelman, Paul, ed. *Race, Law, and American History, 1700–1990: The African American Experience*. 11 vols. New York: Garland, 1992.

Foster, Hal. "What Is Neo about the Neo-Avant Garde?" *Duchamp Effect* 70 (1994): 5–32.

Foucault, Michel. *Archaeology of Knowledge*. Translated by A. M. Sheridan Smith. New York: Pantheon, 1972.

Foucault, Michel. "Of Other Spaces." Translated by Jay Miskowiec. *Diacritics* 16, no. 1 (1986): 22–27.

Fox-Amato, Matthew. *Exposing Slavery: Photography, Human Bondage, and the Birth of Modern Visual Politics in America*. New York: Oxford University Press, 2019.

Fraser, Andrea. "I Am Going to Tell You What I Am Not; Pay Attention, This Is Exactly What I Am." In *Museum 21: Institution, Idea, Practice*, edited by Sophie Byrne, 82–103. Dublin: Irish Museum of Modern Art, 2011.

Fraser, Andrea. *2016 in Museums, Money, and Politics*. Cambridge, MA: MIT Press, 2018.

Fraser, Nancy. *The Old Is Dying and the New Cannot Be Born: From Progressive Neoliberalism to Trump and Beyond*. New York: Verso, 2019.

Freud, Sigmund. *Civilization and Its Discontents*. Translated by James Strachey. New York: W. W. Norton, 2021.

Fusco, Coco. *The Bodies That Were Not Ours: And Other Writings*. London: Routledge, 2001.

Gage, Beverly. "Why Violence Matters: Radicalism, Politics, and Class War in the Gilded Age and Progressive Era." *Journal for the Study of Radicalism* 1, no.1 (2006): 99–109.

Gellman, David Nathaniel, and David Quigley, eds. *Jim Crow New York: A Documentary History of Race and Citizenship, 1777–1877*. New York: New York University Press, 2003.

Gilliland, Anne J., and Michelle Caswell. "Records and Their Imaginaries: Imagining the Impossible, Making Possible the Imagined." *Archival Science* 16 (2016): 53–75.

Girst, Thomas. *The Duchamp Dictionary*. New York: Thames and Hudson, 2014.

Goeman, Mishuana. *Mark My Words: Native Women Mapping Our Nation*. Minneapolis: University of Minnesota Press, 2013.

Gompers, Samuel. *Seventy Years of Life and Labor: An Autobiography*. New York: Dutton, 1925.

Goodnough, Robert, ed. *Artists' Sessions at Studio 35 (1950)*. Chicago: Soberscove, 2009.

Gordon, Lewis. "Disciplining as a Human Science." *Quaderna* 28, no. 3 (2016). https://quaderna.org/3/disciplining-as-a-human-science/.

Grande, Sandy. "Accumulation of the Primitive: The Limits of Liberalism and the Politics of Occupy Wall Street." *Settler Colonial Studies* 3, nos. 3–4 (2013): 369–80.

Gruber, Aya. *The Feminist War on Crime: The Unexpected Role of Women's Liberation in Mass Incarceration*. Oakland: University of California Press, 2021.

Gutiérrez y Muhs, Gabriella, Yolanda F. Niemann, Carmen G. Gonzalez, and Angela P. Harris, eds. *Presumed Incompetent: The Intersections of Race and Class for Women in Academia*. Boulder: University Press of Colorado, 2012.

Haiven, Max. "Finance as Capital's Imagination? Reimagining Value and Culture in an Age of Fictitious Capital and Crisis." *Social Text* 29, no. 3 (2011): 93–124.

Hall, Stuart. "Constituting an Archive." *Third Text* 15, no. 54 (2001): 89–92.

Hall, Stuart. "Minimal Selves." In *Identity: The Real Me; Post-Modernism and the Question of Identity*, edited by Lisa Appignanesi, 44–46. London: ICA, 1987.

Hanlon, Gerard. *The Dark Side of Management: A Secret History of Management Theory*. London: Routledge, 2015.

Harney, Stefano, and Fred Moten. *The Undercommons: Fugitive Planning and Black Study*. Wivenhoe, UK: Minor Compositions, 2013.

Harper, Phillip Brian. *Abstractionist Aesthetics: Artistic Form and Social Critique in African American Culture*. New York: New York University Press, 2015.

Harris, Cheryl. "Whiteness as Property." *Harvard Law Review* 106, no. 8 (1993): 1707–91.

Harris, Leslie M. *In the Shadow of Slavery: African Americans in New York City 1626–1863*. Chicago: University of Chicago Press, 2003.

Harris, Verne. *Archives and Justice: A South African Perspective*. Chicago: Society of American Archivists, 2007.

Harris, Verne. "Hauntology, Archivy, and Banditry: An Engagement with Derrida and Zapiro." *Critical Arts: South-North Cultural and Media Studies* 29, no. 1 (2015): 13–27.

Harris, Verne. "Postmodernism and Archival Appraisal: Seven Theses." *South African Archives Journal* 40 (1998): 48–50.

Hartman, Saidiya. *Lose Your Mother: A Journey along the Atlantic Slave Route*. New York: Farrar, Straus and Giroux, 2008.

Hartman, Saidiya. *Scenes of Subjection: Terror, Slavery, and Self-Making in Nineteenth-Century America*. New York: Oxford University Press, 1997.

Hartman, Saidiya. "Venus in Two Acts." *Small Axe: A Caribbean Journal of Criticism* 12, no. 2 (2008): 1–14.

Heckewelder, John, and William C. Reichel. "Names Which the Lennie Lennape or Delaware Indians Gave to Rivers, Streams and Localities within the States of Pennsylvania, New Jersey, Maryland and Virginia, with Their Significations." *Transactions of the Moravian Historical Society* 1, no. 6 (1872): 227–82.

Henry-Smith, S*an D. *Wild Peach*. New York: Futurepoem, 2020.

Hinshaw, John. *Steel and Steelworkers: Race and Class Struggle in Twentieth-Century Pittsburgh*. Albany, NY: SUNY Press, 2002.

Hong, Grace Kyungwon. *Death beyond Disavowal: The Impossible Politics of Difference*. Minneapolis: University of Minnesota Press, 2015.

Hong, Grace Kyungwon. *The Ruptures of American Capital: Women of Color Feminism and the Culture of Immigrant Labor*. Minneapolis: University of Minnesota Press, 2006.

Honma, Todd. "Trippin' over the Color Line: The Invisibility of Race in Library and Information Studies." *InterActions: UCLA Journal of Education and Information Studies* 1, no. 2 (2005). http://dx.doi.org/10.5070/D412000540.

Huber, Sasha, and Petri Saarikko. "Louis Who? What You Should Know about Louis Agassiz." In *(T)races of Louis Agassiz: Photography,*

*Body, and Science: Yesterday and Today*, edited by Maria Helena Pereira Toledo Machado, 130–38. São Paulo: Capacete, 2010.

Hudson, Peter James. *Bankers and Empire: How Wall Street Colonized the Caribbean*. Chicago: University of Chicago Press, 2017.

Huggins, Nathan Irving. *Voices from the Harlem Renaissance*. Oxford: Oxford University Press, 1976.

Hunter, Tera W. *To 'Joy My Freedom: Southern Black Women's Lives and Labors after the Civil War*. Cambridge, MA: Harvard University Press, 1997.

Hurley, Chris. "Parallel Provenance (If These Are Your Records, Where Are Your Stories?)." *Archives and Manuscripts* 33, no. 1 (2005). https://doi.org/10.4225/03/58057708c6e0e.

INCITE! Women of Color Against Violence. *The Revolution Will Not Be Funded*. Durham, NC: Duke University Press, 2017.

Irmscher, Christoph. *Louis Agassiz: Creator of American Science*. Boston: Houghton Mifflin Harcourt, 2013.

ITPS (Intergovernmental Technical Panel on Soils). *Report of the Fourth Working Session of the Intergovernmental Technical Panel on Soils*. Rome: Food and Agriculture Organization of the United Nations, 2015. https://www.fao.org/3/az979e/az979e.pdf.

James, Joy. "The Womb of Western Theory: Trauma, Time Theft, and the Captive Maternal." *Carceral Notebooks* 12 (2016): 253–96.

James, William. *Brazil through the Eyes of William James: Letters, Diaries, and Drawings, 1865–1866*. Edited by Maria Helena Pereira Toledo Machado. Cambridge, MA: David Rockefeller Center for Latin American Studies, 2006.

Jeon, Joseph Jonghyun. "Neoliberal Forms: CGI, Algorithm, and Hegemony in Korea's IMF Cinema." *Representations* 126, no. 1 (2014): 85–111.

Johnson, Walter. *The Broken Heart of America: St. Louis and the Violent History of the United States*. New York: Basic Books, 2020.

Jones, Stephanie E. *They Were Her Property: White Women as Slave Owners in the American South*. New Haven, CT: Yale University Press, 2019.

Joselit, David. "Molds and Swarms." In *Part Object Part Sculpture*, edited by Helen Molesworth, 156–64. University Park: Penn State University Press, 2005.

Joselit, David. "NFTs, or The Readymade Reversed." *October* 175 (2021): 3–4.

Juguo, Zhang. *W. E. B. Du Bois: The Question for the Abolition of the Color Line*. London: Routledge, 2014.

Kanigel, Robert. *The One Best Way: Frederick Winslow Taylor and the Enigma of Efficiency*. Cambridge, MA: MIT Press, 1997.

Kantarelis, Demetrius. *Theories of the Firm*. 5th ed. Geneva: Inderscience, 2017.

Kantrowitz, Nathan. *Ethnic and Racial Segregation in the New York Metropolis: Residential Patterns among White Ethnic Groups, Blacks, and Puerto Ricans*. New York: Praeger, 1973.

Kapadia, Ronak K. "Up in the Air and On the Skin: Drone Warfare and the Queer Calculus of Pain." In *Critical Ethnic Studies: A Reader*, edited by the Critical Ethnic Studies Editorial Collective (Nada Elia, David M. Hernández, Jodi Kim, Shana L. Redmond, Dylan Rodríguez, and Sarita Echavez See), 360–75. Durham, NC: Duke University Press, 2016.

Kapil, Bhanu. *Humanimal: A Project for Future Children*. Berkeley, CA: Kelsey Street, 2009.

Karuka, Manu. *Empire's Tracks: Indigenous Nations, Chinese Workers, and the Transcontinental Railroad*. Berkeley: University of California Press, 2019.

Kauanui, J. Kēhaulani. "'A Structure, Not an Event': Settler Colonialism and Enduring Indigeneity." *Lateral: Journal of the Cultural Studies Association* 5, no. 1 (2016). https://doi.org/10.25158/L5.1.7.

Kelley, Blair L. M. *Right to Ride: Streetcar Boycotts and African American Citizenship in the Era of* Plessy v. Ferguson. Chapel Hill: University of North Carolina Press, 2010.

Kelley, Robin D. G. *Hammer and Hoe: Alabama Communists during the Great Depression*. Chapel Hill: University of North Carolina Press, 2015.

Kenning, Dean. "Art Relations and the Presence of Absence." *Third Text* 23 (2009): 435–46.

Kester, Grant. "The Device Laid Bare: On Some Limitations in Current Art Criticism." *E-flux journal*, no. 50 (2013). https://www.e-flux.com/journal/50/59990/the-device-laid-bare-on-some-limitations-in-current-art-criticism/.

Kester, Grant. *The One and the Many: Contemporary Collaborative Art in a Global Context*. Durham, NC: Duke University Press, 2011.

Kim, Claire Jean. *Bitter Fruit: The Politics of Black-Korean Conflict in New York City*. New Haven, CT: Yale University Press, 2003.

Kim, Eunsong. "On the Depth of Fakeness." In *Deep Fakes: Algorithms and Society*, edited by Michael Filimowicz, 50–70. New York: Routledge, 2022.

Kim, Eunsong. "We Hope You Can See Your Way Home." In *Divya Mehra: From India to Canada and Back to India (There Is Nothing I Can Possess Which You Cannot Take Away*, n.p. Exhibition pamphlet. Regina: Mackensie Art Gallery, 2021.

Kim, Jodi. *Settler Garrison: Debt Imperialism, Militarism, and Transpacific Imaginaries*. Durham, NC: Duke University Press, 2022.

King, Tiffany. *The Black Shoals: Offshore Formations of Black and Native Studies*. Durham, NC: Duke University Press, 2019.

Kitzmann, Andreas. "Between the Inside and the Outside: Commemorative Tattoos and the Externalization of Loss or Trauma." In *The Tattoo Project: Commemorative Tattoos, Visual Culture, and the Digital Archive*, edited by Deborah Davidson, 39–47. Toronto: Canadian Scholars' Press, 2016.

Klare, Karl. "The Bitter and the Sweet: Reflections on the Supreme Court's Yeshiva Decision." *Socialist Review* 71 (1983): 99–129.

Klein, Ezra. "Jenny Odell and the Art of Attention." Interview. *Vox*, May 23, 2019. https://www.vox.com/ezra-klein-show-podcast/2019/5/23/18636332/jenny-odell-how-to-do-nothing.

Koshy, Susan, Lisa Marie Cacho, Jodi A. Byrd, and Brian Jordan Jefferson, eds. *Colonial Racial Capitalism*. Durham, NC: Duke University Press, 2022.

Kosuth, Joseph. *Art after Philosophy and After: Collected Writings, 1966–1990*. Edited by Gabriele Guercio. Cambridge, MA: MIT Press, 1991.

Krause, Paul. *The Battle for Homestead, 1880–1892*. Pittsburgh, PA: University of Pittsburgh Press, 1992.

Lazzarato, Maurizio. *Marcel Duchamp et le refus du travail*. Paris: Les Prairies Ordinaires, 2014.

Lee, Pamela. *Think Tank Aesthetics: Midcentury Modernism, the Cold War, and the Neoliberal Present*. Cambridge, MA: MIT Press, 2020.

Lenin, Nikolai. "Scientific Management and Dictatorship of the Proletariat." In *Trade Unionism and Labor Problems*, edited by John R. Commons, 179–98. Boston: Ginn, 1921.

Levine, Lawrence W. *Highbrow/Lowbrow: The Emergence of Cultural Hierarchy in America*. Cambridge, MA: Harvard University Press, 1990.

Lipsitz, George. *The Possessive Investment in Whiteness: How White People Benefit from Identity Politics*. Philadelphia: Temple University Press, 1998.

Lowe, Lisa. *Immigrant Acts: On Asian American Cultural Politics*. Durham, NC: Duke University Press, 1996.

Lowe, Lisa. *The Intimacies of Four Continents*. Durham, NC: Duke University Press, 2015.

Lowe, Lisa, and David Lloyd, eds. *The Politics of Culture in the Shadow of Capital*. Durham, NC: Duke University Press, 1997.

Machado, Maria Helena Pereira Toledo. "Traces of Agassiz on Brazilian Races: The Formation of a Photographic Collection." In *(T)races of Louis Agassiz: Photography, Body, and Science: Yesterday and Today*, edited by Maria Helena Pereira Toledo Machado, 20–43. São Paulo: Capacete, 2010.

Machado, Maria Helena Pereira Toledo, ed. *(T)races of Louis Agassiz: Photography, Body and Science: Yesterday and Today*. Exhibition catalog. São Paulo: Capacete, 2010.

MacLeod, Kirsten. "The 'Librarian's Dream-Prince': Carl Van Vechten and America's Modernist Cultural Archives Industry." *Libraries and the Cultural Record* 46, no. 4 (2011): 360–87.

Magat, Richard. *Unlikely Partners: Philanthropic Foundations and the Labor Movement*. Ithaca, NY: ILR, 1999.

Mainardi, Patricia. *Art and Politics of the Second Empire: The Universal Expositions of 1855 and 1867*. New Haven, CT: Yale University Press, 1987.

Marchart, Oliver. "Art Institutions between Politics and the Police." In *Police: Francis Alÿs, Jeremy Deller, Peter Friedl, Rodney Graham, Annika Larsson, Tuomo Manninen, Lisl Ponger, Oliver Ressler, Santiago Sierra, Milica Tomić*, edited by Martin Hochleitner and Gabriele Spindler, 66–85. Exhibition catalog. Weitra, Austria: Publication N1, Bibliothek der Provinz, 2005.

Marcuse, Herbert. *One-Dimensional Man: Studies in the Ideology of Advanced Industrial Society*. Boston: Beacon, 1964.

Markovits, Daniel. *The Meritocracy Trap: How America's Foundational Myth Feeds Inequality, Dismantles the Middle Class, and Devours the Elite*. New York: Random House, 2020.

Marriott, David. "Signs Taken for Signifiers." In *Assembling Alternatives: Reading Postmodern Poetries Transnationally*, edited by Romana Huk, 338–46. Middletown, CT: Wesleyan University Press, 2003.

Marriott, David. *On Black Men*. New York: Columbia University Press, 2000.

Martinez, Rosa. "Entrevista a Santiago Sierra/Interview with Santiago Sierra." In *Santiago Sierra, Spanish Pavilion, 50th Venice Biennial*, 152–211. Exhibition catalog. Madrid: Ministerio de Asuntos Exteriores, Dirección General de Relaciones Culturales y Científicas/Turner, 2003.

Marx, Karl. *Capital*. Vol. 1. Translated by Samuel Moore and Edward Aveling. Edited by Frederick Engels. Moscow: Progress, 1887.

Marx, Karl. *Economic and Philosophic Manuscripts of 1844*. Translated by Martin Mulligan. Moscow: Progress, 1959.

Massey, Douglass, and Nancy A. Denton. *American Apartheid: Segregation and the Making of the Underclass*. Cambridge, MA: Harvard University Press, 1993.

Massey, Douglass, and Nancy A. Denton. "The Dimensions of Residential Segregation." *Social Forces* 67, no. 2 (1988): 281–315.

Matt, Gerald. *Interviews*. Translated by Tom Appleton. Cologne: Walter König, 2007.

McKemmish, Sue. "Placing Records Continuum Theory and Practice." *Archival Science* 1, no. 4 (2001): 333–59.

McKittrick, Katherine. "Plantation Futures." *Small Axe: A Caribbean Journal of Criticism* 17, no. 3 (2013): 1–15.

Melamed, Jodi. *Represent and Destroy: Rationalizing Violence in the New Racial Capitalism*. Minneapolis: University of Minnesota Press, 2011.

Melamed, Jodi. "The Spirit of Neoliberalism: From Racial Liberalism to Neoliberal Multiculturalism." *Social Text* 24 (2006): 1–24.

Meltzer, Eve. *Systems We Have Loved: Conceptual Art, Affect, and the Antihumanist Turn*. Chicago: University of Chicago Press, 2013.

Merkle, Judith A. *Management and Ideology: The Legacy of the International Scientific Management Movement*. Berkeley: University of California Press, 1980.

Mohanty, Chandra Talpade. "Under Western Eyes: Feminist Scholarship and Colonial Discourses." *Feminist Review*, no. 30 (1988): 61–88.

Molesworth, Helen, ed. *Part Object Part Sculpture*. University Park: Penn State University Press, 2003.

Moore, Eli, Nicole Montojo, and Nicole Mauri. *Roots, Race, and Place: A History of Racially Exclusionary Housing in the San Francisco Bay Area*. Berkeley, CA: Hass Institute for a Fair and Inclusive Society at UC Berkeley, 2019. https://belonging.berkeley.edu/rootsraceplace.

Morrison, Toni. *Playing in the Dark: Whiteness and the Literary Imagination*. Cambridge, MA: Harvard University Press, 1992.

Morrison, Toni. "Unspeakable Things Unspoken: The Afro-American Presence in American Literature." In *The Black Feminist Reader*, edited by Joy James and T. Denean Sharpley-Whiting, 24–56. Malden, MA: Blackwell, 2000.

Moten, Fred. *In the Break: The Aesthetics of the Black Radical Tradition*. Minneapolis: University of Minnesota Press, 2003.

Muensterberger, Werner. *Collecting: An Unruly Passion; Psychological Perspectives*. Princeton, NJ: Princeton University Press, 1994.

Mullen, Harryette. *The Cracks between What We Are and What We Are Supposed to Be: Essays and Interviews*. Tuscaloosa: University of Alabama Press, 2012.

Murray, Yxta Maya. "From Here I Saw What Happened and I Cried: Carrie Mae Weems's Challenge to the Harvard Archive." *Unbound: Harvard Journal of the Legal Left* 8, no. 1 (2013): 1–78.

Naumann, Francis. *New York Dada 1915–1923*. New York: Abrams, 1994.

Negri, Antonio, and Michael Hardt. *Multitude: War and Democracy in the Age of Empire*. New York: Penguin, 2004.

Nelson, Maggie. *The Art of Cruelty*. New York: W. W. Norton, 2011.

Ngai, Sianne. *Our Aesthetic Categories: Zany, Cute, Interesting*. Cambridge, MA: Harvard University Press, 2015.

Nichols, Robert. *Theft Is Property! Dispossession and Critical Theory*. Durham, NC: Duke University Press, 2020.

Obrist, Hans Ulrich. *A Brief History of Curating*. Edited by Lionel Bovier and Birte Theiler. Zurich: JRP/Ringier, 2018.

Omi, Michael, and Howard Winant. *Racial Formation in the United States*. New York: Routledge, 2014.

Parikka, Jussi. *A Geology of Media*. Minneapolis: University of Minnesota Press, 2015.

Park, Josephine Nock-Hee. *Apparitions of Asia: Modernist Form and Asian American Poetics*. New York: Oxford University Press, 2014.

Park, K-Sue. "The History Wars and Property Law: Conquest and Slavery as Foundational to the Field." *Yale Law Journal* 131 (2002): 1062–53.

Pearce, Susan. *Interpreting Objects and Collections*. New York: Routledge, 1994.

Perloff, Marjorie. "A Duchamp unto Myself: Writing through Marcel." In *John Cage: Composed in America*, edited by Marjorie Perloff and Charles Junkerman, 100–124. Chicago: University of Chicago Press, 1994.

Perloff, Marjorie. *21st-Century Modernism: The New Poetics*. Malden, MA: Blackwell, 2002.

Perloff, Marjorie. *Unoriginal Genius: Poetry by Other Means in the New Century*. Chicago: University of Chicago Press, 2010.

Perloff, Marjorie. "Whose New American Poetry? Anthologizing in the Nineties." *Diacritics 26*, nos. 3–4 (1996): 104–23.

Phillips, Ulrich B. *American Negro Slavery*. Baton Rouge: Louisiana State University Press, 1966.

Pollard, Riva. "The Appraisal of Personal Papers: A Critical Literature Review." *Archivaria* 52 (2001): 136–50.

Pollard, Sidney. *The Genesis of Modern Management: A Study of the Industrial Revolution in Great Britain*. Cambridge, MA: Harvard University Press, 1965.

Prodanovich, Todd. "Whose Coast Are You Surfing in San Diego?" *Kumeyaay*, August 17, 2020. https://www.kumeyaay.com/news/483-whose-coast-are-you-surfing-in-san-diego.html.

Purifoy, Noah. "African American Artists of Los Angeles Oral History Transcript, 1990: Noah Purifoy / Interviewed by Karen Anne Mason." Oral History Program, University of California, Los Angeles. Charles E. Young Research Library, Department of Special Collections, UCLA, 1990.

Purifoy, Noah, and Ted Michel. *Junk Art: 66 Signs of Neon*. Exhibition catalog. Los Angeles: Watts Art Festival, 1966.

Purnell, Brian, Jeanne Theoharis, and Komozi Woodard, eds. *The Strange Career of Jim Crow North: Segregation and Struggle Outside of the South.* New York: New York University Press, 2019.

Ramírez, Mario H. "Being Assumed Not to Be: A Critique of Whiteness as an Archival Imperative." *American Archivist* 78, no. 2 (2015): 339–56.

Rancière, Jacques. *Disagreement.* Translated by Julie Rose. Minneapolis: University of Minnesota Press, 1999.

Rancière, Jacques. *Nights of Labor: The Workers Dream in Nineteenth-Century France.* Translated by John Drury. Philadelphia: Temple University Press, 1989.

Rancière, Jacques. *The Philosopher and His Poor.* Translated by John Drury, Corinne Oster, and Andrew Parker. Durham, NC: Duke University Press, 2003.

Raymond, Claire. "The Crucible of Witnessing: Projects of Identity in Carrie Mae Weems's *From Here I Saw What Happened and I Cried.*" *Meridians* 13, no. 1 (2015): 26–52.

Rees, Jonathan. "Homestead in Context: Andrew Carnegie and the Decline of the Amalgamated Associated of Iron and Steel Workers." *Pennsylvania History: A Journal of Mid-Atlantic Studies* 64, no. 2 (1997): 509–33.

Richter, Hans. *Dada: Art and Anti-Art.* New York: Thames and Hudson, 1965.

Riding, Laura. *Anarchism Is Not Enough.* Berkeley: University of California Press, 2001.

Robinson, Cedric J. *An Anthropology of Marxism.* 2nd ed. Chapel Hill: University of North Carolina Press, 2019.

Robinson, Cedric J. *Black Marxism: The Making of the Black Radical Tradition.* 2nd ed. Chapel Hill: University of North Carolina Press, 2000.

Robinson, Cedric J. *The Terms of Order: Political Science and the Myth of Leadership.* Chapel Hill: University of North Carolina Press, 2016.

Roediger, David R. *Working toward Whiteness: How America's Immigrants Became White; The Strange Journey from Ellis Island to the Suburbs.* New York: Basic, 2018.

Roediger, David R., and Elizabeth D. Esch. *The Production of Difference: Race and the Management of Labor in U.S. History.* Oxford: Oxford University Press, 2012.

Rogers, Molly. *Delia's Tears: Race, Science, and Photography in Nineteenth-Century America.* New Haven, CT: Yale University Press, 2010.

Rose, Gideon. "James Cuno on Museums." *Foreign Affairs*, May 12, 2015. https://www.foreignaffairs.com/audios/2015-05-10/james-cuno-museums.

Rosenthal, Caitlin. *Accounting for Slavery: Masters and Management*. Cambridge, MA: Harvard University Press, 2019.

Rosler, Martha. "Lookers, Buyers, Dealers, and Makers: Thoughts on Audience." In *Decoys and Disruptions Selected Writings, 1975–2001*, 9–52. Cambridge, MA: MIT Press, 2004.

Rothstein, Richard. *The Color of Law: A Forgotten History of How Our Government Segregated America*. New York: Liveright, 2018.

Sahakian, Rijn. "What We Are Fighting For." *e-flux journal* 84 (2007). https://www.e-flux.com/journal/84/150664/what-we-are-fighting-for/.

Samuels, Helen Willa. "Who Controls the Past." *American Archivist* 49, no. 2 (1986): 109–24.

Sassen, Saskia. *Global Networks, Linked Cities*. New York: Routledge, 2016.

Sawelson-Gorse, Naomi. "Marcel Duchamp's 'Silent Guard': A Critical Study of Louise and Walter Arensberg." PhD diss., University of California, Santa Barbara, 1994.

Schneider, Eckhard, ed. *Santiago Sierra: 300 Tons and Previous Works*. Zurich: Kunsthaus Bregenz, 2004.

Schneider, Suzanne. "Louis Agassiz and the American School of Ethnoeroticism: Polygenesis, Pornography, and Other 'Perfidious Influences.'" In *Pictures and Progress: Early Photography and the Making of African American Identity*, edited by Maurice O. Wallace and Shawn Michelle Smith, 211–43. Durham, NC: Duke University Press, 2012.

Scoville, James G. "The Taylorization of Vladimir Ilich Lenin." *Industrial Relations* 40, no. 4 (2001): 620–26.

Sharpe, Christina. *In the Wake: On Blackness and Being*. Durham, NC: Duke University Press, 2016.

Sholette, Gregory. *Dark Matter: Art and Politics in the Age of Enterprise Culture*. London: Pluto, 2011.

Siegel, Daniel J. *Mind: A Journey to the Heart of Being Human*. New York: W. W. Norton, 2016.

Sierra, Santiago. *Santiago Sierra: Works, 2002–1990*. Birmingham, UK: Ikon Gallery, 2002.

Simpson, Audra. "Consent's Revenge." *Cultural Anthropology* 31, no. 3 (2016): 326–33.

Slobodian, Quinn. *Globalists: The End of Empire and the Birth of Neoliberalism*. Cambridge, MA: Harvard University Press, 2018.

Smith, Cherise. "Carrie Mae Weems: Rethinking Historic Appropriations." *Nka: Journal of Contemporary African Art* 44 (2019): 38–50.

Smithson, Robert. "Production for Production's Sake." In *Conceptual Art: A Critical Anthology*, edited by Alexander Alberro and Blake Stimson, 284–85. Cambridge, MA: MIT Press, 1999.

Sokol, Jason. *All Eyes Are upon Us: Race and Politics from Boston to Brooklyn.* Amherst: University of Massachusetts Press, 2017.

Spalding, Julian. *The Poetic Museum: Reviving Historic Collections.* Munich: Prestel, 2002.

Spencer, David. "Braverman and the Contribution of Labour Process Analysis to the Critique of Capitalist Production—Twenty-Five Years On." *Work, Employment, and Society* 14, no. 2 (2000): 223–43.

Spieker, Sven. *The Big Archive: Art from Bureaucracy.* Cambridge, MA: MIT Press, 2017.

Spillers, Hortense J. *Black, White, and in Color: Essays on American Literature and Culture.* Chicago: University of Chicago Press, 2003.

Spillers, Hortense J. "Mama's Baby, Papa's Maybe: An American Grammar Book." In *The Black Feminist Reader*, edited by Joy James and T. Denean Sharpley-Whiting, 57–87. Malden, MA: Blackwell, 2000.

Spivak, Gayatri Chakravorty. "Can the Subaltern Speak?" In *Marxism and the Interpretation of Culture*, edited by C. Nelson and L. Grossberg, 271–313. Basingstoke, UK: Macmillan Education, 1988.

Spivak, Gayatri Chakravorty. "Scattered Speculations on the Question of Value." *Diacritics* 15, no. 4 (1985): 73–93.

Spivak, Gayatri Chakravorty. "Three Women's Texts and a Critique of Imperialism." *Critical Inquiry* 12, no. 1 (1985): 235–61.

Standiford, Les. *Meet You in Hell: Andrew Carnegie, Henry Clay Frick, and the Bitter Partnership That Transformed America.* New York: Crown, 2006.

Starobin, Robert. *Industrial Slavery in the Old South.* New York: Oxford University Press, 1970.

Starosielski, Nicole. *The Undersea Network.* Durham, NC: Duke University Press, 2015.

Stewart, George R. *Names on the Land: A Historical Account of Place-Naming in the United States.* New York: New York Review of Books Classics, 2008.

Stewart-Ambo, Theresa. "The Future Is in the Past: How Land-Grab Universities Can Shape the Future of Higher Education." *Journal of Native American and Indigenous Studies Association* 8, no. 1 (2021): 162–68.

Stewart-Ambo, Theresa, and K. Wayne Yang. "Beyond Land Acknowledgment in Settler Institutions." *Social Text* 39, no. 11 (2021): 21–46.

Stone, Katherine. "The Origins of Job Structures in the Steel Industry." *Radical America* 7, no. 6 (1973): 19–64.

Sutton, David C. "The Destinies of Literary Manuscripts, Past Present and Future." *Archives and Manuscripts* 42, no. 3 (2014): 295–300.

Tallon, Loic. "Introducing Open Access at The Met." Met, February 7, 2017. https://www.metmuseum.org/blogs/digital-underground/2017/open-access-at-the-met.

Taylor, Frederick Winslow. *The Principles of Scientific Management.* New York: Harper and Row, 1911.

Taylor, Frederick Winslow. *Shop Management.* New York: Harper and Brothers, 1912.

Taylor, Frederick Winslow. "Taylor's Famous Testimony before the Special House Committee." In "Testimony of Frederick W. Taylor at Hearings before Special House Committee of the House of Representatives, January, 1912." Special issue, *Bulletin of the Taylor Society* 11, nos. 3–4 (1926): 95–196.

Thoburn, Nicholas. *Deleuze, Marx, and Politics.* London: Routledge, 2003.

Trinh, T. Minh-Ha. *Woman Native Other.* Bloomington: Indiana University Press, 1989.

Tsinhnahjinnie, Hulleah. "When Is a Photograph Worth a Thousand Words?" In *Photography's Other Histories*, edited by Christopher Pinney and N. Peterson, 40–52. Durham, NC: Duke University Press: 2003.

UNESCO (United Nations Educational, Scientific and Cultural Organization). "Convention on the Means of Prohibiting and Preventing the Illicit Import, Export, and Transfer of Ownership of Cultural Property 1970." UNESCO, November 14, 1970. https://en.unesco.org/about-us/legal-affairs/convention-means-prohibiting-and-preventing-illicit-import-export-and.

Upward, Frank. "Continuum Mechanics and Memory Banks." *Archives and Manuscripts* 33, no. 1 (2005): 84–109.

Vargas, João H. Costa. *The Denial of Antiblackness: Multiracial Redemption and Black Suffering.* Minneapolis: University of Minnesota Press, 2018.

Vatanparast, Roxana. "The Infrastructures of the Global Data Economy." *Harvard International Law Journal Frontiers* 61 (2020): 1–9.

Veblen, Thorstein. *The Theory of the Leisure Class: An Economic Study of Institutions.* New York: Random House, 1961.

Vora, Kalindi, and Neda Atanasoski. *Surrogate Humanity: Race, Robots, and the Politics of Technological Futures.* Durham, NC: Duke University Press, 2019.

Wallach, Allan. *Exhibiting Contradiction: Essays on the Art Museum in the United States.* Amherst: University of Massachusetts Press, 1998.

Wallis, Brian. "Black Bodies, White Science: Louis Agassiz's Slave Daguerreotypes." *Smithsonian American Art Museum* 9, no. 2 (1995): 39–61.

Wang, Dorothy. *Thinking Its Presence: Form, Race, and Subjectivity in Contemporary Asian American Poetry*. Stanford, CA: Stanford University Press, 2013.

Waring, Stephen P. *Taylorism Transformed: Scientific Management Theory Since 1945*. Chapel Hill: University of North Carolina Press, 1991.

Weber, Max. *The Protestant Ethic and the Spirit of Capitalism*. Translated by Talcott Parsons. London: Unwin Hyman, 1930.

Weeks, Kathi, *The Problem with Work: Feminism, Marxism, Antiwork Politics, and Postwork Imaginaries*. Durham, NC: Duke University Press, 2011.

Weinberg, Zoe. "The Incalculable Legacy: Race Science at Harvard in the 19th and 20th Centuries." YouTube, November 7, 2011. https://www.youtube.com/watch?v=K2SoA3p1eHo.

White, Gillian. *Lyric Shame*. Cambridge, MA: Harvard University Press, 2014.

Widener, Daniel. *Black Arts West: Culture and Struggle in Postwar Los Angeles*. Durham, NC: Duke University Press, 2010.

Wilder, Craig Steven. *Ebony and Ivy: Race, Slavery, and the Troubled History of America's Universities*. London: Bloomsbury, 2013.

Williams, Patricia. *The Alchemy of Race and Rights*. Cambridge, MA: Harvard University Press, 1992.

Williams, Raymond. *Marxism and Literature*. Oxford: Oxford University Press, 1977.

Williamson, Oliver E. "The Theory of the Firm as Governance Structure." *Journal of Economic Perspectives* 16, no. 3 (2002): 171–95.

Willoughby-Herard, Tiffany. *Waste of a White Skin: The Carnegie Corporation and the Racial Logic of White Vulnerability*. Berkeley: University of California Press, 2015.

Wilson, Jackie Napolean. *Hidden Witness: African-American Images from the Dawn of Photography to the Civil War*. New York: St. Martin's Griffin, 2002.

Wong, Winnie. *Van Gogh on Demand: China and the Readymade*. Chicago: University of Chicago Press, 2013.

Wood, Erika, and Liz Budnitz, with Garima Malhotra. *Jim Crow in New York*. New York: Brennan Center for Justice, New York University Law School, 2010.

Wu, Chin-Tao. *Privatising Culture: Corporate Art Intervention since the 1980s*. London: Verso, 2002.

Wynter, Sylvia. "Black Metamorphosis: New Natives in A New World." Ca. 1970s. Manuscript 508. Institute of the Black World Papers, Schomburg Center for Research in Black Culture, New York Public Library, New York.

Wynter, Sylvia. "Novel and History, Plot and Plantation." *Savacou*, no. 5 (1971): 95–102.

Yamamoto, Hisaye. *Seventeen Syllables and Other Stories*. New Brunswick, NJ: Rutgers University Press, 2001.

Young, Hershini Bhana. *Illegible Will: Coercive Spectacles of Labor in South Africa and the Diaspora*. Durham, NC: Duke University Press, 2017.

Yu, Timothy. *Race and the Avant-Garde: Experimental and Asian American Poetry Since 1965*. Stanford, CA: Stanford University Press, 2009.

Zadeh, Joe. "The Tyranny of Time." *Noēma*, June 3, 2021. https://www.noemamag.com/the-tyranny-of-time/.

Zakaria, Rafia. *Against White Feminism: Notes on Disruption*. New York: W. W. Norton, 2021.

# INDEX

www.ingramcontent.com/pod-product-compliance
Lightning Source LLC
LaVergne TN
LVHW041113080826
845145LV00007B/1795

* 9 7 8 1 4 7 8 0 3 0 4 8 5 *